Mr. Cheap's
Boston

Bargains, factory outlets,
off-price stores, deep
discount stores, cheap
eats, and cheap fun
things to do.

Mr. Cheap's Boston

Bargains, factory outlets,
off-price stores, deep
discount stores, cheap eats,
and cheap fun things to do.

Mark Waldstein

BOB ADAMS, INC.
PUBLISHERS
Holbrook, Massachusetts

Published by Bob Adams, Inc.
260 Center Street, Holbrook, MA 02343

ISBN: 1-55850-170-3

Printed in the United States of America

J   I   H   G   F   E   D   C   B   A

This publication is designed to provide accurate and authoritative information with regard to the subject matter covered. It is sold with the understanding that the publisher is not engaged in rendering legal, accounting, or other professional advice. If legal advice or other expert assistance is required, the services of a qualified professional person should be sought.

— From a *Declaration of Principles* jointly adopted by a Committee of the American Bar Association and a Committee of Publishers and Associations.

A FEW CAREFULLY-CHOSEN WORDS FROM MR. CHEAP

About this "cheap" business. I'll admit, there are more elegant ways to put the idea.

Just about everyone wants to save money, especially with things being so tough lately. When it comes to low *prices*, few know as many good places as I do. But, strictly speaking, that doesn't make these stores and eateries "cheap," nor does it make anyone who uses this book "cheap." *Thrifty* would be a better word. Or perhaps *frugal*. A cheap person, in my mind, is one who has plenty of money to burn, and refuses to spend it; a thrifty person would probably spend the money if he or she had it. I think more of us fall into the latter category, don't you?

Anyway, most folks do love a bargain, and it's my pleasure to pass these hints along. But this is hardly an exact science; prices change all the time. Since it's taken me a while to put all this information together, a lot will have changed even by the time you read this book. And, in my experience, price changes just *never* seem to go downward.

Stores have to make money to stay in business, after all. They will not always have exactly what I describe, at the prices I mention. Restaurants will come and go, or nudge their rates up, or even change their menus completely. So use this book as a general list of suggestions to check out.

I expect to get mail from readers who insist I've left out their favorite diner, or some resale boutique they frequent. To which I say, Mr. C can't be *everywhere*; but please do pass along the information for our next edition. The address is: Mr. Cheap, care of Bob Adams, Inc., 260 Center Street, Holbrook, Massachusetts, 02343. Please use correct stamp amounts; I can't abide those horrid "postage due" notices.

One last word of caution: You get what you pay for. It's been said many times, and it's usually true. With new merchandise especially, if the price is low, the quality may not be far behind. I have tried to point out, wherever I could, items that are cheap because they are less well made, or because they are irregulars or slightly damaged—which may still be of use to the reader who only needs something to last a short time. Students furnishing a dorm room, for example. Sometimes, that's all you want. And that's fine.

So, get ready to use my book—but be careful how you use my name. As you see, "cheap" can mean many things. Now, on to the goodies!

Mark Waldstein
for I.M. Cheap, Esquire

CONTENTS

SHOPPING

AUTOMOTIVE SUPPLIES

As the old commercial used to say about chickens, parts is parts. There doesn't seem to be a great factory-direct source for things like motor oil and mufflers, other than the local stores and the large chains, which you probably know of already. The big retailers are most likely your best deals, especially when they have a particular item on sale. These include **ADAP/Auto Palace**, **Lappen's**, and **Foreign Autopart**, along with the smaller **Gem Auto Parts** chain in Dorchester and East Boston. Their newspaper ads will alert you to good sales.

For parts, though, there is another road to take. When someone kindly snaps off your antenna, and your dealer says the replacements are $90.00 each—most dealers seem to use the same warehouse as the Pentagon—consider a used part instead. There are junkyards (er, automotive recycling centers) all over the city, filled with perfectly good parts from engines to tail lights, for all makes of cars.

These can cost half, or even one third, of the original retail prices. Most garage mechanics don't mind you bringing along your own parts for them to install; it saves them effort and saves you money.

The best of the bunch (more and more, these days) are even computerized; they can find out in a jiffy whether they have exactly the part you need. Some shops are even linked to each other. As a further convenience, or perhaps because of zoning laws, many yards are clustered together. Good neighborhoods to roam include the area between Union Square, Somerville, and Inman Square, Cambridge; Allston, near the Mass. Pike and along Western Avenue; Massachusetts Avenue and Dorchester Avenue in Dorchester; and Everett Avenue in Chelsea. Here are a few of the bigger yards:

BOSTON

A-M Used Auto Parts — 1149 Harrison Ave., Boston; 442-4629. This South End shop has a large selection of every kind of part for late model foreign and domestic cars, including engines, transmissions, radiators, and accessories. They also have access to stock from their second branch, located in Rowley. A-M specializes in Cadillac parts, of which Mr. C's readers may not need many; but they have plenty of supplies for other makes too. Closed on weekends.

Ellis The Rim Man — 1001 Commonwealth Ave., Brighton; 782-4777. Nothing used here, but this is a particularly big store for accesso-ries to adorn your chariot. Wheel covers, air conditioners, anti-theft devices, roof racks, wiper blades, radar detectors and more are all here, many sold at discount. Ellis is located near the Boston University campus, and is open from 8 a.m. to 6 p.m. weekdays and 8 a.m. to 5 p.m. Saturdays.

CAMBRIDGE

Bucky's Auto Parts — 330 Webster Ave., Cambridge; 354-2255. Bucky's is one of the several yards located near Inman Square; they also have an affiliate store, **Cam-**

Mr. Cheap's Picks

There are no gold mines in this category. For basic supplies, shop the superstore chains. They advertise frequent sales in the newspapers; follow the ads and stock up.

For parts: cruise the junkyards. This is not as bad as it sounds—many such places are grouped together in areas like Inman/Union Squares and Chelsea/Everett, and most have computerized access to their stock. Bring the part in to your local mechanic and have him install it. Save a bundle over dealers' prices.

---

bridge Auto Parts, at 290 River Street, Cambridge (491-0111), near Memorial Drive. Both are hooked up to computers, and thus to each other, for a very comprehensive selection of parts. They can tell you right away whether they have what you need, where it is, and how much it will cost.

Some of the other yards in the immediate area include **Columbia Auto Parts**, 305 Webster Ave., Cambridge (547-1800); **Elm Auto Parts**, 333 Elm St., Cambridge (354-1523), specializing in windshield and glass installation; **Nissenbaum's Auto Parts**, 480 Columbia St., Somerville (776-0194); and **J & A Auto Parts**, 517 Columbia St., Somorville (628-4691). J & A even offers a delivery service!

CHELSEA

Borr's Auto Parts And Sales — 300 Everett Ave., Chelsea; 889-

0091. A huge, older junkyard near Everett Stadium, Borr's will even let you wander around and look at its collection of parts. And they have quite a lot. Nearby, **Emerald Auto Parts and Sales** at 177 Everett Ave. (884-6851) also has a large stock of both new and used parts. They do the installing, too.

WATERTOWN

Watertown Used Auto Parts — 183 Grove St., Watertown; 923-1010. This huge warehouse just off Route 128 specializes in the hard-to-find. They have a tremendous amount of parts in stock, with easy access to late-model stuff. And if they don't have your part at hand, they'll find it pronto—their locator service links them with 140 other businesses in the area. They also have some new items, particularly radiators, at good prices.

TIRES

Tires can be pretty expensive, especially if you need to replace a whole set. They are a very important investment, of course, for your own safety. The best prices on new tires, from Mr. C's research, are at the large chains (no pun intended there); you'll have to shop around and see who's best for the size and grade of tire you want.

Some of the likely places to try for good rates are: **Cambridge Tire Centers**, 290 Albany St., Cambridge (864-7575); also in Braintree, Chelsea, Dedham, Revere and others. **Dedham Wholesale Tire Corporation**, 5218 Washington St., West Roxbury (325-6600). **Liner Tire**, 128 Boylston St., Brookline (232-1014). **Merchants Tire Company**, 1299 Boylston St., Boston (267-9200); also in Everett and Quincy. **National Tire Wholesale**, 21 Needham St., Newton (244-1313); also in Dedham, Everett, Natick and others. **Quirk Tire**, 275 Arsenal St., Watertown (924-8700). **Sears Tire and Auto Centers**, 280

VFW Parkway, Dedham (320-5195); also in Braintree, Natick, Saugus and others.

A further option for low prices on new tires is BJ's Wholesale Club, at 909 The Fellsway (Route 28), Medford; see listing under "Department Stores."

A money-saver on tires, by the way, is retreading. It's like putting a brand-new layer of grooves on an old, worn-out tire. Retreads cost about half the price of new tires; for a small car, that can be as little as $25.00 apiece. Of course, they won't go as far; they are good for twenty thousand miles or so, about half the life expectancy of new economy-level tires. But, if you're short of cash at the moment, or plan to sell your car soon, this can be a good interim move.

The major retread dealer in Boston:

DORCHESTER

Dorchester Tire Service — 1160 Dorchester Ave., Dorchester; 436-0900. Very good service, friendly guys, and cheap tires mounted while-you-wait from their large in-house stock. Their retreads are guaranteed against defects for the life of the tire; of course, that's a little more subjective than new tire guarantees, but it's still very good for a used product.

BOOKS

Save money at many of these used book stores by bringing them the ones you don't want anymore. They'll give you more for your books if you take store credit rather than cash. It's a good, cheap way to keep your libraries lean, or to try out new authors.

Also, check the "Thrift Shop" listings for more places to find used books. Many have good selections at very low prices.

ALLSTON

Diskovery — 127 Brighton Ave., Allston; 787-2640. As the title implies, this is meant to be a record store; but it's pretty evenly divided between used books and disks, all nice and cheap. They're packed into this tiny storefront like sardines. A collection of short stories by Isaac Bashevis Singer was $6.00, in fine condition; Tracy Kidder's award-winning *House* was marked down from an original $17.95 to just $3.50. And there are tons of paperback novels, most $1.00 to $2.00. Comic books, too. See a separate listing under "Records."

ARLINGTON

Arlington Books — 212 Massachusetts Ave., Arlington; 643-4473. A couple of doors down from the (discount) Capitol Theater, Arlington Books is two storefronts' worth of used books of all kinds, including sets from estate collections. Many are rare and unusual. They also specialize in textbooks, foreign language books, and rare children's books, many from decades long past. The store is closed on Saturdays.

BOSTON

Ave. Victor Hugo Bookshop — 339 Newbury St., Boston; 266-7746. Fiction fans, this is your used book store! That's the specialty here, especially science fiction. Most books sell for about half of their current cover value, paperbacks and hardcovers. There are also some new books, many at 10 percent off; also, reviewer copies— a great way to get a current book for about one-third to one-half of the cover price.

You can buy, sell, or trade your own books in. AVH has lots of back-issue magazines too, and estate collections and sets. They're open every night of the week until 8:00 or 9:00.

Barnes And Noble — 395 Washington St., Boston; 426-5502. Also, 607 Boylston St., Boston; 236-1308. One of the country's best-known book discounters, B & N sells all new hardcovers at 15 percent off the cover price, except for those on the New York Times best seller list, which are 30 percent off; all paperbacks are 10 percent off.

There are also remainder books, such as John Updike's recent *Rabbit at Rest*, marked down from $21.95 to $4.99. Robert Parker's latest "Spenser" mystery was seen for $3.98. And then there are the $1.00 shelves, with books by Arthur C. Clarke and Erma Bombeck and a collection of Andy Warhol diaries (now *there's* a combination for ya).

Boston Book Annex — 906 Beacon St., Boston; 266-1090. Also, 705 Centre St., Jamaica Plain; 522-2100. Both locations of the Boston Book Annex are terrific for used books. From the the Boston store's trademark browsing tables outside the front door, with hardcovers for a dollar and paperbacks for 50¢, to the chic library look of the J.P. branch, you'll find plenty of great books in every subject.

Hardcovers are half the cover price, unless otherwise marked. A quick saunter through the "new" shelves—that is, newly arrived recent titles—found Thomas Pynchon's latest novel, *Vineland*. It was half-price, just $10.00. Garrison Keillor's delightful *Lake Wobegon Days* was also on these shelves.

Elsewhere, the Boston store had a major deal on a new Encyclopedia Brittanica set—forty-two volumes, including special science supplements and "Year in Review" editions from 1975 to 1983, all for $400.00—less than $10.00 apiece.

There are as many sections here as in a retail bookstore, from history to philosophy to medicine to humor. There's even a special bargain table, where Mr. C found Shelley Winters's kiss-and-tell Hollywood bio—much lauded by gossip mongers a few years back—in hardcover, reduced from $15.00 to just $4.00.

The JP store focuses more on educational textbooks and sets. It even looks like a library, complete with rolling wall ladders.

Buck A Book — 553 Boylston St., Boston; 266-0019. See listing under "Dollar Stores."

Charlesbank Bookshops — At the Boston University Bookstore, 660 Beacon St., Boston; 236-7425. Up on the fourth floor of this otherwise pricy student "mall," Charlesbank Bookshop—which also sells full-price books on level 2 and textbooks on level 5—sells remainders and overstocks at 60 to 90 percent off retail prices. A paperback edition of Anthony Lukas's landmark *Common Ground* was recently

seen for $3.98; so was Bill James's *1991 Baseball Book*, a definitive guide to the game, reduced from $15.00 to $4.98.

Anne Rice's *The Witching Hour* was less than half-price at $9.98, and a large-edition art book on Monet's water lilies, with color plates, was on sale for $30.00, marked down from $75.00. They also had a number of *Where's Waldo* items.

Goodspeed's Book Shop — 2 Milk St., Boston; 523-5970. Also, 7 Beacon St., Boston; 523-5970. Dealing mostly in antiquarian books, Goodspeed is like buying from the local library. It features rare book sets, like a fifteen-volume set of Rudyard Kipling's works, printed during the author's heyday in 1899, for $50.00.

There are more current books, like Henry Kissinger's *Years of Upheaval* for $10.00, marked down from $25.00; or William Styron's stunner *Sophie's Choice*, for $5.00. Also, a table of $1.00 books, and piles of National Geographic magazines for 25¢ apiece.

BRIGHTON

Commonwealth Bookmart — 918 Commonwealth Ave., Brighton; 232-9565. A good-sized, pleasant new book store on the BU campus, Commonwealth boasts, "All books discounted all the time." Current hardcovers are 15 percent off, paperbacks are 10 percent off, and New York Times bestsellers are 30 percent off. In addition, they have some remainders on sale at further reductions. Videos, books on tape, cards, and calendars are also sold at 10 percent off.

BROOKLINE

Brandeis Bookstall — 12 Sewall Ave., Brookline; 731-0208. Tucked behind the Harvard Street stores in Coolidge Corner, down a flight of stairs, Brandeis Bookstall is a cozy little used bookshop whose proceeds are contributed to the Brandeis University libraries. The prices are great, with most subjects well represented, including (naturally) textbooks. In fact, each month, one subject—such as law books, or medicine—goes on sale for just $1.00 per book, any title. And twice a year, everything goes into a half-price sale.

In general, you'll find most hardcover fiction around $1.00 to $3.00; paperback novels go from 50¢ to $2.00, with a large section at four for a dollar. Bill Cosby's *Fatherhood* was spotted for $3.00. There are also art and travel books; individual sections of French, German, Spanish, Russian, and even Asian books; sheet music collections; lots of Judaica; cookbooks; computer manuals; and sections for senior citizens and children.

Brookline Booksmith — 279 Harvard St., Brookline; 566-6660. This large and hip bookstore sells new books mainly, but always has several tables of remainders at big discounts. A coffee table bio of Jimi Hendrix, originally $27.50, was recently on sale for $9.98; Calvin Trillin's hilarious *Travels with Alice* was marked down from $18.98 to $3.98, and same price for *Summer Game*, a collection of baseball essays by the literary Roger Angell. Booksmith is always fun to browse (*that's* cheap), and has a large selection of funky greeting cards too.

Brookline Village Book Store — 23 Harvard St., Brookline; 734-3519. This shop is not all that cheap, by used book standards. Most hardcovers go from $4.00 to $8.00, rather high, but still well below list prices; and there are a ton of them, stacked literally from floor to ceiling. Many of these are in excellent condition, and the quality and selection reflect the owner's careful tastes.

The series of Dick Francis mystery novels, for instance, were priced at $5.95; these are obviously overstock buyouts, in fine condition, with several copies of each title. Doris Kearns Goodwin's *The Fitzgeralds and the Kennedys*,

source for the TV miniseries, was $7.95. Again, not cheap, but like new.

Royal Discount Book Store — 1354 Beacon St., Brookline; 734-7903. Also, 635 Massachusetts Ave., Arlington; 643-4422. This large store in Coolidge Corner offers everything at discount, including current and recent best sellers. Titles on the New York Times best seller list are sold at 35 percent off the cover price; 25 percent off for paperbacks on the list. All other books in the store are at least 10 percent off, with special tables of discounts up to 80 percent.

Mr. C found (but did not pick up) *Lady Boss*, by Jackie Collins, marked down from $21.95 to just $5.98. On a similar note, Ivana Trump's novel *For Love Alone* (yep, must be fiction) was reduced from $22.00 to $14.30. Robert Ludlum's latest was there. So was Dave Barry's. And on the overstock table, a large-size Bruce Springsteen photo biography was just 98¢, from $10.95. Sorry, Boss.

Royal Discount also has magazines, books on tape, calendars and gift items, all at 10 percent discount.

CAMBRIDGE

Barillari Books — 1 Mifflin Place (Mt. Auburn St.), Cambridge; 864-2400. This attractive new Harvard Square store (complete with coffee bar) claims to offer over one hundred thousand titles; and, with the exception of textbooks, they are all sold at 25 percent off the retail price. Not bad. And, if it's on the current New York Times best seller list, you can get it at 35 percent off.

Go upstairs to the second floor and you'll find a good selection of overstock books at further discounts. Mr. C found *Life* magazine's large paperback book on the history of sports, marked down from $14.95 to $4.98. Also in paperback (the full-size book club edition) was E.L. Doctorow's *Billy Bathgate* for $2.98. You missed the movie, now read the book—which everyone said was better anyway.

There are lots of big, glossy art books, many around $10.00; and *Webster's Illustrated Dictionary Encyclopedia* was on sale for $12.98. Let's see, with ten thousand entries, that comes to about $0.0013 per word. Pretty cheap—and that's not including the five hundred color illustrations!

Helpful tip: Barillari gives you a free hour of parking in the nearby Harvard Square Parking Garage (corner of Eliot and JFK Streets) with a minimum $5.00 purchase. Bring your ticket with you to the store.

The Book Case — 42 Church St., Cambridge; 876-0832. A few doors down from the Harvard Square Cinema, this shop looks tiny from the outside—but downstairs, the large basement is filled with used books on every subject. Best bets here are the hardcovers, most of which are about half the original cover price. Paperbacks, around $2.00 each, are rather dog-eared for that much dough.

Non-fiction dominates the collection, with lots of textbooks and mass-market works. The history section alone divides into general, ancient and medieval, English, U.S., Chinese, French, Russian . . . . They also have a big selection of Cliff's Notes— students, take heed.

Harvard Book Store — 1256 Massachusetts Ave., Cambridge; 661-1515. Right across the street from Harvard Yard, HBS gets high marks for thorough inventory. In addition to the full-price books, there are two discount options here—first, a good-sized table of remainders, ranging from best sellers to literary collections. These, as in many stores, sell for anywhere from 50 to 80 percent off.

Downstairs in the basement, though, is the place to be for any book lover. The used book department has almost as much selection as the main level's regular shelves—or those of any other book store, for that matter. Arts, politics, science,

novels—mostly paperbacks, all sold at half the cover price. Used textbooks are 25 percent off. For students, and any readers on a budget, this is a must.

Harvard Coop—1400 Massachusetts Ave., Cambridge; 499-2000. Actually, you have to go behind the main store to the Palmer Street building, where books take up the ground level. All current books are discounted by 10 percent, except texts; New York Times bestsellers are 20 percent off. Furthermore, several long tables of remainders are always stacked with books on just about any subject, at up to 80 percent off the original prices. Great for browsing.

Parking tip: With a minimum $5.00 purchase, get two free hours of parking at the University Place or Charles Square garages, or one hour at the lot on Church Street. Just bring your sales slip to the cashier's desk on the third floor of the main store.

Kate's Mystery Books — 2211 Massachusetts Ave., Cambridge; 491-2660. Not a discount store *per se*, but one of the best mystery book stores around. Now, as you may know, mystery fans go through novels the way Sy Sperling goes through hairpieces. That means they have a lot of useless books on their hands. And they bring them into Kate's by the carton.

If you're a part of this food chain, Kate's is the place for you. Bring in your old mysteries (hardcover or paperback) for credit toward other new or used books. And if you're just looking to buy, check out the several shelves of used paperbacks, mostly priced from $1.00 to $3.00. Used hardcovers are mixed in with the new ones, so they take a bit more sleuthing.

Whodunnit fans go through books so quickly, in fact, that you can often find current best sellers only a few months after their publication. And mysteries apparently age like wines—a recent used title may actually cost less than an older one. Great way to support your habit—and save!

McIntyre & Moore Booksellers — 8 Mt. Auburn St., Cambridge; 491-0662. Heading out of Harvard Square, you come to several scholarly used book stores—Pangloss, Starr, and this one are all along Mt. Auburn Street, and all have good selections of texts and related nonfiction. M & M specializes in the sciences, history and cultures from around the world, architecture, theology, and similar subjects. They are open every day of the week until 10 p.m.

Pangloss Bookshop — 65 Mt. Auburn St., Cambridge; 354-4003. A used book store for the highbrows. Non-fiction is the specialty of the house, with lots of history, literature studies, pop psychology, and the like. Oh, you may come across the odd novel, like John Le Carre's *The Russia House*, for $5.00; but you're more likely to find journalist Nicholas Daniloff's account of his capture by the KGB, *Two Lives, One Russia*, half-price at $10.00—on a whole shelf of Russian studies. Lots of sets, too.

Reading International Bookstores — 47 Brattle St., Cambridge; 864-0705. Also, 43 Leonard St., Belmont; 484-0705. Another popular stop on the literary tour of the Square, Reading International sells new books at discount. Latest releases are usually gathered on a couple of tables at 20 percent off, while remainders go on another table for up to 70 percent off. During the summer months they even set up tables outside the store, with lots to browse for half-price. You can find authors from Shakespeare and the Greeks to Faulkner and Dorothy Parker, along with the yuppie novels of Jay McInerney. Also, *The Columbia History of the World*, marked down from $25.00 to $10.00, and even *The Doonesbury Dossier*, originally $12.95, now $4.98.

Starr Book Shop — 29 Plympton St., Cambridge; 547-6864. As you've begun to notice, Cambridge is renowned for having one of the highest concentrations of bookstores per square mile in the country. Along Mt. Auburn Street, the Starr shares space in the narrow, oddly-shaped Harvard Lampoon building. Don't worry—the store is much more serious about books than its neighbor.

Most hardcovers are just over half of their original prices, unless they are very old or worn. Generally, the quality here is quite good, and the selection is large. Mr. C saw a like-new copy of Norman Mailer's *Tough Guys Don't Dance*, reduced from $16.95 to $8.50.

Mr. Cheap's Picks

✓ **Ave. Victor Hugo** — Used paperback paradise, especially for fiction (science and otherwise).

✓ **Buck A Book** — this fast growing chain snaps up recent closeouts and overstocks and sells most of them—honest—for a buck. A branch may be opening on your corner even now.

✓ **Harvard Book Store** — the one *in* Harvard Square, that is. Classy overstock tables upstairs, lots of used books downstairs, including textbooks.

✓ **New England Mobile Book Fair** — Nothing mobile about it. Probably the biggest collection of overstocks and new books all at discount in the area.

More diverse are the non-fiction subjects, with a lot to browse through in sociology, psychology, law and medicine, history, art and travel. Open every day from 10 a.m. to 8 p.m., and Sundays from noon to 6 p.m.

Wordsworth Books — 30 Brattle St., Cambridge; 354- 5201. Perhaps the king of Harvard Square bookshops, the two-story WordsWorth looks out over the open plaza at the beginning of Brattle Street. It offers a very complete selection of current books, over a hundred thousand titles under nearly a hundred categories, from Native American studies to linguistics to bestsellers. All are sold at 15 percent off hardcover prices and 10 percent off paperbacks.

On the second floor, by the windows, you'll also find further reductions on leftover editions. *New and Selected Essays* by Robert Penn Warren, originally $25.00, was on sale for $6.25. Gore Vidal's *Hollywood* was reduced from $20.00 to $5.40, and David Attenborough's book based on the TV series *The Living Planet* went for just $7.19, down from $25.00. WordsWorth is open late seven days a week.

JAMAICA PLAIN

Rose Way Books — 470 Centre St., Jamaica Plain. This funky little place in a converted old house is crammed from floor to ceiling with novels, dramas, antique books, and more. Most of the stock is old books, but you may unearth some treasures—like a set of Shakespeare's plays in six tiny volumes, each the size of a pack of playing cards.

Rose Way is also famous—or infamous—for its "outdoor book sale," browsing tables outside the shop that are covered over with plastic and left out at night. Hardcovers are 50¢, paperbacks a dollar; if you're browsing after hours, just drop the money through the mail slot in the door. The honor system lives!

NEWTON

New England Mobile Book Fair
— 82 Needham St., Newton; 964-7440. One of the largest, most amazing bookstores in the Boston area—truly, a book lover's paradise. Blink as you cruise Newton's commercial strip and you'll miss this plain wooden warehouse; but go inside, and you'll find what seem to be acres and acres of shelves.

The store divides into two halves: books currently in print, most at 20 percent off, and remainders at greater discounts. The current section is organized by publishers and titles, with both hardcovers and paperbacks. The knowledgeable staff can help you find, or look up, almost any book you want. And yet the overstock area of the store is just as big, if not bigger. It's packed with hundreds of titles in every subject: history, literature, children's, travel, cooking.

Find David Halberstam's excellent account of the Red Sox-Yankees rivalry in *The Summer of '49*, marked down from $21.95 to $4.98. Eric Lax's popular biography of Woody Allen is just $7.95; and an oversized photo essay book on Hemingway, with a cover price of $39.95, sells for $9.98. There are lots of computer user's books, like *Advanced DOS 4.0*, reduced from $22.95 to $5.98. There are also many collector's edition books, such as the giant, sealed *Art of Walt Disney*—originally $60.00, here $39.95.

CDs, RECORDS AND TAPES

Like used book shops, many of these places allow you to trade in music you no longer want (some, alas, don't accept LPs anymore). You can get cash for the deal, but you'll get more by taking store credit instead. Besides, this is an easy way to check out artists you may not want to try at full price.

ALLSTON

CD Spins — 187 Harvard Ave., Allston; 787-7680. Staffed only by its two owners, this tiny walk-down shop keeps a low overhead in many ways—but what they save on rent and staff gets passed on to the customers. They have lots of good music, on cassettes as well as CDs, and some very liberal return policies. Rock is the main course here. You may find Paul Simon's *Graceland* on tape for $3.99; there is also a section of used cassettes that have been traded in without boxes—so, if you don't mind handwritten packaging, you can get perfectly good tapes for a mere $1.00 to $3.00.

On discs, the Grateful Dead's double set *Without a Net* was on sale for $18.99; a couple of unopened Genesis CDs were each $8.99. New discs, mixed in with the used ones, are marked with a blue dot. Better yet, there is a large rack of bargain CDs, priced from just $1.00 to $6.00; even there, you'll find such names as Robert Plant, George Michael, and LL Cool J.

Now, here's the best part. All CDs are fully returnable for seven days—even used ones—for full credit (keep that receipt!). So your music shopping is essentially risk-free. A further bargain: If you buy four CDs, you can get a fifth one at half-price.

Diskovery—127 Brighton Ave., Allston; 787-2640. As noted in the "Books" section, this is a store with an identity crisis—is it a used book store or record store? No matter; there are lots of both. Most cassettes and LPs are priced from $2.50 to $4.50; records are the most plentiful, mainly in rock 'n roll. What makes this store more interesting, for those who bring stuff to trade in, is the option of using store credit for both music *and* books. There is even a bit of room for wheeling and dealing. Get creative!

BOSTON

In Your Ear! — 957 Commonwealth Ave., Boston; 787-9755. Also, 72 Mt. Auburn St., Cambridge; 491-5035. One of Boston's many great used music stores. In Your Ear! recently moved its Boston location to larger quarters, near the Paradise rock club, which gives you some idea of the music they carry. Rock 'n roll, both new and old, is ably represented here—from vintage sixties records to tapes by Boston's local bands. They have other kinds of music, but these sections are not extensive.

Most records and cassettes are reasonably priced, from $3.99 to $5.99; compact discs are in the $5.99 to $7.99 price range. They also have lots of boxes filled with records and tapes for $1.00, and some for 50¢. Most of these are junk, of course, but they're still fun to rummage through—every once in a while, you find something interesting hidden in there.

In Your Ear! also sells new and used music videos, lots of rock and movie posters, and accessories.

Looney Tunes — 1106 Boylston St., Boston; 247-2238. Also, 1001 Massachusetts Ave., Cambridge; 876-5624. Yet another large selection of used albums, tapes and CDs. The main store is located in the music schools area; and so in addition to lots of rock and pop, Looney Tunes has a healthy offering of classical music at both stores. Most discs are $2.00 to $5.00; cassettes, $3.00 to $6.00; CDs, $6.00 to $8.00. Check out the bargain section, where records are 99¢, tapes are $1.49, and CDs are just $4.99.

Nuggets — 486 Commonwealth Ave., Boston; 536-0679. Also, 1354A Beacon St., Brookline; 277-8917. Of Kenmore Square's many used record stores, Nuggets has always been one of the largest. In the last few years it has both spawned a branch in Coolidge Corner and moved its original location into newer, even more spacious digs next door.

There you can find plenty to choose from in cassette, CD and good ol' LP formats. Rock is their primary seller (including lots of local bands), but there is a good selection of jazz too.

Most of the tapes sell around $3.00 to $5.00 for popular titles; some are higher, especially if they are recent. Still, if you find one that's new and unopened, it may cost less than in retail stores. One drawback about Nuggets' tape section is that all kinds of pop music—rock, jazz, soul, etc.—are mixed together alphabetically by artist. Most stores don't do that. Nuggets doesn't even do it with records and discs. Oh well.

There's plenty of vinyl here, priced from $1.99 and up. The Rolling Stones' *Hot Rocks* is $5.99. And there is a sizeable collection of

45 rpm records, all 99¢ each.

Most CDs are in the $7.00 to $10.00 range. Tracy Chapman's *Crossroads* was spotted for $8.00; Eric Clapton's *Crossroads*, on the other hand, was $35.00—for a four-disc set. There are new CDs mixed in too, usually $11.00 to $12.00.

Nuggets has a separate area filled with racks of $1.00 tapes and $2.00 CDs, and if you're patient, you may find a deal. They also sell T-shirts, posters, wooden racks, and even old copies of *Rolling Stone* for $1.00 apiece.

The Brookline outpost is smaller and more cramped, but draws from the same overall stock as its parent store. It's hidden down an alley off of Beacon Street, behind the Royal Discount Book Store (see listing under "Books").

Planet Records — 536 Commonwealth Ave., Boston; 353-0693. For a small store, this longtime favorite packs a lot in— plenty of records, tapes, and CDs. Like anything in Kenmore Square, rock 'n roll is big here—but Planet is also strong in soul, jazz, and R & B.

A couple of years ago it looked like they were getting out of vinyl, going mainly with CDs. But that's not proven to be the case. In fact, to make the used 33s more competitive, many of the popular titles are labeled with a sound quality rating—"8.5 out of 10"—done by the store. Great idea.

Most good or new LPs are priced around $4.00 to $8.00. Planet also has a good variety of imports, rare LPs and special sets. Singles, including lots of oldies, are 49¢ to $2.99. And then there's the vintage stuff, kitschy albums from the fifties and sixties—it's hilarious just to look at the covers.

Tapes and CD's are reasonably priced—many cassettes are $4.00 and $5.00, and discs are usually $7.00 to $9.00.

Tower Records — 360 Newbury St., Boston; 247-5900. Also, 95 Mt. Auburn St., Cambridge; 876-3377. Huh? What's this doing in here, Mr. C? Tower may be big, they may be

Mr. Cheap's Picks

✓ **Cheapo Records** — What did you expect? Mr. C's favorite name in town, and one of his favorite spots for any kind of music.

✓ **Nuggets** — Recently expanded into new digs, you can spend hours in one of Boston's largest used music stores.

✓ **CD Spins** — Dedicated primarily to compact discs, the best way to get good quality used tunes. Very liberal return policy.

✓ **Disc Diggers** — Lots of hip used music, especialiy jazz and world beat.

open 365 days a year and all, but are they cheap? Well, no, not for new music. But many shoppers aren't aware that Tower has a large cutout album section—overstocks that won't sell at full price anymore. It's a whole row near the other records, with quite a good variety of stuff. Many of these albums are $2.99 to $4.99 for big-name artists like Stevie Wonder, Fleetwood Mac, and Steely Dan, as well as some jazz and folk.

For cutout tapes you have to go to the tape section. Jazz and folk remainders are mixed in with the full-price tapes; classical is in its own section. The tape selection may be smaller, but you can often find good stuff for $3.99.

CAMBRIDGE

Cheapo Records — 645 Massachusetts Ave., Cambridge; 354-4455. Well, this has to be Mr. C's favorite, from the name alone. Fortunately, there's more to recommend it than just that! Cheapo has a huge collection of records and tapes, and a growing section of CDs too. It's a long, narrow store crammed from floor to ceiling on two levels. When you come in, you're looking at new, opened, and some used stock— but go downstairs for the real fun.

Here you'll find most LPs and tapes from $1.99 to $5.99, with CDs a bit more. But there is a special rack of CDs under $5.00, with some selection, not to mention a box of cassette singles, 50¢ each. Cheapo gets high marks for variety; both floors have every kind of music you can think of. Rock, of course (*lots* of oldies), jazz, Latin, country—often in great detail. From the South alone there are sections for Dixieland, Cajun and zydeco, blues—and how many places have an entire three-section bin dedicated to "Louisiana Swamp Music"?

Discount Records — 18 J.F.K. St., Cambridge; 492-4064. Don't be fooled by names. This tiny shop in Harvard Square has lots of good music, but it ain't that cheap. They barely even have records, for that matter, thanks to the CD revolution. This is all new merchandise, with a small section of remainders at discount. Have a look, but . . . .

Mystery Train Records — 1208 Massachusetts Ave., Cambridge; 497-4024. Also, 306 Newbury St., Boston; 536-0216. As you may guess from the name, this place can really give you the blues. Rock too, of course. Mainly on tapes and CDs, though; the original Cambridge store, in particular, is tiny.

Most records and tapes are nice and cheap, priced around $3.00 to $5.00. Compact discs are about $8.00 to $9.00 for most popular bands.

Mystery Train also has a large selection of homemade concert tapes of many major groups, like Led Zeppelin, the Beatles, and the Kinks; these are $6.50 and up. Video concert tapes of such artists as John Lennon and the Rolling Stones start at $15.00 and up. Collect every city!

And there are lots of rare records, British imports and the like, starting around $15.00 to $20.00.

Skippy White's Records — 555 Massachusetts Ave., Cambridge; 491-3345. A definitive store for all kinds of black music, from rap and urban pop to soul, R & B, and lots of gospel. New and used recordings are mixed together; the LPs tend to be cheap but also well used. The digs are a bit small, but Skippy's has an extensive collection in these special varieties of music. Lots of hard-to-find artists and out-of-print discs. Not that much in CDs here, and most tend to be new and full-price; but for tapes and especially records, boogie on over.

Stereo Jack's Records — 1704 Massachusetts Ave., Cambridge; 497-9447. Yet another of Cambridge's many fine used music shops, Stereo Jack's specializes in jazz, straight-ahead blues, and R & B. Records, which are still a vital format in this area of music, are mostly $1.00 to $4.00; most CDs average from $7.00 to $10.00. Jack's doesn't seem to concentrate that much on tapes. There is also a bargain bin of records for $1.00. "Some people come in here and only look there," says Jack. "They always walk away with something." He is more proud, though, of the extensive jazz selection. Open seven days. Knowledgeable staff.

EAST BOSTON

Boston Beat — 80 Bennington St., East Boston; 561-4790. This store keeps the beat by specializing in dance music—reggae, hip-hop, rap, and even good ol' disco from the seventies. Most of the discs are current stuff, though—Boston Beat sells both new and used music. In the used category they sell only records and CDs; no cassettes. Most LPs are priced at $2.00 to $3.00, with many as low as 99¢. Compact discs range from $5.00 to $9.00 for current sounds. They boogie from noon to 8 p.m. on weekdays, 11 a.m. to 8 p.m. on Saturdays, and noon to 6 p.m. on Sundays.

SOMERVILLE

Disc Diggers — 401 Highland Ave., Somerville; 776-7560. This big outpost in Davis Square has a fine selection of pop music, jazz, and happening sounds from all over the world. In fact, they claim to have the largest selection in New England; but you won't find records there. Yes, vinyl die-hards, they've made that dreaded move. Only CDs and cassettes spoken here.

The selection and prices are good, though. Used CDs are about $7.99 on average, with some new ones mixed in at only $9.99. They also have lots of those cute little CD singles for 99¢ to $1.09. Most cassette prices are around $3.99, with many at lower prices.

Open seven days, from 11 a.m. to 9 p.m., except noon to 6 p.m. on Sundays.

CAMERAS AND PHOTOGRAPHY EQUIPMENT

Apart from big sales in department stores, the best way to save big money on a camera is to buy one used. Well cared for, a good camera will last longer than a good car; most used models still have several years of snaps left in them. Downtown Crossing is one of the best places to shop, with many stores in the same area.

BOSTON

Bromfield Camera Company — 10 Bromfield St., Boston; 426-5230. This store has perhaps the largest selection of used cameras around; the display cases are filled with them, and the salesman is happy to show you one or all. $140.00 can get you a Konica TC 35mm camera with semi-automatic features. It originally retailed for around $250.00. Stepping up just a bit, they had a Canon AE-1—"the most popular camera of the seventies," said the salesman—for $175.00. These cameras come with lenses, and there are other used lenses to choose from as extras (they twist on and off). Add a used leather case for another $10.00.

Nikons start around $250.00 and up. At the other end of the range, Mr. C saw a Polaroid "One-Step" for just $25.00. All cameras here come with a thirty-day full warranty; or you can buy a four-year extended warranty from the store for an additional $50.00.

General Photographic Supply Co. — 71-73 Canal St., Boston; 742-7070. This large store near North Station has a large selection of new and used photo equipment, mainly in 35mm still cameras. There are always lots of brands to choose from, including Minolta, Canon, and especially Nikon. New cameras are usually priced just above cost; used equipment is even less. A used Nikon 5005, with auto focus, may be around $300.00. General Photo is very choosy about used cameras; they only sell stock that is in good to excellent condition, and all items have a thirty-day warranty.

They also have used enlargers and tripods; and new supplies, like chemicals, paper, and film, all sold at 30 percent off list price.

International Camera, Inc. — 4 Bromfield St., Boston; 423-2968. One of the few camera stores that seems to have compact automatic cameras among the used stock. A Nikon "One Touch" 35mm camera, the kind with the sleek body that fits into the palm of your hand, sells for $89.00. It's a point-and-shoot type. Other SLR's start around $100.00, with such brands as Pentax, Olympus, and Minolta. This store had the least number to choose from in the area, but just enough. All cameras have a thirty-day warranty, with the option of purchasing a longer warranty plan. Sales help here is on the brusque side.

Sherman's — 11 Bromfield St., Boston; 482-9610. (See listings under "Electronics".)

Stone Camera, Inc. — 42 Bromfield St., Boston; 542-6928. A nice staff here, and some good options under $200.00. For as little as $90.00, you can get a Ricoh KR-5 manual 35mm camera with a

55mm lens. Even at this low price, you'll get a through-the-lens light meter and focusing system. Moving up some, Mr. C looked at a Chinon, also with lens, for $130.00; they had several other choices in this price range.

Stone guarantees used cameras for thirty days, full parts and labor, as the other stores do; but their warranty continues at 50 percent for the rest of one year. They'll cover half of any repair work you need them to do. A unique deal.

CAMBRIDGE

Cambridge Camera Exchange — 2032 Massachusetts Ave., Cambridge; 497-2300. Also, 727 Revere Beach Pkwy., Revere; 284-2300. A full-price camera and film developing shop, with a selection of used and discontinued cameras and lenses at reduced prices. Mr. C found an old Nikon "F" camera, with manual exposure and focusing, for $160.00; also a more recent Minolta 7000, with manual or automatic functions, for $290.00 with lens. This was an unused, discontinued model; the version that has replaced it sells around $500.00 today.

You'll also find used lenses and filters and even a box of outdated film (all varieties, $2.00 each). The equipment comes with a thirty-day full warranty; you can purchase a one-year warranty for $20.00 extra. Knowledgeable staff, too.

Kenmore Camera — 50 Church St., Cambridge; 661-6643. "We have everything," says the owner of Kenmore Camera, which sounds like it should be under the Citgo sign instead of in Harvard Square. He went on to recite a litany that proved his point: Kenmore has 35mm cameras, movie cameras, lenses, tripods, projectors, and even some video camcorders (which don't stick around for long).

You'll find all major brands— Nikon, Olympus, Minolta, Kodak, Leica, Bell and Howell . . . almost all of the stuff is used, which is the specialty here. There are plenty of items under $100.00. Some cameras start as low as $30.00, as do some of the movie and slide projectors. These may, of course, be older models, which are sold as is; more recent ones carry a thirty-day warranty.

Closed on Sundays.

NEWTON

Newtonville Camera And Video — 249 Walnut St., Newton; 965-1240. Perhaps the largest selection of new and used cameras in the area, from current models to the old and unusual. This shop is frequented by amateur photographers and professionals, making for a strong selection in the used department. Cameras start around $40.00 or $50.00 for basic point-and-shoot models. They also have lots of tripods and lenses. Used

Mr. Cheap's Picks

✓ **General Photographic Supply Company** — A big place with good bargains on high-quality used 35mm cameras and darkroom equipment.

✓ **Kenmore Camera** — What are they doing in Cambridge? Selling used cameras of every shape and kind under the (filtered) sun.

✓ **Newtonville Camera** — Not only used cameras, but one of the only places selling used *video* camcorders—a good way to save on an expensive item.

cameras carry a full ninety-day warranty, much longer than most other stores offer.

More interesting yet is Newtonville's selection of used video equipment. Camcorders by Sony, JVC, and others are available in the range of $200.00 to $300.00, a substantial savings over new models,

which remain stubbornly high in this market. They have used VCR's too. These have a thirty-day warranty.

As far as Mr. C knows, this is the only major collection of used video equipment around; though when it comes to saving money, he is always happy to be corrected.

CLOTHING

Know what kind of clothes you're buying! Clothing, like anything else, is sold at discount for many reasons. Let's go over some terms: *"First quality"* means brand-new merchandise that has no flaws. It may be reduced in price as a sales promotion or because it's overstock or from a past season. *"Discontinued"* is self-explanatory; but again, these items are new and most are perfectly good.

"Seconds," or *"irregulars,"* are new clothes that have some slight mistakes in their manufacture or that have been damaged in shipping. Often these blemishes are hard to see. A reputable store will call your attention to the problem area with a piece of masking tape or such.

"Consignment shops" sell clothing they call "gently used"—by one owner who wore the article only a few times and chose to resell it. This merchandise is of high quality, and it's a great way to save lots of money on a designer piece that looks like new. *"Vintage clothing"* is usually well-worn but may still cost you a bit—being from a past era, or of a particularly hot "retro" style. Nevertheless, there are great bargains for the persistent vintage hound. *"Thrift stores"* sell used merchandise that has seen a lot of duty, often donated for charity. Quality and selection are strictly grab-bag, but you can get a lot of stuff super-cheap.

NEW CLOTHING

The purpose of this book is to direct your attention to smaller, lesser-known stores; big chains with high visibility are given less ink here. You already know about them. There are some exceptions, of course—how could someone called Mr. Cheap fail to mention the downtown **Filene's Basement**, after all? You'll notice, though, that the watered-down suburban branches are omitted.

Here's another exception. Several of Mr. C's female shopping hounds love two major chains: **Marshalls**, at 275 Needham St., Newton (964-4987), Arsenal Mall, Watertown (923-1044), Meadow Glen Mall, Medford (391-1331), and in many outer suburbs; and **T.J. Maxx**, at the Fresh Pond Shopping Center, Cambridge (492- 8500), 300 VFW Parkway, Dedham (329-8162), and 750 The Fellsway, Medford (393-0027). They cruise through as often as they can, finding well-known name brands at good savings—whether they're stocking up on the basics or going for a splurge. While these stores once had a bit of a stigma attached to them, they have grown to be acceptable for quality as well as price.

Both have men's clothing too, of course; and another chain worth mentioning for the guys is **Milton's**, at 174 Boylston St. (Route 9), Chestnut Hill (969-4547); also in Braintree, Natick, and Peabody. True to its commercials, Milton's has a huge selection of new clothing for men and women at substantial reductions. Designer names and lesser-known brands as well.

Now, on to the rest of the bargains!

ALLSTON

Boston Sweats Outlet — 16 Brighton Ave., Allston; 782-0480. The main business here is custom-printed clothing; T-shirts and caps with your team's name on them, silk-screen designs, etc. But they do have display racks with samples, leftovers and irregulars, which you can grab for a song. "Cheers" T-shirts are $6.00. Sweat pants and shirts with a variety of college logos are $10.00 and under; baseball hats are $5.00.

Chain Bargain Store — 20 Harvard Ave., Allston; 254-4590. The last outpost of a chain store that was very popular earlier in the century, before the mall mentality took over. Just walking in is like going back fifty years, to a time of good, basic men's clothes at affordable prices. Personal service, too. Here, you'll find jeans, work shirts, sneakers and boots, jackets, and accessories.

Painter's pants are $12.00 to $15.00; a Windbreaker cotton-polyester jacket goes for $25.00; and cotton walking shorts are just $11.99. Not everything here can compete with big-name stores, but as the name implies, there are bargains to be found.

Brand-new Converse All-Stars, the classic high-top sneakers, sell for $25.00, about $10.00 below department store prices. Wrangler jeans (irregulars) are $14.99; and Georgia "Oxford" shoes, at $43.00, look exactly like the popular "Dr. Marten's" black leather uniform shoes that sell around $70.00 on Newbury Street.

BOSTON

Eddie Bauer Outlet — 230 Washington St., Boston; 227-4840. People who know and wear Eddie Bauer clothing swear by it, and so they love this store—where you can buy almost the same popular clothes at savings of 30 to 70 percent over retail prices. Most of the stock is made up of seconds and irregulars from the factory; but the boo-boos are so miniscule as to escape notice.

Find dresses for as little as $19.99 that had originally retailed for anywhere from $42.00 to $68.00, or sweaters for $10.00, and all kinds of other sportswear, outdoor gear, and shoes. Open seven days a week.

Fashion Avenue — 97 Salem St., Boston; 723-1628. For twenty years, Fashion Avenue in the North End has been an insider's haven—quietly selling name-brand and designer apparel for women at savings of 60 to 90 percent off retail prices. The owner has lots of connections with factories and gets merchandise from them directly; in many cases, this is the only place they can be found at discount. Most are seconds and irregulars, but the blemishes are hard to find. Serious damages are clearly indicated; you know what you are getting.

But what you can get is incredible. To protect his contacts, the owner requested that no names be given here—but take it from Mr. C, you'll know the names. One popular store's line of heavy cotton T-shirts, in bright pastels, was marked down from $25.00 to just $5.00. A white cotton bodysuit from a well-known lingerie store was also $5.00, originally $48.00. And a minidress from an international designer was on sale for $50.00, from $175.00.

There are many racks of blouses and slacks priced at $5.00, $10.00 and $15.00; also a clearance rack of items for $2.00 (or three for $5.00).

All sales, of course, are final.

Filene's Basement, Jordan Marsh Basement — Downtown Crossing, Boston. See listings under "Department Stores."

Freedberg's Of Boston — 112 Shawmut Ave., Boston; 357-8600. Not much here is *cheap* in the strictest sense—but it's all at drastically reduced prices. What is it? Superior-quality men's suits. Freedberg's makes clothes for the best: Louis of

Boston, Saks Fifth Avenue, and the like. Way upstairs, on Saturday mornings from 8:00 to noon only, you can peruse the racks yourself for the current season's fashions at anywhere from 40 to 70 percent off.

The styles range from European cuts to conservative Wall Street looks; there are also ties, sweaters, and some women's suits and dresses. Men's suits are the main item, though. They start around $300.00, which sounds like a lot, but these would easily cost twice as much in trendy stores. The range goes up to about $450.00, for suits that would retail at well over $1,000.00.

Gentlemen's Wear House — 161 Newbury St., Boston; 236-4220. Also, 257 Crescent St., Waltham; 647-0858, and in Hingham, Danvers and Burlington. At Gentlemen's Wear House, the main thing is suits, suits and more suits. These are made in GWH's own local factories for distribution to major department stores; but you can buy them here directly for less. The look here is ultra-conservative— strictly business.

There is a huge selection of single- and double-breasted suits in wools, silks, and synthetics. They also have a wide range of sizes, including big and tall. Most of the suits are sold at certain price levels; you have your $99.00 suits, your $129.00's, $159.00's, and so on. All of these prices are savings of $35.00 to $50.00 and more. And, periodically, they run a two-for-one sale for even better deals.

Harry The Greek's — 1136 Washington St., Boston; 338-7511. This South End shop—which looks more like an indoor version of selling off the back of a truck—has attained legendary status for cheap clothes and shoes. Don't expect much in the way of niceties; the aisles are narrow and cluttered with boxes and people. But the deals . . .

Most of the clothes are seconds and irregulars. As usual, this is hardly noticeable in most of the items. Recent bargains (ever-changing) included solid-color T-shirts for $2.00 each, with "roll-up" styles for $4.00; Hanes sweatshirts and pants for $7.50 to $8.50; men's "unbranded" sneakers for $12.00; and white painters' pants for $10.00. They also carry lots of children's sizes (kids' Wrangler jeans, two pairs for $18.00).

Then there are the shoes— well, mostly sneakers and work boots, plus hiking boots by Timberland and Herman's. Adidas basketball sneakers were $40.00; a pair of Asics "Gel" running shoes was marked down to $35.00. Pick up six pairs of tube socks to go with them for $5.00.

Harry's makes a few nods to fashion, like "Rude" jeans— artistically tattered, patched, and dyed in hot colors—for $35.00. There are also some used clothes; Mr. C saw a nicely-faded pair of Levi's jeans for $8.00.

Take cash with you—because Harry's "doesn't take checks and he doesn't take American Express" . . . or any other credit cards, for that matter.

Hit Or Miss Clearance Center — 91 Franklin St., Boston; 338-1208. Shoppers don't always know that this branch of the popular chain has its own bargain basement near Downtown Crossing. Prices on these career clothes for women are automatically reduced every three weeks. You may find a Boston Classics linen skirt, half-price at $20.00; a two-piece nylon running suit, marked down from $50.00 to $30.00; or a silk-type paisley blouse, originally $33.00, now just $5.00.

There are some big-name brands, like an Oleg Cassini linen blazer reduced from $90.00 to $40.00; or a D'Albert cotton dress in a houndstooth check, same price, from an original $140.00. As usual, these are mostly seconds and last season's leftovers.

Kingston Textiles — 116 Kingston St., Boston; 542-8140. Mainly a silkscreening shop, where you can get

---

Mr. Cheap's Picks

✓ **Back Door Warehouse** — Behind Somerville's Davis Square, these folks snap up overstocks and slightly-damaged coats, boots, work clothes, and jeans, and sell 'em dirt cheap.

✓ **Burlington Coat Factory** — Two area stores as big as any clothing department stores, but all at discount. Bargains on last season's lines.

✓ **Fashion Ave.** — Tucked into the North End, Mr. C can't divulge the women's designer names you'll find here at tremendously-reduced prices. Experienced shoppers know its the real goods as soon as they walk in.

✓ **Frugal Fannie's** — Out in the 'burbs, a gold mine in past-season clothing; ask any woman who's been there—or her husband who gets to wait in the holding tank. Weekends only.

✓ **Harry The Greek's** — This South End joint is like Filene's Basement, only packed in much tighter. Good place to take the kids for jeans and sneakers.

---

all sorts of activewear printed up with anything you like; they will also sell you "plain" clothing by Fruit of the Loom, Hanes, and others at below-retail prices. Hanes solid-color sweatshirts and pants are $7.99 each; and their 50/50 cotton-poly T-shirts are $3.99 in a variety of classic colors. There are neon T's, too, for $6.99; and Lee "Superweight" cotton sweatshirts—boy, are they heavy—are $25.00, almost half of what they cost in department stores.

Super Socks — 10 Winter St., Boston; 482-3750. Also, 520 Commonwealth Ave., Boston; 247-7092, and 360 Longwood Ave., Brookline; 734-9366. Women love this chain of tiny shops—it's a good place to stock up on stockings, socks, lingerie, and exercise wear. Cotton slouch socks are $2.99 a pair, as are nylon trouser socks; Hi-Performance tights, sold for $8.00 elsewhere, are $4.99 here. Exercise body suits are marked down from $15.00 to $10.00. There is usually a good selection of stuff in the $1.00 bin, too.

BRAINTREE

ABC Warehouse Outlet — ABC Industrial Park, Braintree; 843-0552. Also, Caldor Plaza, Route 1, Saugus; 233-5566. Worth a drive out to the 'burbs. ABC has a large selection of women's and girls' clothing, firsts and seconds, in both current and past seasons' styles.

Browning blazers were recently on sale for $25.00, originally $60.00; designer T-shirts with gold applique were half-price at $19.00; so were Adolfo jackets at $29.00. Stretch pants with stirrups and polka dots were reduced from $24.00 to $8.00, and a bathing suit sale set one price—$12.00—for every item in that department, including current models.

BRIGHTON

Snyder Leather Outlet — 42 Western Ave., Brighton; 782-3300. Also in Braintree and Framingham. Not really a factory outlet, as it once was, Snyder sells many lines of leather apparel at 20 to 40 percent below other specialty and department store prices. Most of the items are first quality, with occasional seconds mixed in. The best bargains come in late spring and early summer, after the heavy part of the "leather season" (Christmas).

That's when you can find a men's brushed-leather bomber jacket in a soft forest green, marked down from $199.00 to just $99.00. Slightly blemished models—a bit faded from being on display—go for $49.00.

The store is vast, with racks and racks of leather and suede jackets, long coats, pants, skirts, bags, and gloves, as well as cleaning and care products. For obvious reasons, Snyder's closes down for the month of July and then reopens with a bang for the fall season.

CAMBRIDGE

Surman's Clothing — 8 Central Square, Cambridge; 492- 7665. "We have one price for everybody—the lowest price," said the gentleman. He clearly meant it—he works to strike a bargain with his customers. "You like the jacket? Take two, I'll give you twenty dollars off." Surman's is an old-style men's clothier—suits, accessories, and tailoring at reasonable prices.

Casual suits start as low as $69.95. A recent closeout on Pierre Cardin suits brought the price down from $195.00 to $80.00. Marquis dress shirts, complete with bolo ties, were $15.00; slacks ranged from $20.00 to $30.00, as did sportcoats. Jeans and corduroys were $10.00 to $25.00. The service is what makes the store as much as the prices; take your time, try whatever you like, don't worry about the alterations. As the man said, "Show people a little kindness and they'll come back."

FRAMINGHAM

Frugal Fannie's Fashion Warehouse — 55 New York Ave., Framingham; 508-872-5800. Also,

24 Wilson Way (off Route 1), Westwood; 329-8996, and 1 General Ave., Reading; 942-2121. Bargain hunters have come to swear by Frugal Fannie's as much as any basement for women's clothing at big discounts. They wait for sale announcements in the mail and jump in the car. The stores are warehouse-style, with common dressing rooms and vast racks of career and casual wear. The clothing includes both first quality and seconds.

Here you can find an irregular Albert Nipon dress of 100 percent silk, marked down from $298.00 to $120.00; a Jones New York skirt suit reduced from $350.00 to $170.00; or a shoulder-padded Liz Claiborne blouse for $17.00, originally $40.00.

$60.00 jogging suits were $24.00, Gloria Vanderbilt jeans were half-price at $20.00, and a Stanley Blacker navy blue trenchcoat was marked down to $90.00, from $220.00. There are also basement-style bargain tables of jewelry, hosiery, and other accessories.

Adding to the offbeat nature of the store is a waiting area for all the guys who've been dragged along; there is a TV as well as toys for the kids. Looks more like a holding pen. Also of note, the stores are only open on Friday evenings, Saturdays and Sundays. FF is truly geared to the working woman.

MILFORD

Nobody's Perfect — 327 West St. (Route 140), Milford; 508-634-3824. Okay, so this isn't in Boston; it's not even close. Hey, nobody's perfect. But what a deal this is—they've gathered up first-quality overstocks and slight irregulars from several national specialty stores. Every so often, when they've collected enough to fill up this Milford warehouse, they open their doors to the public for one blowout weekend. Only then can you buy these clothes at 50 to 90 percent off their original prices.

Would you believe ladies'

blazers, valued at $60.00 to $190.00, selling for $8.00 to $16.00? Of course you wouldn't. Well, no one would ever have paid that $190.00 price, but still . . . . How about skirts and leggings for $8.00, mens' and ladies' pants, all at $12.00, or childrens' knit separates for $3.00 each? Got to be worth a road trip.

As noted above, this warehouse is not open on a regular basis; call or write to get on their mailing list. Then, if you don't have a car, borrow one.

NATICK

Burlington Coat Factory — Cloverleaf Marketplace (off Route 9), Natick; 508-651-2526. Also, 705 Granite St., Braintree; 848-3200. Big as a department store, everything here is at discount— and it's not just coats. Men's and women's clothing, shoes, and accessories, as well as linens, are all at bargain prices every day. Women's overcoats range in price from $70.00 to $180.00; blazer suits for $29.95, and Leslie Fay dresses were marked down from $150.00 to $60.00.

For men, Henry Grethel knit shirts were recently on sale for $20.00, originally $45.00; down parkas by Fox Run were reduced from $140.00 to $50.00; and a Nino Cerruti suit was nearly half-price at $130.00. An Adolfo overcoat was an incredible $30.00, from $160.00; and a selection of athletic shoes were all $30.00, including Reebok and L.A. Gear.

Linens are 20 to 50 percent off; you can find goose down comforters for $60.00 (twin size), cotton flannel sheet sets, reduced from $25.00 to $15.00, and blankets from as low as $11.88.

NEEDHAM

Calvert's Family Clothes — 938 Highland Ave., Needham; 444-8000. True to its name and tradition, Calvert's is an inexpensive

place to outfit yourself or a whole family. The lines are pretty conservative, mostly good ol' classic names and styles. Just about everything is discounted in this large store—actually, it's two stores in adjacent buildings.

For men, there are Arrow shirts for $6.99; $25.00 Bugle Boy shirts were reduced to $15.00; and Lee denim jackets were marked down from $45.00 to $23.00. Among irregulars, there are John Weitz slacks for just $12.99, and Alexander Julian "Colours" dress socks for $3.99, reduced from $8.50.

Women's fashions included a Boston Classics blazer and skirt set for a mere $30.00; this retailed for $98.00 originally. There were many racks of seconds and irregulars, with blouses, slacks, lingerie, jackets, and just about anything else. One pair of burgundy corduroy pants was on sale for $4.99.

Plenty of stuff for the kids, too, and lots of athletic clothing for all. Each department had bargain bins of further reduced prices on various items. It's almost the "Metro-West" Filene's Basement.

NEWTON

Dress Barn—241 Needham St., Newton; 332-8710. Also, 948 Great Plain Ave., Needham; 449-5260. 1092 Lexington St., Waltham; 891-9019. This chain of stores specializes mainly in "career dresses" and gear for the working professional woman. Most clothing is first quality. Liz Claiborne dresses sell around $40.00 and up; white cotton short-sleeved blouses with lace detail, for $20.00. Suits, from various designers with values up to $135.00, were on sale recently for $70.00; and $38.00 pleated skirts for half-price. Some special sales offer a second item at half price when you buy two. They also sell jewelry and accessories.

SOMERVILLE

The Back Door Warehouse — 42
Grove St., Somerville; 628-8722. Located at the rear of 401 Highland Avenue in Davis Square, Back Door has lots of work clothes, shoes, sneakers and boots, coats, and more. These are surplus buyouts and irregulars of well-known brands. The stock is always changing.

A pair of Converse sneakers was seen for just $7.99; indeed, most footwear is 50 to 60 percent off, such as black leather western boots for $35.00 and Wear Guard work shoes for $20.00. Other WG items seen included two-color waterproof ski parkas for $19.99, and all-cotton pullover sweaters for $6.00.

Lee sweat pants for $9.00, Levi's work jeans for $10.00, satin-look baseball jackets for $15.00 to $20.00, heavy-cotton plaid work shirts for $8.00—much of the clothing is sold at up to 80 percent off original prices. There are also quantity discounts for purchases over $50.00.

By the time you read this, Back Door hopes to have made it to the front door; at the time of Mr. C's visit they were looking to acquire space on Highland Ave. itself, next to the great Disc Diggers record store. That means two of this book's entries in a row—thanks for making it easier on bargain hunters, folks!

Mayan Mercantile Outlet — 322
Somerville Ave., Somerville; 776-0908. Here's a switch: This company's primary location is in Ogunquit, Maine, while the outlet branch is here in Somerville. In fact, these folks import handmade clothing and accessories from artisans in Central America for trendy stores across the country, like Nomad on Newbury Street.

At this outlet you can find woolen sweaters from Ecuador for $30.00 in bright native American colors of purple, red, blue, and gold. Pants from Guatemala sport the same look, as do crocheted handbags. In the bargain bin area,

a friend of Mr. C's found one in purple and green for just $5.00. There was also an embroidered leather bag for $25.00, marked down from $55.00, and a tie-dyed cotton pullover shirt, with a hood, for $12.99. They also have handcrafted jewelry and tapestries on sale.

Wearguard Outlet Store — 21
McGrath Hwy., Somerville; 776-1010. WearGuard specializes in work clothes of all types, from surgical smocks (so trendy for those pre-med students, too) to good old flannel work shirts in bold colors. At this branch they sell their full-price clothing, plus other brands; but they also clear out their own overstocks and leftovers at huge savings.

Tultex 50/50 cotton sweatshirts, regularly $5.95, are $3.99; WearGuard cotton windbreakers are reduced from $14.95 to $10.00; and a $100.00 Carhartt Arctic Parka was seen after the winter selling season for $53.75. Also, Wear-Guard's classic yellow rubber rainslickers were marked down from $20.00 to $13.50.

Most items are discounted by at least one-third; remainders are even lower. Mr. C found vast racks of those popular black/blue and black/red flannel shirts as low as $2.00 each, originally $16.95; nylon baseball jackets from $6.00, leftovers printed with the names of various businesses; Wrangler misses' jeans for $9.95; and WearGuard's acid-wash jeans, with leather trim, for $6.50.

There are also lots of work boots and shoes, like Timberland boots marked down from $100.00 to $33.50 and Nurse Mates shoes reduced from $55.99 to $20.00. Open seven days a week.

WALTHAM

Newton's Of Waltham — 410
Moody St., Waltham; 891-5776. One of a cluster of discount shops on Moody St., Newton's of Waltham specializes in sports and casual clothing seconds. They sell what-

ever they can get, but that may include fleece sweat shorts or Boston Celtics long sweat pants for $5.00 each, baseball caps with major league team insignias for $3.99, Bike compression shorts for $9.00, and lined Adidas jackets for $25.00.

Ladies' L.A. Gear sneakers were found for $28.00, and men's insulated duck boots for $35.00; men's and ladies' Wrangler jeans, irregulars, for $10.00; Dickie's painter pants for $12.00, and a pack of tube socks, six pair for $4.99. All sales are final.

WATERTOWN

Gap Outlet — Watertown Mall, Arsenal St., Watertown; 926-5858. In spite of its casual clothing, Mr. C has always found the Gap's prices anything but casual; at the Gap Outlet they are at least reasonable. Men's rugby shirts, originally $34.00, may sell for $10.00; khaki jeans are half-price at $20.00, and walking shorts in colorful stripes are just $10.00.

Banana Republic, the Gap's sister brand, also sells overstock here. Cotton pants were recently marked down from $45.00 to $25.00; for women, BR print blazers were reduced from a snooty $148.00 to a respectable $40.00. Like about half of the stock here, these were all irregulars. Other ladies' stuff included denim shorts for $17.00 and cotton scoop-neck T's

reduced from $17.00 to $4.00. Lots of socks and underwear, too—a good place to stock up.

WESTWOOD

The Clothing Wearhouse — 425 Providence Hwy. (Route 1), Westwood; 329-5621. Off of exit 15B from Route 128, along the Norwood/Westwood line, is a whole cluster of discount shops that are well worth the trip. Clothing Wearhouse is a national manufacturer and distributor of tailored clothes for men; here at their showroom you can find factory seconds—along with women's career clothing (not their own), also at discount.

The selection is as large as any major department store. Men's suits, retailing for $250.00 to $350.00, are as low as $80.00 here, including longs, shorts, and irregular sizes. A recent closeout on 100 percent silk sportcoats found some $160.00 jackets on sale for $30.00. European design and athletic-fit suits too.

For women, a rack of 100 percent silk paisley skirts, originally $150.00, was reduced to $29.00 each; wool skirt suits were $99.00, down from $250.00, in varieties of checks and houndstooths. A Boston Classics tweed skirt was reduced from $69.00 to $19.00.

Clothing Wearhouse is open seven days a week; items may be returned for credit or exchange only.

CONSIGNMENT AND RESALE CLOTHING

Consignment shops are a step above vintage clothing stores. They get most of their merchandise from people who, for various reasons, can only "be seen" in such clothes once or twice. They bring it to the consigners, who resell the items and split the money with the original owner. Each shop has its "sources"— society figures who go to gala fundraisers, television personalities, etc. The clothes are usually quite classy.

BOSTON

The Bargain Box — 117 Newbury St., Boston; 536-8580. Given the neighborhood, you'd expect the fancy names on these labels—but

not the basement prices. Would you believe an $800.00 Alan Bilzerian dress—used maybe once or twice—for $185.00? Or an Escada

Mr. Cheap's Picks

✓ **Bargain Box and The Closet** — Cheap clothes on Newbury Street? Yes, if you don't mind that they were worn once or twice. In *this* neighborhood, that can work out to great advantage.

✓ **Encore Exchange** — Hidden away in the Coolidge Corner Arcade is another gem of a resale shop, with designer gowns, coats and jewelry at a fraction of original prices. Two other great consignment shops in this neighborhood are Silk Road Consignerie and Zazu.

✓ **Second Time Around** — Continuing to the west, this Newton shop is actually two shops on the same street—one for men, one for women. Again, the affluent suburbs yield big catches for the budget buyer.

floral silk print skirt and blouse, originally priced at $500.00 and $380.00, respectively, here just $225.00 for the set?

Not all the items are this sky-high. There are plenty of blouses for $10.00 to $25.00, blazers for $25.00 to $55.00 and dresses for $18.00 to $68.00; as well as evening gowns, shoes, jewelry, and accessories. Many sport popular names such as Liz Claiborne, Adolfo, and others.

The Bargain Box has some men's clothing, but not a whole lot; it also has a limited rack of new clothes at discount. All purchases benefit the Junior League of Boston, a non-profit women's organization that sponsors volunteer programs around the city. They've operated the store for over forty years.

The Closet — 175 Newbury St., Boston; 536-1919. Another fun place to find designer names cheaply. A pair of Ellen Tracy slacks, originally $42.00, was seen here at half price. Also, a pair of Papagallo shoes for just $16.00 and an Ann Taylor dress of 100 percent silk for $59.00.

There is a bit more of a selection of men's clothing here than at the Bargain Box, such as a Giorgio Armani sportcoat for $165.00—a splurge, probably, but a great deal.

Perhaps a Christian Dior dress shirt for $26.00 to go with it.

A few doors down, the Closet Upstairs is this store's lower-priced, vintage flip side (see listing under vintage clothing).

Deja Vu — 222 Newbury St., Boston; 424-9020. The third and most recent of Newbury Street's consignment shops, Deja Vu yielded fewer real bargains than the others—one good example seen there was a Ralph Lauren blouse for $50.00. Again, the stock here consists only of clothing for women; much of it is very fancy stuff.

BROOKLINE

Encore Exchange — Harvard Arcade, 318 Harvard St., Brookline; 566-4544. This Coolidge Corner boutique is filled with incredible bargains for the sophisticated shopper. Some of the designer dresses, furs, jewelry, and accessories are new; more often, "gently used."

A new leather jacket by Andrew Marc, meant to retail for $650.00, was on the racks for just $250.00. A fancy Diane Fres dress was reduced from $600.00 to $175.00. Most gowns start at $60.00, with other clothes from $30.00 and up.

There is also quite a selection of semi-precious and costume jewelry, some one-of-a-kind creations, like a locket made with Swarovski crystal by a California artist—it would sell for $450.00 on Rodeo Drive, and here it's $150.00. At the other end of the price spectrum, there are lots of $5.00 and $10.00 earrings too.

KidsWorld Consignment Shop — Harvard Arcade, 318 Harvard St., Brookline; 232-0141. For kids from toddlers to adolescents, KidsWorld has used clothing and accessories at great prices. Get designer pants from $5.00 to $10.00; Levi's corduroy overalls for $4.50; or a white lace wedding dress for a flower girl, originally $125.00, here just $30.00.

Babies' car seats, as available, are usually priced around $12.00 to $18.00, and there are often strollers, books, and toys as well. The tiny store is packed from floor to ceiling with shirts, sweaters, jeans, dresses, jackets, and more. There is also a reduced price rack at the rear of the store, where you can save 50 percent off the already cheap prices. It's enough to make parents not mind how fast kids grow out of their clothes.

Silk Road Consignerie — 1386B Beacon St., Brookline; 739-3399. "Designers charge too much, for what? Their names," says Miki Boni, the artist who created her own shop in response to high prices. She's filled that shop with beautiful clothes, thanks to women who empty their closets of these fancy things.

Giorgio Armani, Escada, Ann Klein, and Valentino are just a few of the names you'll find here, at a fraction of their original costs. In many cases these are salesmen's samples—display pieces they took to major stores for a season and then had no more use for. These, obviously, have never been worn. Ms. Boni is very big on recycling; why should such clothes go to waste? "You can look better for your career without having to pay a lot."

Indeed, some examples bear this out. A black leather jacket and skirt by Avanti was on sale for $75.00; Bandolino open-toe dress shoes were $12.00; a pair of Ann Klein linen slacks were $25.00. There is also jewelry, including many antique and one-of-a-kind pieces.

Through The Looking Glass — 1682A Beacon St., Brookline; 731-0111. This tiny walk-down shop sells contemporary women's clothing, never more than two years old. Many items are one-of- a-kind, originally sold in specialty boutiques; the selection covers all sizes, from 2 to 26. Larger sizes and maternity wear are specialties.

There is plenty of unique crafted jewelry, as well as shoes, handbags, and other accessories. The store is closed on Mondays.

Zazu Designer Consigner — 395A Harvard St., Brookline; 739-5876. One of the first of the many consignment shops in the Coolidge Corner area, Zazu has a large selection of very attractive clothing and accessories. A 100 percent silk wraparound dress by St. Gillian was seen for $35.00; a pair of Ann Taylor pleated slacks with a fine houndstooth pattern was $18.00.

There is a "Designer's Corner" with such names as Ann Klein and Ellen Tracy; a gold lame blouse by Oleg Cassini was on this rack for $40.00. All merchandise in the store goes through periodic markdowns, à la Filene's Basement, until it sells; Zazu also has occasional "bag sales" in which you can fill a bag for $15.00.

CAMBRIDGE

Chances Resale Boutique — 2324 Massachusetts Ave., Cambridge; 876-6919. This small shop outside of Porter Square deals mostly in women's and children's clothing. A pair of Guess jeans was seen for $8.00; other jeans, in decent shape, ran $4.00 to $8.00. There was a good selection of ball gowns in time for prom season; a red satin number, with spaghetti straps, was just $25.00.

A Saville linen blazer was $18.00. For kids, there were quite a lot of baby clothes at very cheap prices, like $3.00 for a two-piece sweatshirt and pants. Also some toys and accessories.

NEWTON

One More Tyme — 1271 Washington St., West Newton; 969-2959. For almost twenty-five years this tidy, friendly shop has been selling used and consignment women's clothing in excellent condition. There are many designer labels, like a Kasper blazer for $25.00, or a Liz Claiborne sweater for $40.00. A recent visit even turned up a St. John strapless evening gown, retailing for $500.00, on sale for $195.00—its original owner purchased it for the one-time-only occasion of meeting Princess Di!

The shop also has a selection of belts, jewelry, shoes, and handbags. Senior citizens receive a special discount.

Second Appearance — 801 Washington St., Newtonville; 527-7655. There is quite a selection for men and women at this consignment shop, but the quality of the items is mixed. Some are new or in good shape; others have marks or stains on them, but these are clearly pointed out. A new Ralph Lauren denim jacket sold for $40.00; a Gap shirt and pants set, for $28.50. Mr. C's expert liked a Laura Ashley "sailor suit" in light blue, only $45.00 and a pink linen "mother of the bride" dress with lace trim for $75.00. Helpful staff.

Second Time Around — 1169 Walnut St. (women's shop), Newton Highlands; 964-4481. Also, 39A Lincoln St. (men's shop), Newton Highlands; 244-3164. Second Time Around is well established and fun to browse through. The place is not large, but you can get lost in the many "nooks and crannies," as a friend of Mr. C's put it. Things are kind of disorganized, but that's the charm of it. In the ladies' shop, a two-piece casual skirt and blouse ensemble had the original tag still on it; the retail price had been $156.00. Here, it was on sale for $58.00. A pair of Henri Bendel woolen tweed pants was $78.00, and a unique-looking blazer with a tapestry print was $46.00. Some items are never-worn; most everything is top-quality stuff.

The sister branch (or should it be "brother"?), opened more recently down the block; it's one of the few consignment shops for men. Apparently there isn't that much out there to consign, since men tend to keep clothes longer than women. Still, this place has a big selection of designer clothes at about one-third of the retail prices. Mr. C saw a Harris Tweed sportcoat for $48.00, an Armani suit for $150.00, a Bill Blass robe for $16.00, and a Lacoste sweater vest for $6.00. As you may guess, the merchandise is a bit on the snooty side, but that goes with the territory. Good bargains, though, if this is your style.

WALTHAM

Fred's Rethreads Consignment Shop—402 Moody St., Waltham; 891-1720. A small, cozy store with a variety of items, including clothes, belts, sports watches, jewelry, and things for the home. Recent items included a pair of men's (size 8 1/2) Frye boots, almost like new, for $30.00; girls' Esprit blouses in purple and pink, $6.00 each; and soft, handmade afghan blankets for $25.00. There is also a 50 percent-off rack with more bargains.

VINTAGE CLOTHING

ALLSTON

Hot Sugar — 107 Brighton Ave., Allston; no phone. A small, funky store upstairs in the "Allston Mall" with some great prices on vintage wear and paraphernalia. Find a silk-lined smoking jacket for $18.00 or a hot-pink chiffon dress for $14.00. Jeans are just $8.00, and costume jewelry includes earrings for $4.00 and rings for $6.00. Plus platform shoes, movie posters, and other kinds of fun period stuff.

Strutter's — 202A Harvard Ave., Allston; 277-8323. Also, 257 Newbury St., Boston; 247-7744. Strutter's has literally made a name for itself among the vintage clothiers in Boston; it's become a line of clothing that you may find in other vintage stores, such as Sadye's Antiques in Cambridge. More interestingly, the company even competes with itself, with prices that are higher on Newbury Street than they are in the Allston shop.

This may not be enough for the die-hard bargain hunter, though. Strutter's commands fairly high rates for its merchandise, no matter where you buy it. Yes, these are authentic period clothes, most in fine shape; but $45.00 is still a lot to pay for a men's blazer, as is $22.00 for a wide print tie to go with it. A linen skirt suit was fair at $60.00; women's slacks are $20.00 to $30.00. You can find some bargains among the shoes, such as oh-so-trendy black patent leather military shoes for $35.00.

BOSTON

Astoria — 50 Concord Square, Boston; 859-0509. "We are not a thrift shop," Astoria's owner emphatically states. Indeed, a good look around this small but fascinating shop just off Columbus Avenue in the South End reveals clothes that aren't just old—they're genuine antiques. The 1960s are about as recent as you'll find here, and many pieces date back to the turn of the century.

This makes the store a bit more expensive than your average vintage shop; but Astoria's prices are actually well below true market value. So, you can get a 1940s grey and black linen skirt suit for $58.00 (tough to match, even new). Open-toed platform shoes from that period are $85.00, which may seem like a splurge—yet copies of these sell for twice as much at stores on Newbury Street. Every style comes back, after all; and here you'll get the real thing.

Men can find a "sharkskin" shirt from the 1950s for $20.00, Hawaiian shirts from $10.00, and sportcoats for $20.00 to $30.00. Astoria also specializes in things like antique "daywear" lingerie, hats and gloves, lots of jewelry, and even women's separates made of all-silk velvet—which, these days, is only the realm of glitzy designers.

All items are neatly arranged, and many sport helpful notes on their tags—telling you which period a piece is from, what would go well with it, or where a bit of repair may be needed.

Bertha Cool — 528 Commonwealth Ave., Boston; 247-4111. One flight above Kenmore Square, Bertha Cool has lots of great stuff to wear down on the street—in Kenmore, Copley, Harvard, or any other place where it's hip to be square.

The clothing is a bit on the pricey side for used, but it's of great quality and still less than what you'd pay for new. A nicely broken-in pair of Levis is $15.00; a new pair of men's patent-leather uniform shoes can be found for $40.00. For women, a long, black sequined dress is $75.00; other dresses range down to $55.00 and less. A really sharp-looking leather jacket was also $75.00.

You'll find vintage jewelry here, too—a man's tie tack, with a horsehead design, is $9.00; women's ankle bracelets are $14.00. And don't forget cool sunglasses and hats. The shop is small, but crammed from floor to ceiling.

The Closet Upstairs — 223 Newbury St., Boston; 267-5757. Direct kin of The Closet, the Upstairs version has clothing that is a bit more used. Lots of jeans, shoes, belts, jewelry, and other accessories here, with stuff for men and women. A ladies' cashmere winter coat, in good condition, was seen for $25.00; men's tuxedo jackets start around $75.00, $135.00 for a full suit. Lots of leather jackets too, in the $35.00 to $95.00 range.

There are some never-used pieces here as well, also at discount.

King Of Records — 54 Queensberry St., Boston; no phone. A record shop in the vintage clothing section? Yes. This eclectic hodgepodge is run by a collector who has branched from music into all kinds of other things, like costume jewelry, funky shoes, framed art, and some clothing items. It's all very cheap, and his use of rare music memorabilia gives the place a vintage feel.

BRIGHTON

Cinderella's Closet — 370A Chestnut Hill Ave., Brighton; 566-8511. Perhaps the name fits best because Cinderella's fairy godmother made so much out of so little at hand. This small, cozy shop in Cleveland Circle has a limited selection of nice clothing, like dresses for $10.00 to $20.00 and jeans for $9.00; plus hats, shoes, funky horn-rimmed sunglasses, and more. Most of the stock is women's stuff, with a few items for the guys.

BROOKLINE

Cafe Society — 131 Cypress St., Brookline; 738-7186. Like so many vintage shops, the woman behind

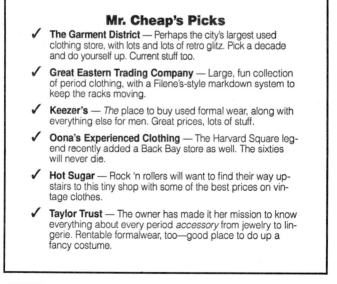

Mr. Cheap's Picks

✓ **The Garment District** — Perhaps the city's largest used clothing store, with lots and lots of retro glitz. Pick a decade and do yourself up. Current stuff too.

✓ **Great Eastern Trading Company** — Large, fun collection of period clothing, with a Filene's-style markdown system to keep the racks moving.

✓ **Keezer's** — *The* place to buy used formal wear, along with everything else for men. Great prices, lots of stuff.

✓ **Oona's Experienced Clothing** — The Harvard Square legend recently added a Back Bay store as well. The sixties will never die.

✓ **Hot Sugar** — Rock 'n rollers will want to find their way upstairs to this tiny shop with some of the best prices on vintage clothes.

✓ **Taylor Trust** — The owner has made it her mission to know everything about every period *accessory* from jewelry to lingerie. Rentable formalwear, too—good place to do up a fancy costume.

the counter here is the one who owns the store, and finds the great clothing. Cafe Society has fancy retro styles, like tuxedos for $50.00, a black chiffon ruffle skirt for $28.00, and men's brown and white wing-tip shoes for $40.00. There are lots of hats, fedoras for men and veiled Victorians for women. All sorts of handbags and costume jewelry, too.

In more contemporary styles, there was a Laura Ashley jumpsuit, in a floral print, for $22.00, and many dresses from $20.00 and up. Jeans for men and women were mostly around $15.00, in nicely broken-in condition. The store is clean and bright, and all the clothing is well-marked and displayed.

Taylor Trust — 111 Marion St., Brookline; 566-8126. Another one-woman-show, Taylor Trust specializes in period clothing and accessories, as much for rental as for sale. Rent a 1920s flapper dress for $35.00; for $50.00, you can add all kinds of costume jewelry, gloves, hats, even lingerie—a complete outfit for any special occasion. Same with tuxedos.

The jewelry is really Taylor's claim to fame, as the owner put it; and there is quite a lot to see. She happily takes the time to explain what was worn in any period, and how it was made.

Of course, many items are for sale too, like men's and women's blazers (usually in the fall) for $15.00 to $35.00, 1940s and 1950s cocktail dresses for $25.00 to $75.00, and much more that's packed into this tiny shop near Coolidge Corner. It's only open Wednesdays through Saturdays.

CAMBRIDGE

The Garment District — 200 Broadway, Cambridge; 876-5230. Probably the biggest and best vintage clothing store around. The place is huge, with vast stocks of every kind of clothing. The merchandise ranges from super-cheap (the $1.00 T-shirt bin) to fancy vintage dresses at reasonable prices. They even have a Filene's-type markdown system.

There is usually a big rack of blue jeans for $9.99; men's sport jackets from $8.00 to $16.00; long tweed winter coats for as little as $20.00, especially off-season; skirts from $5.00 to $20.00, and much more, including a children's section.

And that doesn't even touch the period stuff. You won't find a larger collection of Hawaiian shirts ($5.00 to $10.00), taffeta prom dresses ($10.00 to $25.00), platform shoes ($8.00), go-go boots ($12.00), and other styles that should have died out years ago.

Another interesting line is "restyled" clothing by the quirky local designer Eddie Kent. He takes vintage clothes, cutting and sewing them into new creations that blend the present with the past. They are wild. Dresses run from $25.00 to $50.00; a pair of black velour hot pants with a rhinestone belt was $28.00; and a flowered minidress was $26.00.

Finally there is the phenomenon known as Dollar A Pound. On Saturday and Sunday mornings from 7:45 a.m. to 1:00 p.m., the first level of this warehouse opens up to sell old clothes that would have been made into rags for the shipping industry but may still have some value if you're into the worn look. And it goes for, you guessed it, $1.00 a pound.

Great Eastern Trading Company — 49 River St., Cambridge; 354-5279. Here is a vintage shop with lots of fun stuff "from the 20s to the 90s", attractively laid-out and easy to see and try on. The owner clearly takes a lot of care with her merchandise, and has been doing so for over twenty years.

She employs a Filene's-like markdown system, dropping prices by 20 percent after each month until the items sell. Thus, you can find lots of men's sportcoats from $5.00 to $15.00, cotton shirts as low as $2.50, Hawaiian shirts for $12.00, and tuxedo jackets for $25.00 to $45.00.

Good deals on leather jackets too. For women, there is a delightful variety of evening dresses from $10.00 to $30.00—lots of sequins and lace. Skirts are $5.00 to $25.00, and blouses range from just $3.00 to $18.00. There is also fine handcrafted jewelry from around the world, including sterling silver hoop earrings for as little as $1.00 to $3.00; plus handbags, and men's and women's hats from various decades from the Victorian era onward.

Justin Tyme — 91 River St., Cambridge; 661-7149. A small but packed shop with a basement of clothes that lean heavily on the 1960s. Garishly yellow sleeveless dresses for $10.00 to $20.00, a flower-print jumpsuit for $12.00, silver lame sandals for $10.00, and big plastic flower earrings for $4.00 can outfit you for any college reunion or Halloween party.

For men, how about those great 1970s silk print shirts? There's quite a bunch here, all $10.00. Or jeans for $8.00, men's and women's, in contemporary styles as well. Lots of period bric-a-brac, too.

Keezer's Harvard Community Exchange — 140 River St., Cambridge; 547-2455. Across the street from Great Eastern and Justin Tyme is one of the granddaddies of the clothing resale biz, Keezer's. They've made their name in discount formal wear for men, but also sell more everyday stuff as well. Certainly, guys should start here for all kinds of tuxes; used tuxedo jackets are just $40.00 to $50.00, and tails are $85.00. Pants are $18.50, and there are even new tux shirts for just $5.00 to $10.00. And they have all the accoutrements: bow ties, suspenders, the works. You can rent tuxes here too, for as low as $40.00.

Keezer's has lots of men's suits for $30.00 to $50.00; a Brooks Brothers pinstripe, for example, was $42.50. Givenchy and Yves St. Laurent blazers were also seen for around $30.00. Plenty of wool overcoats too, like a Burberry model for $55.00; also trenchcoat-style rainwear and leather bomber jackets.

A large selection of chino pants, in all sizes, was recently on sale for $4.50 each; same price for a rack of new silk ties. There are used shoes, like a pair of Bally ankle-high brown leather boots for $22.50.

Oona's Experienced Clothing — 1210 Massachusetts Ave., Cambridge; 491-2654. Also, 1110 Boylston St., Boston; 536-6388. Perhaps the earthiest of Boston's vintage clothing stores, Oona's manages to be funky without even trying. The original Cambridge location winds from room to room, each filled with one kind of clothing—dresses, men's suits, and their famous $5.00 leather jackets.

In fact there is a ton of clothing here, most for $10.00 and under; sweaters $5.00 to $10.00, men's sportcoats $5.00, genuine 1960s shirts $9.00, long Indian wrap skirts $4.00 to $6.00. There are leather jackets, in better shape, from $75.00 to $125.00; the $5.00 ones are, well, heavily broken in. Oona's also has lots of handcrafted bead and silver jewelry.

Reddog — 1737 Massachusetts Ave., Cambridge; 354-9676. Nearly twenty years in Cambridge, Reddog is one of the must-sees on the vintage clothing circuit. There is some new stuff, about 20 percent; but the real bargain is the used clothing, which goes as far back as the Victorian era.

Evening dresses, many from the 1940s, start around $50.00 and go up to $150.00. Plenty of costume jewelry to adorn these outfits, too—fancy rhinestone pieces for about $20.00. Interesting and unique sweaters, with beaded appliques, are around $50.00.

Reddog also has a selection of furniture and collectibles from the same periods.

Sadye & Company Antiques — 182 Massachusetts Ave., Cambridge; 547-4424. See listing under "Used Furniture."

Vintage, Etc. — 1796 Massachusetts Ave., Cambridge; 497-1516. While Vintage Etc. carries much of the clothing found in any vintage store, it's the "etc." part that offers unique values. More than other stores, Vintage specializes in new hosiery bargains: Berkshire opaque tights for $5.00 in a range of sizes and hot colors, Danskins for $6.00, Hue socks for $5.00 and tights for $10.00.

They also have a selection of the offbeat, such as Voila pantyhose—hand silkscreened in various designs for $12.00. There are, of course, all kinds of great clothes to "go with" these accessories.

BRIDAL WEAR
BOSTON

Filene's Basement — 426 Washington St., Boston; 542-2011. Four times a year, Filene's Basement in Boston runs a most unusual sale. At these magical moments you can buy designer wedding gowns, valued from $400.00 to $3,650.00—discontinueds, irregulars, and floor samples—for the single low price of two hundred bucks.

Word gets around, and this has become a hallowed event. On the appointed date the doors open at 8 a.m., and hundreds of brides-to-be frantically rush in and start grabbing. They yank whatever they can off the racks, jumping in and out of dresses (in plain view), bartering with each other until they find the right one. All five hundred gowns are gone in about thirty minutes, and the sale is over.

Is this any way to get married? Probably. After going through all that, you'd think twice about a divorce. If this is for you, call Filene's to find out the next sale date, or keep an eye on the newspaper ads.

DEDHAM
Manhattan Bridal And Tux Warehouse
— 283 Washington St., Dedham; 326-9888. Calling itself "New England's Largest Wedding Complex," the downstairs level of this store has over one thousand gowns in stock, many one-of-a-kind, all sold at off-price rates. It's kind of like a bridal department store, as opposed to a personalized boutique, but it may do if you want to save some money. Located in the Dedham Mall, its hours are 10:00 a.m. to 8:30 p.m. Mondays through Thursdays, and 10:00 to 4:30 on Fridays and Saturdays.

EVERETT
Something Old, Something New
— 362 Ferry St., Everett; 389-4696. Near Glendale Square in Everett, this full-service shop is a must if you're searching for a bridal bargain. They sell new and used gowns and accessories, all at low prices. Many of the new dresses are closeouts from other stores, selling at perhaps half their original

---

Mr. Cheap's Picks

✓ **Filene's Basement** — Did you know? Four times a year they have a one-day sale of dresses off the rack, $199 each. More like a one-hour sale, before they're gone. Check the papers for ads.

✓ **Something Old, Something New** — This Everett shop combines used dresses with designer closeouts. Full service, friendly folks.

costs. Some are as low as $100.00, but most are in the $200.00 to $500.00 range. Used, professionally cleaned gowns cost about the same, and you'll find such names as Alfred Angelo, Mary's, and Jazzman. If you don't see something you like, or if you want to match an entire party, these folks can order dresses at good prices too.

Hours are rather offbeat: The store is open mornings and evenings on weekdays, and all day Saturday.

NEWTON

Zazu Resale Bridal Boutique —
118 Needham St., Newton; 527-2555. A separate branch of the Brookline consignment shop, this Zazu deals exclusively in bridal gowns and headpieces that have been used, once, but are in fine shape. Many of the gowns are designer pieces, from Yolanda, Galina, Bianchi, and more.

There is a good selection of sizes, and styles range from traditional to modern, conservative to funky, for any season and taste. And with any purchase you get 20 percent off related services.

COSMETICS

BOSTON

Boston Beauty Supply — 59 Temple Place, Boston; 426-0921. This second-floor walkup sells professional-grade hair care supplies at discount; the general public is also welcome. Colors, perms, shampoos, sprays; they're all here, in brands such as Clairol, L'Oreal, and Wella. Many items cannot be found in retail stores. L'Oreal hair color, for example, is sold by the bottle for just $2.75. Instead of buying the usual kit, you can assemble the materials yourself and save.

They also carry several generic copies of expensive name brands; a copy of Paul Mitchell shampoo is just $2.95, about half of the real thing and every bit as good. A thirty-two-ounce generic bottle of peroxide is a low $1.75. Service is friendly and helpful, too. Open weekdays, plus Saturday from 9:30 to 5:30.

Perfumania — 201 Newbury St., Boston; 437-9410. Also, Meadow Glen Mall, Medford; 396-8430. "America's Fragrance Discounter" has opened a Boston branch on—where else?—Newbury Street. Indeed, you will find well-known designer perfumes here, most at 20 to 60 percent below retail. The secret is buying in bulk and passing the savings along. A recent promotion featured half-a-dozen women's fragrances, all with suggested retail prices from $40.00 to $60.00, selling for $29.95 each. These included Opium, Liz Claiborne, and Oscar de la Renta.

For men, a Perry Ellis after shave and cologne gift set, $39.50 elsewhere, was on sale for $24.95.

Perfumania also sells beauty products, such as the Episauna skin cleansing device—it retails for $24.00, and sells here for $12.95. The salespeople are very friendly and helpful, too.

Status/State Beauty Supply — 328 Newbury St., Boston; 236-1477. Also, 242 Harvard St., Brookline; 232-1626. Status is a professional beauty supply store that sells to the general public as well. You can buy salon-quality hair care products, perfumes, and cosmetics here, all top-quality stuff—at everyday prices that are lower than most department stores. Many of these products, in fact, can't even be found in the bigger stores. Check out the in-store specials, like a selection of hair sprays and conditioners for $2.00 each.

They also carry generic copies of expensive name brands: "Exact" shampoo, a copy of the Nexus luxury line, sells for $4.20—about half the price of the salon brand, with all the same ingredients.

Perfumes and makeup are sold at about 20 percent below department store prices, with just as much personal service to make sure you get what's best for you.

BROOKLINE

The Beauty Connection — 326 Harvard St., Brookline; 734-2114. Also 749 Beacon St., Newton Centre; 969-3333. These small but packed shops sell just about anything you could need, most at some discount. The prices are quite reasonable.

Mr. Cheap's Picks

✓ **Boston Beauty Supply** — Stock up where the salons buy their stuff. Sure, you can go in, too.

✓ **Perfumania** — A chain that's sweeping through the region, applying the "How do we do it? VOLUME!" approach to designer fragrances at discount for men and women.

Sally Beauty Supply—1360 Beacon St., Brookline; 277-0095. Also, 180 Alewife Brook Parkway (Fresh Pond Mall); 876-9880, and 1530 VFW Parkway, West Roxbury; 323-2530.

Sally Beauty Supply is a chain with over 1,500 stores nationwide; their parent company is Alberto Culver, the "VO5" folks. So they have a lot of factory-direct products, many of which are for professional use only. This means high quality, large sizes, and good prices.

TRESemme is Alberto's salon brand, and you can get a sixteen-ounce can of their hair spray for $1.49—about half-price. A thirty-two-ounce bottle of TRESemme conditioner, also half-price, is $2.39. Other brands sold at discount include Aussie Moist shampoos, Jheri Redding "Volumizers," Infusium, and Faberge.

Sally also has a number of generic products that have exactly the same ingredients as expensive name brands. Aura products, which copy the Aveda line, save you about half the cost of those salon exclusives. Seven ounces of Aura Cherry Almond Bark conditioner cost $3.99. You'll find generic versions of Paul Mitchell and Sebastian hair products too.

There are also nail and skin care items, full lines of ethnic hair products, and discounted professional hair dryers and curling irons. Be sure to check the "Reduced for Quick Sale" and "Cheaper by the Case" sections.

SOMERVILLE

Flammia Beauty Supply — 363 Highland Ave., Somerville; 628-0249. Flammia is not necessarily a discounter, but it does sell beauty products in professional-size large quantities, making for some very good deals. After all, if you shampoo every day, why not buy it a liter at a time? Especially when you can get such a bottle for $3.95, in a variety of brands. You may be spending that much on a regular bottle now.

How about a gallon of Wella Balsam conditioner for $12.95? Okay, maybe Mr. C is carrying this a bit too far. But, there are ways to save money here. If you use L'Oreal hair color, for example, the folks at Flammia will show you how to assemble the individual ingredients for less than the packaged kit.

They also carry a line of generic copies of expensive name brands, like Paul Mitchell, for about half the price. The recipe is the same in both! And you'll find everything you'll need for nail sculpturing—tools and polishes.

Flammia also has professional-quality accessories, including hair styling appliances, that are more durable than department store brands—so you won't need to replace them anytime soon. That saves money down the line.

DEPARTMENT STORES AND RELATED OUTLETS

DEPARTMENT STORES

Not all of these are fully-stocked department stores; some are resellers of overstock merchandise at discount. They are often organized like department stores but carry only what is available to them at any given time. In other words, you may not always find what you're looking for; but if you prowl them regularly, you'll come up with some super deals.

BOSTON

Filene's Basement — 426 Washington St., Boston; 542-2011. Undoubtedly the granddaddy of all discount shopping in Boston. Here is where you'll find die-hard bounty hunters diving onto tables piled high with clothing, hurling item after item into the air in the hope that some greater prize lies hidden underneath. Once the treasure has been unearthed, it is clutched tightly, before anyone else even has a chance to consider it, and the search goes on.

For Mr. C's more demure readers, don't worry—not everyone is like that here. Just plunge in and find yourself some bah-gains. The stock comes from many quality stores and manufacturers—overstocks, leftovers, irregulars, things from last season. Not everything is super-cheap, but you never know what may turn up. That's why Basement veterans try to cruise through on a regular basis. And of course every few weeks, prices on unsold items are marked down further.

Going from section to section, you may find men's dress shirts for $8.00, valued at $17.00 to $24.00; tennis and basketball shoes, normally $52.00 to $70.00, on sale for $39.00; women's pleated shorts for $14.00; "career" dresses for $35.00; a $120.00 misses' silk blazer for $59.00; not to mention jewelry, leather belts and handbags, men's tailored suits.

Of course, there is more here than clothing—many shoppers never even venture down to the second level, where there are similar reductions on housewares, linens, home decorations, children's items, and more.

Jordan Marsh Basement — 450 Washington St., Boston; 357-3000. Fewer people seem to rave about the Jordan Marsh Basement across the street from Filene's. The atmosphere is more subdued, like that of an ordinary department store. The discount system doesn't have the automatic markdowns, but it too offers good bargains.

Levi's "Dockers" jeans for men were recently on sale for $20.00 a pair, reduced from $42.50; a rack of Geoffrey Beane sweaters, left over from the previous season, went for $6.00 apiece. For women there were Evan Piccone print slacks marked down from $84.00 to $27.00, and a blue blazer/black skirt set by Chad Stevens, reduced from $110.00 to $56.00; plus earrings from $3.99, and lots of underwear to stock up on from $3.00 to $6.00.

There is also a selection of personal accessories, and linens for bedroom and bathroom. For other items for the home, check out JM's Clearance Center in Framingham (listing below).

CAMBRIDGE

Economy Hardware — 438 Massachusetts Ave., Cambridge; 864-3300. Also, 219 Massachusetts Ave., Boston; 536-4280. (See listing under "Housewares".)

Friendly Family Centers — 576 Massachusetts Ave., Cambridge; 492-4435. Also, 245 Elm St., Somerville; 623- 9048. 22 Bennington St., East Boston; 561-0460. 441 West Broadway, South Boston; 269-7287. 1618 Blue Hill Ave., Mattapan; 298-9668. 20 Corinth St., Roslindale; 325-9595. If you needed to furnish your place with housewares quickly and cheaply, FFC would be one place to do it. Similar to a Woolworth's, they have things like plastic kitchen utensils for 99¢, a six-pack of men's athletic tube socks for $3.99, kids' printed T-shirts for $2.99, and flannel-backed tablecloths for $1.99.

Flex shampoos and conditioners were recently on sale at two for $3.00, mix and match; a thirty-ounce bottle of Shout stain remover, $1.69; Regal heavy aluminum frying pans, $3.59; and eighty-one-inch tall sheer window curtains for $2.69 a panel. You know, basic stuff, low prices.

Harvard Cooperative Society — 1400 Massachusetts Ave., Cambridge; 499-2000. Founded way back when as a money-saving service by and for the academic community, the Coop now sells to everyone. However, the original "mission" continues, and all students, faculty, alumni, and employees of Harvard are eligible to become members—as well as those of M.I.T., Wheelock College, the Massachusetts College of Pharmacy, and personnel at the hospitals affiliated with Harvard Medical School.

For an annual fee of $1.00, members receive an annual rebate based on their purchases throughout the year. Currently, the amount is about five percent of the total each member has spent. They may also take advantage of special members-only sales, such as a recent one featuring an extra 15 percent off regular prices on compact discs.

Meanwhile, the Coop sells everything from clothes to TVs to toothpaste, like any department store. They also buy back textbooks (you can be from any school for that, member or not) for cash on the spot. And the Insignia Shop, on the street level of the main building, is a good place to check for clearance sales of leftover "Harvard" stuff—like a heavy maroon hooded sweatshirt reduced from $30.00 to a more respectable $19.99.

Lechmere — 88 First St., Cambridge; 491-2000. Also in Danvers, Dedham, Framingham, Weymouth and Woburn. No, it's not the regular store merchandise that attracts Mr. C—though sometimes, their sales are good. What many shoppers aren't aware of is that Lechmere frequently takes items that have been returned and sells them at discount. They are usually gathered on a table in the appropriate department. You may find a Panasonic computer printer for half-price, or a Sony Walkman, or a boom-box tape deck. Some of these were defective and have been repaired, with a limited warranty. Occasionally they have simply been opened and returned unused; the box is damaged, but the item is perfectly good.

EVERETT

Mark's Discount Outlet — 2050 Revere Beach Pkwy., Everett; 381-0669. Set back from the highway by a parking lot that's bigger than the store, Mark's has a crazy but useful array of overstocks and irregulars in clothing and house-wares.

You'll find lots of socks, sneakers, and T-shirts, including plenty of children's sizes; kids' ballet slippers and tap shoes, too, for $4.00 to $6.00 a pair. Shampoos and cosmetics, including generic copies of perfumes; housewares; and a large section of hardware and tools. All good 'n cheap.

FRAMINGHAM

Jordan Marsh Clearance
Center — Shoppers World Mall, Routes 9 and 30, Framingham; 508-879-0100. Here's where leftover Jordan Marsh merchandise goes to be sold at further reductions. There is no clothing here; that stays in the Basement store in Downtown Crossing (see above). The Clearance Center deals mainly in furniture, beds, rugs, and home electronics.

Most of the items on sale here are only available in very limited quantities, so you never know what you'll find. But a recent sale featured $400.00 recliner chairs for $97.77; queen-size beds marked down from $799.00 to $377.00; a $600.00 Stearns and Foster twin mattress set for $97.00; Smith-Corona electric typewriters for $47.77; same price for a $150.00 Southwest Bell cordless phone; and Magnavox VHS camcorders for just $397.00, less than half-price.

In some cases what you're getting is a returned item that may have been repaired; all sales are final, so you do take your chances. But at these prices the gamble may pay off.

HINGHAM

Building 19 — 100 Derby St., Hingham; 749-0019. Also, 1450 Providence Hwy. (Route 1), Norwood; 769-3700. 810 The Lynnway, Lynn; 581-1910. 9/27 Shopping Plaza, Route 9, Natick; 508-653-1900. Plus Burlington, Haverhill, Worcester, New Bedford, Manchester and Pawtucket, R.I. Well, if Filene's is

the traditional bargain basement, Building 19 is the next generation—the new kid on the auction block. They snap up manufacturers' overstocks, discontinued lines, and irregulars in clothing, furniture, home decor, hardware, toys, kitchenware, paper supplies, and anything else they can get their hands on, and sell them dirt-cheap.

So when a ladies' shoe manufacturer goes out of business, B-19 grabs what's left; and first quality shoes that would have retailed for $47.00 to $55.00 go on sale for $16.99 and $19.99. Pleated summer skirts, perfectly good but from the previous summer, are $4.99. You can get a pair of $75.00 men's Nike sneakers for $14.99, a $50.00 nylon four-suit garment bag for $19.99, kids' tie-dyed shirts or shorts for $2.99, an upholstered wicker loveseat marked down from $400.00 to $200.00, a woodgrain TV/VCR cart for $22.99, and even genuine wool oriental rugs (8' x 11'), half-price at $199.00.

Many of the stores also have a "Sample Department," in which they sell designer clothing that has been used only by the salespeople who take it on the road to show to buyers. They are finished with the samples, so B-19 can buy them and sell them at super-cheap wholesale prices.

There is a sort of irreverent attitude at Building 19; the idea is that anyone who wants to shop at these prices won't mind the wacky signs, jammed racks and dirty floors. They seem to be correct in this assumption, as the chain just keeps growing.

MEDFORD

BJ's Wholesale Club — 909 The Fellsway (Route 28), Medford; 396-0235. Also in Weymouth, Stoughton, Danvers. What used to be a more exclusive club, for members of certain professions and unions, recently changed hands and has thrown open its doors to the general public—for a $25.00 annual fee, that is. Non-members can get a one-day trial pass, to look around; if you want to buy something, you'll pay a 5 percent surcharge.

The deal here is that once you join, you can buy all kinds of clothing, food, household, and automotive items at wholesale prices. The best bargains, though, often tend to involve large quantities. For example, a four-quart container of Breyer's ice cream is $4.98; less than supermarket prices, but you need a big freezer. Mr. C had never seen a fifty-eight-ounce bottle of Plax before, but there it was, a bargain at $6.89; same price for a bag of fifty Bic disposable razors.

If you own a car (and a garage), you may want to pick up a case of Mobil motor oil, twelve quarts for $10.99. You can even buy name-brand tires, which BJ's will mount for you on the premises at no charge.

Appliances and clothing, of course, do not present the quantity problem. A Sharp four-head VCR, with on-screen display, is $230.00; and a six-pack of Sony VHS blank tapes is just $13.49. Men's jeans by Lee sell for $16.99, while a woman's spring jacket in pastel colors by Gloria Vanderbilt was seen for $15.00.

BJ's also has a bakery, a butcher, and a huge grocery section. How about a case of Coke for $6.19—that's a quarter a can, folks . . . Or, a twenty-pound bag of Friskies dry cat food (for dry cats?) at $9.98.

The impression at a place like BJ's (or its competitor, Costco, which has no stores closer than Avon, on the South Shore) is that everything must be at tremendous savings. Not so. You have to look carefully to find the true bargains; many items are not that much less than they would be at other discount stores. The selection here is often limited; if you're shopping for TV's, there may only be half a dozen to choose from, and not all of them are at rock-bottom prices. It's best to go in knowing what you want and how much it should cost. Then you can pick out the best deals.

REVERE

Inner City Discounters — 590 Revere Beach Parkway, Revere; 289-7833. In spite of the name, this place requires a trip out of town; perhaps the name best describes the store as a city in itself. It's certainly one of the largest of the independent discount department stores. Aisle after aisle is crammed with everything you could ever need, mostly overstocks at 40 percent to 60 percent off original prices.

It's too much to describe in

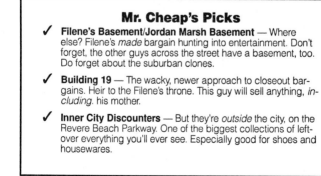

Mr. Cheap's Picks

✓ **Filene's Basement/Jordan Marsh Basement** — Where else? Filene's *made* bargain hunting into entertainment. Don't forget, the other guys across the street have a basement, too. Do forget about the suburban clones.

✓ **Building 19** — The wacky, newer approach to closeout bargains. Heir to the Filene's throne. This guy will sell anything, *including*, his mother.

✓ **Inner City Discounters** — But they're *outside* the city, on the Revere Beach Parkway. One of the biggest collections of leftover everything you'll ever see. Especially good for shoes and housewares.

detail. The first section is shoes and sneakers, with many name brands mixed in—Perry Ellis, Sporto, Etonic, Giorgio Brutini, and Sperry. Nothing seems to go over $30.00. Socks and such too. Also at the front is the clothing section, where a Gap madras shirt was reduced from $28.00 to $11.00; Van Heusen shirts for $3.99; various college sweatshirts, $9.99; same price for women's swimsuits.

Now move on into the main halls. Housewares, grocery items, hardware, toys, car products, you name it—it's here somewhere. A sixteen-piece dinnerware set, $15.99 . . . all books $2.99 . . . candy, five for a dollar . . . Armitron watches, $9.00 . . . even new furniture: A matching upholstered sofa and loveseat for $440.00, or a vinyl recliner for $160.00. It goes on and on; worth a trip, to stock up.

SOMERVILLE

Jimmie's Discount Outlet — 79 Bow St., Somerville; 625-5605. This new, two-room shop near Union Square offers mostly overstocks and buyouts at very cheap prices—if they have something you want. One entire room features clothing at $3.00 a piece—shirts, vests, chino pants, work clothes and uniforms, and sports T's. Some were irregulars and some seemed to be used.

The other half of the store has lots of household items, sporting goods, and toys. Roller blades were the big sell, made by Seneca, $15.00 a pair. Or, for young girls, a pair of Barbie roller skates for $6.00 and a pink tricycle for $22.00.

There were also kids' Reebok sneakers ($20.00), women's leather shoes ($8.00), bath towels ($3.99), a three-piece set of microwave bowls ($1.29), a Westclox wall clock ($9.00), a six-pack of white tube socks ($4.99), and neon sunglasses ($2.99).

Among the more unusual items were many bolts of fabric at $1.00 per yard, and collector's baseball cards at $1.00 each.

WALTHAM

The Half-Price Store — 97 Linden St., Waltham; 899-6198. There are several stores in the Waltham area that are worth a look for inexpensive clothing and household items. The Half-Price Store offers just what it promises: overstocks and odd lots of all kinds of things, at half the original retail price. Much of the stuff comes in name brands you'll recognize. A small fraction is damaged goods, sold at greater discount (if you don't mind a shirt with a tear in it, you can get one for a dollar).

Clothing is at the front. Mr. C saw Fruit of the Loom T-shirts for $1.88 each, boys' camouflage-style pants for $5.00, kids' sneakers for $10.00, and Wear Guard rain slickers for $8.00. Any clothing that has gotten dirty from handling is reduced by $1.00.

The hardware and automotive section included STP engine treatment, reduced from $4.50 to $2.00; a four-pack of light bulbs for $1.75 (a generic brand—you can save money *and* be politically correct), paints by the gallon and the spray can, and a two- drawer metal toolbox for $18.00.

Going on: A twenty-four-inch-tall soft vinyl suitcase for $25.00, a batch of clocks and telephones under $20.00; cassettes and compact discs for $2.00 each; tapered candles, four for a dollar; same deal on a huge selection of used paperbacks with major titles. Plus hand-painted coffee mugs for a dollar, kitchen items, cleaning products, sunglasses, toys and more.

Moe Black's — 140 Lexington St., Waltham; 894-4933. Moe Black's is comparable to Building 19; warehouse-style presentation of closeouts and irregular merchandise. It's not as big as B-19, but it does have plenty of stuff and good prices.

A recent sale featured ladies' swimwear from a "well-known" catalog. One- and two-piece suits, valued up to $44.00, were on sale for $9.99. A three-pack of ladies' crew socks by Fruit of the Loom was half-price at $1.99. Cotler men's casual slacks were reduced from $30.00 to $9.99, and a selection of Levi's jeans for men were on sale for $14.99.

In home furnishings, exterior lighting fixtures were priced at $4.19 to $35.99, while a Universal ceiling fan with light sold for $39.99. For cars, you could get a gallon of Prestone anti-freeze for just $3.49, about half-price; and pet lovers were loving four cans of 9-Lives cat food for a dollar.

Black's also has a large section of hardware supplies, as well as a separate building for gardening and sporting goods. There you may find a forty-pound bag of Garden King topsoil for just 69¢ (with a rebate coupon), or Spaulding and Franklin baseball mitts as low as $9.99.

Trader's Outlet — 899 Main St., Waltham; 894-4041. You can find some great deals on real clothes here. The emphasis is on casual and activewear. Not everything is super-cheap, but poke around. Levi's men's chino pants, $12.99, L.A. Gear hi-top sneakers for $22.99, and a good selection of men's, women's and children's sneakers from $25.00 to $40.00—including Reebok and Avia, first quality, in current models.

College and professional sports team T-shirts are $3.99, as are women's applique oversize T's. Also for women there are racks of blouses, bright cotton dresses, pants, and more, with prices of $6.99, $9.99, etc.

There is a pretty good selection of furnishings for men and women—socks, underwear, and other basics. Also, a hodgepodge of household items at overstock prices, such as toothpaste, toys, photo frames, etc. Many are gathered in a "99 cent" section.

Value Village — 413 Moody St., Waltham; 899-7771. Also, 1902 Centre St., West Roxbury; 327-3733. Value Village has an ever-changing variety of knick-knacks, clothing, and some furniture, at overstock prices. A wall full of kitchen gadgets, for example, were mostly 99¢ each. Hanes socks for men were $1.99 a pair, and Lee khaki pants, slightly damaged, were $5.00 each. There were lots of childrens' sweatshirts and pants for $2.99 each.

An oak-finish coffee table, meanwhile, was $70.00; while a dinette table and chairs was $125.00. Some of the furniture is damaged. There were books for a dollar, sewing supplies, and cheap decorative housewares. The West Roxbury store also carries lots of sporting goods and camping equipment, much at up to half the original price.

"DOLLAR" STORES

This seems to be the new rage for the recession: Stores selling retail overstocks for a single price—the almighty dollar. The word, or some variant, appears in the name, and everything in the store sells for a dollar, or three for a dollar, or sometimes a higher even figure, like two dollars.

ARLINGTON

The Buck Stop — 449 Massachusetts Ave., Arlington; no phone. This is a good example of the species. They have a good supply ranging from basic household items to packaged food to toys and books.

Here Mr. C found packaged cookies, dishwashing liquid, hair spray and accessories, four-packs of those tiny individual cereal boxes, yarn and sewing supplies, and a cassette tape that makes your answering machine sound like Porky Pig.

You never know what you'll find, but it's always fun.

Balich 5 & 10 — 1314 Massachusetts Ave., Arlington; 648-3707. Also, TAD'S 5 & 10—185 Massachusetts Ave., Arlington; 643-6158. In the old days they didn't have dollar stores; they had five and dime stores. Not many 5 & 10's are left, but Arlington boasts two of the last remaining examples; in each, you'll find greeting cards, linens, vacuum cleaner bags, cooking utensils and kitchen gadgets, hardware, toys, and probably everything else under the sun.

The prices are well above five cents nowadays, of course, but they are still cheap. Get a bath towel for $3.00, a pair of sunglasses for $3.99, a microwaveable food container for $1.29, a tablecloth for $5.00. And unlike more modern department stores, you can even find helpful service. It's like a trip into the past. If you find this kind of shopping fun, though, a word of warning: A nickel here and a dime there can still add up!

BOSTON

All For A Dollar — 95 Summer St., Boston; 426-4008. Also in the Cambridgeside Galeria Mall, Cambridge; 494-0241 and the Fresh Pond Mall, Cambridge; 497-0223. This appears to be the most upscale of the dollar stores, being one of a chain. The store itself is clean and bright and gets a lot of people browsing through, as it is located halfway between Jordan Marsh/Filene's and South Station.

Again, you know the price; the items include hardcover books, hair products, snack foods, stationery, sewing and knitting, party supplies, accessories for pets, cooking and cleaning stuff, toys, socks. . . .

It has probably the largest selection of any of the dollar stores, and has more brand names than most. You'll find Revlon nail polish, Gerber baby food, Pepperidge Farm and Keebler cookies, Del Monte foods, and more.

Buck A Book — 553 Boylston St., Boston; 266-0019. Also at 636 Beacon St., Boston, 266-7219; 42 Court St., Boston, 367-9419; and 1001 Massachusetts Ave., Cambridge, 876-3519. They mean what they say. What kinds of books can you get for a dollar? All kinds—when this large chain snaps up bookstore returns, overstocks, hardcovers that don't sell once the paperback comes out, and the like.

Recent novels by Larry McMurtry and Jackie Collins, nonfiction in all subjects, dictionaries, children's activity books, and more are all creatively displayed. There is also an upstairs section, where some books are *a few* bucks each, but still cheap.

The big arrival during Mr. C's visit was Ronald Reagan's autobiography—quite a thick tome for someone who has such a poor memory. A buck may be too much for this one. Upstairs, though, his speechwriter Peggy Noonan's hot tell-all, *What I Saw at the Revolution*, was also on sale, reduced from $20.00 to just $5.00. Good balance.

Upstairs features include large-size art and coffee table books, from $3.00 to $10.00; and computer software guidebooks, like *The Wordperfect Bible*, half-price at $15.00. The store also sells office supplies at discount—computer paper, envelopes, Rolodexes. Greeting cards are two for a buck.

The store has cheap videos, cartoons, and self-help programs, from $1.50 to $5.00; and books on tape (audiocassettes) for $2.00 each.

CAMBRIDGE

Buys For A Buck — Twin City Plaza, McGrath-O'Brien Hwy., Cambridge; 628-6651. One of the most recent entries into the dollar derby, Buys for a Buck is one of the brighter, nicer-looking shops. It has all the usual stuff: Glassware and mugs, kitchen gadgets, books, toys, lots of brightly-colored plastic earrings and necklaces, cosmetics, stationery, party supplies, small clothing accessories, and much more. All, you guessed it, for a buck. Everything is neatly laid out on stacking shelves.

WESTWOOD

Dollarama — 214 Providence Hwy., Westwood; 461-1117. Well, this is a bit out of range for Boston, but Mr. C found it right on Route 1 near a lot of other discount stores along the Westwood/Norwood border. If you're in the area, try it out.

It's a true dollar store, with a big selection of greeting cards and wrapping paper, sewing supplies, silk flowers, and porcelain giftware, stuffed animals, coffee mugs, kitchen gadgets, and baby toys. They have a lot of small items at two or three for a dollar. As usual, you never know what you may find!

ELECTRONICS

HOME AND OFFICE APPLIANCES

For starters, two mega-store chains have cropped up in the greater Boston area: Staples (branches at 25 Court St. and 1249 Boylston St., Boston, 1660 Soldiers Field Rd., Brighton; also in Waltham, Natick, Saugus, and Cambridge) and OfficeMax (Twin City Plaza, McGrath-O'Brien Hwy., Cambridge; also in Natick). Both of these stores offer phones, answering machines, fax machines, computers, copiers, etc. at savings of about 30 percent to 70 percent off list prices. Of course, no one really pays list prices; but these discounts are indeed very good. Another chain worth checking out for electronics and home appliances is Service Merchandise (Twin City Plaza, Cambridge; also in Saugus and Natick). The selection is usually limited in these places, but what they do have may be at good savings. All three publish catalogs of their wares.

Look for more appliances in the "Department Stores" section of this book.

BOSTON

Sherman's — 11 Bromfield St., Boston; 482-9610. In addition to all kinds of cameras and electronics (see listing under "Stereo"), Sherman's in Downtown Crossing has bargains on phones, fax machines, refrigerators, air conditioners, and smaller home appliances—irons, rechargeable razors, water filtration devices, and the like. A factory-refurbished Smith Corona word processor, which would normally retail for $400.00, sells here for $199.00—and it is guaranteed. Be sure to pick up their latest circular at the front of the store for the best deals.

Trotman Office Machine Service — 6 Clearway St., Boston; 424-7143. This shop, which mainly sells and services new IBM typewriters and word processors, also sells reconditioned models at good prices. Most of what they have in the used department are typewriters, both manual and electric. Prices for electric models, such as the IBM Selectric, start around $100.00 and up;

manuals are a bit less. They will try to match you up with just the features you want. All reconditioned machines come with a sixty-day warranty.

BRIGHTON

Grossman's Bargain Outlet—217 North Beacon St., Brighton; 783-1906. Also, 129 Bacon St., Waltham; 894-5100, and in Braintree, Framingham and Malden. See listing under "Housewares."

BROOKLINE

Commonwealth Builders Supply — 375 Boylston St., Brookline; 731-1800. Everything here is sold at discount—from small appliances like toaster ovens and boom-boxes to the big-ticket refrigerators and washer/dryers. All items are new and fully warrantied.

A Black and Decker iron, normally $22.00, sells here for $14.00; a Braun "Flex" rechargeable razor, retailing for $164.00, is just $90.00. Get a good-sized Welbilt microwave oven for $139.00; or a Eureka "Hot Shot" upright vacuum cleaner for $79.99. Not to mention air conditioners and heaters, televisions, and much more in this large showroom.

Wyatt's Office Machines — 999 Beacon St., Brookline; 232-7660. Just on the Boston/Brookline border, this small and friendly shop sells new and used word processors, telephone products, typewriters and other such tools. They accept trade-ins, so they have an ever-changing stock of used machines available. You can usually find a few varieties of word processors, for example—the kind with the eight- or sixteen-line LCD display and 3.5-inch floppy disk drives—for $200.00 to $300.00. These carry a limited warranty. Lots of typewriters to look at, too. Wyatt's also does excellent and quick repair work.

CHARLESTOWN

Mystic Appliance — 135 Cambridge St., Charlestown; 242-9679. Mystic sells reconditioned refrigerators, washers, dryers and ranges, by all major brands, for as much as half their original cost. These generally start in the neighborhood of $150.00; it can be more or less, depending on the age of the machine. Some are only a year old. All

carry a ninety-day warranty on parts and labor for service performed at the store.

NEWTON

Appliance & Kitchen Showroom — 345 Boylston St.
(Route 9), Newton; 527-4884. The owners of this spiffy little shop belong to a "buying group" which allows them to get bulk prices on refrigerators, stoves, washing machines, TVs and more. Thus, they can compete with major department stores, and with lower overhead, offer better prices.

Sure, the chains may run a special on a particular item—for one week only, and it may not even be in stock. The prices here are consistently low, without special sales; and you can always get the item right away. In fact, they have access to local warehouses with over $14 million of inventory. So even if you don't see what you want in the store . . . ask.

Appliance & Kitchen Showroom carries most major brands, but another way they can save you money is with models made by the big brand under lesser-known names. Whirlpool, for example, has its own subsidiary, Roper; all the working parts are by Whirlpool, as is the service warranty. But buying a Roper can save you as much as $50.00 or more off the big-name prices in major department stores.

A & K is big on service, too. After twelve years in business, the

---

Mr. Cheap's Picks

✓ **Commonwealth Builders Supply** — Good selection of everything from razors to refrigerators, all at discount.

✓ **Grossman's Bargain Outlet** — Along with the lumber and paint, these outlet stores carry cheap closeouts on lamps, vacuum cleaners, phones, toaster ovens, and more.

✓ **Sherman's** — Vast array of home appliances, stero, and housewares at good discounts.

---

folks here know their stuff. They can find exactly what you want or need without wasting your time on salesmanship. They also carry plumbing fixtures at discount, and specialize in custom cabinet design and installation. Open late on Thursdays, closed Sundays.

ROSLINDALE

Ashmont Discount Home

Center — 4165 Washington St., Roslindale; 327-2080. Ashmont is a general merchandise store, carrying everything from small appliances to furniture and bedding. They are keen on beating competitors' prices—if you bring in an ad for a particular item, they will match the price.

Meanwhile, their own prices are pretty good to begin with. On sale recently were a Proctor-Silex iron for $9.99, a Toastmaster two-slice toaster for the same price, and a ten-cup Mr. Coffee machine for $16.99. In larger appliances, a Whirlpool dryer sells for $299.00, and a Welbilt eleven-cubic-foot re-frigerator was on sale for $299.00 as well—reduced from $349.00. Open seven days a week.

SOUTH BOSTON

Broadway Appliance — 77 Dorchester St., South Boston; 268-7080. Located in Perkins Square, where East meets West (Broadway, that is) Broadway Appliance sells new and used refrigerators, washers and dryers, stoves, etc. Most of the stock is used and has been fixed up on the premises—with a ninety-day warranty. During that period they will repair your purchase for free, or replace it, if necessary.

There are at least three or four models of each kind of appliance; most items are only a year or two old, and they look quite good. A Frigidaire side-by-side refrigerator/freezer, with twenty cubic feet of space, which probably retailed for over $1,000.00 a couple of years ago, was seen here for $300.00. Other fridges were on sale for $250.00. Good deals.

COMPUTERS

Like any big-ticket item, computers are a tricky purchase. There are ways to save money, but you should be careful in dealing with salespeople; make sure you're getting the features *you* want, and that the unit has a warranty for service. Most computers work fine—even used—but you want to be covered. Another note: The computer market is extremely volatile—one of the few in which prices may drop, seemingly overnight. Use the figures quoted here as a general comparison.

BOSTON

Boston Computer Exchange — 55 Temple Place, Boston; 542-4414. Not a store, really, but a telephone service. Boston Computer Exchange is a buying and selling network for used computers. Their staff of operators will guide you through an international listing of computers for sale by individuals, businesses, and manufacturers. They will try to find exactly the system you wish, at a substantial discount.

BCE's listings note the condition of each item, the specifications, and the location. They can access IBM-types, Macs, lap-tops and more. If they find something you like, you can arrange to have it shipped directly to you. Inspect it for forty-eight hours, make sure it's good, and pay BCE. They take care of the seller. If anything is wrong with the machine, you can renegotiate the price or send it back—postage is paid by the seller.

The listings are extensive, and chances are they can find what you need, or something comparable.

Laptop Superstore — 28 Battery-march St., Boston; 330-1666. Also, 218 N. Main St., Natick; 508-650-9800. In addition to brand-new merchandise, this store sells factory-refurbished laptop and notebook computers at bargain rates. These, of course, are the latest rage in word processing: personal computers small enough to carry around with you, battery-operated, to use wherever you may happen to be.

"Refurbished" means items that were found to be defective and were returned to the manufacturer. The defects have been taken care of, and now the computers can be resold at discount— with none of the wear and tear of other used computers.

Notebooks on display recently included a Sharp 286, with one megabyte of memory. It originally sold for about $1,500.00; here, it was $779.00. Another notebook, an NCR 386, also with 1MB of memory, was $1,095.00, reduced from $1,800.00. Laptops are less frequently in stock, but they tend to be even lower in price, starting around $700.00.

All computers come with their manufacturer's warranty, generally three months or six months, depending on the model. Laptop Superstore is open weekdays from 9:00 to 5:30, and Saturdays from 10:00 to 3:00.

Rentex Office Equipment — 337 Summer St., Boston; 423-5567. Here's a slightly different take on the used computer market. Rentex, which leases PCs to businesses, refurbishes them when they come back in. They "scrub" the hard disk, replace worn-out parts, and fix anything that needs it. This means you can get current models, in like-new condition, for $400.00 to $500.00 below retail prices.

A Macintosh "Plus" system, complete and ready to use, costs $475.00. At present only Macs are available, but by the time you read this, Rentex hopes to have added IBMs to its sales inventory. Higher-end Macs, all the way up to the "FX" system, are all for sale—as are Imagewriter printers, laser printers, modems, and scanners.

So well are these restored that Rentex offers a full one-year warranty for parts and service, along with a ten-day money-back guarantee. They do their business over the phone; call Monday through Friday between 9:00 and 5:30.

Schneider Leasing — 451 D Street, South Boston; 261-6060. As the name implies, this company leases out computer systems of all kinds; when the systems are returned, you can buy them cheap. There's always a lot in their ever-changing inventory. Like Boston Computer Exchange and Rentex, they prefer to work over the phone rather than in person; the salespeople are very helpful and will figure out what you need and what they have to match.

In general, complete systems start around $500.00 for an IBM-compatible PC. That would get you a 286 unit; 386's start closer to $800.00. Schneider has Apple systems too, like a "Mac Classic" for $900.00. And they have printers from $150.00; even the occasional laser printer (they go fast at these prices), as low as $700.00.

All equipment carries a ninety-day warranty. Hours are Monday-Friday, 8:30 to 5:30 only.

BRIGHTON

A.L.S. Computer Systems — 121 North Beacon St., Brighton; 254-0003. How'd a new computer place get in with all these resellers? Since 1984 A.L.S. has been assembling its own IBM-compatible systems right here in Brighton, shipping them all over the world. It's like a factory-direct outlet for computers. And unlike many of the used dealers, you can go in and see these for yourself.

Mr. Cheap's Picks

✓ **Boston Computer Exchange** — Not a store, really, but a phone service that can hook you up with individuals and offices around the country that are looking to sell off equipment as they upgrade.

✓ **Progenius** — Not just new and used computers, but one of the only stores selling used software.

✓ **Rentex** — Another service selling off used equipment, but these guys refurbish the machines themselves and guarantee them.

A basic 286 package, with a 12mhz processor, 1 megabyte of RAM, a 40 MB hard drive, a 5.25" floppy disk drive and an amber monochrome monitor, sells for $695.00. You can, however, order any specific upgrades you want: More memory, a bigger hard drive, a full-color monitor. In fact, A.L.S. prides itself on upgrade service done on the premises—"while-U-wait."

The basic 386 package starts at $995.00. All computers carry a one-year parts and lifetime labor warranty. They also sell printers, modems, and other peripherals.

Progenius, Inc. — 71 Washington St., Brighton; 789-4122. Progenius sells new and used computers. In their showroom you can see a complete IBM-type 386 system for as little as $720.00. And yet you can also get an IBM clone—older, of course—for less than half of that, $325.00. It has 640K memory and a monochrome monitor. Makes for a cheap entry into the world of chips and bytes.

Used printers start at around $50.00 for a nine-pin model, and $125.00 for a twenty-four-pin (letter quality). Progenius also sells used software (they don't carry any new), for $5.00 and up—about half of the retail price. Accessories, too.

Used merchandise has a thirty-day warranty, with repairs done in the store. They're open every day except Sunday, including Thursday and Friday evenings until 9.

CAMBRIDGE

Computer Exchange — 401 Massachusetts Ave., Cambridge; 868-8998. This bright, tidy shop in Central Square offers a lot of cheap options for the budget computer. Because the industry changes so quickly, perfectly good systems can go from expensive to cheap in just a couple of years—just because the newer ones are faster or have more memory. But you can find an IBM system here (not a clone) that retailed for $2,500.00 when it came out and now sells for $159.00. It has a monochrome monitor, of course, and a small memory; but if all you need is a simple little system, this could do it. Great for students or for kids just getting started.

Many of the pieces are newer, of course—like an Apple Imagewriter II printer for $250.00, about $100.00 under retail. You can get nine-pin printers as low as $60.00, keyboards, and other peripherals.

CX has lots of choices under $500.00, and you can see everything in the store up and running. You get three days to check a piece out at home and return it if necessary, but they've already weeded out most of the duds. They also offer service, upgrades, and trade-in or consignment options.

CHARLESTOWN

A.P.C. Computer Rental Co. —
142 Cambridge St., Charlestown;
241-0900. Another leasing/reselling
outfit, again doing business over
the phone. IBM-type systems with
a 286 processor start around
$500.00, complete; Macintosh SE-
20s are in the same ballpark. Printers start as low as $10.00 (!),
ranging up to around $100.00. All
carry a thirty-day warranty. Call between 8:30 and 5:00, weekdays.

WILMINGTON

Computer Haus—332 Lowell St.,
Wilmington; 508-657-7959. Further
afield, Computer Haus is located at
the junction of Routes 93 and 128
(Exit 38), so it may be convenient
for readers who live on the North
Shore or who work in that sea of
suburban office buildings.
    This shop sells new and used

systems, including an IBM 286
clone for $595.00. Used IBM-type
systems, though, start around
$250.00; they also have Macs, like
an Apple II-C for $350.00. All in-
clude a ninety-day warranty on
parts and labor. Open Monday
through Friday, 9:00 to 5:00, Saturday
day 10:00 to 3:00.

WOBURN

CompUSA — 335A Washington St.,
Woburn; 937-0600. Closest Boston
branch of this fast-growing chain,
offering some of the best prices on
up-to-the-minute hardware and software. CompUSA features technical
assistance by phone also. The best
thing about the store, according to
Mr. C's personal computer guru:
"Everything's out on display, so you
can really play with things and get
a feel for different models."

STEREO EQUIPMENT

ARLINGTON

Audio/Video Exchange — 204
Massachusetts Ave., Arlington; 646-
4243. Despite its name, this is not a
place to swap 'n shop; it is a consignment dealer for anything and
everything in home entertainment.
People bring items in, either for cash
on the spot or to go on display in the
store. Profits are then split between
the store and the seller.
    The quality ranges from basic
models to high-end brands. A pair
of $1,500.00 Polk speakers recently
sold for $500.00; a Bang & Olufsen
turntable, with a tonearm that actually moves across the record, sold
for $230.00—it originally retailed for
$795.00. And a studio-quality Tas-
cam reel-to-reel deck, $1,600.00
new, was available for $495.00.
    Among the more down-to-
earth items are, a Sanyo cassette
deck, which sells for $79.00, and a
twenty-five-inch Quasar color TV for
$127.00; a Panasonic hi-fi stereo

VCR goes for $199.00. There are
even a few computers, refurbished
to like-new running condition; you
can get a complete 512K system
for just $189.00. Everything in the
store is up and running.
    And then there are the un-
usual items, like video games and
CB radios. A combination
AM/FM/TV/shortwave radio, with a
three-inch TV screen, for $89.00; or
a one-inch TV screen with AM/FM
(the kind people take to sports
events) for $59.00.
    They also carry used records,
tapes, CD's, and music equipment,
like guitar amplifiers. Audio/Video
Exchange claims to be the only
business in town selling all these
kinds of things under one roof. The
hours are funky too: Tuesday-Friday
from 5:00 to 9:00 p.m., and Saturday from 10:00 to 5:00.

BOSTON

Sherman's — 11 Bromfield St., Boston; 482-9610. On the basement level of this large Downtown Crossing store, Sherman's displays a wide range of electronics and photo equipment. Televisions and VCRs, cassette decks, receivers and speakers, boom boxes, Walkmans, and more. A recent sale featured a Denon compact disc player, originally priced at $300.00, now $219.00; and a Panasonic cordless phone marked down from $120.00 to $88.00. Some items are factory-refurbished returns; all equipment is guaranteed.

Sherman's is also a good place to stock up on blank tape of all kinds; one or two major brands of video cassettes are usually on sale for $2.99 (even high-grade!), and they have many brands of audio cassettes at low prices too.

Tweeter Outlet Center — 874 Commonwealth Ave., Boston; 738-4411. At the rear of Tweeter Etc.'s branch at the Boston University campus is a big room with shelves and shelves of demos, discontinued and returned stereo and video equipment, at savings of 20 to 70 percent off the list prices. You may, for example, find a Mitsubishi fifty-inch projection TV, listed at $3,800.00, on sale for a paltry $1,999.00. Even the ultra-fancy Bang & Olufsen can be found at discount, their sleek silver CD player priced at $750.00, a savings of $350.00.

Okay, so Tweeter tends to traffic in high-end. Not to worry. How about a Kenwood double cassette deck, marked down from $300.00 to $180.00, or a Yamaha CD player with a five-disc carousel, reduced from $300.00 to $200.00. And Mr. C spotted a system of Proton mini-components: CD player, receiver, and cassette deck, all fastened into one fine-looking black metal unit for $700.00.

They may not necessarily be cheap, but you can save a bundle. Tweeter offers the original manufacturer's warranties on all merchandise, which varies according to the item.

CAMBRIDGE

Audio Lab — 36 J.F.K. St. (Garage Mall), Cambridge; 864-1144. If you can work your way to the top of this silly circular mall in Harvard Square and find Audio Lab, you may find a few bargains in used stereo components. They sell mostly new products but do repair work as well, and so they have a couple of shelves of refurbished items—an Onkyo cassette deck, for example, at

---

Mr. Cheap's Picks

✓ **Audio Replay** — A tiny Harvard Square nook with an excellent repair department and lots of used stereo components they've fixed up.

✓ **Audio/Video Exchange** — Not a swap shop, but a consignment store with plenty of regular and high-end stereo, TVs, VCRs, and more.

✓ **Cambridge Soundworks** — For some reason, it's in Newton. Anyway, they have lots of closeouts on great tape decks, CD players, and speakers at bargain prices.

✓ **Tweeter Outlet Center** — Again, lots of closeouts to choose from in audio and video, many at substantial discounts.

$110.00. Not a lot of choices, but worth a look if you're shopping around.

Audio Replay — 8 Bow St., Cambridge; 492-4604. This tiny shop near Harvard Square does expert stereo and VCR repair and has a full range of components that have been refurbished into fine working order. You can always check the board out front (it may be easier than squeezing into the shop), with listings of the many pieces currently for sale.

Among them on Mr. C's visit were a JVC dual cassette deck with auto reverse for $75.00; a pair of JBL three-way tower speakers for $180.00; a Yamaha preamp with equalizer for $225.00; and, for vinyl die-hards, a JVC direct-drive turntable with automatic return for $80.00.

All items are warrantied for ninety days, parts and labor. Some great finds here—plus several "Best of Boston" awards.

Q Audio — 95 Vassar St., Cambridge; 547-2727. It's a natural—a used audio place on the MIT campus. Right on the corner of Vassar and Mass. Ave., Q bills itself as "the world's smallest hi-fi shop" but actually has quite a lot of equipment, with plenty of options for the budget audiophile. New, used, and "B-stock," or factory blemished items, are all sold at discount. The brands cover the spectrum, from Technics to Sony to Bose to Luxman.

Among the used items, Mr. C saw a Technics receiver for $89.00—a few years out of date, but working ably. A used cassette deck by the high-end Nakamichi, retailing originally for $650.00, was just $250.00. B-stock items included a Sony dual cassette deck for $170.00, as well as a Sony CD player for $120.00. Most of these new, slightly blemished machines come from Sony; Q makes sure they work smoothly and gives you two weeks to return them if problems crop up. And just try to find the scuffs.

The sales folks are friendly and helpful, solicitous but not heavy on the pressure. New and B-stock items carry full one-to-three year warranties; but they'll even cover used equipment for at least a few months. You can also bring in your own pieces for cash (if they can sell them), trade, or consignment.

NEWTON

Cambridge Soundworks — 154 California St., Newton; 332-9461. Henry Kloss, the engineer who founded the high-end company KLH, has started a new speaker company that has again attracted a lot of attention from hi-fi enthusiasts. At his store you can buy high-tech SoundWorks speakers at factory-direct prices, starting as low as $150.00 a pair.

For greater savings, though, check the stock of other stereo components—with many discontinued or factory-refurbished items. The brands most frequently seen are Pioneer, Denon, and Philips. Examples: CD players reduced from $250.00 to just $109.00, and forty-watt receivers marked down from $225.00 to $159.00. You never know what may turn up; there are almost always incredible bargains in very limited quantities. The salespeople are very helpful, and will also leave you alone if you prefer. No "hard sell."

SOMERVILLE

Used Sound — 31 Holland St., Somerville; 625-7707. This Davis Square shop buys, sells, trades, and repairs stereo equipment, as well as electric guitars and amps. Cassette decks by Technics and Pioneer were in the $65.00 to $75.00 range; a Kenwood receiver was also $75.00, and a Sony CD player was $90.00. A special note for collectors of old radios: Used Sound specializes in tubes and has a good stock of these hard-to-find items. All stereo equipment carries a ninety-day warranty. Closed Sunday and Monday.

FOOD

WHOLESALE FOOD MARKETS AND SHOPS

Producers of all kinds of foods sometimes sell directly to consumers as well as to their business clients. In Boston, these kinds of shops tend to be clustered together. A stroll through Chinatown, for instance, will take you past many vendors of fruits, exotic vegetables, and prepared meats—all pretty much at bargain prices.

Here are four other parts of town for great prices on foods—some well-known, some less so.

THE HAYMARKET AREA

The Haymarket is a Boston tradition that stretches back to the 1700s. Every weekend produce vendors cram this stretch of North and Blackstone Streets, just outside of Quincy Market, with wagonloads of fruits, vegetables, flowers, fish, and more. You can buy direct, stock up, and save money. Be strong, though; sometimes you just have to muscle your way through the crowds. It's like the Filene's Basement of fruit. By Monday, the entire bazaar is somehow miraculously cleaned up and you'd never know it had been there.

Several discount food shops line the area, open all week:

C & C Thrift — 118 Blackstone St., Boston; 248-0828. One of the string of basement shops along this Haymarket street, C & C sells leftover packaged foods that are near their "sell by . . ." dates—but are still good if you're going to use them promptly. This store deals mostly in baked goods, such as "Vermont All-Natural Bread" at 89¢ a loaf, reduced from $1.99. You can get three bags of Green-Freedman rolls for a dollar, or boxed apple pies marked down from $2.69 to $1.25. There are also bags of uncooked pasta, usually $1.25 for two bags. Lots of cookies, too.

Haymarket's Famous Bargain Basement — 96A Blackstone St., 723-5859. A few doors down is the butcher's equivalent of C & C. You can find a sixteen-ounce package of bacon for 99¢, pork shoulder for 99¢ a pound, and whole chickens for 89¢ a pound.

If you can buy in large quantities, you'll save even more. A ten-pound bag of chicken drumsticks is $6.90; or, you can get three pounds of ground beef for $4.00. The surroundings are no- frills, and so are the burly men behind the counter, but hey, it's the Filene's Basement of meats.

Puritan Beef Company — 90 Blackstone St., Boston; 523-1419. Next along the block is Puritan Beef—a few steps up, for a change, rather than down. Again, bargain prices, especially in bulk: Turkey wings by the bag, or unsliced bacon. Pork spareribs for $1.89 a pound, sirloin tips for $1.99 a pound, and steak cuts for $2.49 a pound. Also a good source for goat meat, ox tail, and pig's feet.

NEWMARKET SQUARE

Newmarket is a wholesalers' enclave between the South End and the Southeast Expressway. Most of the businesses are meat distributors that deal only with other businesses; but tucked in are two adjacent shops offering wholesale foods to the general public.

Basics Food Warehouse — 132 Newmarket Square, Boston; 442-1414. It's like a supermarket warehouse—only they don't have everything you may need. What they do have is cheap, much of it in large quantities. You can get a five-pound bag of frozen French fries for $2.99; Kraft barbecue sauce for $8.99 a gallon, to go with ten pounds of baby spareribs for $19.00.

Don't worry—not all the meat is for armies. There are Tyson cornish game hens, $1.59 a pound; pork loin is $1.79 a pound, and steak from $2.79. These two stores may also become your headquarters for soul food—chitterlings, ox-tail, smoked neck bones, and goat meat are all here and cheap. You can even buy a whole pig—just $1.50 a pound. Also, fresh vegetables like collard greens, 59¢ a pound.

Lord Jeff's Beef Place — 129 Newmarket Square, Boston; 445-7000. Next door, Lord Jeff's is similar but a little larger. Again, being at Newmarket, the emphasis is on meats: five-pound boxes of deli franks or frozen all-beef hamburger patties are each $8.90, while fifteen pounds of pig's feet are a mere $5.90.

Jeff's has more variety, including a soda and liquor section; the soda can be a bargain, like a twelve-pack of Coke in cans for $2.99, or five cans of Cott sodas for a dollar. Some of the beer tends to be cheap as well—a Budweiser suitcase for $14.99— but otherwise the liquor didn't seem that much of a deal.

Meanwhile, back in foods: get a box of 2 1/2 dozen eggs for $1.19, a pound box of sliced bacon for 69¢, and a five-pound box of Domino sugar for $2.39. Like most warehouse sales, though, you may see different items at different times.

NORTH END

You know, the North End. Italian. "Anthonyyyyy!" running down Prince Street. Wandering through the narrow streets is like a day trip to Rome, and you'll turn up all kinds of inexpensive bakeries, butchers, pizzerias, etc. Here are just a few examples to get you started.

Bay State Lobster Company — 395 Commercial St., Boston; 523-7960. Along the waterfront, this is the supermarket of cheap fish. The quality may not compare with the small shops along Northern Avenue's docks (Bay State's stuff is not always local), but the prices are good.

All kinds of fresh and frozen seafood can be found here, along with various condiments. Bay State's own cocktail sauce is $2.29 for a one-pound container, and it'll go well on fresh small shrimp at $2.99 a pound. Extra-large cooked shrimp, by the way, are $9.99 a pound. Or get a tub of clam chowder base and some fresh quahogs at 69¢ a pound. Swordfish chunks are $4.99 a pound, perch and cod around $3.00 a pound, and breaded fish cakes $1.69 a pound.

Bay State's lobsters come from Maine and start around $5.00 a pound off-season. During the summer they can go under $2.00.

Bova's Bakery — 76 Prince St., Boston; 523-5601. Bova's has many varieties of breads and Italian pastries, baked on the premises. Prices are as good as the aroma. Best of all, the shop is open 24 hours a day!

Dairy Fresh Candies — 57 Salem St., Boston; 742-2639. One of those great little tucked-away places for which the North End is so famous. They sell nuts and candies at discount, both fresh and imported. For example, it's a good source for Perugina chocolates, that heavenly stuff made in Italy. Perugina is always expensive, but you can save a couple of bucks on it here. Nuts are reasonably priced, too—a pound of cashews for $7.99.

Frocione's Butcher Block — 379 Commercial St., Boston; 742-4999. Brrr! Wear a sweater or jacket in here—it's cold as a meat locker. In fact, it *is* a meat locker, where you can get packaged meats and cuts made to order at good prices. Grade A whole turkeys are 49¢ a pound; homemade Italian sausages are $1.79 a pound, sweet or hot. A packaged pound of sliced bologna is just 99¢, salami $1.49. There are also national brands at discount, like Hillshire Farms, Kahn's, and Weaver.

Of course, you may not see these exact products or prices. But going on, Mr. C noted a pound of Chinese-style boneless pork spareribs or teriyaki chicken breast, each for $3.59. And at the butcher section they'll cut you steak tips or top round roast beef at $2.99 a pound; or chicken breasts at $1.79 a pound.

There are also cheeses, pastas, soups, and more; and next door, a gourmet shop with prepared salads, soups, subs, and bread.

Mike's Pastry — 300 Hanover St., Boston; 742-3050. Mr. C couldn't get out of this North End section without mentioning at least one of the many fine bakeries along Hanover Street, the neighborhood's main drag. Mike's does both wholesale and retail business, and its pastry cases are filled with colorful cakes and cookies. There are over a dozen varieties of cannoli alone! They also have table service, if you prefer to while an hour away over pastry and an espresso.

J. Pace & Sons — 42 Cross St., Boston; 227-9673. Walk underneath the Central Artery from Faneuil Hall to the North End, and one of the first things you see is Pace's. This packed, bustling market is not a wholesaler but has lots and lots of fresh fruit, produce, bread, and pasta—as well as imported specialty items, like olives and Nutella—that sinfully yummy Italian chocolate-hazelnut sauce. The prices are very reasonable, making this a sort of microcosm of the North End all in one stop.

A few doors down, La Fauci & Sons at 46 Cross Street (523-1158) offers more great prices on fresh fruits and vegetables, particularly if you're buying in bulk.

NORTHERN AVENUE

Northern Avenue runs right along Boston's waterfront, from the Central Artery behind the Children's Museum area past the World Trade Center. Along with some very expensive restaurants, the route is lined with shops where you can get seafood inexpensively, sometimes practically off the boat. Seafood prices rise and fall like the tides, so Mr. C suggests you compare prices and selection.

James Hook And Company — 15 Northern Ave., Boston; 423-5500. On the Boston side of the Northern Avenue bridge, James Hook is a large operation specializing in shellfish. Hook brings in its lobsters from Maine and Canada, selling them for around $3.00 to $4.00 a pound in season. Huge buckets of scallops and steamers are also on view,

$2.00 a pound or less.

Neptune Lobster And Seafood — 88 Sleeper St., Boston; 426-0961. As you cross over that fine old trestle bridge, the first stop you come to is the tiny but choice Neptune Seafood. Here you can find steamers, all varieties of lobster from "chicks" to culls to jumbos, or just lobster meat. Also scallops and

Mr. Cheap's Picks

✓ **Bakery Thrift Outlets** — Several famous brands of commercial bakeries offer their products at direct-to-you discounts. Fresh packages are marked down slightly, day-old returns from the supermarkets (still good) are even better deals. Best of the lot are Entenmann's in Norwood and Pepperidge Farm in Cambridge.

✓ **Borden Candy Outlet** — Yup, they make it right here. Boxed chocolates in quantities from one pound to five.

✓ **Clear Flour Bakery** — This tiny, no-frills bakery sells wonderful fresh breads for as little as a dollar a loaf.

✓ **Frocione's Butcher Block** — Another good place to stock up on chicken and chops. Also, lots of cheeses and ethnic foods at discount.

✓ **Haymarket Shops** — In addition to the weekend Haymarket itself, for all your fruits and veggies, there are several tiny shops lining Blackstone Street that are open all week. Haymarket's Famous Bargain Basement and Puritan Beef Company sell fresh meats; C & C Thrift offers day old breads and cookies.

✓ **Pasta Del Palato** — A find in Oak Square. Freshly-made pastas in a wide variety of exotic flavors, plus homemade sauces. These guys supply some of the best restaurants in town.

tiny shrimp in bags of one hundred to two hundred.

During the warm months, the chic dockside restaurant Venus Seafood in the Rough (426-3388) operates out of the same building. Huge, crispy fish and chips, lobster rolls, fried clams, and special fillets like mako shark abound. It's not too expensive and gives you good-sized, delicious portions.

Paul's Lobster Company — 148 Northern Ave., Boston; 482-4234. Another place to check out for lobsters, is in front of the Anthony's Pier 4 parking lot. From small culls and chicks up to three-pounders.

Yankee Lobster Company — 272 Northern Ave., Boston; 542-1922. Yankee's lobsters are local, fresh off the boat. They can go for as little as $1.99 a pound in season. Shrimp, crab, and scallops too.

BAKERIES AND THRIFT OUTLETS

ALLSTON

Boca Doce — 182 Harvard Ave., Allston; 787-5555. This tiny step-down, which has been open for only a few months, does a brisk business. Boca Doce is a Brazilian take-out bakery, offering warm and yummy pastries filled with beef, chicken, or shrimp. Most of these hand-sized pies go for 95¢ each. They are excellent.

There are also various Brazilian sweet pastries, tea cookies, and meringues; frankly, Mr. C found the cookies rather dry. But then there are slices of cheesecake and flan, as well as little homemade candies. A recent special featured a muffin or pastry with fresh, strong Brazilian coffee for 95¢. Perfect to grab on your way to the trolley at the corner.

BROOKLINE

Clear Flour Bread — 178 Thorndike St., Brookline; 739-0060. The minute you walk into this bakery, you'll be floating on air. It smells fabulous. Clear Flour is not a real shop—more a humble bakery for restaurants and markets—but they are happy to sell to you directly. Baguettes are the best deals here, with prices that haven't gone up since 1988. The small ones, well over a foot long, are just $1.00; large ones, which are gigantic, are $2.00. They come in French and sourdough, with great crunchy crusts.

Round loaves of buckwheat, sourdough, and herb varieties are $2.50. Clear Flour also makes scones and "Morning buns," with or without walnuts on top; these are all $1.00 each.

Kupel's Bake And Bagel — 421 Harvard St., Brookline; 232-3444. Most bagel mavens agree that Kupel's makes some of the best bagels around. Since lots of restaurants and specialty food shops make a proud point of importing them, it must be true. So go to the source, near Coolidge Corner—where you can get a dozen for $3.75, hot from the oven, in about twenty varieties from poppyseed to "Tomato Veggie Onion."

Better yet, peruse their "day-old" rack. This includes bags of eight bagels for 95¢, depending on what's left over and when you check it. Usually they have the more popular flavors—poppyseed, sesame, pumpernickel. Eight fresh ones would cost you $2.70; but

when they start out as good as this, yesterday's batch is still terrific.

Just a few doors down, by the way, is longtime rival Eagerman's Bakery (415 Harvard St., Brookline; 566-8771), which also has great bagels as well as loaves (which Kupel's no longer bakes). They offer a half-dozen day-old bagels for 70¢, and various loaves for under a dollar.

CAMBRIDGE

Casal Bakery — 1075 Cambridge St., Cambridge; 547-6282. At this Inman Square bakery you can buy bread and rolls directly before they go out to the supermarkets. A loaf of scali bread is $1.08, saving you about a quarter; a dozen rolls, about $2.40 in stores, goes for $1.70 here. And, of course, you're getting the stuff as fresh as it can possibly be.

Pepperidge Farm Thrift Store — 87 Blanchard Rd., Cambridge; 661-6361. Wow. Near Fresh Pond, close to the border of Belmont, this is more like a discount mini-supermarket. Not only bread but all the Pepperidge Farm products and a few others too. Check the tag colors: Red is for fresh items at 25 percent off retail. Black is just past the expiration date, but still good, at 40 percent off; and blue means closeouts and lesser-quality food—though never spoiled—at 50 percent off.

Lots of bread loaves and rolls to choose from, as low as 87¢; a large chocolate layer cake, reduced from $2.49 to $1.86; bags of soft-baked cookies, in the gourmet varieties, marked down from $2.59 to $1.94; and of course, Goldfish. A recent sale offered them at two bags for the price of one ($1.04).

There is also a freezer case, with PF cheese and pepperoni pizzas at two for $3.00; as well as Le Menu Chicken Cordon Bleu, reduced from $3.79 to $2.75. The store has weekly specials, and senior citizen discounts on Tuesdays and Wednesdays. Stock up!

MEDFORD

Hoff's Bakery — 134A Mystic Ave., Medford; 396-7918. Hoff's supplies many of Boston's finest restaurants with pastries, calzones, and specialty items. By going to their bakery, you can buy these directly at considerable savings. Ten- inch cheesecakes, whole or sliced (and reassembled), carrot cakes, Italian rum cakes, mocha tortes, apple crisps, key lime pies, and, of course, Boston cream pies are all made here. Because of Hoff's relationships with area restaurants, they requested that no prices be printed in this book—but they are good. Hoff's also makes large sheet cakes to order, suitable for parties and banquets. They are open all day Monday-Friday, and Saturday mornings.

NATICK

Wonder-Hostess Bakery Thrift Store — 330 Speen St., Natick; 508-655-2150. Seems kind of funny to make a fuss over Wonder Bread, that most ordinary of loaves. You can get such a loaf here for only 60¢—fresh and direct from the bakery. But there's a lot more here than white.

Hostess Cupcakes and Twinkies are 25¢ a pack; cinnamon crumb cake, fat-free, is reduced from $2.99 to just 99¢. A dozen assorted doughnuts is marked down from $2.49 to the same 99¢. Most of these are reaching their expiration date, but rarely are they past it.

Other brands and products here include Home Pride Butter Top Wheat Bread, 50¢ a loaf; Beefsteak Rye, same price, marked down from $1.69; a box of Uncle Ben's stuffing mix for 99¢. There are also various soup mixes, rice, popcorn, and candies.

NORWOOD

Entenmann's Outlet Store — 105 Providence Hwy. (Route 1), Norwood; 769-6635. Readers in the south and west suburbs, especially those with a sweet tooth, may want to take advantage of the chance to get Entenmann's baked goods at tremendous savings—in many cases, over half-off. This outlet has large quantities of cakes, cookies, pastries and bread, plus some other items.

There are three levels of discount on boxed pastry. Fresh goods are sold at bakery-direct prices: French crumb cake, for example, sells at $2.99 in supermarkets and $2.30 here. Market returns, which haven't yet reached their expiration dates, are about half-price: A box of six blueberry muffins was reduced from $2.99 to $1.50. The markdown section includes goods that can be anywhere from two to eight days old, all priced at $1.00. Here you may find a lemon danish twist that retailed for $2.99, or a box of chocolate chip cookies that had been $2.39. Entenmann's stuff is made well enough, though, that it doesn't go stale very quickly. At these prices, people snap them up.

The store also gets products from other area companies at discount, such as Sealtest ice cream for $1.89 a half gallon and Arnold rye bread for 85¢ a loaf. And the local Brothers Bakery trucks in bags of fresh Italian bread and dinner rolls each day, 95¢ each. For senior citizens there is a further 10 percent discount off the total at the register.

QUINCY

Nissen Bakery Thrift Shop — 715 Washington St., Quincy; 773-9230. As you've gathered by now, these outlets for major commercial bakeries are terrific places to stock up on essential supplies. As Nissen trucks bring fresh bread to supermarkets each morning, they collect whatever was left over from the day before and bring it here. So, you can get perfectly good loaves, most of which haven't reached their expiration dates, at half of the supermarket price. Even less, sometimes, if the item is closer to expiration.

Nissen Thrift also carries

other lines, such as Drake's Cakes. They also have fresh, current merchandise as well; even this is below retail prices. Open Monday through Friday from 9:30 a.m. to 5 p.m. and Saturday from 8 a.m. to 4 p.m.

SOMERVILLE

Neighborhood Restaurant And Bakery — 25 Bow St., Somerville; 623-9710. This extremely popular Union Square restaurant (see listing in the dining section) also bakes its own mouth-watering Portuguese sweet bread. You can buy it here directly for just a dollar a loaf; early in the day you may even be able to grab one of yesterday's loaves for a mere 75¢. Heavenly.

Roma's Bakery — 201 Somerville Ave., Somerville; 776-0869. Roma's bakes bread for supermarkets all over the area. Buying at the bakery couldn't be simpler; nearly everything is priced at $1.20—large, round soft loaves, sliced scali bread, whole-grain loaves, or a bag of a half-dozen sandwich rolls. You only save a bit over the stores, but the best part is that after three o'clock you can get the bread straight out of the oven. "So hot it'll burn your hand," says Mr. Roma. This continues until about 8 p.m.; closed Saturdays and holidays.

Up the avenue toward Union Square is a larger, similar establishment: La Ronga Bakery, at 599 Somerville Avenue (625-8600) also distributes to area markets, but you can get it fresh from the source. A sliced cinnamon-raisin loaf is $1.29. They sell day-old bread, such as three baguettes for a dollar; and they also bake up fresh, hot calzones about the size of a football for $2.50, filled with spinach, mushrooms, or broccoli and cheese.

SOUTH BOSTON

Green & Freedman Bakery — 75 Old Colony Ave., South Boston; 269-4700. Their bread goes out to supermarkets and restaurants all over the city; but if you're near Southie, you can stop in and get some for less. Onion rolls are sort of a specialty of the house, and a dozen of these aromatic treats costs just $2.76 here—about a dollar and a half less than in supermarkets. Loaves of rye bread are also lower here.

The shop serves sandwiches and soups, as well as pastries; G & F no longer makes its own sweets, but the ones they sell are good!

WATERTOWN

Sevan Bakery — 598 Mt. Auburn St., Watertown; 924-3243. You've got to love this neighborhood just outside of Cambridge. Lined with Middle Eastern restaurants and markets, there is nevertheless a McGonagle's Bar and Stella's Pizza mixed in. Anyway, Sevan's specializes in great breads of all kinds, from basic Italian loaves ($1.00) to something called Zaahtar— large, round Syrian bread with a topping of thyme, sesame seeds, sumac, and other spices baked in. $2.00 gets you a pair of these zesty breads. They also have a large case of spinach and feta cheese pies (75¢), baklava made with walnuts or pistachios ($1.00), and many more delicacies.

While you're in the area, check out Massis Bakery across and down a bit at 569 Mt. Auburn St. (924-0537); and, walking down Dexter Avenue to the corner of Nichols Avenue, Marash Bakery (924-0098), for more Middle Eastern baked specialties. Diagonally across from Marash is Gennaro's Italian Food Center, 107 Nichols Avenue (924-9550), where you can get great calzones piping hot from the oven. Making a big circle, head back to Sepal Falafel at 555 Mt. Auburn St., a newcomer offering twelve pieces of falaffel to take home for $6.85. Big sandwiches, too.

FRUIT, NUTS AND CANDY

CAMBRIDGE

Borden Candy Outlet — 134 Cambridge St., Cambridge; 498-0500. Ah, to stroll through the sugary, sweet-smelling air of . . . East Cambridge? Land of factories, buses, and sub shops? Yes, this is one factory no one can complain about—Borden Candy. From a no-frills front corner room they sell gobs and gobs of the stuff. Long glass counters show you what's currently available, and the shelves above are lined with boxes ready to go. You can't ask for a quarter-pound of this and a half-pound of that; some of the boxes are, well, for the industrial-size sweet tooth.

The bargains vary from week to week, with a "specials" blackboard out front. You may find a two-pound bag of caramels for $1.75, or the same size of chocolate peanut clusters for $2.50. And, just like clothing, candy has "irregulars"; these are sold in five-pound boxed assortments for just $4.80. So what could be irregular about chocolate? They taste the same, no matter how they look.

Sometimes there are smaller sizes, like four ounces of chocolate-covered raisins or Haviland thin mints—60¢ each. There are also sugar-free chocolates, which taste very much like the real thing.

You'll also find disounted bags of candy bars, Snickers, and Kit Kats, especially around Halloween; where better to stock up. Of course, this is one of Mr. C's favorite haunts any time of year.

Superior Nut Outlet — 225 Msgr. O'Brien Hwy., Cambridge; 876-3808. Every kind of nut imaginable is processed here and trucked out all over greater Boston. In a tiny office in front of the factory, anyone can walk in and purchase fresh nuts by the bag or jar, at discount. There are usually a few specials, like a twenty-ounce jar of honey-roasted cashews for just $2.50—

very cheap. A one-pound bag of filberts, almonds, cashews, Brazil nuts, and pecans was $4.00. You can get pound bags of raw, blanched almonds for baking, whole, sliced or slivered, for $3.00 to $4.00, or Cajun-spiced peanuts for $1.75 a pound.

Processed nuts and candies include butter toffee peanuts, $2.00 a pound; jumbo dried peaches, $4.00 a pound; and all-natural sun-dried raisins, $1.50 a pound. Also, a four-pound jar of real old-fashioned peanut butter for $8.50.

JAMAICA PLAIN

Allandale Farm — 259 Allandale St., Jamaica Plain; 524-1531. The only honest-to-goodness working farm within the city limits. At Allandale you can get the freshest apples (and cider), tomatoes, sweet corn, and whatever else happens to be in season. What's more, you can see the fields these came in from. Talk about buying factory-direct. Don't you love Boston? Try getting out to the country this easily in New York.

SOUTH BOSTON

American Nut And Chocolate Company — 230 West Broadway, South Boston; 268-0075. Cashews, $3.99 a pound . . . pistachios, $2.99 a pound . . . dry roasted peanuts, half a pound for 69¢. These delicious items are roasted and processed on the premises and sold in a no-frills shop at the front. They also have chocolates and candies, though these are not made in their factory; get a pound of chocolate-covered jellies for $1.59, or a large bag of Three Musketeers mini-bars for $2.23.

WATERTOWN

A. Russo And Sons — 560 Pleasant St., Watertown; 923-1500. Outside of Watertown Square, Russo's is about as beautiful a warehouse as you're likely to see. The store at the front is modern, architecturally designed in brownstone, and offers direct prices on fruits, vegetables, flowers, and plants.

It's tough to delve much into exact prices, since they fluctuate by season. In summer, though, you may find cantaloupes under a dollar and squash for 49¢ a pound. In any case, this is definitely a good place to stock up if you live in the burbs and don't want to deal with the hustle and bustle of Haymarket. In fact, it's so handsome and mellow, it's almost *relaxing* to shop there.

MEAT

There are, of course, plenty of good butcher shops all over town. Recently, though, a newcomer came into the business— famous restaurants trading on their name and buying power to give great prices on meats. Here are the two biggies in butchery:

BRIGHTON

The Stock Market — 149 Market St., Brighton; 782-9499. A few years ago, the popular Stockyard Restaurant added a retail butcher shop on the premises, offering their diners a chance to buy from the same distributors as the restaurant. There is a large selection of beef, pork, and chicken, at just above "insider" wholesale prices.

SAUGUS

Hilltop Marketplace And Butcher Shop — 901 Broadway (Route 1), Saugus; 231-2300. Also, 210 Union St., Braintree; 848-2899. You know, the Hilltop. The one with the giant cactus and the hour-long wait for a table. Their mega-market approach to retail meats offers great prices on their own cuts of beef and chicken, as well as swordfish steaks, ham, and franks. In addition they have fruits and vegetables, paper products, and just about everything else you'd find at your local supermarket. Open seven days a week.

PASTA

BRIGHTON

Pasta Del Palato — 579 Washington St., Brighton; 782-7274. Fresh rolled pasta in Oak Square? Believe it! In this clean, spare kitchen, yards and yards of noodles are spun out in all kinds of innovative flavors. Among the buyers are Rocco's, in the Back Bay, and On the Square—Watertown. Both are known for their fancy cooking, and fancy prices.

Here, for $3.00, you can get a pound of egg, spinach or tomato pasta, cut into any of four thicknesses: Angel hair, linguine, tagliatelle, and fettucine. For $6.00 a pound (you can order by the half pound), you get into the more exotic varieties. Lemon, ginger, chipotle, scallion, and roasted garlic are just some of these pungent pastas. Unfortunately, depending on how much of each has been prepared on a given day, your first choices may be gone by the time you get there. PDP sells fresh sauces, too.

EAST BOSTON

Spinelli Ravioli & Pastry Shoppe — 282 Bennington St., East Boston; 567-1992. East Boston's Day Square is a haven for Italian food lovers. There are several good restaurants and, in a big building across the square, Spinelli's. They make all kinds of pasta right there in the factory and sell it directly to the public. The pasta comes uncooked—shells, fusilli, bow ties, and more—or as prepared dinners.

Ricotta cavatelli is $1.99 a pound, chicken cacciatore is $3.75, and chicken tortellini is $4.00 a pound. You can even get a tray of chicken wings cooked in wine ($3.29) or stuffed peppers ($3.00 a pound).

Spinelli also serves up hot foods in the store, like ravioli and meatballs ($4.99) or veal parmigiana with spaghetti ($6.25). And they specialize in large quantities, for parties of as many as twenty-four people.

SEAFOOD

ALLSTON

Rose Fish Market — 162 Harvard Ave., Allston; 783-3034. In addition to good prices on fresh fish to prepare at home, Rose's cooks up its own fried fish plates really cheap. A single order of fish and chips is $1.50, good and greasy. Fried fish dinners, with French fries and cole slaw, are $3.00; fried scallop, shrimp or clam dinners are $4.50. Take-out only.

Cao Palace — 137 Brighton Ave., Allston; 783-2340. This Vietnamese restaurant (see listing in the "Restaurant" section) also sells fresh fish—from the basics, like haddock, flounder, and scallops, to the more exotic, such as catfish and sometimes shark. Prices are usually very reasonable. You can also have them prepare your fish to go, in their wonderfully tangy ginger or caramel sauces.

CAMBRIDGE

Court House Seafood — 484 Cambridge St., Cambridge; 876-6716. Just down Cambridge Street from its namesake in East Cambridge, Court House Seafood specializes in whole fish to take home. They generally have low prices on standards and more, like redfish, porgy, and monk fish. If you don't want to do the dirty work, by the way, they will fillet the fish for you.

A few doors down is the Court House Seafood Restaurant, at 498 Cambridge Street (491-1213), which offers complete seafood dinners for $7.00 and under, along with homemade clam and fish chowders.

FARMER'S MARKETS

Most towns in the Boston area hold weekly farmer's markets at set locations throughout the summer and early fall. Like mini-Haymarkets, these are places to buy fresh produce directly from the folks who grow it. You'll often find prepared foods, too, like jellies and preserves, homemade pies, etc.

To find out this year's exact schedules, call your town hall; or the helpful staff at the Massachusetts Department of Food and Agriculture at 727-3018, extension 175.

BOSTON

Back Bay — Tuesday and Friday afternoons, in Copley Square Park (St. James Ave. side). July through November.

Government Center — Monday and Wednesday afternoons, at City Hall Plaza. July through November.

BRIGHTON

Saturdays, 9 a.m. to 1 p.m., in the Bank of Boston parking lot at 5 Chestnut Hill Avenue. Mid-July to September.

BROOKLINE

Thursdays, 1:30 p.m. to dusk, in the town parking lot on Webster Street in Coolidge Corner. June to October.

CAMBRIDGE

Mondays, noon to 6 p.m., in the parking lot on Norfolk Street in Central Square. Mid-June to Thanksgiving.

EAST BOSTON

Tuesdays, 11 a.m. to 3 p.m., at the Holy Redeemer Church, 63 London Street. Mid-July through October.

JAMAICA PLAIN

Tuesdays, noon to 7 p.m., in the Curtis Hall parking lot at 20 Centre Street. Mid-July through October.

NEWTON

Tuesdays, 2 p.m. to 6 p.m., in Cold Spring Park, Beacon Street (near Walnut Street). July to October.

SOMERVILLE

Wednesday afternoons in Union Square. July to October.

FOOD CO-OPS

There are three major food cooperatives in the Boston area, each separate but all operating in a loose confederation. They are **The Boston Food Co-op** at 449 Cambridge St., Allston (787-1416); **The Cambridge Food Co-op**, better-known as The Central Square Market, at 581 Massachusetts Ave., Cambridge (661-1580); and **The Arlington Food Co-op** at 7A Medford St., Arlington (648-3663).

The idea behind a co-op, of course, is that you become a member, pitch in a few hours regularly behind the register or stocking the shelves, and get big discounts because of the low overhead costs. You can save an average of 5 to 15 percent on your grocery bills compared to regular supermarkets.

However, you don't have to be a member to shop at these places. The prices are still quite reasonable, even without the member discounts, and the merchandise is closer to Bread and Circus than Star Market—lots of organically-grown produce, health foods, and bulk-size packages.

For members the savings can be tremendous, though, and the requirements are minimal. Just for paying a small membership fee you get a 2 percent discount off shelf prices. By volunteering a mere two hours a month, you save 10 percent. And if you choose to work a regular shift for two hours a week, you'll get food at cost—24 percent off the non-member prices.

The foods here offer lots of unusual options. The prepared food counter has delicious stuff like curried peanut chicken salad by the pound. There are bulk dispensers of everything from coffee beans to sesame seeds to instant falaffel mix. Bring in your own container to fill with pure water for 19¢ a gallon. The spice shelves have hundreds of jars—chives, licorice root, mustard seeds, bee pollen—sold by weight. And perishable foods, like cheese, fruit, and vitamins, are sold at reduced prices when they get a little past their prime.

Now, co-ops may not be for everyone. They are in many ways a world unto themselves; these are politically active community organizations. They run several non-food activities, including recycling programs, a clothing exchange, child care, and even free lectures and movies. But again, you can always choose how much or how little you wish to participate.

FURNITURE

NEW FURNITURE

There are a few acknowledged giants in the discount furniture game, but you probably don't need Mr. C to tell you about them. After all, even a five-year-old can probably recite the directions to **Jordan's Furniture**: "In Waltham, take Main Street to Moody Street . . ." You may hate their cloying commercials, but ol' Barry and Elliot do have very good prices on quality furniture. They're at 289 Moody Street, Waltham (894- 6100) and on Route 24 in Avon (508-580-4900).

Coming up on the inside "personality" track is **Bernie and Phyl's Furniture Discount**, nearby at 320 Moody St., Waltham (894- 6555). It's less well-known that their branch at 2010 Revere Beach Parkway, Everett (389-3430) includes an upstairs "attic" of leftovers and one-of-a-kind bargains at further price reductions.

Meanwhile, here are some places to check out that are further off the beaten (media) path:

ALLSTON

Bernstein Furniture Co. — 154 Harvard Ave., Allston; 782-7972. One of the several furniture stores along this stretch of Harvard Avenue, Bernstein's has a large selection of beds, sofas, bookcases, lamps, and accessories. The service is friendly and complete—they will assemble and/or deliver pieces within the Boston area.

You can find a three-piece bed set of mattress, foundation, and frame for as little as $120.00 (twin size) or $150.00 (full). Add a headboard of unfinished wood for $90.00. Futon frames of 1¼" heavy pine are $109.00 in full size, and they have futon mattresses too.

A 2' x 3' butcher block kitchen table, with two drop leaves, is just $50.00; a full dining table and chair set is $220.00. There are several styles of lamps, such as a white-lacquered three-lamp tree for $40.00.

Mr. C also noted an "entertainment center" for $40.00, with room for stereo and records or a television and VCR. This was made with pressed wood board and veneer—a less sturdy, but still practical, alternative to real wood. Most of the furniture here, though, is made from solid wood. And, if you really poke around, you may find a slightly damaged piece at a further-reduced price.

Boston Paint And Supply Co. — 151 Harvard Ave., Allston; 254-1060. You wouldn't guess from the name, but a walk past tells you that this place too is a discount furniture store. It also sells lamps, rugs, mirrors, window shades, and, of course, paints.

Here you can find a full-size futon and frame for $160.00, or a study desk in walnut veneer for $70.00; same price for a black metal cocktail table with a smoked glass top. Mr. C also saw a four-drawer dresser of unfinished pine for $80.00.

Several rolled-up rugs or carpet remnants are usually leaned up outside the store—you may find a 6' x 9' bound remnant of 100 percent wool in a beige pinstripe pattern, for $80.00. Nylon rugs are even less, like an 8' x 10' carpet remnant for $60.00.

Factory Carpet And Furniture Inc. — 137 Harvard Ave., Allston; 787-5064. Further along the same street, Factory Carpet and Furniture offers another good selection of discount furniture, beds, rugs, and carpet remnants. The selection is more limited here, but there are some good finds.

A recent closeout offered futon frames for just $49.00. A full-size futon frame in black lacquer finish is $130.00. Most of the furniture is unfinished, such as a student desk with three drawers for $90.00, or a five-drawer dresser for $140.00. Lots of unfinished pine bookshelves and cassette racks, too. Be sure to poke around the basement room for more bargains.

In carpeting, you can find a big selection of 2' x 3' Oriental rugs for just $7.00 each, or Oriental runners for $3.95 a foot. A 7' x 12' rug was selling for $30.00.

Home Design Furniture Clearance Center — 244 Brighton Ave., Allston; 254-5040. Home Design's outlet sells furniture at discount, but be warned—it still ain't cheap. This is finely made designer stuff, and it is gorgeous; the kind of living room, dining room and bedroom pieces you see in an *Architectural Digest* photo spread. So if you're looking to tone up the place with an $1,100.00 cherry wood dining table, you can get it here for half-price. Or a black metal futon frame, full-size, for $199.00. Plus sofas, beds, armoires, hutches, and the like. Most of the pieces are leftovers in perfect condition; some are slightly worn floor models—"one-of-a-kind" bargains. Well, *upscale* bargains.

Sallet Furniture Co. — 44 Harvard Ave., Allston; 782-1891. This is one of the biggest discount furniture stores around. Room after room, on

the street level and in the basement, is filled with many styles of furniture for the living room, dining room, and bedroom. The quality ranges, too, from solid wood pieces to the pressed-wood and veneer type, which often require assembly at home. Can't beat the prices, though.

How about a walnut veneer television table for $30.00, with a shelf for your video tapes underneath? To go with it, on sale recently was a solid oak and glass end table, reduced from $150.00 to just $70.00.

Also on sale was a complete living room set, with a sofa, love seat, and chair, all cloth-upholstered, along with a cocktail table and two end tables, for $500.00. A three-way folding wall mirror framed in solid walnut for $75.00.

Sallet's also has beds, mattresses, lamps, kitchen table sets, bookshelves and much, much more.

ARLINGTON

Irreverent Relics — 106 Massachusetts Ave., Arlington; 646-0370. This is known as a popular antiques shop, and Mr. C has declined to enter the pricy and subjective world of antiques. So what's it doing in this book, and this section? Well y'see, Don, the owner, noticed that antiques weren't selling as they once had in pre-recessionary days. So he decided to add some new things to his line. The first is unfinished furniture; there are several pieces in the store, or you can have one custom made to your specifications. A three-shelf cabinet with a swinging door is $35.00, and a 3' x 6' bookcase is $60.00. These are well-made, with solid joints and rounded corners.

The more interesting additions, however, straddle the line between new furniture and used. One set comes from a source in Maine, where they make "old" hutches, jelly cabinets, and the like. These are actually new pieces in rustic

---

Mr. Cheap's Picks

✓ **Boston Interiors! Warehouse** — A drive out of the city in
Randolph, but you can save hundreds on trendy sofas and
stuff.

✓ **Maverick Designs** — For unfinished furniture. If they don't already make what you need, they'll create it for you.

✓ **Office Furniture Bargain Center** — Again, a schlep out to
the burbs (Westwood), where you can become an important-
looking exec behind an imported mahogany desk at 50 to 80
percent off. Regular auctions, too.

✓ **Sallet's** — Big selection of living room and bedroom furniture,
some of it prefab, but cheap.

---

nineteenth-century American styles,
painted and then scuffed to look
like primitive country antiques. Of
course, they cost much less (and
are in better shape) than the real
thing; a $495.00 hutch would cost
over $2,000.00 as an antique.

Another line comes from
Amish country: Some folks there
have been collecting wood from
old barns that have been torn
down, and using it to make furniture. The results are handsome bur-
nished wood pieces that, again,
have the rustic look of antiques at a
fraction of the cost. Another advantage to this approach: You can be
the first among your friends to own
an "antique" CD rack or coffee table—things that were never made
until this century.

BOSTON

Eastern Butcher Block — 381
Congress St., Boston; 423-2173.
Also, 630 Worcester Rd. (Route 9),
Framingham; 508-879-8636. For
high-quality hardwood furniture,
Eastern Butcher Block offers factory-direct pieces that are still somewhat expensive, even at discount,
but will probably last forever, to be
passed down to your children and
theirs. In fact, they carry a lifetime
factory guarantee.

If you catch one of Eastern's
inventory clearance sales, you can

save even more—like a 3' x 4' drop-
leaf kitchen table, in hard rock maple, for $189.00. Or contemporary
European-style oak chairs for
$49.00 each. A set of three nesting
oak tables was on sale recently for
$139.00. All of their prices are well
below fancy retail stores. Some of
the items are factory seconds;
though they are not returnable, they
are still guaranteed.

BRIGHTON

Maverick Designs, Inc. — 1117
Commonwealth Ave., Brighton; 783-
0274. The folks at Maverick Designs must never stop working.
Their tiny shop, right at the junction
of Commonwealth and Brighton
Avenues, smells of fresh sawdust
and is packed with bookcases, record racks, dressers, desks, stools,
futon frames, and much more.

There are dozens of book-
shelves in all sizes, like a 2' x 6' unit
in unfinished pine for $56.00. Get a
12" x 16" wood-frame mirror for
$17.00, a pair of speaker stands for
$12.00, or a wall rack that holds
ninety-six cassette tapes for
$16.00. Curiously, these display
racks actually contain used records, tapes and CDs, which you
can buy for $1.00 to $4.00 each.

Larger items include a six-foot
tall, thirty-inch-deep armoire for
$159.00, a computer center desk

for $79.00 and even an oak park bench for $59.00. Everything is solid and well-made. If you buy something that isn't quite the right fit, you can trade it for a piece that is; and if you need something to fit exact dimensions, they'll custom design it for you.

CAMBRIDGE

Bookcase Factory Outlet — 453 Massachusetts Ave., Cambridge; 547-0802. You've probably noticed this crazy hodgepodge of a store in Central Square—the one with the colorfully-painted roll-down shutters. Venture inside and it's a combination hardware store, tool rental center, and unfinished furniture dealer. All sizes of shelving units, chairs and stools, bedroom furniture, and more are on display or can be made to order. There is also a basement with further-reduced bargains on both finished and unfinished pieces.

Tri-fold futon frames, in high-quality hardwood, range from $89.00 to $110.00, depending on size. Add a twin, all-cotton futon for $84.00. A finished pine round kitchen table, with drop-leaf sides, was seen for $129.00, and a five-drawer pine dresser for $160.00. There are usually several slightly-damaged items out in front of the store, very cheap—like a maple bar stool for $20.00.

DEDHAM

Home Furniture — 450 Providence Hwy. (Route 1), Dedham; 329-4770. Also, 461 Broad St. (Route 1A), Lynn; 595-7113. These stores call themselves the "Home of the Package Deal," and they do offer some very good ensemble sets. A recent sale included a mattress, foundation, frame, and wood headboard, a dresser with mirror, and a tall chest with swinging doors up top and two wide drawers below, all for $497.00.

They have a free layaway plan, as well as offering financing, and they're open seven days, including weeknight evenings.

FRAMINGHAM

Oriental Furniture Warehouse — Route 9, Shoppers World, Framingham; 508-872-1986. And now for something completely different—Oriental furniture. This is the real stuff, imported from the East; that means expensive, even at discounts of 30 to 40 percent. But if this is your taste, it's worth the trip.

Six-foot tall shoji screens—you know, with the rice paper and black lattices—are just $89.00. A black lacquer chest, with ornate figures painted on the front, was reduced from $329.00 to $229.00. A similarly-decorated white lacquer jewelry box, with three drawers hidden behind swinging doors, was $189.00, marked down from $299.00.

A ceramic stand for a flower pot, shaped like an elephant with trunk raised, was $119.00; they also have real bonsai plants and ficus trees, or silk versions of the same.

There is also an "Oriental Garage Sale" section at the back, where slightly-damaged items are further reduced for a chance—a $350.00 chair for $99.00, or four-foot mirrors framed in black or white lacquered wood for $75.00.

MEDFORD

Pine And Baker — 546 Boston Ave., Medford; 628-4733. Pine and Baker is one of those great places for unfinished furniture, made on the premises and sold at factory-direct prices. The merchandise consists primarily of freestanding bookshelf units, as well as dressers, in a wide range of sizes and dimensions. Prices for pine bookshelves start under $15.00, going only up to about $100.00 for the largest size, 4' x 6'. Dressers are priced from $75.00 and up.

NORWOOD
Office Furniture Bargain Center
— 375 Providence Hwy. (Route 1),
Westwood; 329-1662. Just off exit
15B from Route 128, amid the dozens of auto dealers, this vast liqui-
dation warehouse offers all kinds of
new office furniture for at least 50
percent off. Some of the stuff is
slightly damaged, some is just overstock, but there is quite a lot to
choose from. Mr. C found a rolltop
desk, a bit nicked but otherwise
fine, marked down from $450.00 to
$225.00. A brown leather office
chair, retailing for $800.00, was just
$299.00. And a veneer-topped
computer desk, with room for PC
and printer, was $149.00, reduced
from $308.00.

If you're furnishing an office,
there is a further 10 percent discount for buying in bulk. They also
have back-saver chairs, file cabinets,
drafting tables, cutting boards, and
some supplies—like a 250-sheet box
of computer paper that retails for
$8.95, on sale for $2.85.

The Bargain Center has another, larger warehouse nearby at
194 Vanderbilt Street, off Route 1 in
Norwood, where you can find items
that are more damaged—at even
lower prices. This location also has
periodic auctions, which include
pieces of office machinery such as
copiers. Call to find out dates and
times.

RANDOLPH
Boston Interiors! Warehouse —
24 Teed Drive, Randolph; 986-
7404. Merchandise left over from
the several Boston Interiors! stores
is brought to this warehouse, and
sold at 20 to 70 percent off its original prices. They also sell floor models and slightly marked seconds.
BI's stock is contemporary living
room, dinette and bedroom furniture and accessories; you may find
a three-piece "Bistro" set—a glass-
top table with two rattan chairs—
selling for $150.00 instead of the
original $400.00.

First-quality Bauhaus sofas, in
perfect condition, were on sale for
$399.00 each, reduced from
$599.00. In the seconds area, a
writing desk in natural ash finish, a
bit scuffed, but not enough to notice easily, was reduced from
$400.00 to just $120.00. All sales,
of course, are final; the store is only
open Tuesdays-Saturdays from
9:30 to 3:30.

READVILLE
Nationwide Warehouse & Stor-
age — 67 Sprague St., Readville;
364-6630. Also, 134 New Boston
St., Woburn; 932-3338. Not far from
Randolph—you could hit this on
the same swing as Boston Interiors—Nationwide serves as liquidators for major manufacturers of
furniture and bedding and has a
large, ever-changing selection of
bargains. A recent sale offered mattresses for as little as $19.00
apiece; the super-firm deluxe
model was all of $99.00, for a king-
size mattress with a twenty-year
warranty. Brass headboards to go
with these were $39.00, all sizes.

Other items on sale were a
two-piece sectional sofa for
$328.00, or a sofa, loveseat and
armchair set for $268.00. A five-
piece bedroom set went for just
$398.00, with dresser, mirror, chest,
headboard, and night table. All of
the merchandise is new. Nationwide offers free layaway and is
open seven days.

ROSLINDALE
Ashmont Discount Home Center
— 4165 Washington St., Roslindale;
327-2080. As noted in the "Appliances" section, Ashmont sells just
about everything for the home. In
addition to large and small appliances, housewares, plumbing fixtures, and the like, they sell new
furniture very inexpensively. And,
as mentioned elsewhere, they work
to stay close to competitors' prices;
they will meet or beat any advertise-
ment you bring in.

They have, for example, a bunk bed set, with mattresses, for $200.00 complete; recently, it was even on sale for $160.00. Twin mattresses start at $65.00, and may also go lower on sale. And a dinette table and chairs, made from solid wood, sells for $159.00. They are open Monday through Saturday from 8 a.m. to 9 p.m., and Sunday from 11:30-5:30.

SAUGUS

The Comfort Store — Godfried Plaza, Route 1, Saugus; 231-0414. Also, Mattress Warehouse I, 281 Washington St., Norwell; 659-4961. These stores may be a bit out of your way, but they both have good prices on new furniture for the bedroom, living room, and dining room. Much of it is sold at factory prices; it's all first quality, undamaged, and there is a good selection of styles. Find sleep sofas, valued at $599.00 to $999.00, on sale for as low as $399.00; or dinette sets for $195.00 to $595.00.

In bedding, twin-size platforms start as low as $98.00; there are also futons and traditional mattress sets on sale. Sealy mattresses in sets start at $57.00 per piece. Simmons "Maxipedic" firm beds start at $164.00 for mattress, box spring, and frame. Most other sizes are also at good discounts. Both stores offer free delivery throughout the Boston area on larger items.

SOMERVILLE

Union Square Furniture — 337 Somerville Ave., Somerville; 776-0716. While all of the furniture in this large store is sold at discount—like a complete thirteen-piece bedroom set for $699.00 (including mattress and foundation)—there are better bargains to be found upstairs in the clearance room. These are one-of-a-kind pieces at 50 to 80 percent off.

Some are damaged, some are out of date, but you never know what may turn up. A plush corduroy loveseat was found here, originally priced at $599.00, marked down to $299.00. A 2' x 4' mirror with a wood frame was reduced from $128.00 to $59.00. And a walnut dining table with four chairs went for $699.00, reduced by $1,000.00.

STONEHAM

Love's Furniture Warehouse — 426 Main St. (Route 28), Stoneham; 438-9191. For luxurious contemporary furniture and bedding at discount prices, Love's is worth a drive. Their large showrooms are filled with bargains; their selection of closeouts, floor samples, and overstocks offer further reductions for really good prices. For example, you may find a solid cherry cocktail table for $99.00, marked down from $149.00; or a sleeper and matching loveseat, originally $1,199.00, for just $699.00. Even a four-piece bedroom set of dresser, chest, queen-size headboard, and mirror, half-price at $799.00. Also, Sealy queen mattress sets reduced from $449.00 to $249.00. Open daily from 10 a.m. to 9 p.m., Saturdays 9 a.m. to 5:30, Sundays noon to 5 p.m.

USED FURNITURE

BRIGHTON

Cort Furniture Clearance Center — 155 North Beacon St., Brighton; 254-5455. Cort rents fine-quality home and office furniture to businesses, model homes, and the general public. When these are returned, still in good shape but maybe not sparkling-new, they go into the Clearance Center at the rear of this large showroom. You can then buy a $325.00 comfy designer chair, upholstered in striped cloth, for just $89.00. Or a huge, arc-shaped sectional sofa for $629.00, marked down from $1,100.00.

These are not all inexpensive, but you can save a lot. Most pieces are in fine shape and are good-looking contemporary fashion styles. The stock changes all the time. There was a "whitewash look" queen-size headboard, reduced from $235.00 to $99.00, and a matching nightstand for $39.00; large ceramic-base lamps, $29.00; as well as wall units, dining tables, chairs, and more. On the office side, there were plenty of desks and fancy chairs, such as a 30" x 60" oak desk, marked down from $550.00 to $179.00. There is also a "damaged" area, with further reductions for items that are scratched or dented (these flaws are pointed out for you). Mr. C saw a solid cherry dining table, reduced from $875.00 to $175.00, and an executive's desk for $59.00.

Goldstein Office Furniture — 156 Lincoln St., Brighton; 787-4433. Goldstein's is quite possibly the largest collection of desks, filing cabinets, and chairs you'll ever see in your life. Step into their cavernous warehouse: they are stacked two stories high on shelves above shelves. It seems that everything that was ever discarded from every office in the country has ended up here, and that's pretty much the story.

For over thirty years the folks at Goldstein's have been snapping up used office furniture and reselling it for one-third of its original cost or less. They do stock new furniture at discount as well, but the used bargains are truly amazing. How about a $250.00 rolling office chair, upholstered with a posture backrest, for $49.00—or a $525.00 Steelcase file cabinet, fireproof, with extra-deep drawers, lock and key, for just $149.00?

And there's so much more.

Computer tables and printer stands for $29.00. Oak office desks for $69.00. Metal locking desks with walnut tops, by Shaw-Walker, for $99.00. And whatever it is, there are literally hundreds of each. Some items go for as little as five cents on the dollar.

All sales are final, of course; but if something goes wrong, they will send a repair person out to you. They even offer painting and re-topping services, to match your office or your tastes. Though Goldstein's is open Monday to Friday, it is advisable to call ahead to make sure they have exactly what you're looking for.

CAMBRIDGE

Cambridge Greenhouse
Antiques — 2301 Massachusetts Ave., Cambridge; 876-1430. Everything in this tiny shop is piled high, like in Grandma's attic; poke around and you may find maple dining chairs for $25.00 each, or an oak-framed mirror for $20.00. The stuff is not always in great condition: a neat-looking art deco dresser was unfortunately discolored, but sold for just $85.00.

Cambridge Office Furniture — 113 Richdale Ave., Cambridge; 876-6614. Located off of Walden Street outside of Porter Square, COF mainly sells used office furniture at discount. Some pieces are new or barely touched; a large leather executive's chair was seen for $159.00, reduced from $268.00; an executive's desk, never used, was on sale for $299.00, from $500.00. You can even buy a whole conference room set. These were in very good shape.

Downstairs, though, are the big bargains. This stock may be a bit more worn, but there is a lot of it—nearly all on sale for more than half-off the original retail price. A Steelcase swivel chair, worth $450.00 new, for $100.00; a $300.00 wood-and-tweed guest chair for $89.00; computer tables for $75.00 and up; file cabinet after file cabinet for $50.00 and up. If you're setting up one of those modular offices with free-standing panel walls, you can get used panels here for just $25.00 per linear foot; new panels can cost as much as $500.00 apiece.

There are almost no price tags on the items. COF salesmen are very knowledgeable about the value of each piece and their own costs; within that range, they will negotiate a bit on prices in order to make a sale.

Consignment Galleries — 2044 Massachusetts Ave., Cambridge; 354-4408. Also, 1276 Washington St., West Newton; 965-6131. As the name implies, these shops sell estate furniture on behalf of its owners; there are lots of very nice pieces, including antiques, which are at good (and firm) prices, though still not "cheap." However, it's fun to browse, and you may yet find a bargain.

Mr. C saw a mahogany dresser with an attached mirror, slightly scratched, for $295.00; and an oak chair with a caned seat for $22.50. The key is to check out the basement, where items that have not sold are marked down; lamps for $20.00, mirrors for around $50.00, and many more pieces.

Organic Furniture Cellar — 25 Decatur St., Cambridge; 492-5426. You'll have to look carefully for this place, at the corner of Pearl and Decatur Streets in the heart of Cambridgeport (between Central Square and the river). It's only open on Saturdays from 10 a.m. to 5 p.m., except Wednesdays through Saturdays in September, and it's closed in July and August; still, for over ten years bargain hunters have beaten a path to its door.

Here you'll find a vast selection of antique and vintage furniture without fancy antique store prices—mainly because it's a one-man operation with almost no overhead costs. Get a big teacher's desk in solid oak for $95.00; a spruce clothing chest from Sweden, $125.00; coffee tables from $35.00 to $75.00; a cherry headboard for your bed, $25.00; plus chairs, lamps, dressers, mirrors, and even the occasional old-time wooden radio.

Everything is well displayed and clean, and much of it is in very good condition.

Putnam Furniture Outlet — 556 Massachusetts Ave., Cambridge; 354-1742. Also, 815 Somerville Ave., Cambridge; 354-6172. Like Cort, Putnam leases new home and office furniture and sells much of what comes back in order to keep styles current. PFO, however, has more stock; and a lot of it is "everyday"-type furniture, as opposed to fancy designer styles. You can profit nicely by this system; one recent example was a bedroom

---

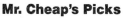

Mr. Cheap's Picks

✓ **Organic Furniture Cellar** — Hard to find, only open on Saturday, but a collector's collection of really nice pieces—*nearly* antiques.

✓ **Cambridge Office Furniture/Office Furniture Liquidators** — Two related warehouses, one in Porter Square, one in Somerville. Tons of desks, chairs, file cabinets, you name it.

✓ **Goldstein Office Furniture** — The biggest of the bunch. It's like a small city inside this warehouse. Something for every price range, with enough stock to fill a couple of Hancock towers.

---

set—wooden headboard, double dresser, tall chest and mirror—for $298.00. The stock is primarily of high quality, like a large mahogany executive's desk reduced from $1,600.00 to just $448.00. There was also one in walnut for $144.00.

Living room suites start around $500.00; and an imported marble-topped Italian kitchen table with six chairs was seen for $988.00—valued at around $2,000.00. Of course, you can buy individual pieces as well; there's quite a good selection, and the sales pitches are not heavy-pressure.

Sadye & Company Antiques — 182 Massachusetts Ave., Cambridge; 547-4424. Not necessarily cheap, Sadye nevertheless has a huge selection of estate furniture—as well as vintage clothing, old radios (well, it is near the MIT campus) and other collectibles. There are a few bargains among the several rooms, and it is just a lot of fun to browse. Most of the furniture dates from the 1920s to the 1940s, not quite old enough to be antiques, so the prices are fairly reasonable on some pieces. Friendly, no-pressure service too.

FRAMINGHAM

Universal Clearance Center — 1590 Concord St., Framingham; 508-788-0700. Another company in the furniture rental business. When leased items come back, their warehouse sells it—from slightly used to very worn—at rock-bottom prices. There is a huge selection to choose from, either in sets or as individual pieces.

Seven-piece living room sets start as low as $125.00; this includes a sofa, two matching chairs, a cocktail table, two end tables, and two lamps.

Styles are mostly contemporary. Find a sleep sofa for $79.00, or a modern black leather sofa and easy chair set for $299.00. There are "entertainment center" units for $99.00, table lamps from just $5.00 and up, office furniture, and even

appliances. A nineteen-inch color TV sells for $139.00; microwave ovens for $59.00. They are guaranteed, and you can even test them on the spot.

The Big Deal of the Day, worthy of Monty Hall himself, has got to be the "Complete Apartment" set. Start with the living room detailed above, and add a dinette set, a bedroom dresser and mirror, headboard, nighttable and two lamps. The entire package was on sale recently for a mere $299.00. Run down, but usable.

The stock changes frequently, and there are special sales a few times a year; but there is always plenty to see. Universal is open Monday through Friday from 9 a.m. to 5 p.m., and Saturday from 10 a.m. to 3 p.m. Delivery is optional, for a fee—they encourage you to take the items yourself, to save the most money.

SOMERVILLE

Office Furniture Liquidators — 519 Broadway, Somerville; 625-7060. A huge selection of new overstocks and used furniture for any office. A new 20' x 60' executive's desk, in a handsome oak finish with two drawers down each side of the chair area, was marked down from $599.00 to $299.00. New two-drawer file cabinets were on sale for $59.00; used ones were $29.00, and there were even some wood-veneer ones for $69.00.

There are tons of chairs, including an upholstered rolling secretary's chair for $69.00; and lots of large-quantity sets for conference rooms. A wooden workstation with a white drawer was $79.00, and large wooden bookcases were $69.00. Some items are damaged seconds. Cash and carry is the method of business here.

Porter Square Furniture — 95 Elm St., Somerville; 625-9744. Just on the Somerville side of the big Porter Square shopping center, this shop has a nice collection of antiques, used furniture, and also new unfinished pieces, all reasonably priced.

Among the used items, Mr. C saw a maple headboard and bed frame for $45.00, and a drum-style coffee table for $29.00. Also, lots of lamps, decorative items, and some carpet remnants. New furniture included a three-drawer nighttable for $49.00, and a five-foot-tall dining room hutch for $119.00. They also carry futons and frames; twin-sizers are $98.00 each.

Whalen Furniture — 311 Somerville Ave., Somerville; 666-5100. For over thirty-five years, Whalen Furniture in Union Square has been selling some new, mostly used, furniture and appliances. Three large rooms are filled with sofas, kitchen tables, chairs, lamps and bric-a-brac. There are various styles, from classic to hopelessly outdated, in various conditions.

A handsome colonial-style writing desk, with four drawers down the side, was seen for $85.00; it did have a few scratches, but it's solid wood. A nice sturdy chest was $75.00, and a six-shelf bookcase, painted white, was $65.00. A long, low walnut dresser and mirror set was $250.00; a beige-fabric sleep sofa was $200.00, and so was a dinette table with two center add-in leaves and four captain's chairs.

In appliances, there was a large Litton microwave oven for $100.00, and a Kenmore washer for $200.00; both looked like new. A Toastmaster toaster/broiler oven was $20.00. There was even an old photocopy machine for $25.00. Not to mention books, records, and old movie stills.

Many pieces can be delivered free in the immediate area; for larger items, you can either lend a hand or pay a reasonable fee. All sales are cash or check only.

SOUTH BOSTON

John's Used Furniture — 373 West Broadway, South Boston; 269-1238. This little corner shop is so packed with furniture that it spills out onto the sidewalk. The antique pieces are quite nice, but still a bit expensive; however, Mr. C did see an art deco dresser for $100.00, in less-than-pristine condition. Among the more recent used wares, there was a good selection of uphol-stered chairs from $5.00 to $50.00, and coffee tables for $25.00 to $35.00. They're not all in great condition, but they're cheap.

Lenox Super Saver Store — 272 West Broadway, South Boston; 269-0333. This new small storefront takes a very personal approach to thrift furniture. The prices are low, for merchandise that is usually well-worn but still useable; the idea is to help out folks on a very limited budget. They offer a fifteen-day lay-away plan with no interest or fee, as well as a thirty-day warranty.

You may find a bedroom set—including a full-size bed with head-board and mattress, a dresser, and a nighttable—all for $100.00. The one Mr. C saw was antique art deco; though not in great shape, it still had plenty of life left. Lenox also has kitchen sets at similar prices and a limited selection of clothing, stereo equipment, and ap-pliances—like a Hotpoint refrigera-tor for $150.00.

BEDS

ALLSTON

Bernstein Furniture Co. — 154 Harvard Ave., Allston; 782-7972. See listing under "New Furniture."

Boston Paint And Supply Co. — 151 Harvard Ave., Allston; 254-1060. See listing under "New Furniture."

Factory Carpet And Furniture Inc. — 137 Harvard Ave., Allston; 787-5064. See listing under "New Furniture."

Home Design Furniture Clearance Center — 244 Brighton Ave., Allston; 254-5040. See listing under "New Furniture."

Sallet Furniture Co. — 44 Harvard Ave., Allston; 782-1891. See listing under "New Furniture."

Sofa And Futon Outlet — 244 Brighton Ave., Allston; 254-5040. See "Home Design Furniture Clearance Center" listing under "New Furniture."

ARLINGTON

Royal Slumber Discount Shop — 397 Massachusetts Ave., Arlington; 648-0933. Also, 660 Arsenal St., Watertown; 923- 6021. Also in Natick, Norwood, Peabody. Royal Slumber will save you as much as half off the retail prices of name brand (although, as we all know, *no one* ever really pays full "retail" price). You can get a Sealy Posturepedic set here for $320.00 in twin size; lower Sealy grades sell at just $60.00, $80.00, and $100.00 per piece, especially during their frequent sales.

There are several brands to choose from here, but Royal tends to feature Sealy—sofa beds too, from $399.00 to $799.00, with a variety of fabrics to choose from. Also futons and frames, bunk beds and headboards. A recent special was a twin-size metal headboard, in any of four different colors, for $29.00. Fun for the kids' room.

A big bonus is free delivery, setup, and removal of your old bed; another is the six-month price guarantee. If you buy something and see it somewhere else for less, they will refund you the difference, plus ten dollars. Royal Slumber is open seven days a week—including weeknights until 9:00.

BOSTON

Mattress Discounters — 757 Boylston St., Boston; 437-6633. Also, 872 Commonwealth Ave., Brighton; 738-0033. Fresh Pond Shopping Center, Cambridge; 354-0118. 180 Needham St., Newton; 527-3692. And in Braintree, Dedham, Framingham, Natick, Saugus, and others. How do they do it? VOLUME! That's the basic idea with this rapidly expanding national chain. They certainly do carry known brands at low prices. Their best deals are on closeout models, perfectly good leftovers from previous seasons. Among these, you may find Simmons deluxe firm sets for $135.00 in twin size, or $225.00 in full size. Or Beautyrest extra firm sets for $198.00 twin, $340.00 full, $459.00 queen.

The stores are huge, and they also have kids beds with colorful metal frames, day beds, brass headboards, adjustable beds, and much more. Open seven days a week, and Monday through Wednesday evenings until 9:00.

BRIGHTON

Sleep-Rite Factory Outlet — 1113 Commonwealth Ave., Brighton; 782-3830. Sleep-Rite is one of the largest manufacturers of bedding in the country. At this outlet shop near BU, you can buy their "Ther-a-Pedic" brand at factory-direct prices. A queen-size set, including a very firm mattress, box-spring, frame, and local delivery, is just $469.00. The same set in department stores can cost as much as $700.00!

They also sell futons and frames, such as a full-size futon and frame for $178.00. Though Sleep-Rite only makes the mattresses, the frames are made of high-quality wood (no pine). Most are guaranteed for ten years. All mattresses are also guaranteed for up to twenty years, depending on the type.

Mr. Cheap's Picks

✓ **Big John's Mattress Factory** — Yes folks, they make 'em upstairs and sell 'em downstairs. Good prices on all kinds of bedding, including waterbeds that look (and behave) like regular mattresses.

✓ **Mattress Discounters** — An ever-growing chain; their buying power works out well for you, especially during special sales.

✓ **Sleep-Rite Factory Outlet** — These guys make their own too, for high quality at very reasonable prices. Friendly service.

CAMBRIDGE

Big John's Mattress Factory — 121 First St., Cambridge; 876-6344. It's all here in one place, folks—the factory is upstairs and the showroom is downstairs, where Big John (there really is a Big John, the salesman said) sells directly to the public. Which is all they do. The mattresses, in a huge variety of sizes and firmness, are of very high quality. The top-of-the-line model, the "Ultra 1000," uses ten layers of coils and padding. The twin-size set is $339.00; full-size is $429.00.

At the other end of the spectrum, mattresses start at just $48.00 (twin) and $68.00 (full). Double those prices for sets. Even the lower-priced models, though, are guaranteed and sturdy. Many mattresses are engineered to meet specifications detailed by chiropractors for firm support.

Also interesting is Big John's "New Generation" waterbeds—a truly innovative design that looks exactly like a normal bed. The water-filled part is covered by an outer layer, which is upholstered like any other mattress; it has a wooden frame, so the edge of the bed doesn't sag, and it easily lifts up for changing the standard-size sheets. It also needs no heater. These start at $288.00 for twin and $348.00 full.

The store also carries headboards, frames, bunk beds, and roll-aways. There is a thirty-day exchange period, immediate delivery,

and full warranties. Big John's is open seven days, including most evenings.

Bookcase Factory Outlet — 453 Massachusetts Ave., Cambridge; 547-0802. See listing under "New Furniture."

DEDHAM

Home Furniture — 450 Providence Hwy. (Route 1), Dedham; 329-4770. Also, 461 Broad St. (Route 1A), Lynn; 595-7113. See listing under "New Furniture."

LYNN

Waterbed Warehouse — 315 The Lynnway (Route 1A), Lynn; 581-6900. For traditional-style waterbeds, check WW for prices. Their "Contempo" line sells for $150.00—any size. Three other models are under $300.00, some of which feature bookcase headboards. These models use solid pine, not a wood for the ages; they do carry more expensive styles with oak or cherry woods. All sets include frame, pedestal, heater, liner, and other necessary apparatus. Open seven days; Thursdays and Fridays until 8 p.m.

MEDFORD

Mystic Bedding Company — 81 Mystic Ave., Medford; 396-7878. Also, 1351 Massachusetts Ave., Arlington; 646-7878. Mystic Bedding manufactures its own line of high-quality mattresses, which top the big-name brands for workmanship and durability. The materials used combine a high coil count, heavy-gauge wire, and extra padding to give what the woman in the store called "a Mercedes for the price of a Chevy."

Their "Bostonian Luxury Firm Orthopedic" queen-size mattress and box spring, priced at $550.00 for the set, is lower in price and better in quality than a comparable Simmons Beautyrest, which can sell for as much as $700.00 in department stores. The fifteen-year warranty includes free repair or replacement during the first year; after that, repair charges are based on the length of ownership. Mystic offers free delivery in twenty-four hours in the Boston area.

RANDOLPH

Boston Interiors! Warehouse — 24 Teed Drive, Randolph; 986-7404. See listing under "New Furniture."

READVILLE

Nationwide Warehouse & Storage — 67 Sprague St., Readville; 364-6630. Also, 134 New Boston St., Woburn; 932-3338. See listing under "New Furniture."

ROSLINDALE

Ashmont Discount Home Center — 4165 Washington St., Roslindale; 327-2080. See listing under "New Furniture."

SAUGUS

The Comfort Store — Godfried Plaza, Route 1, Saugus; 231-0414. Also, Mattress Warehouse I, 281 Washington St., Norwell; 659-4961. See listing under "New Furniture."

SOMERVILLE

Futon Outlet — 360 Mystic Ave., Somerville; 776-9429. Hidden in this three-story wooden building, in the shadow of Route 93, is a family business that turns out high-quality futon mattresses at factory-direct prices. You can save $50.00 or more over department stores, with a variety of sizes and styles to choose from—frames are sold at discount too, though they are not made here.

The basic twin-size futon set goes for $209.00, including the mattress, tri-fold pine frame, pillows, covers, and delivery in the Boston area. Frames are also available in birch and maple. There are also bargains on floor models and irregulars, like a queen-size futon mattress for $109.00, or futon covers at half-price. The folks here are friendly and offer great service; custom orders can be made up and delivered by the next day.

Porter Square Furniture — 95 Elm St., Somerville; 625-9744. See listing under "Used Furniture."

Union Square Furniture — 337 Somerville Ave., Somerville; 776-0716. See listing under "New Furniture."

WALTHAM

Bernie And Phyl's Furniture Discount — 320 Moody St., Waltham; 894-6555. Also, 2010 Revere Beach Pkwy., Everett; 389-3430, and 373 Washington St., Weymouth; 331-4500. See "New Furniture" introduction.

WATERTOWN

Mariner Sleep Shop — 222 Arsenal St., Watertown; 923-4000. Mariner's factory in Brockton makes wooden bed frames, platforms, headboards and more in solid, one-inch-thick wood. This factory-direct shop, down the road from the Arsenal Mall, combines these with good deals on Eclipse and Spring Air mattresses.

Headboards start at just

$59.00. Frames and platforms come in a wide variety of shapes and sizes, including custom sizes. They have waterbeds, too, as low as $200.00 for everything—pedestal, deck, frame, mattress, liner, heater, and thermostat. Just add water. All wood frames are finished with two coats of lacquer and one coat of sealer; some are stained in a rich, dark brown.

Tri-fold futon frames are $99.95 in twin; save 10 percent on futons when you buy them with the frames.

Mattress deals include specials from other factories, such as a full-size set for $230.00. One closeout featured a queen set, originally $750.00, here just $299.00. Other mattresses start around $70.00 for twin pieces; you don't have to buy in sets. All mattresses have quilted tops; no cheap-quality grades here. They all carry factory warranties, and the wood products carry a lifetime warranty.

HOUSEWARES AND LINENS

See also listings under "Department Stores" and "Dollar Stores."

BOSTON

Bed & Bath — 361 Newbury St., Boston; 421-9442. Also, 1 Porter Square, Cambridge; 491-5431. 350 Western Ave, Brighton; 787-1030. 1450 Highland Ave., Needham; 444-2506. Yes, it's a chain, and many of their items are high-priced designer furnishings; still, Bed & Bath is a good place to check out when you're on the prowl for good-quality linens at sale prices. B & B's sales are very good indeed, but they usually have lots of unadvertised specials in many departments also.

Thus, you can find such goodies as 100 percent goose-down comforters for $99.00 in all sizes, or cotton-flannel sheets from $8.00 and up. Some of the sale items are seconds, but the imperfections are hard to find; $30.00 Martex flannel sheet sets were recently on sale for $9.99, twin size, including pillowcase.

First-quality Fieldcrest bath towels, originally $10.00, were a closeout at $3.99, and even a Ralph Lauren twin sheet was on sale for $9.99, marked down from $24.00. There are always good prices on pillows of various thicknesses, from goose-down (values of up to $80.00, reduced to $30.00) to polyester ($5.25, standard size).

But wait, there's more. If you can high-tail it out to Norwood, you'll find the **Bed & Bath Outlet Store**—38 Vanderbilt Avenue, off Route 1 (near Boch Oldsmobile); 769-5895. They have even more seconds and closeouts, all at drastically reduced prices.

Economy Hardware — 219 Massachusetts Ave., Boston; 536-4280. Also, 438 Massachusetts Ave., Cambridge; 864-3300. Remember the hardware stores we all grew up with? The place you'd go to with your dad to get a pipe fitting or a light bulb . . . a dingy, dimly-lit store with wooden floors and seemingly endless aisles with bins and bins of nails . . . . Well, Economy Hardware ain't like that. Oh, they have nails and bulbs, and caulk and window screens; but then there's furniture, boom boxes, coffee makers, VCR's and more—all cleanly and brightly displayed like a mini-department store.

The prices on many of these are competitive and worth a look. One or two items in each section are usually on sale, too: like $20.00 off a Southwestern Bell cordless phone, at $159.00, a Goldstar nineteen-inch color TV for $229.00, or a Queen Anne-style writing desk in solid dark-stained pine for $75.88.

Other furniture includes butcher-block and crate-style pieces, traditional chairs and a "Princess" sleeper loveseat in striped cloth for $299.00. Among housewares, there are bathroom linens and cooking utensils; kitchen appliances included a West Bend hot-water pot for $14.00, various irons and toasters, and a microwave casserole dish reduced from $39.00 to $29.00.

Pier 1 Imports — 114 Boylston St., Boston; 542-8874. Also, 1351 Beacon St., Brookline; 232-9627. One

Porter Square, Cambridge; 491-7626. 799 Broadway (Route 1), Saugus; 233-8500. Sure, you all know Pier 1. They get all manner of housewares, clothing, and trinkets made in distant countries, fresh off the boat. As the chain has expanded, their prices have gotten a bit higher; but there are still many nice things for the kitchen, dining room, and around the house that are reasonably priced.

Tall iced tea glasses with bright color stripes are $2.49 each; linen placemats, made in India, are $2.99; same price for pieces of basic white chinaware; and lots of empty picture frames, in wood, metal and acrylic.

There are always lots of items on clearance, so you can save a bit more. This can be an inexpensive way to give your place a whole new look.

BRIGHTON

Grossman's Bargain Outlet —
217 North Beacon St., Brighton; 783-1906. Also, 129 Bacon St., Waltham; 894-5100, and in Braintree, Framingham and Malden. Though these warehouses sell mostly lumber, electrical supplies, flooring, paints, and the like (at great discount, even from their regular stores), you can also find bargains on other kinds of items for the home.

Recent specials have included vertical mini-blinds in several sizes, all $4.88; picture frames, in wood, metal, and acrylic, at 50 percent off retail prices; ceramic-base table lamps for $6.88; ultrasonic humidifiers for $22.00; a

Regina upright vacuum cleaner, valued at $90.00, for just $48.00; a Black & Decker ten-cup coffee-maker for $35.00, marked down from $54.00; and a phone with built-in answering machine for $38.73.

Most of these are surplus, returns, and closeouts; some are factory-refurbished. Appliances and lamps are guaranteed to work, or they can be returned.

BROOKLINE

China Fair —
1638 Beacon St., Brookline; 566-2220. Also, 2100 Massachusetts Ave., Cambridge; 864-3050; and 70 Needham St., Newton; 332-1250. China Fair is a longtime favorite for diningware and kitchen accessories. They seem to have just about anything you could want in that area, from complete dinner sets and silverware to glass candy jars, coffee makers and tea kettles, pots and pans, Pyrex cookware for the microwave, and even wicker baskets and bamboo shades.

A six-cup ceramic teapot, imported from France, is $8.99; a three-cup espresso maker is $9.99. A forty-piece dinner set, with everything you need for eight people, is $50.00. Or, you can buy individual items piece by piece. Wine glasses with leaded crystal stems were recently on sale for 99¢ each, in all sizes. Service is minimal; you're left to poke around on your own.

CAMBRIDGE

Friendly Family Centers —
576 Massachusetts Ave., Cambridge; 492-4435. Also, 245 Elm St.,

---

Mr. Cheap's Picks

✓ **Bed and Bath Outlet Store** — Out in Norwood, a good place to stock up on linens, gadgets and stuff.

✓ **China Fair** — Shelf after shelf of dishes, silver, teapots, cookware and more. Two locations.

Somerville; 623- 9048. 22 Bennington St., East Boston; 561-0460.
441 West Broadway, South Boston;
269-7287. 1618 Blue Hill Ave., Mattapan; 298-9668. 20 Corinth St.,
Roslindale; 325-9595. See listing
under "Department Stores."

JEWELRY AND CRAFTS

BOSTON

Elements — 18-20 Union Park St., Boston; 451-9990. Also, 103 Charles St., Boston; 227-3029. For unique, hand-crafted jewelry at prices you can afford, Elements is a refreshing alternative in two expensive areas of town. Rings, bracelets, pins, and all kinds of jewelry created by local artisans sell here at a fraction of the prices seen at chic boutiques. Lots of other crafted items too, including clocks, pottery, mirrors, and some clothing items, all hand-made or designed.

Freedman Jewelers — 333 Washington St., Boston; 227-4294. Freedman's is part of the wonderful old Jewelers Exchange building in Downtown Crossing. It's eight floors of jewelers, dozens of them, packed into a single address. Not all sell to the public, but it is fun to walk around in here. And if you're trying to hunt down a bargain on a diamond, Freedman's may be the hidden jewel in the treasure box.

Located in Suite 408 on the fourth floor, Freedman's has been in the jewelry business for over forty-five years. They specialize in highly personal service, especially with diamonds. They have a huge stock of unmounted stones, each with its own documentation of size and color ratings; there is also an extensive collection of diamond engagement and wedding bands already made up. There are other kinds of jewelry and watches as well.

By manufacturing most of these themselves, Freedman's sells well below other jewelers—some prices are as much as 50 to 75 percent lower. It's the kind of place whose regular customers come in, having seen something in the bigger stores, to get what they want at a big discount. There is no sales pressure from the friendly staff, though it is advisable to call ahead and make an appointment.

Pier 1 Imports — 114 Boylston St., Boston; 542-8874. Also, 1351 Beacon St., Brookline; 232-9627. One Porter Square, Cambridge; 491-7626. 799 Broadway (Route 1), Saugus; 233-8500. Pier 1 always has a bright and colorful selection of handcrafted jewelry from faraway places, generally at very inexpensive prices. Earrings can be as low as $2.00 to $4.00, and necklaces around $8.00 to $12.00. These range from the exotic to the funky; hammered brass designs, tiny wooden elephants, strung beads, vividly painted ceramics. Many are clearance items, marked down even further.

BROOKLINE

Gateway Crafts — 62 Harvard St., Brookline; 734-1577. Gateway Crafts is a wild place—a combination workshop and store, humming with activity and sparkling with handmade jewelry and ceramics. It's a non-profit venture for the developmentally disabled, who make the wares and get the satisfaction of seeing them sold. The designs are often outrageous, in bright colors, and often tinged with a sense of humor.

And with all that, the prices are terrific. Bead necklaces, strung with offbeat shapes, are usually

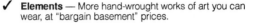

Mr. Cheap's Picks

✓ **Cambridge Artists Co-op** — Beautiful, funky creations in Harvard Square, direct from the artists to you.

✓ **Elements** — More hand-wrought works of art you can wear, at "bargain basement" prices.

✓ **Freedman's Jewelers** — For that *special* ring (and other be-jeweled items), this shop imports its own diamonds and eliminates the middleman. Highly-attentive, personal service.

$8.00 to $12.00; there are also bolo ties, with abstract ceramic clasps, for $3.00. Ceramic pins, made from irridescent pieces into bold and shiny collages, are $7.00. Put one on your dress or lapel—these eye-catching works could easily have come from a ritzy Soho boutique.

Gateway's artisans also create funky hand-painted clothing. T-shirts from $10.00 to $15.00, longjohns and leggings, even boxer shorts for $7.00! The designs range from hearts and flowers to the abstract. Open weekdays from 9 a.m. to 4 p.m. and Saturdays from 11 a.m. to 3 p.m.

CAMBRIDGE

Cambridge Artists Cooperative
— 59A Church St., Cambridge; 868-4434. Among the many fine crafts in this beautiful Harvard Square shop are cases of "wear-able art"—rings, pins, earrings, necklaces and other unique jewelry. Each display is by a different member artist, with a description of his or her technique.

These may not be the cheapest prices you'll ever pay for jewelry, but they're pretty good, considering the high quality and the fact that no one else will ever have a piece that looks exactly like yours. Perhaps a pair of brightly-colored ceramic fish earrings for $15.00, graceful sterling silver rings for $35.00, or large, hammered bronze earrings for $24.00.

Not to mention wild ceramic

housewares, clocks, handmade clothing, prints, and more. The collections are ever-changing, and the place is staffed by the artists themselves, who are delighted to talk about the work and the co-op.

NORWOOD

Jewelry Forum Of Boston — 145
Providence Hwy. (Route 1), Norwood; 769-2100. Jewelry Forum may be a bit of a drive (exit 15B from Route 128), but it can prove worth the distance. A direct importer of diamonds and manufacturer of jewelry, the store offers many items at prices well below those of other retail stores. Gold chains, for example, often selling for around $40.00 a gram at your local mall, are just $16.50 a gram here. Other chains and bracelets may be as much as 50 percent lower than fancy shops.

A pair of diamond stud earrings, which may cost $150.00 and up in big stores, starts around $70.00 at Jewelry Forum. And a bracelet made of black onyx freshwater pearls was recently on sale for just $19.00.

Jewelry Forum offers all the personal service you'd get in a big-name place, if not more. Merchandise is returnable within thirty days for credit or an exchange; all jewelry carries a lifetime guarantee. Payment can be in cash, by check, or by any of several major credit cards.

SOMERVILLE

Mayan Mercantile Outlet — 322 Somerville Ave., Somerville; 776-0908. In addition to handmade clothing, the Mayan Outlet sells a fascinating and offbeat array of jewelry handcrafted in Central and South America. Beaded necklaces, silver earrings, bracelets, and more are sold here at very modest prices.

A selection of silver beaded hoops, for example, are $10.00 to $14.00. Or, for something really funky, how about a pair of fish earrings, handcarved from wood and painted in bright colors? These are just $6.00. Lots of fun stuff here, and well below Newbury Street prices too.

LIGHTING

BROOKLINE

Renovator's Supply — 1624 Beacon St., Brookline; 739-6088. This is a retail showroom for the popular mail-order company, which specializes in recreations of lighting and plumbing fixtures from the Victorian, Colonial, and other periods. Some examples include Windsor wall sconces, with turn-key switch and amber glass shade, $69.00; the famous banker's desk lamp, with brass base and green glass shade, $99.00; solid brass wall lantern, $35.99; and, for a bit of the contemporary, black halogen desk lamps from $49.00.

For homes decorated in a classic manner, Renovator's has brass faucet sets from $25.00; plus brass coat trees, doorknobs and switchplates, wrought-iron fireplace tools, copper weathervanes, and all kinds of architectural accents. All in stock at reasonable prices. Open seven days.

NEWTON

Newton Electrical Supply Co. — 44 Mechanic St., Newton; 527-2040. Here's a great place to look for bargains on fine- quality lighting fixtures and lamps—if you can find it. Coming from Route 9, take Elliot Street south and wind your way around to Mechanic Street in Newton Upper Falls.

This full-service store has a large selection of classic and contemporary fixtures. Most prices are nearly half of the list price, which ain't bad. But look around for special deals; there are usually a few in each area. Mr. C saw a Tiffany-style ceiling light with a retail price of $530.00, on sale for $260.00; a swing-arm brass floor lamp, originally marked down from $335.00 to $200.00, on final sale for $99.00. And a shiny brass chandelier, listed at $1,050.00, was reduced to $520.00.

On a more approachable level, a mauve contemporary table lamp was just $39.00 (from $96.00). They also have mirrors, door chimes, bath fixtures, ventilator fans, and more. Very helpful staff, too.

SOUTH BOSTON

Ralph Pill Electric Supply Co. — 307 Dorchester Ave., South Boston; 269-8200. Also, 312 Mystic Ave., Medford; 391-0180, and 219 Washington St., Quincy; 471-7500. This warehouse-style lighting chain has a lot of pull (sorry!). They are distributors for several decorator brands, which you can buy here with very low markups. These are top-quality fixtures at everyday "sale" prices.

Choose from a wide range of styles, from Colonial to art deco to modern. Some are priced as low as $10.00, but even in the $30.00 to $40.00 range you have lots to look at. They also have things like ceiling fan lights, starting around $60.00; as well as shades, special bulbs, and more.

LIQUOR

Like any major city, Boston seems to have a liquor store on about every block. It's virtually impossible to see them all and compare them; furthermore, they are there more for convenience than price. While any of them may have a great price on a certain wine, or a special sale, most have a hard time beating the big guys on a day-to-day basis.

For low prices, the major chains to check out include:

Atlas Liquors, 156 Mystic Ave., Medford (395-4400), 591 Hyde Park Ave., Roslindale (323-8202) and 661 Adams St., Quincy (472-1573); **Blanchard's**, 103 Harvard Ave., Brighton (782-5588), 741 Centre St., Jamaica Plain (522-9300), 418 Lagrange St., West Roxbury (327-1400) and 286 American Legion Hwy., Revere (289-5888); **Kappy's**, 10 Revere Beach Pkwy., Medford (395-8888), 215 Alewife Brook Pkwy., Cambridge (547-8767), 120 Liverpool St., East Boston (567-9500), also in Malden and North Reading; **Macy's**, distributing through Murray's, at 747 Beacon St., Newton Centre (964-1550) and **Rotary Liquors** at 1826 Centre St., West Roxbury (325-9200); **Martignetti's**, at 64 Cross St., Boston's North End (227-4343), 1650 Soldiers Field Rd., Brighton (782-3700) and Parkway Plaza, Chelsea (884-3500); **Marty's** at 193 Harvard Ave., Allston (782-3250) and 675 Washington St., Newtonville (332-1230).

Without wishing to be unfair or leave anyone out, here are just a few other individual stores that offer discount prices on wine and spirits. As always, prices change and claims vary, so you should compare values for yourself.

ALLSTON

Brookline Liquor Mart — 1354 Commonwealth Ave., Allston; 734-7700. Right on the Allston/Brookline border, this store includes a "Bargain Basement" of wines and holds free wine tastings on a regular basis. For info, ask to be put on their mailing list.

BRIGHTON

Dollar Saver Warehouse — 165 North Beacon St., Brighton; 254-7071. The name says it all; Mr. C was unable to see the store, though, as it has been closed for several months while transferring its license. Should be open again as you read this.

BROOKLINE

Gimbel's Discount Liquors — 1637 Beacon St., Brookline; 566-1672. Small but packed, Gimbel's is a friendly place where they will help you—but not pressure you—with your choices.

Reservoir Wines And Spirits — 1922 Beacon St., Brookline; 566-5588. A large selection of wines at discount prices, for the student crowd in Cleveland Circle.

CAMBRIDGE

Boyle's Buy-Rite Liquors — 2440 Massachusetts Ave., Cambridge; 354-1000. Always some wines on special sale, like a 1987 Cabernet Sauvignon marked down from $24.99 to $19.99.

Mall Discount Liquors — 202 Alewife Brook Pkwy., Cambridge; 864-7171. Lots of bargain wines in this large store next to the Stop & Shop; vintage wine sales, too, like a 1988 Beaujolais-Villages, usually $8.49 per bottle, recently seen at two for $9.99.

EAST BOSTON

Bargain Basement Liquors — 944 Bennington St., East Boston; 567-3100. Good prices on beer, if you're on this side of the Callahan.

NEWTON

Upper Falls Discount Liquors — 150 Needham St., Newton; 969-9200. Fits right in on Newton's "discount mile" between Route 9 and Route 128.

SOMERVILLE

Sav-Mor Discount Liquors — 13R McGrath Hwy., Somerville; 628-6444. A huge, warehouse-style place with monthly specials, saving you $2.00 to $3.00 on 1.75-liter bottles of such brands as Jim Beam or Dewar's White Label. Prices often match the big chains.

MUSICAL INSTRUMENTS

ALLSTON

Mr. Music — 128 Harvard Ave., Allston; 783-1609. Mr. Music has a huge selection of used guitars and basses, primarily Fenders and Gibsons. Japanese-made Fender Stratocasters can be found for as low as $199.00, and range up to around $650.00. A Strat "Squire" of black maple was seen for $299.00.

Their prices on new instruments are pretty good too, and may get even better if you're good at haggling a bit. "It's just like buying a car," says one of Mr. C's music experts. The sales staff here can be alternately brusque or helpful, so be thick-skinned about it.

Mr. Music warranties used guitars for the first couple of weeks, during which they will do repairs for free; they also buy used instruments. They sell drum stuff too, as well as accessories, CDs and tapes.

BOSTON

A.A. Rayburn Musical
Instruments — 263 Huntington Ave., Boston; 266-8164. The first sight that greets you upon entering Rayburn's is a wall of autographed photos from giants of the music biz—George Benson, Sonny Rollins, Henry Mancini, Tom Jones (?), Woody Herman—all thanking and blessing Emilio Lyons. He is also known as the "Sax Doctor," a guru among musicians for keeping their horns in perfect shape.

Rayburn's sells new and used instruments, mainly saxes, flutes, and brass. Many of the used horns are rentals that have been refur-

bished under this expert care to "like-new" condition. A basic alto sax that would sell for $650.00 new would be $525.00 used. Trumpets start at $175.00 and up. They do carry some guitars—electric, acoustic and classical—starting around $125.00.

Daddy's Junky Music Store — 165 Massachusetts Ave., Boston; 247-0909. With access to inventory from eleven stores, Daddy's probably has the largest selection in Boston of new and used guitars, amps, keyboards, drums, etc. You may find a used Yamaha electric guitar for as little as $80.00; new models start around $190.00 (for a Peavey "Predator"). Acoustic guitars start in the same price range. Daddy's is a Gibson dealer, but they have many other brands as well.

There are plenty of used guitars under $200.00, and lots of amps in the $50.00 to $100.00 range. You can also save a bit more by negotiating a package deal; a guitar and amp for as low as $100.00. All used guitars include a free set-up, a sort of basic examination that normally costs $35.00.

Used equipment carries a warranty of thirty days on parts, sixty days on labor. Daddy's does a heavy business in trade-ins, using computer stats from their other stores to help determine their offer. Of course, you get more for your axe by using it as credit toward a purchase rather than for cash.

DJ Price Music—1116 Boylston St., Boston; 536-4205. Affiliated with

Daddy's, DJ Price is a dealer for new Rickenbacker guitars and Marshall amps; but most of their business is in all kinds of used guitars and amps. They are also renowned for the quality of their service, as confirmed by both Mr. C and his guitar expert.

They always maintain a handful of decent, basic guitars, like Nationals, for $99.00. After that, you can find Epiphone acoustics around $150.00, and Ovations starting at $250.00—these are the kind with the round fiberglass backs. Electrics, such as Fender Strats, are in the $500.00 range.

DJ Price also has a sizeable collection of unusual items, like jazz guitars from the 1930s and 1940s, preferred by serious musicians over newer versions. These sell for $1,000.00 to $5,000.00— not cheap, but much less than in, say, New York shops. Used amps, meanwhile, are in the $350.00 to $550.00 price range.

The warranty on parts is thirty days and labor, sixty days (twice that of many other stores); they also offer thirty-day price protection on new instruments. Repairs are not done on the premises; however, they will give you a comparable loaner while your guitar is in the shop—and that's available for the life of the instrument, even after the warranty is expired.

As for trade-ins, DJ Price loves 'em—and while they may not offer as much as other stores for your instrument, they will probably give you a better discount on the one you're trading for. It keeps their inventory moving. And the friendly salespeople are always willing to "talk."

Tosi Music And Sporting Goods
— 250 Hanover St., Boston; 227-2349. A music store in the North End? Why not? Established in 1905, this old-world shop is not as up-to-the-minute as the places near the music schools, but you can find some inexpensive guitars and such here. A Yamaha six-string guitar sells for $210.00 and a Fender Stratocaster for $850.00, but you can find other acoustics from just $60.00, and other electrics from $150.00. These may make good options for children or anyone just starting out.

Mr. C's visit yielded a used Gemeinhardt flute for $150.00 and a snare drum kit, with stand and sticks, for $80.00. Tosi's also carries accessories—reeds, guitar cases and strings, etc.

And they have a selection of more unusual (Italian-style) instruments, like a Hohmer accordian ($325.00), a Premier mandolin ($250.00), and ukeleles for $19.95.

Strangely, half of the store is devoted to music, while the "sporting goods" half seems to consist largely of a vast selection of rifles. A bizarre combination, si?

CAMBRIDGE

Cambridge Music Center—1904 Massachusetts Ave., Cambridge; 491-5433. Also, 4 Hemenway St., Boston; 247-1747. A dealer primarily of used guitars and amps, priced to move. Fender "Squires"

Mr. Cheap's Picks

✓ **Daddy's Junky Music Stores/DJ Price Music** — Two related companies with a vast stock of used guitars and amps for the as-yet-undiscovered rock star. Good service, too.

✓ **A.A. Rayburn Music** — A legend in the jazz world, lots of good horns and reed instruments, new and used.

---

start as low as $175.00 and up; a Japanese-made Ibanez recently went for $100.00. Used amps tend to be "classic" tube models from the 1960s and 1970s, as well as new Crate amps, which are modestly priced.

CMC offers good service, with repairs done on the premises. Used guitars are warrantied for as long as the buyer owns them; chances are, any bugs have already turned up and gotten fixed. Amps, being older, are warrantied for thirty days. Lots of strings, straps, and accessories; friendly help.

Central Sales Company — 1702 Massachusetts Ave., Cambridge; 876-0687. Central Sales began thirty years ago as a small family business selling all kinds of used items. Over the years, musical instruments won out as the main line of trade. Here you can find a student guitar for as little as $50.00, or a full-size Yamaha for $100.00. There are some new guitars for sale as well, but all other instruments come used only.

Band instruments do a brisk trade as well: Trumpets start as low as $40.00 ("or $100.00 without dents"), saxophones from $250.00, and violins from about $100.00 with bow and case. The occasional drums go for around $300.00 to $400.00 for a five-piece set. These are all sold "as is," but electric guitars are warrantied for thirty days, as are pads and springs on band instruments.

An interesting remnant of the store's history is the fact that they still get other kinds of things in trade; jewelry, stereos, televisions. So not only can you trade up for your flute, you can actually trade in appliances, jewelry, etc. toward an instrument—and vice versa.

Sandy's Music — Massachusetts Ave., Cambridge; 491-2812. This tiny shop between Central and Harvard Squares has a loyal following among the folk music crowd, and it's easy to see why. One wall is lined with all kinds of acoustic and electric guitars, banjos, ukeleles and violins; the other has racks of folk records and tapes, some used, for as little as $3.00. Used cases, too, and some amps.

During Mr. C's visit, a man was sitting on a stool in the middle of the shop (not easy in the narrow clutter) playing a banjo. He turned out to be a customer, not in-store entertainment, of course; and he was raving about the instrument, saying, "I can't believe this is so much better than the one in that other store—and it's a hundred dollars less!" 'Nuff said.

SOMERVILLE

Used Sound — 31 Holland St., Somerville; 625-7707. In addition to used stereo equipment (see listing in that section), Used Sound has guitars and amplifiers starting as low as $90.00 or so. These include a ninety-day warranty. The store is closed on Sundays and Mondays.

PARTY SUPPLIES

See also the listings under "Dollar Stores."

BROOKLINE

Paper Annex — 1638 Beacon St., Brookline; 566-2220. Also, 70 Needham St., Newton; 332-1250. Part of the China Fair housewares stores, Paper Annex has a full line of supplies and decorations for all your party needs. From decorator paper plates at $2.19 a pack, to plastic "Happy Birthday" banners at 79¢ a foot, they have shelves and shelves of the stuff.

Bags of colored tinsel, $1.20; packs of eight invitations with envelopes, $2.00; paper American flags for 49¢. Even "prismatic" reflective top hats for $1.59, as well as mylar balloons with cartoon characters on them and even pinatas.

SOMERVILLE

Paperama — 43 Foley St., Somerville; 625-5900. Also, Burlington, Danvers, Natick, Norwood. More than just party supplies, Paperama is like a festivities department store. Not only can you get a twenty-five-pack of heavy paper plates in bright colors for $1.99, with a matching paper tablecloth for $2.49—they can even sell you the table! A six-footer with folding legs is as low as $32.99, and stacking metal/vinyl chairs are $9.99 each.

Plenty of kitchen stuff too, like a variety of Ecko baking pans, $1.99 each; stemware from 77¢ apiece; and linen napkins and placemats, two for $3.00.

Not to mention silk flowers and vases, stationery supplies, cards, gift wrap, balloons (with portable helium tank), snack foods, and more.

SAUGUS

Brenner's Party Supply Store — 31 Osprey Rd., Saugus; 231-0555. Also, Route 1 (South), Chelsea; 884-2888. Brenner's is a full-service store for parties from small to gigantic. Related to two adjacent businesses, Exclusive Millinery and the Saugus Shoe Barn, the trio be-

---

Mr. Cheap's Picks

✓ **Brenner's Party Supply Store** — Up in Saugus (be sure to call for directions), a place to take care of your every whim. Excellent service; big on weddings.

✓ **Party Needs Warehouse Outlet** — Acres and acres of everything from color-coordinated paper plates to silly kiddie favors.

---

comes a complete outfitter for weddings, banquets, and holiday celebrations.

From party favors and cake decorating to invitations, banners, and aisle runners, the folks at Brenner's will help you plan just what you'll need. The prices are very reasonable, leading to the long list of regular customers on the North Shore.

WALTHAM

Party Needs Warehouse Outlet

— 411 Waverly Oaks Rd., Waltham; 893-9101. Ready to party? Want to do it up? Get this—Party Needs has over 28,000 items, from the practical to the frivolous, in a showroom that covers a quarter of an acre. Whatever you need, they've got it. There are three hundred different designs of napkins alone, to match any theme or decor. Not to mention plates and cups, streamers, favors, and all the rest. There are lots of unique items, some incredibly cheap: Little rubber fish for a nickel, and lots of other toys and favors under a dollar.

It's also worth noting that you can purchase items by the case for a discount of between 15 percent and 25 percent off, depending on the item. Party Needs is open daily from 9 a.m. to 6 p.m. (Thursdays and Fridays until 9 p.m.), and Sundays from noon to 5 p.m. It's a bit out of the way—look for the sign outside an industrial park, off Route 60.

PETS AND PET SUPPLIES

PETS

When it comes to buying pets themselves, you shouldn't expect to go on the cheap. Owning a pet is a serious, ongoing proposition, and there are constant expenses for food and health care. Still, one way to save some money initially is to adopt a pet rather than buying one in a pet store. Adoption is not free; there are various up-front fees. But these are usually less than in the stores, and you get the satisfaction of giving a home to a pet who really needs one. Here are two options:

BOSTON

Animal Rescue League Of Boston — 10 Chandler St., Boston; 426-9170. The Animal Rescue League shelter has dogs, cats, rabbits, guinea pigs, hamsters, and a few birds. Most of their animals are full-grown, though they occasionally have puppies or kittens. All are examined by veterinarians, even more thoroughly than in many pet stores—and that includes studying the animal's behavior as well as its health, so you know they are safe for adoption.

The fee for adopting a dog is $41.25 as of this writing; cats are $30.75. These costs include spaying/neutering and shots. Smaller pets are $5.25. The shelter is open seven days a week, from 10 a.m. to 4 p.m.

JAMAICA PLAIN

M.S.P.C.A. Animal Shelter — 350 South Huntington Ave., Jamaica Plain; 522-5055. Again, a selection of dogs, cats, rabbits, gerbils and birds. Dogs and cats may be adopted for an initial fee of $45.00 each; there is an extra fee of $63.00 to complete the necessary vaccinations. The fees here are a bit higher because they include a donation to the Society. The shelter is open Tuesdays through Saturdays only, from 11 a.m. to 4 p.m.

PET SUPPLIES

Mr. C was hoping to find you some inexpensive places to stock up on the basics for your pets, namely food; however, it seems the markup is so small on this stuff, that you may prefer to stick with the supermarket. Many pet owners don't like the quality of those foods, though, and there are a few shops that offer good prices on specialized items.

BROOKLINE

Commonwealth Pet Center — 362 Boylston St., Brookline; 232- 0067. This is a fun place just to walk around in—packed with pets

---

Mr. Cheap's Pick

✓ **Pet Supply Depot** — A chain store ringing the suburbs. Stock up on basic supplies at discount.

---

and supplies everywhere you look, as you wind around each nook and cranny of the store's layout. The walls and ceilings have been painted with underwater murals; indeed, the whole interior feels like some deep-sea grotto.

One room is in fact filled with fish tanks. New tanks come as a complete one-price package with filter, heater, gravel, pH kit and florescent light, as well as a gift certificate for fish of $10.00 to $25.00, depending on the tank. Further, they offer price breaks whenever you buy fish in multiples of two; the fish are, after all, happier that way.

That sums up the style at Commonwealth Pet. The service is very personal for owners and conscientious about the pets. New kittens are also discounted in pairs.

There are several unadvertised specials in the store, such as a fifty-lb. bag of cat litter for $7.99, or an electronic pet feeder (for when you take short trips), marked down from $69.99 to $49.99. They're open seven days a week.

CAMBRIDGE

Boston Pet Center — 119 First St., Cambridge; 868-3474. Also, 922 Main St., Waltham; 647-1120. A huge, very complete store with live animals and everything you'll need for them—whether you're into dogs, cats, birds, or exotic fish. The Cambridge store even has a flowing, landscaped pond right in the middle. There is a large in-house stock of tanks and cages, as well as several aisles of animal foods. These include most of the well-known premium brands such as Science Diet and Iams, at competitive prices. BPC also offers grooming services by appointment.

DEDHAM

Pet Supply Depot — 820 Providence Hwy. (Route 1), Dedham; 320-9700. Also, 395 Worcester Rd. (Route 9), Natick; 508-651-9229. Also, 682 Broadway (Route 1), Saugus; 231-2088. Also in Avon, Shrewsbury, and Weymouth. This growing chain of suburban stores has good prices on premium food brands like Eukanuba, Fromm, and Nutro-Max. Since these are more nutritious than average brands, they say, you get a better value because you can use less at a time— not to mention fewer vet costs down the road. Forty-pound bags of dry dog food here start around $24.00; eight-pound bags of cat food from about $7.00.

Pet Supply Depot also has grooming and health care items, toys, leashes, and the like, at lower prices than many independent stores. No pets sold here; just the supplies. Open seven days.

NEWTON

Cherrybrook — 66 Needham St., Newton; 332-8525. Not really an inexpensive store, Cherrybrook caters to "serious pet people"—such as professional animal breeders. They do have good prices on kennels and cages; more significantly, they have a big selection of everything from shampoos to instructional books and videotapes, which you can even rent as you would at any video store.

WESTWOOD

Pet Provisions — 917 High St., Westwood; 329-7414. Also in Salem and Beverly. Another suburban store, taking a personalized approach in selling supplies only. In addition to selling food and related products for dogs, cats, birds, and small animals, they offer grooming and even "pet-sitting" services. They have a loyal clientele, which attests to their low prices and dedication.

Foods sold here are only the professional brands, like Iams, Science Diet, and Old Mother Hubbard. "We don't have supermarket foods," the woman said. "That's just leftover people food." You can get the stuff in tiny milk-container boxes or up to fifty-pound bags. The store is closed on Sundays; the Salem branch is open seven days.

PICTURE FRAMING

Mr. C doesn't really have the space to deal with services, but this category is an important part of home decoration—and it's such a fun way to save money if you're good with constructive projects.

Yes, he means none other than do-it-yourself picture framing! There are several businesses in the Boston area dedicated to letting you mount and frame pictures and posters— with their expert guidance, of course, so you can't mess up. Depending on the size of your picture, and the materials and styles you choose, you can usually save anywhere from $25.00 to $50.00 over stores that do the framing for you.

Don't be scared—the staff usually do the trickiest parts for you, like cutting the glass. They explain everything with remarkable patience and let you take all the time you need. In the end, you have something you are proud to hang on your wall; and not only because of the money you've saved.

Two of these are **Framer's Workshop**, 64 Harvard St., Brookline (734-4995) and 115 Parkingway, Quincy (472-0995); and **Frameworks**, 2067 Massachusetts Ave., Cambridge (868-6798).

Still, as long as we're on the subject, there are several stores that advertise "less than do-it-yourself prices." They may also be worth investigating. Among them are:

Copley Art and Framing, 150 Huntington Ave., Boston (267-6060). **Frame King Express**, Porter Square Shopping Center, Cambridge (661-8661) and 118 Needham St., Newton (527-9330). Hamill Studio, 2164-rear Washington St., Boston (442-0403). **Warehouse Picture Framing**, 49 Highland Ave., Needham (449-4412).

With a bit of comparison shopping you should be able to save a bundle one way or the other.

This is probably a good place to mention stores in which you can save on pictures themselves. Among the best: **The Harvard Coop**, 1400 Massachusetts Ave., Cambridge (499-2000). The Coop shop is actually in the Book Building, behind the main store, on Palmer Street. It has an impressive collection of art prints, from Wyeth to Warhol, most priced at a mere $4.50. Also, movie still blowup posters from 50¢ to $5.00. **Mostly Posters**, 1022 Commonwealth Ave., Brighton (232-7335), along the BU campus; movies and rock 'n roll are the house specialty, at line-your-dorm-room prices. **Pix Poster Cellar**, 99 Mt. Auburn St., Cambridge (864-7499) specializes in original movie posters, most priced at a modest $12.00. They also have movie stills from $2.50 to $5.00. And rock *rules* at **Stairway to Heaven**, "Boston's Rock 'n Roll Supermarket," 48 Winter St., Boston (338-9835).

PLANTS AND FLOWERS

BRIGHTON

Warehouse Flowers — 370 Chestnut Hill Ave., Brighton; 277-0054. Also, 68 Chestnut St., Needham; 449-4882. The claim to fame for this shop: A dozen roses for $9.52. Indeed, it's the lowest price Mr. C has found in town. Warehouse also has a nice, chilly walk-in where you'll find carnations or irises for $3.99 a dozen, tulips for $4.99 a bunch, orchid corsages for $3.99, and other assortments—or make up your own.

Lily plants and azaleas are $5.99, and large floor plants are mostly $14.99. The reason for the low prices is in the name; this is a no-frills, high-volume establishment. They make no deliveries, to keep costs below retail florists.

They also extend the warehouse approach to an eclectic mix of cards, posters, artistic gift bags, baskets, and teddy bears.

CAMBRIDGE

The Grower's Market — 889 Memorial Dr., Cambridge; 661-6194. Not the cheapest garden center around, but certainly one of the most complete, for everything from apartment planters to backyard farms. Catch a sale, though, and you may find a twenty-five-pound bag of Toma's vegetable and garden fertilizer marked down from $20.00 to $12.00. Or four-inch pots of geraniums for $4.29.

Various potted herb plants, like sage, garden cress, spearmint, and even chocolate mint (yes, that's what it smells like!), are each $2.99. Among larger plants, a four-

foot-tall ficus tree is a reasonable $19.99. Grower's Market also offers a 10-percent student discount all the time.

ROSLINDALE

City Farm — 721 American Legion Hwy., Roslindale; 469-2992. What name could be more appropriate for this urban haven? All you need for creating your own farm, or just a nice window box, is here. By working cash-and-carry, City Farm saves lots of money over most other gardening centers. Better yet, they offer quantity discounts when you buy six or more of any plant.

Annuals, for example, are $1.98 each; this is already half a dollar less than most retail places. Buy six or more and the price drops to $1.75. Small change, perhaps, but it adds up in a big garden!

There are lots of vegetable plants, too; and starter fruit trees—apple, cherry, peach, plum—at $15.00 each. CF also has cut flowers at wholesale prices, including a boxed dozen long-stem roses for $15.00.

Another good deal is on foliage plants for the house. During the summer months, when City Farm can stock large quantities and keep them outside, these decorative large-pot plants are reduced from $35.00 to just $19.98. And a very helpful feature on all house plants is the color-coding tags, to tell you which plants want lots of light and which ones want to hang out in the shade.

Mr. Cheap's Picks

✓ **Ricky's Flower Market** — Located in the heart of Somerville's Union Square (literally), a good place to get your geraniums and a few gardening tips.

✓ **Warehouse Flowers** — Lowest price on a dozen roses in town. Lots of other cut flowers at cut prices, too.

City Farm is open daily from 9 a.m. to 6 p.m., except Sundays until 5 p.m.

SOMERVILLE

Ricky's Flower Market — 283 Washington St., Somerville; 628-7569. Ricky's is located in the heart of Union Square—literally. Whichever direction you travel through that crazy course of roads, you'll be looking right at the open-air stand. It's been there for over four years, with good prices on all kinds of plants and flowers.

The big promotional deal is a dozen long-stemmed roses for $9.98. But there is also a wide variety of annuals, ready to replant, at $1.98 each—petunias, marigolds, violets, begonias, and more. Larger-sized annuals are $3.25 each. $1.98 is also the basic price for herbs and vegetable plants like tomatoes.

Ricky also has a "Bargain Basement"—around the side, actually—with tables of pansies and "Tom Thumbs" for a dollar, and a sea of impatiens in pink, purple, red and white, at $2.00 each. Taking advantage of rush-hour business, the shop is open on weeknights until 8:00. There is a parking area on the Washington Street side.

WALTHAM

Moe Black's — 140 Lexington St., Waltham; 894-4933. As mentioned in the "Department Stores" section, this discount store also has a separate garden center. Get a three-cubic-foot bale of peat moss for $4.99; flower or vegetable flats as low as 69¢ apiece; potted rose bushes as low as $4.99; and all kinds of garden care products. A recent sale featured Ortho insect killer spray bottles at two for $7.00, normally $5.00 each.

WATERTOWN

Ann & Hope — 615 Arsenal St., Watertown; 924-3400. This king of cheap department stores also has a large garden shop, entered separately from the parking lot. It's more like a warehouse, filled with just about anything you might need for house and outdoor plants. Good prices and large quantities on fertilizer, lime, bark chips, planters, tools, sod, and more.

The plants themselves are dirt-cheap—couldn't resist!—small annuals and vegetables from 99¢, larger ones for $1.50, and indoor plants from $1.50 to $7.50. Rose bushes in two-gallon pots are $8.99, and one-gallon evergreen shrubs are $4.99.

Unfortunately, this is a department store, not a true nursery; the plants are not well taken care of, and many are wilted—especially the more delicate flowering plants. You do always get what you pay for; still, at these prices, perhaps you can afford to take a chance on rescuing these neglected children.

RUGS AND CARPET

ALLSTON

Able Rug Company — 20 Franklin St., Allston; 782-5010. Also in Natick and Hanover. This giant carpeting store, located across from the Sports Depot restaurant at the beginning of Harvard Avenue, sells imported rugs, wall-to-wall and remnants, most at good discounts. You may find a 5' x 8' hand-knotted rug from India, valued at $1,000.00, on sale for $399.00; or a 3' x 5' hand-made Dhurrie for as little as $39.00.

Upstairs you'll find more bargains, particularly in remnants of all kinds. One overstock sale on Mr. C's visit was a 4' x 6' bound contemporary rug—beige with two bold diagonal stripes of maroon and turquoise across the middle. It was valued at $458.00, and reduced to $115.00. A 6' x 9' bound rug in grey, with diamond shapes cut into it, was $89.00. And a 3' x 6' Oriental-style rug—actually made in Belgium, with a country floral design on 100 percent wool, was marked down from $150.00 to $99.00.

Able has lots more to see. They are open seven days, and also provide padding and installation.

Boston Paint And Supply Company — 151 Harvard Ave., Allston; 254-1060. See listing under "New Furniture."

Factory Carpet And Furniture Inc. — 137 Harvard Ave., Allston; 787-5064. See listing under "New Furniture."

BROOKLINE

Warehouse Carpet — 479 Harvard St., Brookline; 277-2565. You know the old saying, "I can get it for you wholesale"? This shop, up the street from Coolidge Corner, is like that.

They install commercial and residential carpeting at 25 to 30 percent below most other retailers (their estimate; you should compare for yourself). Meanwhile, hundreds of remnants are left over, which they sell at $6.00 to $10.00 per square yard, bound. Just about all of these are nylons of various types. Check 'em out!

CAMBRIDGE

Lechmere Rug Company — 200 O'Brien Hwy., Cambridge; 876-9700. Lechmere Rugs is a small place that deals directly with several mills, in high volume, to offer discounts on first- quality factory surplus and closeouts. You can find nylon carpeting from just $7.99 per yard and wool blends from $21.99 a yard—about half of retail.

A 6' x 9' remnant may go for $60.00, a bit more if you want one that's bound. Orientals start around $150.00. Lechmere also offers full service throughout the Boston area and beyond, with padding and installation available; they are open seven days a week.

CHELSEA

Ben Elfman Carpet — 124 Second St., Chelsea; 884-7330. This warehouse has been in business since 1907, selling carpets and rugs of

---

Mr. Cheap's Pick

✓ **Ben Elfman Carpet** — Over the bridge and through Chelsea to carpet a house we go . . . . Tons of bargains, open evenings and weekends.

---

every kind. Whether you want an Oriental rug or polyester by the yard, Ben's got it cheap. Find Du-Pont "Stainmaster" for $11.99 a square yard; it retails for $19.00 elsewhere. Sculptured-texture nylon carpeting is as low as $7.99 per yard, and 6' x 9' bound remnants are $29.00 in a large variety of colors. Oriental rugs of the same size, valued at up to $150.00, sell for just $39.00. Periodically, they run a 25 percent off sale on every item in the store.

Elfman's also offers padding and installation. They're open seven days, and weekday evenings until 9:00.

DORCHESTER

C & S Carpet — 756 Dudley St., Dorchester; 524-7479. C & S installs carpets throughout Boston and has lots of great remnants to look at; over four hundred colors, by their estimation. These all sell for $5.00 per square yard—period. Most of them are nylon weaves, and come unbound (they will do binding for you at $1.00 per linear foot). They also have some imitation Oriental rugs, a less-expensive alternative to the real thing. A 9' x 12' rug sells for $150.00. C & S is open from 9 a.m. to 5 p.m., Mondays through Saturdays.

FRAMINGHAM

Carpet Mill Outlet Store — 1602 Concord St., Framingham; 508-877-8002. If you're planning to carpet a room or a house, check out these folks for an estimate. Their prices may not be much lower than other retail stores, but the same amount of money here gets you higher-quality materials that will ultimately last longer and look better. They will also try to save you money by measuring the yardage as efficiently as possible; a hidden seam here or there may mean less scrap to pay for.

They also have a big selection of unbound remnants, in over one hundred varieties of materials, thickness, and colors. At $5.00 a yard and up, these can be up to 50 percent less than retail prices. Open seven days a week.

SEWING AND FABRICS

Beware: for the sew-it-yourselfer, buying fabric heedlessly can sometimes make a project more expensive than if you had bought the item ready-made. Here are places where you may find good, off-price deals. Price your whole project thoroughly.

BOSTON

Clement Textiles — 54 Kneeland St., Boston; 542-9511. A very small, old shop, crammed with bolts and remnants for as little as $1.00 per square yard. A good place to start from as you search out the bargains, but be sure to wander around to the other shops listed below; this neighborhood is a sewing fan's paradise.

New England Textiles — 50 Essex St., Boston; 426-1965. This cozy little corner shop has entrances on both Essex and Chauncy Streets. It has lots of cotton and polyester remnants from 99¢ a yard, velvet from $1.49 and linen from $2.99 a yard. Bolts of lace in many colors and patterns start at $3.29; polyester crepes, in various prints, are reduced from $5.99 to $3.99 a yard; same price for polyester taffeta.

There is also satin for $2.99 a yard, lycra for $5.49, and "fancy" velvets from $12.99 a yard.

North End Fabrics — 31 Harrison Ave., Boston; 426-2116. Across Essex Street, heading into Chinatown, is the inappropriately named North End Fabrics. Must have moved at some point. No matter. These friendly folks cut you good prices on fine designer fabrics. One woman in the shop was saying that she had combed the suburbs searching out a particular embroidered lace for her daughter's wedding dress. Not only was this one of the only stores that had what she wanted; it was ten dollars less per yard than any other she'd seen.

North End has little in the way of remnants, but they say their everyday prices are $2.00 to $3.00 below even the sale prices of most other stores. Mr. C also noted many special items, such as Ellen Tracy textured silks for $20.00 a yard.

Winmil Fabrics — 111 Chauncy St., Boston; 542-1815. Perhaps the largest of the Downtown Crossing/Chinatown area showrooms, Winmil has a lot to see beyond the basic cottons and synthetics. Metallic lames at $3.98 a yard, chiffons for $3.19 a yard, sequined lace for $9.98, cotton/lycra in solids and wild patterns for $4.98. Several varieties of crepe du chine were marked down from $6.98 a yard to $3.98; various linens for men's suits were $3.98, and calico was reduced to $1.98.

Also, lots of designer fabrics and patterns for draperies and slipcovers, reduced from $10.98 to $5.98, with remnants at $3.98. Plus patterns, pillow forms, lace trim, thread (four spools for a dollar) and buttons.

Yarn And Craftworks—151 Lincoln St., Boston; 357-5391. Here's something a bit different from the above—everything for the do-it-yourself *knitter*. Let's talk yarn! The walls and aisles are lined with bin upon bin of wools, cottons, mohair, and acrylics; thin, thick, brushed, multicolored . . . .

Full-price yarns are all sold at discount. Brand-new two-color cotton by Linsey, just into the store, was marked down from $3.75 a skein to $2.99. In addition there are always several bargain tables, where you'll find things like Icelandic wool for $2.99 a skein. A basket of 100 percent Irish wool was $19.50 per one-pound roll; two of these are enough for a large sweater. And a grab-bag of eighteen assorted wool skeins was just $22.50.

Y & C also carries all the patterns and tools you'll need, as well as printed canvases for latch rugs, needlepoint pillows, and crewel embroidery. Service is personable and helpful.

BRIGHTON

The Fabric Showroom — 319 Washington St., Brighton; 783-4343. The owner of the Fabric Showroom, whose family has run the company for over seventy years, is justly proud of his store. They have over thirty thousand different fabrics, from domestic cottons to imported velvets. "We inspect every roll that comes in here, to make sure they're all first quality," he points out. "No one else does that."

There's a lot to see. Designer fabrics for reupholstering chairs and making slipcovers for sofas, draperies, or bedspreads. They buy direct from the mills and sell at 30 to 70 percent off retail. By keeping prices below even the places only the pros can use, this store makes designers of *all* its customers. Fabric Showroom also does custom work, or you can buy the

materials for yourself; they will even let you borrow two-foot wide sample swatches to take home and test. "No one else does that, either," says the owner.

Cotton fabrics start around $7.95 per square yard. They have a special rack of fabrics for just $2.99 a yard, or 50 percent off the last markdown; and a remnants table with more bargains.

Ralph Jordan Textiles — 332 Washington St., Brighton; 254-5852. Across the street, Ralph Jordan is another longtime area fabric house. The selection is not as large, nor is it discounted; but they do have lots of remainder fabrics from past seasons, sold at about half the original prices. Polyester jacquards and moires are $4.98 per square yard, and some cottons and wools are as low as $2.00 to $4.00 a yard. There is also a basement area with even older stuff, priced for clearance at 98¢ to $1.98 a yard. Think of it as vintage clothing that hasn't been made yet; also good for making costumes for the school play, or for anything you may want to cover over a large area. Cheap!

CAMBRIDGE

Sew-Fisticated Discount Fabrics — 264 Msgr. O'Brien Hwy. (Twin City Plaza), Cambridge; 625-7996. Also, 735 Morrissey Blvd., Dorchester; 825-2949, and in Dedham and Brockton. Sew-Fisticated is a complete store for the sewing fan, with fabrics, supplies, and patterns, all at discount. A recent sale, in fact, had several Simplicity and McCall's patterns at 60 percent off. They also run regular "Dollar Day" sales, when remnants of calico, cotton-knit prints and sol-

---

Mr. Cheap's Pick

✓ **The Fabric Showroom** — Blows the competition away. More designer material, at rock-bottom prices, than you can shake a yardstick at.

---

ids, broadcloths, and more are $1.00 to $1.50 a yard.

Regular store displays always feature items on sale, such as forty-two-inch wide velvet remnants in solid colors, marked down from $8.00 to $4.99 a yard. They also have lycra blends and spandex.

Threads were on sale at seven spools for a dollar, usually 55¢ apiece; there are also tools, lace trim, dyes and more. Open evenings, and Sundays from noon to 5 p.m.

Sew-Low Fabrics — 473 Cambridge St., Cambridge; 661-8361. Lots to look at here. Sew-Low features many of the usual fabrics but also has lots of unique materials. Fake fur, as low as $9.99 a yard; velveteen; corduroy, recently on sale for $2.99 a yard; imported Italian tapestries, marked down from $25.99 to $19.99 a yard; plus upholstery and drapery fabrics, yarns and knitting supplies, Simplicity patterns, and more. Friendly, expert advice too. Open seven days.

SHOES AND SNEAKERS

ALLSTON

Footwear Marketplace — 2 Harvard Ave., Allston; 787-9858. This no-frills shop on the corner of Cambridge Street has grown from a weekends-only secret into a thriving everyday goldmine. The main attraction is shoes and sneakers; you can find current brand names at discount and last year's leftovers at closeout prices. There are also bargains in clothes and accessories.

For top-line sneakers like Reebok, Nike, Fila, and Adidas, there is a good selection of current styles sold at about 30 percent off retail. A pair of men's Reebok pumps, which would be over $90.00 downtown, goes for $65.00 here. For women, Tretorn ankle-high soft leather exercise shoes are marked down from $65.00 to $40.00.

At the back of the store the racks are filled with more sneakers, perfectly good, at prices from $10.00 to $45.00. You'll still find brand names like LA Gear, Spalding, and Asics. You can even rummage through $10.00, $5.00, and $3.00 bins. And there are lots of shoes: men's loafers from $9.99, a pair of red patent leather dancing shoes by Juliano's (with gold tips!) reduced from $35.00 to $15.00, Pierre Cardin suede loafers ($65.00 down to $30.00) and more.

Casual clothing varies from slouch socks (three pair for $5.00) to Harvard sweatshirts ($16.00 down to $5.00), tie-dyed women's leggings for $5.00 and cotton sundresses for $6.95. Most everything in the store has a good selection of sizes.

Chain Bargain Store — 20 Harvard Ave., Allston; 254-4590. See listing under "New Clothing."

BOSTON
Cobbie Shop Clearance Center
— 12 Winter St., Boston; 542-8655. Located right in Downtown Crossing, the Cobbie Shop outlet carries overstocks from its other branches. These are first-quality shoes at a straight 50 percent off, with such names as Cobbie, Selby, Joyce, Leslie Fay, and Easy Spirit.

Many of these brands are rarely found on sale elsewhere. A pair of Selby dress pumps that originally retailed for $69.00 was just $34.50 on a recent visit; and a pair of Easy Spirit shoes was marked down from $74.00 to $37.00. There is a good selection of sizes, including special sizes from A to EE.

BRIGHTON
New Balance Factory Store —
61 North Beacon St., Brighton; 782-0803. The very popular New Balance line of athletic shoes is made right here, folks—and this popular store is filled with racks after rack of seconds and closeouts. They proudly state that their seconds meet high enough standards to match other makers' best. Indeed, the tiniest of blemishes—you'd do worse to the shoes after wearing them for a week—can land them in the discount pile. There are all kinds of models: Running shoes,

walking shoes, hiking shoes, basketball, tennis, cross-trainers.

Most of these are at least $20.00 to $30.00 below the prices you'd pay in other stores. Ah, but then there are the closeouts. In this section you can find a $90.00 pair of men's running shoes—in stylish purple, yet—for a mere $19.99. In fact, most of the dozen or more men's and women's shoes here were $19.00 and $29.00. Lots of shoes for kids, too, at $19.99. Remember, though, in the closeouts area, sizes can be very limited. Most shoes can be returned for exchange or store credit.

Athletic clothing and accessories are discounted here, too—running tights, cotton socks, neon windbreakers. A rack of Gore-Tex jogging suits, with the New Balance insignia, was reduced from a price range of $250.00 to $350.00 down to $180.00 to $230.00. At the other end of the scale, a bin of women's nylon running shorts was $1.99 each. You may even find a box of assorted shoelaces by the door—free!

CAMBRIDGE

City Sports Outlet Store — 105 First St., Cambridge; 868-9232. This is not really an outlet store but a regular branch of the popular local chain with a special section of leftover sizes and last year's closeouts. The choices are limited, but you may find something terrific, like Avia ladies walking shoes, marked down from $70.00 to $40.00.

Men may find such reductions as Nike "Air 180" basketball shoes for $90.00, reduced from $120.00. In many cases the only difference between these and the current models is something like the color of the trim.

You'll also find a good selection of closeouts on athletic clothing, such as Nike men's running tights, half-price at $20.00; Body Wrappers nylon windbreakers for $7.99; or Moving Comfort lycra shorts for women, a purple swirl de-

sign, reduced from $25.00 to just $10.00.

David's Famous Name Shoes — 75 First St., Cambridge; 354-3730. For over thirty years David's has been a fixture in East Cambridge; now, thanks to the Galleria Mall, the neighborhood has come alive in a whole new way. Still, David quietly sells Rockport, Timberland, Dexter, and the British Clark's shoes for 20 percent off retail prices. Thus, a current model of RocSports, in brown suede, sells for $80.00 instead of $100.00.

At the rear of the store are even better bargains—closeouts and irregulars at 40 to 80 percent off. Men can find Oleg Cassini tasseled loafers for $40.00; or Nunn Bush leather wing-tips for $30.00. Other shoes on the racks, in most sizes, start at $19.98.

For women the prices are similar, with names like 9 West, Bass, and more. Some of these are in a limited range of sizes only. David's also has sneakers, boots, and some leather items, also at discount. He's open seven days a week.

Hyde Factory Outlet — 1066 Cambridge St., Cambridge; 547-4397. This small Inman Square shop has some great bargains. All of the shoes, mostly Hyde and Saucony, are irregulars, but they seem fine. In some cases, only certain sizes are available. Recently, for example, a man with a size nine foot could have stolen bases in a pair of cleats that were a steal themselves at $10.00.

Other lines are more flexible, and there are many kinds of shoes to see—aerobics, tennis, basketball, running—for men and women. Men's Saucony "Master Control" running shoes were marked down from $70.00 to $40.00. Women's "Jazz 2000," good for daily mileage training, were half-price at just $30.00.

There are sneakers for kids as well; Mr. C saw PF Flyers (they never looked like this in his youth) for $9.88. The Hyde Outlet also has

Mr. Cheap's Picks

✓ **The Barn** — Vast selection of overstock shoes, boots, and sneakers for men, women, and kids.

✓ **Footwear Marketplace** — Primarily good for sneakers and athletic gear, cheap.

✓ **Gerry's Shoes** — Designer names at outlet prices. Women's stuff only.

✓ **New Balance Factory Store** — Dozens of models of these popular sneakers, designed for every sport and made on the premises. Bargains on athletic clothing, too.

✓ **Joan and David Outlet Store** — Up in Everett. J & D fans find it well worth the trip.

a variety of running clothes and accessories at slight discounts.

The shoes are not guaranteed, and sales are final, except for exchanging sizes.

Irving's Shoe Shop — 3 Central Square, Cambridge; 492-2919. This tiny shop sells mostly new shoes for men and women, most at a bit of a discount; men's Buffalino casual leather shoes are $50.00, for example. They do, in addition, have clearance racks with a few bargains. Men's shoes were $10.00 to $30.00, again in casual styles, leather loafers and the like; women had a bit more to choose from, dress and casuals, all priced at $15.00.

EVERETT

Joan & David Outlet Store — 1935 Revere Beach Pkwy., Everett; 389-8655. Fans of this line of shoes, imported from Italy, are loyal devotees. Most are already frequent visitors to this outlet, where first-quality J & D shoes are sold at up to 30 to 40 percent off the retail prices. Many are leftover styles from recent seasons, but all are undamaged and unused. For men there is the companion line, David & Joan's Shoes, which you'll find here too.

The store also sells women's J & D clothing—suits, blazers, skirts, belts, handbags, etc., also at discount. They preferred not to quote prices here, but the bargains are good and the quality is first-rate. All sales are final; the store is open seven days a week.

MALDEN

Converse Shoe Outlet — 35 Highland Ave., Malden; 322-1500. If you've headed out to Everett, you may as well continue on to Malden for your sneaker needs too. The Converse outlet sells its durable brand of basketball, tennis and other athletic shoes at great prices. In new shoes, the ever-popular "Chuck Taylor High-tops" sell for as much as $10.00 less than in retail stores. The "Accelerator" leather basketball shoe, a mid-high style, is marked down from $84.95 to $56.99.

There are also plenty of last year's models, overstocks, and slightly damaged seconds at further reductions. There is a whole "clearance wall" with all kinds of sneakers selling for around $20.00 a pair. Also lots of Converse clothing: T-shirts with the famous Converse All-Star patch for $5.00, sweats, shorts, tank-tops, and more. Open seven days.

NEWTON

The Barn — 25 Kempton Place, Newton; 332-6300. This *is* a big barn of a place, down a little alley off of Washington Street as it runs along the Mass Pike. Watch for the sign as you approach West Newton! The Barn has a huge selection of closeouts and irregulars (all sales final), some at great prices, with many name brands for men, women, and kids.

Ladies may find Italian leather dress shoes by Vanelli, marked down from $90.00 to $59.00, or 9 West high heels in bright red for just $29.00. Another 9 West style, a "boot shoe" with a strap heel, was seen for $45.00. The suggested retail was $61.00, but Mr. C's expert had seen them for even more than that elsewhere.

For men, Bally tassel loafers were marked down from an astronomical $235.00 to a more manageable $145.00. Mr. C was more cozy with Dexter leather walking shoes, reduced from $70.00 to $54.00; and Coleman hiking boots ($44.00, from $64.00).

There are similar savings on athletic shoes, such as men's Asics "Gel" cross-trainers reduced from $72.00 to $54.00, or women's Nike Air tennis shoes for $50.00. Lots of sneakers for kids, too, by Stride Rite and Keds.

Both genders get closeout racks of even bigger savings, with some good shoes as low as $20.00. One assortment of leather pumps was just $5.00; take your chances, but you will find good bargains at the Barn.

Gerry's Shoe Store — 333 Walnut St., Newtonville; 527-2330. Also in Natick and Milton. Gerry's has first-quality women's shoes at discount. Many of the brands are upscale designers, so the bargains are relative, but great. A pair of navy dress pumps by Mr. Seymour, studded with rhinestones, would retail elsewhere for over $200.00; here, it was $89.00.

Bandolino sandals were $40.00, marked down from $70.00; and a stylish European-looking black leather flat by Christiane Perez was $55.00, marked down from $110.00. So, you may want to search among the racks for the one deal that's right for you. Gerry's is small, with an emphasis on service. There is also a selection of other leather products, such as belts and handbags.

Shoe Outlet — 318 Walnut St., Newtonville; 527-6115. Across the street from its own parent store, the Shoe Horn, is the Shoe Outlet. This is the kind of place Mr. C could love (if he needed women's shoes): all shoes here are priced at either $19.90 or $29.90. There are some great deals on the racks. A pair of Evan Picone sandals, in silver or gold lame, had a suggested retail of $73.00; here they were $19.90.

Among the $29.90 styles, Mr. C's companion found "Sport Pumps" by 9 West (retail price— $57.00); Naturalizer black patent leather heels ($50.00); and an artsy pair of multicolored suede flats by Nina ($75.00).

Another recent special had an even lower price: Calvin Klein Sport deck shoes, retailing for $25.00, on sale for just $12.90.

Shoe Town — 241 Needham St., Newton; 965-7849. Also in Norwood, Quincy and Stoneham. This national chain has lots of fine shoes for men, women and kids, all at discounts of up to 20 to 50 percent off. Men's Jordache docksiders, in two-tone brown and white, are marked down from $45.00 to $25.00; for ladies, a pair of Ann Taylor beige strap heel pumps was seen for $55.00, and casual loafers by Saks Fifth Avenue went for just $35.00. Plenty of sneakers as well.

Shoe Town has something else to offer: sales staff. Unlike many of the outlet stores listed here, this is a full-service store, and the folks are quite helpful.

REVERE

Inner City Discounters — 590 Revere Beach Pkwy., Revere; 289-

7833. See listing under "Department Stores."

SAUGUS

Saugus Shoe Barn — 31 Osprey Rd., Saugus; 233-1295. Saugus Shoe Barn offers a vast selection of dress shoes, dyeable shoes for bridal parties (which they can do for you in the store), dance shoes, nurses' shoes, hosiery, handbags, and accessories, all at incredible savings. In order to respect their sources they declined to have prices mentioned here; but big crowds attested to the store's popularity.

SSB is part of a three-store complex off of Route 99, including Exclusive Millinery—makers of bridal headpieces—and Brenner's Party Supplies. Together they make a complete outfitting center for major parties and banquets, or just a place to find just the right shoes for that new dress.

SOMERVILLE

George's Shoe Store — 259 Washington St., Somerville; 623-7363. Also, 669 Centre St., Jamaica Plain; 524-4866. Here are a couple of hole-in-the-wall places to discover. They aren't fancy, but the shoes are—and the prices are amazing. The selections are limited, but you never know what may be hiding on the shelves.

Most of the shoes are for women; brands like Joan & David, Calvin Klein, and Jordache. A pair of J & D dress pumps in black leather, with a gold lame interior, was found for $37.00; suede flats by the same maker were just $18.00. Many of the shoes are seconds or irregulars; there is also a rack of damaged shoes at further discounts.

For guys, a pair of Dexter penny loafers goes for $31.00; more interesting was the exclusive line of shoes by European designer Andre Assous. These are slip-on boot shoes of soft leather in a variety of colors. George's apparently imports these directly at considerable savings; they retail for $145.00 to $185.00, and sell here for $49.00 to $55.00.

SPORTING GOODS

ALLSTON

Bicycle Bill — 253 North Harvard St., Allston; 783-5636. Heading out of Allston toward Harvard Stadium, Bicycle Bill is worth stopping in to see. They have a fairly good-sized selection of racing and mountain bikes, with many leftovers from last year at further discounts. Several of the brands are American-made. Mr. C saw an Iron Horse all-terrain bike for $225.00, and a Diamond Back city bike, with an alloy frame, at $299.00.

International Bicycle Center — 89 Brighton Ave., Allston; 783-5804. Also, 66 Needham St., Newton; 527-0967. One of the area's most complete bicycle stores, geared mainly to the pricier brands, such as Cannondale, Trek, and Univega—though they do carry Schwinn, Bridgestone and lesser-priced names. Their prices are even with, or slightly below, most other bike dealers; it's a high-volume business. Which means good luck getting a salesperson on weekends during the bicycling season.

Best bet for prices here is to look for leftover models from the previous year; on these, you can find big savings, like $100.00 off a Trek mountain bike. Open seven days a week.

Laughing Alley Bicycle Shop — 51 Harvard Ave., Allston; 783-5832. Taking up two storefronts along the antiques stretch, Laughing Alley carries the upscale bicycle brands at competitive prices. A Trek 8000 mountain bike with an aluminum frame was marked down from $870.00 to $750.00. A similar bike by Miyata, originally $650.00, was on sale for $530.00. Several kids' bicycles as well. The sales staff is very friendly, laid-back, and knowledgeable.

Laughing Alley carries rollerblades (make that "in-line skates") at discount; previous year's models were marked down 25 percent, reducing a pair of Bauer XS-5 skates from $230.00 to $175.00. They also have clothing, much of which again is clearance stuff at 25 to 85 percent off. Jerseys from $5.00, lycra shorts from $12.00, and more.

BOSTON

Beacon Street Bicycle — 842 Beacon St., Boston; 262-2332. Along with current new bicycles by Trek, Fisher, and Univega, Beacon has a lot of last year's models on sale at discount prices. A Trek 1100 road bike, with an aluminum frame, sells for around $600.00 new; but you can get last year's version for $499.00. A Sterling city bicycle was seen for $280.00, marked down from $320.00. It's a tiny shop, crammed with cycles. Poke around.

Bob Smith Sporting Goods — 9 Spring Lane, Boston; 426-4440. Hidden away in the Financial District, Bob Smith's is, well, hard to hide. It's so big—one of the largest sporting goods stores in the area. They specialize in the arena of individual sports: Running, skiing, tennis, fishing, rollerblades, and more.

While these sports are non-competitive, Smith's everyday prices are—lower, in fact, than most department stores. It's not all rock-bottom; their main claim to fame is selection and service. Still, they do get special closeout stocks, where you can really save. Reebok sneakers for $29.00 to $39.00, Nike clothing, and lots of tennis racquets—as low as $24.95 for a fully-strung Kennex.

And every February they hold their annual "Ground Hog Ski Sale" to clear out their surplus on skis, boots, parkas and accessories by all the big-name makers. Some are reduced 80 to 90 percent off their original prices, with skis starting at just $20.00. Keep an eye out for the ad in the sports section.

Nevada Bob's Discount Golf And Tennis — 10 Post Office Square, Boston; 523-0177. Also in Hanover, Westboro, Westwood, Woburn and others. A national chain, Nevada Bob's carries a huge selection of golf club sets, gloves and shoes, tennis and squash racquets, and apparel— lots of equipment for men, women, and children too. Tommy Aaron and Lady Aaron golf sets are as low as $240.00 for eight irons and $150.00 for three metal woods. Or get a complete set of irons, woods, bag, and head covers, by Cyclone, for $300.00. Spikeless golf shoes start at $20.00; Stylo waterproof shoes are $60.00, about a third of their pro shop price.

Prince tennis racquets are as low as $80.00, even lower during special closeout sales. And they have tennis socks for 99¢ to $1.99 a pair, along with clothing for both sports. Bob's also offers racquet restringing, as low as $10.00 for synthetic gut. Open seven days a week.

Sports Replay — 860 Commonwealth Ave., Boston; 731-9128. Located in a basement behind the Ski Market store, Sports Replay is the outlet for all the equipment that people trade in upstairs and at the other Ski Markets. This varies according to the season but generally includes bicycles, tennis racquets, lots of skiing stuff, and sailboards, all at 30 to 50 percent off retail. They also rent out water sports equipment, bikes, and rollerblades.

There are also some closeouts, like a group of wetsuits that had never sold at retail, just $50.00 and up. Used ski equipment includes racks and racks of boots, like Nordica 997 rear-entry boots, originally $300.00, now $189.00; or Lang front entry boots for $79.00, down from $189.00. Lots of boots for kids, from $19.95, and plenty of skis for all.

Bicycles on display during Mr. C's visit: A Peugot ten-speed, with quick-release wheels, for $80.00, and a closeout on CCM "Auto Bikes"—they shift automatically as you accelerate, like a car. Never used, these were marked down from $310.00 to $200.00. There were Bell helmets, also new, half-price at $20.00.

Tennis racquets start from about $50.00; and there are lots of accessories for all sports, from sunglasses to ski socks. You can buy, sell or swap your own equipment. Used items are not guaranteed, but Sports Replay does its own servicing and will try to fix anything within a reasonable period of time.

BRIGHTON

New Balance Factory Store — 61 North Beacon St., Brighton; 782-0803. See listing under "Shoes and Sneakers."

CAMBRIDGE

The Bicycle Exchange — 2067 Massachusetts Ave., Cambridge; 864-1300. This new shop in Porter Square is not really a place to swap bikes, but they do have very competitive prices on current models in stock. Mr. C found a mountain bike by Mongoose on sale for $250.00, one of the lowest prices around for new mountain bikes. Going up a little bit, a Fuji "Thrill" mountain bike was $319.00. Low prices on service, too.

The Bicycle Workshop — 259 Massachusetts Ave., Cambridge; 876-6555. Low prices on new bikes, with relaxed salespeople

---

Mr. Cheap's Picks

✓ **Bicycle Workshop** — Good prices on new bikes and one of the larger selections of used bikes around.

✓ **Play It Again Sports** — A consignment store for sports equipment. Find a bargain for yourself, or bring in that tennis racquet you bought on a whim and never used.

✓ **Sports Replay** — Behind and below the Ski Market near BU, this place sells all kinds of equipment that folks have traded in upstairs. Good for skis, bikes, tennis, and rollerblades.

---

and good service. BW also has one of the larger selections of used bicycles around; you may find a Raleigh ten-speed racing bike for $110.00, a Vista ten-speed for $75.00, or a girls' Huffy ten-speeder for $110.00. They offer servicing on the premises. Many of the new bikes are marked down, too, including mountain bikes.

Broadway Bicycle School — 351 Broadway, Cambridge; 868-3392. This is in fact a school for anyone who wants to learn how to fix bicycles from the ground up. Since there are always projects being worked on, they often have used bikes on sale for $50.00 to $150.00. These tend to be older-style bikes, reconditioned with good-quality parts; and you can bring yours back in after one month for a free checkup, just to make sure you haven't gotten a lemon. Occasionally they have deals on a new bike or two; Mr. C saw a Yokota mountain bike with alloy wheels for $230.00.

City Sports Outlet — 105 First St., Cambridge; 868-9232. See listing under "Shoes and Sneakers."

Hyde Factory Outlet — 1066 Cambridge St., Cambridge; 547-4397. See listing under "Shoes and Sneakers."

CHELSEA

Golf Day Outlet Store — 395 Beacham St., Chelsea; 887-2616. Golf Day specializes in—you guessed it—golf equipment, all brand names at discount. Their low prices go even lower during their frequent sales, when you can get accessories like a dozen golf balls for $9.95. Same price for golf shoe bags. Shoes themselves include brands like Nike, Stylo, and GoreTex for as low as $29.95; and a recent sale added cedar shoe trees for $5.00 with the purchase of shoes. For serious duffers who like to practice at home, a 7' x 9' net for working on your swing in the backyard is just $49.95. Of course, they also have clubs, bags, and even instructional videotapes to improve your game further. Open Monday through Friday, 9 a.m. to 5 p.m., and 9 a.m. to 4 p.m. on Saturday.

DEDHAM

Play It Again Sports — 626 Washington St. (Route 1), Dedham; 320-8114. Also, 62 East Montvale Ave., Stoneham; 438-2399. A consignment shop for sporting goods, where you can buy items in very good condition for about half of their original price. You can also trade in, or offer items for cash or resale. They carry a wide range of equipment, from baseball, football, and basketball stuff to scuba gear, tennis, and rollerblades.

There are no guarantees on used equipment, but if something turns out to be defective right away, Play It Again will try to give you a suitable replacement; or, if they can't, a refund. Open seven days a week.

NEEDHAM

Bike Nashbar Outlet Store — 26
Wexford St., Needham; 444-6118.
Just inside of Route 128, off of the
Needham Street stretch of discount
stores, Bike Nashbar runs a retail
outlet for its popular mail-order line
of bicycles and accessories. Nashbar bikes are generally $30.00 to
$100.00 less than comparable
brands like Trek and Cannondale.

In addition to their competitive
everyday prices on parts, helmets
and apparel, Nashbar has frequent
closeout sales—and they often get
first dibs on leftovers from other
well-known manufacturers. A recent
sale featured Specialized tires, originally $25.00, for just $5.95; Time
Sport Carbon racing shoes were
marked down from $108.00 to
$45.00, and Nashbar's own black
spandex shorts, with bright-color
striping down the sides, were
$10.00 off at $13.88. Previous
year's clothing is further reduced,
by as much as 50 percent—shorts
for $5.00, tights for $10.00.

Bike Nashbar prides itself on
friendly, helpful service, especially
for the enthusiast who does his or
her own maintenance. Open seven
days a week.

RANDOLPH

**American Fitness Equipment
Outlet** — 36 North Main St., Randolph; 963-2856. Here's one for you
workout fanatics. American Fitness
in Hingham manufactures its own
line of bench presses and lifting
equipment. This is professional-
grade machinery, made with heavier gauge steel and cables,
more-durable parts, and crafted by
hand to be sturdier than the stuff
you'll find in department stores.

At their Randolph outlet they
sell equipment below retail prices.
Basic benches, for example, which

would retail for as much as
$169.00, are $90.00 here. Add a
simple curling attachment for another $45.00. It gets more sophisti-
cated from there; you can even
have machinery customized for
your workout room. All equipment
carries a full one-year warranty for
parts and labor.

SOUTH BOSTON

AAA Discount Stuff — 54 Thayer
St., South Boston; 451-6181. In the
shadow of the Southeast Expressway, AAA offers new sporting
goods at discount, closeouts and
used equipment as well. Water
sports are the specialty of the
house; surfboards, windsurfing,
boogie boards. They also have
some snow boards and rollerblades.

A recent closeout sale was a
beginner's windsurfing package:
board, mast, sail, booms, and wet-
suit, all for $399.00. Used Mistral
boards, a top-line brand, are well
under half-price at $300.00 to
$500.00.

Ultra Wheels in-line roller
skates sell around $70.00; other
new rollerblades are about 15 percent lower here than many retail
stores. Servicing is done on the
premises. Open seven days.

WATERTOWN

The Ski Warehouse — 137 Mt.
Auburn St., Watertown; 924-4643.
Having moved in the last year to
this new, larger location, Ski Warehouse offers new equipment at discount. The main focus here is
skiing, of course, and tennis, too.
There is a lot to see, including
equipment for children as well as
adults. Hours can be kind of loose,
so you may want to call ahead.

THRIFT SHOPS

Like commercialized yard sales, thrift shops offer you a crazy hodgepodge of stuff—clothing, housewares, and the ever-popular "bric-a-brac" (what *is* that, anyway?). Remember, the descriptions below are a very loose guide; quality, selection and prices can vary widely over time. Each of these places may toss a surprise your way for just a few bucks . . . ya never know.

ALLSTON

Amvets Thrift Store — 80 Brighton Ave., Allston; 562-0720. One of the newest, and nicest, thrift shops to arrive in the Boston area, Amvets suddenly appeared, fully stocked, this year. It's big, bright, and has lots of very cheap clothing. Long racks of suits, pants, shirts, sweaters, coats, dresses and more—for women, men and kids— all seem to be priced between $2.00 and $10.00. Much of the merchandise is well-worn, but there's enough clothing in good condition to make scouring the racks worthwhile.

There is also a good amount of furniture, mostly chairs and tables—as well as books, TVs and radios, etc. Again, these are not in great shape, but useable. Amvets is open seven days a week, and every Monday is senior citizen's day, when seniors get 25 percent off purchases of clothing.

BOSTON

Beacon Hill Thrift Shop — 15 Charles St., Boston; 742-2323. A somewhat limited collection of nice clothing at very low prices. Men's three-piece suits, in good condition, are $35.00; however, there may only be a handful to choose from at any one time. Add a silk tie for $2.00. A pair of ladies' Gap jeans was seen for $8.00; several brightly-colored dresses for $15.00. Plus shoes, antique jewelry, books and some furniture, and decorative antiques. All purchases benefit the New England Baptist Hospital Nurse Scholarship Fund.

Ern's Thrift Shop — 509 Columbus Ave., Boston; no phone. Ernie's is a holdout of the old South End: a tiny walk-down store crammed from floor to ceiling with clothes, books, and magazines. Ernie himself will be there, a pleasant man who likes to talk about jazz music. In fact, he sells old jazz records for 59¢ each, along with cassettes for $3.00 and CDs for $5.00.

The clothing is super cheap, though much of it is in "well-used" condition. Still, an ardent prowl through the racks may reward you with an Esprit cotton dress, looking just fine, for $8.00; a pair of black Sasson jeans for $7.00, or khaki Bugle Boys for $5.00.

Most dresses are just $3.00 to $5.00, and blouses are two for $5.00; for men, suits are $25.00 to $35.00, pants are $3.00 to $10.00. And when there's not enough room in the store, Ernie picks an item— say, shoes—and puts them on tables outside at half the marked prices. Would you believe a pair of Oscar de la Renta embroidered slippers for $8.00? Or Converse cleats for $4.00? That's what thrift shopping is supposed to be all about.

Five Crows Thrift Shop — 131 Jersey St., Boston; 262- 0259. Undoubtedly one of the funkier thrift shops you'll find— but then, it's located in the Fenway. Lots of rock 'n roll-oriented stuff, clothing that's like a vintage store at thrift prices, along with all the usual bric-a-brac.

Dresses range in price from $3.00 to $10.00, including some wild-looking ones. A guy's black satin "roadie" jacket was $5.00. Yes, they've seen better days, but at these prices you can afford to get them pressed and stitched a bit. Costume jewelry is mostly $1.00 to $3.00; so is the large collection of used books, records, and tapes. Also glassware and silverware, toys, and some sports memorabilia (a Bill "Spaceman" Lee photo button for $5.00).

Goodwill Bargain Basement — 1010 Harrison Ave., Boston; 445-1010. Also, 520 Massachusetts Ave., Cambridge; 868-6330. 461 Salem St., Medford; 391-7867. 230 Elm St., Somerville; 628-3618. 315 West Broadway, South Boston; 268-7960. Morgan Memorial Goodwill Shops have taken an aggressive approach to thrift shopping for fun and (non-) profit. A chain of large shops, relying on a mix of donations and wholesale buyouts, has

sprung up in the last few years. The South End store, Goodwill's home base, is the largest; but they all offer much of the same merchandise.

At Goodwill you find lots of used clothing, of course—men's suits for $15.00, ladies' skirts and blouses for $5.00 and up, children's clothing for $2.00 to $3.00. But now you can also see racks of new, name-brand clothes: ladies' blazers for $12.00, suede skirts for $30.00, dresses for $25.00, ski jackets, jogging clothes and more. The stock turns over quite rapidly and is worth checking out on a regular basis.

The used stuff can be more fun, though. During a recent sale, a whole rack of sweaters went for $1.00 apiece, and Mr. C came up with a Henry Grethel all-wool pullover. Furthermore, Goodwill often runs one-day sales—when all items with blue tags, for example, are 30 percent off the already-low prices. You can really find some incredible bargains.

Goodwill also has comforters and linens, often new; the books, housewares, and appliances are usually quite worn out. All sales are final, but clothing can be returned within seven days for store credit.

St. Vincent De Paul Thrift Store — 1280 Washington St., Boston; 542-0883. Also, 50 Prospect St.,

---

Mr. Cheap's Picks

✓ **Amvets Thrift Shop** — Big, basic selection of clothing in good condition.

✓ **Goodwill Bargain Basement** — Who ever figured a chain store of donated clothing? Actually, unused overstocks and remainders are mixed in. The downtown base of operations is the best of the bunch.

✓ **Hadassah Bargain Spot** — Near BU, this huge store has lots of clothes, lots of housewares and junk, lots of furniture, and all the rest. Good prices on all but the furniture.

✓ **Salvation Army Thrift Store** — They, too, have opened a fancy downtown "headquarters" store that borders on the boutique.

Cambridge; 547-6924. Run as a charity to benefit this society's programs for the poor, the main store in Boston is three floors of clothing, furniture, and appliances. The Cambridge branch is smaller, and focuses more on clothing.

In the Boston store, clothes are sold by the pound from piles on tables. It's all $1.25 a pound. Better here are the home furnishings, most of which have seen better days, but there are some finds among the clutter. Mr. C saw a brown leather reclining chair, a contemporary style, for $65.00; and a long, cloth sofa for $89.00, maroon with a pattern of tiny white dots.

There was also an Admiral twenty-five-inch color TV in a wood console; the picture was fine, but the on/off switch needed replacing. For $50.00, that's not so bad. A white formica kitchen table, with wrought-iron legs and four ice-cream parlor chairs, was $99.00. There are also many tables covered with pots and pans, dishware, toasters, crock pots, and popcorn makers.

Salvation Army Thrift Store — 26 West St., Boston; 695-0512. Like Goodwill, the Salvation Army has taken a step up in the thrift world with this boutique-style Downtown Crossing mega-store. At the front there are fancy dresses, leather coats ($8.99!), and even some buy-outs, like a batch of imported Italian wool women's blazers for just $6.00 each.

Further in there are racks and racks of shirts, pants, suits, skirts, and coats, most in fairly good condition. Lots of everything to browse through, and the prices can't be beat. Jeans for $5.00. Sweaters, $1.00 to $2.00. Men's trousers, two for $8.99. Three-piece suits, $20.00. Shoes and boots from $4.00 to $10.00 a pair. A ladies' Oscar de la Renta sweater, with a sporty nautical look, was seen for $7.99.

A separate room has furniture and housewares. These are all well used, but not terribly so. Easy

chairs are mostly $25.00; a bedroom set of two dressers and a mirror was $150.00. And there are tons of glasses, dishes, and small appliances. Upstairs they have a "toddlers" department.

Meanwhile, the Army's other outposts— at 328 Massachusetts Avenue, Cambridge, and 1295 River Street, Hyde Park, continue to sell good ol' super-cheap clothing. Rummage through the racks and tables of jeans for $2.00, shirts for $1.50, jackets for $5.00, men's suits for $10.00, and the like. Some toys and furnishings here, too.

BRIGHTON

Hadassah Bargain Spot — 1123 Commonwealth Ave., Brighton; 254-8300. This is one of the larger thrift stores around, two floors of clothing, housewares, and furniture. Clothing prices tend to be good; poke through the racks and you may find a two-piece blazer and skirt set by Jones New York for $25.00, or ladies' Gap jeans for $7.00. Men's jackets are around $20.00, with lots of dress shirts at $6.00 to $8.00. Shoes for both, including kids, are around $10.00 to $20.00. Also, a selection of linens for the home.

Speaking of which, there is a lot of furniture to see. There are a few good pieces, but much of it seems a bit overpriced for the condition. Mr. C did spot a nice floral print loveseat for $85.00, several nice dressers at $75.00, and lots of chairs for $20.00. Try haggling a bit. Tons of lamps, most at $25.00, and various small appliances, like a Black and Decker hand vacuum for $6.00. Even a spiffy white individual capuccino maker by Salton for $25.00; the pot was missing, but any other would probably fit.

They also have sporting goods—bicycles, skis, tennis racquets—old but usable. And, at the counter, several cases of costume jewelry, priced from $2.00 and up. The Bargain Spot is closed on weekends.

BROOKLINE

Beth Israel Hospital Thrift Shop
— 25 Harvard St., Brookline; 566-7016. Located in Brookline Village, the BI Thrift Shop has a big selection of clothing, mostly in good condition. Men's jackets ranged in price from $15.00 to $25.00; shirts were $4.00 and up, and so was a rack of new-looking women's bathing suits. On Mr. C's visit, he even noticed a Nipon Boutique dress with the original price tag of $130.00 still on it; BI's price was $20.00. Of course, those are more rare.

There are also lots of children's clothes, as well as household items, books (three for a dollar), and—can you believe it—8-track tapes too!

CAMBRIDGE

O.R.T. Value Center
— 458 Massachusetts Ave., Cambridge; 868-0618. This tiny, cramped Central Square shop has a lot of junky clothes cheap, but there are a few nicer pieces mixed in. A brand-new lace minidress was available in a couple of different colors for $9.99. There were also several men's Brooks Brothers blazers at $25.00, though it's helpful if you really like forest green.

Skirts were as low as $3.99 for some nice linen ones; men's pants were around $5.00 to $10.00; and they also have lots of kid stuff. There were some accessories too, like sunglasses for $2.00.

JAMAICA PLAIN

Thrift Shop Of Boston
— 640 Centre St., Jamaica Plain; 522-5676. Quite a large thrift store, with lots of furniture, housewares, and clothing. And lamps, lots of lamps. The general quality of most stuff is on the low end, but it's always worth a look and it's fun to browse. Hours are 10:00 a.m. to 3:45 p.m. daily, except Sundays. Proceeds from the store benefit several charities, including Children's Hospital and the New England Home for Little Wanderers.

ENTERTAINMENT

ART GALLERIES

Boston is filled with art galleries for every style, from historic canvases to the latest abstract splashes of color. Most of the city's galleries are concentrated into two centers: Newbury Street, of course, and the more recent enclave along South Street, near South Station. Both are lined with galleries, and since they don't charge admission, you can have a sublime afternoon for merely the cost of a capuccino at a nearby cafe, if you're so inclined for a breather.

By the way, keep an eye out for Art Newbury Street, a Sunday afternoon event happening each spring and fall. The street is closed off to cars, and all the galleries put on their very best. Live music, balloons, face painting for the kiddies, etc.

Of course, there are plenty of interesting galleries scattered around in other parts of the area. Here are a few of Mr. C's favorites:

ALLSTON

88 Room — 107 Brighton Ave., Allston; 442-8736. Upstairs in this "mall" of vintage clothing and funky specialty shops, the 88 Room has month-long exhibits of avant-garde paintings, photography, and installations. Also, periodic sales of "affordable art." Open Thursday and Friday evenings, and Saturday afternoons.

BOSTON

Artists Foundation Gallery — CityPlace Atrium, 8 Park Plaza, Boston; 227-2787. The Artists Foundation is a statewide agency that helps fund visual artists of all kinds, through grants. Its gallery in the Massachusetts Transportation Building may show paintings, ceramics, masks, sculpture, and more by our best and brightest. Open Tuesday through Saturday afternoons.

Boston Center For The Arts — 539 Tremont St., Boston; 426-7700. In the South End, along with all the antique shops, boutiques, and chic bistros, the BCA is a large red-brick complex with artists' studios, thea-

ters, the Boston Ballet offices, the Mills Gallery (426-8835), and the famous Cyclorama, a large exhibition and performance space. Among other things, the Cyc hosts the annual Boston Drawing Show each fall.

Boston Public Library — Copley Square, Boston; 536-5400. Don't forget the BPL for art! In addition to contemporary painting and photography exhibits in its Great Hall, venture upstairs in the old building for everything from American artists' self-portraits to early baseball photos to rare manuscripts. Look for giant murals by John Singer Sargent on the hallway walls.

Chinese Culture Institute — 276 Tremont St., Boston; 542-4599. This gallery and school next to the Wang Center specializes in folk art by Chinese and American artists. See rustic paintings, calligraphy and more. Open Tuesday through Saturday, 9:30 a.m. to 5:00 p.m.

French Library Gallery — 53 Marlborough St., Boston; 266-4351. Along with its reading collection, lectures, films, and language instruction, the *Libraire Francaise* has

---

Mr. Cheap's Pick

✓ ***The Library Has More Than Just Books*** — Don't forget about the Boston Public Library when looking for something to go out and see. The BPL's main branch at Copley Square offers a wide selection of movies, lectures, and photography exhibits every month, and many of the outer branches do too. Of course, all events are free and open to everyone.

---

regular exhibitions of paintings and photography by French and American artists. Open Tuesday through Saturday from 10 a.m. to 5 p.m., and until 8 p.m. on Wednesday and Thursday evenings.

Genovese Gallery — 535 Albany St., Boston; 426-9738. Art galleries and industrial warehouses just seem to go together, don't they? Genovese is located in that part of the South End near the expressway, along with auto body shops and flower distributors. Check it out for the latest of work by American artists. They now have a gallery "annex" on South Street also.

Mobius — 354 Congress St., Boston; 542-7416. Down a bit from the Children's Museum, Mobius is a collective of many different kinds of artists: They work in painting, sculpture, graphics, theater, sound, and more. Exhibits here are often environmental installations combining several of these, including performance. There's a lot going on all the time; it's always challenging and offbeat, and sometimes humorous. The gallery is open Wednesday through Saturday afternoons, along with evening performance times. Call them for a schedule.

Photographic Resource Center — 602 Commonwealth Ave., Boston; 353-0700. On the campus of Boston University, this gallery offers monthlong exhibits, often on controversial subjects such as AIDS and Vietnam. This gallery does charge admission: $2.00 general, $1.00 for students and seniors. Open Tuesdays through Sundays from noon to 5 p.m., and Thursday evenings until 8 p.m.

Piano Factory Gallery — 791 Tremont St., Boston; 437-9365. Converted from an actual piano factory, this large South End building now houses low-cost studios and apartments for artists. Work by different residents is always on display in the gallery, open Fridays from 6 to 9 p.m., Saturdays and Sundays from 2 to 6 p.m.

Signature & Grohe Glass Gallery — Dock Square, Boston; 227-4885. Here in the North End, see ceramic craftwork and glass sculpture from around the world— as far away as London and Japan, and as close as the United States. Many crafts for sale as well. Open seven days a week, including evenings (except Sundays).

BROOKLINE

Alon Gallery — 1665A Beacon St., Brookline; 232-3388. A small gallery and framing shop in Washington Square, with very impressive exhibits every month by Boston-area artists. Open Tuesdays through Saturdays from 10 to 6 p.m., Thursday evenings until 8 p.m.

CAMBRIDGE

Cambridge Art Association — 25 Lowell St., Cambridge; 876-0246. Exhibitions by CAA members, as well as by members of other groups and individual artists. Painting, sculpture, crafts, jewelry, and more. Open Tuesday through Saturday afternoons.

Cambridge Multicultural Arts Center — 41 Second St., Cambridge; 577-1400. In addition to its dance, theater, and music events, CMAC offers a variety of art exhibits, highlighting many different processes and heritages. Hours are from 10 a.m. to 4 p.m. Mondays through Fridays, and 1 to 5 p.m. on Saturdays.

Ten Arrow Gallery — 10 Arrow St., Cambridge; 876-1117. Arrow Street leads off of Massachusetts Avenue, just outside Harvard Square. In this gallery you can see craft work by American artists from Boston and around the country. Open daily from 10 a.m. to 6 p.m., and Thursday until 9 p.m.

NEWTON

Newton Arts Center — 61 Washington Park, Newton; 964-3424. Just off Walnut Street in Newtonville, the Newton Arts Center offers classes in painting, drawing, and photography; its spacious gallery shows work by different area artists every month. Open from noon to 4 p.m., Tuesdays through Saturdays.

SOMERVILLE

Rugg Road Gallery — 1 Fitchburg Street, Somerville; 666-0007. The Brickbottom Building is another of Boston's several industrial buildings converted into artists' studios. Their gallery reflects the diversity of the residents, moving from landscape paintings one month to graphic prints the next.

CHILDREN

ARLINGTON

Arlington Center for the Arts —
41 Foster St., Arlington; 648-6220.
This center offers a wide range of
children's activities and shows at
some of the best rates around. A recent program on basic movement
and dances for ages three through
five was just $55.00 for eight
weekly sessions; another, teaching
acting on camera at the Arlington
cable TV studio, for ages six
through twelve, was $60.00 for
eight weeks. Classes for teens, too;
call for a current schedule.

BOSTON

Boston By Little Feet — Various
locations. Info: 367-2345. This company puts together hour-long walking tours along the Freedom Trail,
but adds games and activities to
make history fun. It's geared toward
ages six through twelve; children
must be accompanied by an adult.
Events are usually held on Saturday mornings and Sunday afternoons. Admission is $5.00 for all
ages.

**Museum Of Fine Arts "Drop-In"
Workshops** — 465 Huntington
Ave., Boston; 267-9300, ext. 300. In-
troduce your kids to the MFA in an
easygoing way with these on-going
gallery programs for ages six
through twelve. As the name im-

plies, there is no formal registration;
just drop in on Wednesdays, Thursdays, or Fridays at 3:30 p.m. for an
hour-long look at pictures on a
theme, which changes periodically.
The workshops are free, but a donation is suggested; call for more info.

BROOKLINE

**Peanut Butter And Jelly Dance
Company** — At the Church of
Our Saviour, Monmouth and
Carlton Sts., Brookline; 738-7688.
Another opportunity for kids to strut
their stuff, with cheap rates for sea-
son-long courses. Children ages
three through eleven can learn creative movement; a ten-week class is
around $80.00. Fall and spring ses-
sions. Call for more information.

Puppet Showplace Theater —
32 Station St., Brookline; 731-6400.
This long-running theater across
from the "T" in Brookline Village offers very creative puppet shows of
all kinds, from masks to marionettes
to traditional puppetry, presented
by a repertory of different troupes
in the region. Performances during
the school year are held on weekends at 1 p.m. and 3 p.m., and on
Thursdays at 10:30 a.m. and 1:00
p.m. in the summer. One day each
month is sign-language interpreted.
Tickets are $5.00 for all ages.

COLLEGE PERFORMING ARTS

Boston is blessed with many colleges whose performance spaces range from fine halls to experimental stages. The work presented at these places runs the same spectrum, and you can often see terrific performances—or be adventurous—at little or no cost. Most schools have brochures listing upcoming programs, and may even put you on their mailing lists. Here is a selection.

BOSTON

Berklee College Of Music — 136 Massachusetts Ave., Boston; 266-1400. In addition to being one of the city's main venues for major pop concerts, Berklee Performance Center (along with the Berklee Recital Hall next door) hosts weekly shows by faculty and student groups. Many teachers at Berklee are members of prominent local jazz bands or lead their own groups on the club scene; the students they teach sometimes go on to become tomorrow's stars of jazz and rock. Hear anything by new songwriters from gospel to twentieth century American choral music. Concerts are at 8:15 on weeknights; admission is often free, or may range from $1.00 to $4.00, with general seating.

Boston Conservatory — 8 The Fenway, Boston; 536-6340. The lesser-known of the two major conservatories recently marked its 125th anniversary season. At Seully Hall, you can catch piano recitals, modern dance, and even *West Side Story*. Tickets range up to $12.00.

Boston University — Boston (various locations); 353-3345. The BU Symphony Orchestra, the Muir Quartet, or master classes in opera at the new Tsai Performance Center, 685 Commonwealth Avenue. Free organ concerts on Sunday afternoons in Marsh Chapel, 735 Commonwealth Avenue. Faculty and student recitals in the BU Concert Hall, 855 Commonwealth Avenue. A student production of Arthur Miller's *The Crucible*, led by nationally known director Jacques Cartier, at the Huntington Theatre, 264 Huntington Avenue. There's always something doing, and most of it is free or as much as $5.00 to $8.00.

Emerson College — 69 Brimmer St., Boston; 578-8785. The Brimmer Street Studio has two intimate-sized theaters for student productions as well as local professional troupes who rent the stages for their own works. The college also owns, of course, the recently rescued Majestic Theatre, across from the Wang Center, and this hall hosts major fall and spring productions by the theatre department.

New England Conservatory Of Music — 290 Huntington Ave., Boston; 262-1120. Jordan Hall, at 30 Gainsborough Street (diagonally across from Symphony Hall) is one of the city's biggest and best concert halls. Along with major concerts, though, you can go there to hear student ensembles, the NEC Symphony Orchestra, and touring professional groups. Most performances are free; some concerts charge admission of $3.00 to $6.00.

CAMBRIDGE

Harvard University — Harvard Square, Cambridge (various locations); 495-1000. Harvard has several theaters—the Loeb, of course, which it shares with the American Repertory Theatre; the Agassiz; and the Sanders, which presents lots of commercial concerts. But each of these also offers student productions by both Harvard and Radcliffe groups. In fact, the A.R.T. has its own Institute for Advanced Theatre Training, presenting shows by its apprentice company, many of whom also land smaller roles in the main productions (call the A.R.T. directly for that info at 547-8300).

Longy School Of Music — 1 Follen St., Cambridge; 876-0956. One of the small music schools in the Harvard Square area, Longy presents student and faculty concerts in the Pickman Concert Hall at 27 Garden Street. Hear piano recitals, vocal music, chamber groups using period instruments, and more. Almost all concerts are free and open to the public.

Massachusetts Institute Of Technology — 77 Massachusetts Ave., Cambridge; 253-2826. The MIT chapel and Kresge Auditorium, which face each other in front of the student center on Massachusetts Avenue, as well as Killian Hall at 160 Memorial Drive, present a packed program through the school year. Hear chamber music, jazz, student composers, guest artists-in-residence; plus Gilbert and Sullivan operettas, the MIT Shakespeare Ensemble, the MIT Dance Workshop and more. Most concerts are free; theater and dance events range from free up to $9.00.

New School Of Music — 25 Lowell St., Cambridge; 492-8105. This small, ambitious school offers regular classical concerts by students and faculty. They are generally free and open to the public.

CHESTNUT HILL

Boston College — 140 Commonwealth Ave., Chestnut Hill; 552-4800. The Robsham Theatre Arts Center hosts music, theatre and dance performances from around town and around the world. Visits by Russian choral groups or the Boston Ballet, as well as plays and dance concerts by student groups, are among the many cultural offerings held here. Admission is modestly priced.

Pine Manor College — 400 Heath St., Chestnut Hill; 731-7118. Tucked away behind Route 9 near the malls, Pine Manor has a peaceful green campus, lots of free parking, and a lovely concert hall. They boast an active year-round program of classical concerts, theatrical offerings, and lectures, just about all of it for free.

MEDFORD/SOMERVILLE

Tufts University — Medford/Somerville Campus; 627-3493. The Arena Theatre presents an ambitious program of drama all year, including both new works and classic plays. These are generally performed by students and directed

---

Mr. Cheap's Pick

✓ **Student Concerts** — Two of Boston's famous music schools present free or cheap ($1.00 to $2.00) concerts on an almost daily schedule. **The Berklee School of Music** specializes in jazz and world-beat pop, while **The New England Conservatory** has classical ensembles. The faculty, prominent musicians in their own right, often perform too.

---

by the faculty. Tickets range from $3.00 to $6.00, with subscriptions available.

WALTHAM

Brandeis University — 415 South St., Waltham; 736-4300. The Spingold Theatre Center actually contains three different stages of various sizes and shapes; and the quality of the student productions is very high. Most are directed by faculty or major Boston-area directors, and the casts usually feature seriously dedicated and talented MFA students who are not far from Broadway. Elsewhere on campus, the Slosberg Music Center offers faculty and student recitals, as well as concerts by such professional groups as the Lydian String Quartet; these are usually free, or range up to $7.00 to $10.00.

COMEDY

It seems that a new comedy club is opening somewhere in Boston almost every week. Going to a club can be an expensive proposition, between the cover charge and the drinks. Mr. C can't do anything about the price of beer, but don't forget that the larger comedy clubs have shows throughout the week and that the price of admission is lower on, say, a Tuesday night than on Saturday.

Many of these shows are open-mike nights, with a steady stream of new performers trying out their wings. Or, you'll see local comedians who've reached the next level, on their way to becoming regulars. Sure, you may sit through the occasional bomber, but these shows are always hosted by a headliner who keeps things rolling and always gets the last slot. Prices and showtimes change constantly, but among these are many lesser-priced options.

BOSTON

Comedy Connection — Charles Playhouse, 74 Warrenton St., Boston; 426-6339. One of the longest-established comedy clubs in town, the Comedy Connection has a top price of $10.00 on weekends. On Monday through Wednesday nights admission is only $5.00; and it's $7.00 on Sunday nights. Good way to get ready for the work week.

Nick's Comedy Stop — 100 Warrenton St., Boston; 482-0930. A few doors down, Nick's is another club that's been dishing out laughs for years. The upstairs comedy room is more like a hall, and in fact it was once a dance ballroom. Top price here is $12.00; but Monday, Tuesday, and Wednesday nights are $6.00.

Stitches — 835 Beacon St., Boston; 424-6995. Just outside Kenmore Square on the way toward Brookline, Stitches is a well-lit, comfortable room—one of the nicer ones in town. Their top ticket is $10.00, and you can save a bit at $6.00 on Sunday through Thursday nights.

CAMBRIDGE

Back Alley Theater — 1253 Cambridge St., Cambridge; 576-1253. For something completely different from the clubs, try a bit of comedy troupe sketches; this tiny theater in Inman Square has been home to several over the past year or so, in-

---

Mr. Cheap's Pick

✓ **Cheap Gags** — An inexpensive alternative at the Boston area's many comedy clubs is the Open Mike show. These tend to run early in the week, and tickets are about half the price of the big weekend shows. There are usually a few diamonds in the rough; after all, every standup star began the same way.

---

cluding ImprovBoston and Guilty Children, two of Boston's longest-running improvisational groups. Shows are on Fridays and Saturdays at 10:30 p.m.; tickets are usually $3.00 to $6.00, depending on the troupe.

Catch A Rising Star — 30 J.F.K. St., Cambridge; 661-9887. This outpost of the successful New York club has all the hallmarks of the trendy comedy clubs: namely, an intimate room with a fake backdrop of exposed brick. Meanwhile, you can save as much as $7.00 off the top ticket price by going on Sunday through Thursday nights. You may see an open mike night, an improv troupe, or locals on their way up the ladder. Be open-minded!

DANCE

Unfortunately, there are not many opportunities for inexpensive dance in town. Tickets for most performances start around $12.00 to $15.00 and go up from there. Your best bets are mainly at the colleges (see that section), which include both student and faculty shows. Here are a few other options.

Boston Ballet offers student rush tickets to many of its performances at the Wang Center, 275 Tremont St., Boston. Though these are in the neighborhood of $12.00, it's a considerable savings over standard ticket prices of $20.00 to $50.00 a pop. You must show a valid student ID at the box office one hour before the performance. Info: 964-4070.

BB also presents several free performances during the summer in the Hatch Shell series at the Charles River Esplanade. These are usually modern works by some of their smaller ensembles. Call 727-5215 for Hatch Shell info.

The Cambridge Multicultural Arts Center at 41 Second Street, Cambridge, offers many contemporary dance concerts throughout its season. Call 577-1400 for schedules.

The New Dance Complex, 536 Massachusetts Ave., Cambridge, is the three-story Central Square building formerly occupied by Joy of Movement. NDC continues to run the facility as a place to take dance classes, but they have end-of-term performances in which you can see lots of young, talented dancers and choreographers in everything from modern *pas de deux* to tap ensembles. Call 547-9363 for details.

LECTURES

BOSTON

Boston Public Library — Copley Square, Boston; 536-5400, ext. 212. The BPL's large Rabb Lecture Hall is the site of many free lectures, from "The Boston Sports Scene" to "Images of Violence in Our Society" and "Planning Your Retirement." They take place on a varying schedule, usually at 2 p.m. or 6 p.m. on weekdays. Stop in for a schedule; lectures are given at several of the BPL branch libraries, too. Check in with the one near you.

Boston YWCA — 140 Clarendon St., Boston; 536-7940. The Boston "Y" offers free programs focusing on women's issues, relating these to life here and in other parts of the world. These take place on weekday evenings and are open to men as well as women.

Community Church Of Boston — 565 Boylston St., Boston; 266-6710. This forward-thinking Copley Square church explores not only theological matters, such as the existence of God for atheists, but also topics much closer to home, like health care. These are held on Sunday mornings at 11:00, and are free and open to all.

The Ethical Society Of Boston — 44 Commonwealth Ave., Boston; 739-9050. This organization holds free lectures on topics from "Another Look at Henry VIII and the Women in his Life" right up to present-day dilemmas. Weekly discussions are held on Sunday mornings at 10:30; admission is free and open to all.

Ford Hall Forum — Various locations; 437-5800. For almost a century Ford Hall Forum has made "freedom of speech" a reality. The organization presents well-known speakers on a variety of topics, free and open to the public, so that all may learn from experts about vital matters. They have presented political cartoonist Paul Szep, explaining his approach to razor-sharp satire, and U.S. Secretary of Health Louis Sullivan discussing health care reform. FHF made big waves last year when it gave David Duke an evening, but that's their mission— no judgments, just a platform.

Events take place at the Old South Meeting House, 310 Washington St., Boston, and Blackman Auditorium, 360 Huntington Avenue on the Northeastern University campus. Most lectures take place on Sundays or Thursdays at 7 p.m.; all are followed by a question and answer session. Call to get on their mailing list for schedules.

French Library In Boston — 53 Marlborough St., Boston; 266-4351. Topics from world travel to French cooking are presented in regular lectures at this elegant Back Bay center. Some are given in French, some in English. Most lectures are free to the public, though reservations are recommended. Receptions follow the talks.

Kennedy Library Forums — John F. Kennedy Library, Columbia Point, Boston; 929-4554. Another impressive series of discussions on important issues, from the "Big Dig: Progress Report" to "Why Americans Hate Politics." Speakers have included Gov. Michael Dukakis, Boston Police Commissioner Francis Roache, Washington Post re-

---

Mr. Cheap's Pick

✓ **Big Issues, Big Names** — Two organizations in town present a steady diet of food for thought: lectures and panel discussions featuring prominent authors, politicians, and policy makers. The Ford Hall Forum and the John F. Kennedy Library Series events are free to the public, with events scheduled just about every month. Get on their mailing lists.

---

porter E.J. Dionne, Jr., and public opinion pollster Lou Harris. A reception follows each forum. All events are free and open to the public, but reservations are strongly recommended.

Museum Of Afro-American History — 46 Joy St., Boston; 742-1854. This historic church-turned-into-museum (see listing under "Museums") sponsors free lectures on Saturday afternoons at 3:00. Topics cover all facets of black culture.

Old South Meeting House — 310 Washington St., Boston; 482-6439. One of Boston's earliest public gathering places (see listing under "Museums") continues to serve this purpose with its "Middays at the Meeting House" lecture series. These take place on Thursdays at 12:15 p.m. through the year, and are free with regular admission of $2.00 (students and senior citizens, $1.50). Each month examines a single theme, with different topics from week to week. Subjects have included "Boston's African-American Railroad Workers," "Treasures in Your Attic," and "History of Boston's Chinatown."

Society Of Arts And Crafts — 101 Arch St., Boston; 345-0033. This venerable art organization frequently presents talks by artists about their work in painting, sculpture, ceramics, and more. They are free and open to anyone, held at various times and dates. Call for details.

CAMBRIDGE

Cambridge Center For Adult Education — 56 Brattle St., Cambridge; 547-6789. The range of top-

ics covered in the various series here seems to be endless. Hear world travelers recount their experiences in remote lands. Learn about meditation, the psychology of relationships, and much more. Most of these informal gatherings are held in the evenings, with some in the mornings; admission is usually $1.50.

Cambridge Forum — 3 Church St., Cambridge; 876-9644. An ongoing series of discussions on weighty matters, such as "How the Third World Shapes Our Lives." Lectures are held on Wednesdays at 8 p.m. in this Harvard Square church; admission is free to all.

Cambridge Public Library Author Series — 449 Broadway, Cambridge; 349-4040. The main branch library frequently presents authors of significant new books, free and open to the public. These are generally held on Thursday evenings at 7 p.m.

Colloquium Series — Radcliffe College, 34 Concord Ave., Cambridge; 495-8212. Every Wednesday at 4 p.m., the Bunting Institute presents a talk on a different topic from the areas of art, history, politics, and women's issues. Free and open to the public.

Radcliffe also offers a weekly Career Services Forum, dealing with various aspects of job hunting and planning for women. Admission is usually $5.00, with talks held on Tuesdays at 4 p.m. in Agassiz House, Radcliffe Yard. Info: 496-1855.

NEWTON

Newton Free Library — 30 Homer
St., Newton; 552-7145. Across the
street from its town hall, Newton
has a gorgeous new main library,
which includes an art gallery and
lecture hall. Speakers usually have
a book to plug, but these have included such luminaries as Rep.
Barney Frank, Pulitzer Prize-win-
ning poet Maxine Kumin, and ani-
mator Janet Perlman, an Oscar
nominee, showing and discussing
her work. Lectures are free and
open to all.

MOVIES

GENERAL

ARLINGTON

Capitol Theatre — 204 Massachusetts Ave., Arlington; 648-4340. A grand old moviehouse, regrettably converted into a five-screen complex; but, it is one of the nicer renovations of this sort, with brass rails, comfortable seats, and running lights in the aisles. The developers took care to make each cinema a complete one, so you don't feel like you're sitting in an oddly-shaped shoebox. Besides popcorn, the lobby snack bar sells things like frozen yogurt and coffee, and even has tables and chairs. The Capitol shows second-run hits (not that long after their departure from the big houses), with a top price of just $4.00. Senior citizens pay $3.00, and before 6 p.m. kids under twelve get in for $2.50. You can also buy books of five tickets for $18.00.

Regent Theatre — 7 Medford St., Arlington; 643-1198. Not far away along Mass. Ave., the Regent is another historic moviehouse—still with one big screen. They, too, show second-run features, with an admission price of $3.50 and $2.50 for seniors. They usually offer separate matinees for children on the weekends.

BROOKLINE

Coolidge Corner Moviehouse — 290 Harvard St., Brookline; 734-2500. Though no longer the great repertory cinema it once was, with double-features of classic films, the Coolidge remains one of the city's fine art houses, often showing exclusive runs of foreign films, documentaries, and concert films. Ticket prices have gone up to first-run rates, but you can always go to the first showing of the day for either of their two screens for just $4.50. They also offer books of tickets at discount.

CAMBRIDGE

Brattle Theatre — 40 Brattle St., Cambridge; 876-6837. The Boston area's mother of all repertory cinemas, the Brattle puts out a massive calendar every two months with dozens of classic films, series of tributes to stars and directors, and occasional premieres. Most dates offer double features, with ticket prices of $5.50 for the pair. If you only make the last showing, that's $4.50. You can get a book of six tickets for $28.00; or better yet, for $50.00, become a Brattle member and get in for $4.00 anytime for a year. Members also get two free guest passes and various other goodies.

DEDHAM

Community Cinemas — 578 High St., Dedham; 326-1463. They twinned this old cinema into two, and now show a mix of recent hits and classics for an admission price of just $4.00, $3.00 for senior citizens and kids under twelve. All tickets are $2.00 at the first screening of the day.

HINGHAM

Loring Hall Cinema — 65 Main St., Hingham; 749-1400. If you're on the South Shore and love old-time movie palaces, check out the Loring Hall. They show second-run features soon after their main runs, with general admission of $5.00 and $3.75 for senior citizens.

NORWOOD

Norwood Cinemas — 109 Central St., Norwood; 762-8320. Sister theatre to the Dedham Community Cinemas, the Norwood has a similar

lineup of second-runs, usually two pictures on each of two screens. Admission is just $2.00 for the first showings of the day on weekends; otherwise, $4.00 for adults and $3.50 for seniors and children.

SOMERVILLE

Somerville Theatre — 55 Davis Square, Somerville; 625-5700. A great old movie palace in the heart of Davis Square, the single-screen Somerville is one of the few such theaters that still uses its stage for live concerts along with movies. The films are a mix of foreign films, classic oldie double features, and very popular midnight movies. Tickets are $5.00; $3.00 for senior citizens.

LIBRARY FILMS AND SPECIAL SERIES

BOSTON

Boston Public Library — Copley Square, Boston; 536-5400. The BPL has a beautiful auditorium, the Rabb Lecture Hall, which shows all kinds of movies for free, usually on Monday afternoons and evenings. Each month has a theme; recent series have included a tribute to Frank Capra and movies "Made in Massachusetts." The library's senior citizens club, the "Never Too Late Group," also shows weekly films. Call or stop in for a flyer.

The Boston Public Library also offers free films at many of its branches. Here are some of the regular locations; call to find out what's on, and where.
- **Brighton Branch Library**, 40 Academy Hill Rd., Brighton; 782-6032.
- **Fields Corner Branch Library**, 1520 Dorchester Ave., Dorchester; 436-2155.
- **South Boston Branch Library**, 646 East Broadway, South Boston; 268-0180.
- **West Roxbury Branch Library**, 1961 Centre St., West Roxbury; 325-3147.

Free Friday Flicks At The Hatch Shell — Charles River Esplanade, Boston; 727-9547. Every summer, from June to August, the City of Boston sponsors a free movie on Friday nights on a big screen in the Hatch Shell. They start at 8 p.m., and seating is first-come, first-served. Bring a blanket. Past offerings have ranged from *The Wizard of Oz* and *Yankee Doodle Dandy* to *Raiders of the Lost Ark* and even *Wayne's World.* Party on, dudes.

French Library In Boston — 53 Marlborough St., Boston; 266-4351. The Cine Club offers films in French, with English subtitles, every Friday, Saturday, and Sunday at 8 p.m. Classic and current cinema from the folks who invented the New Wave. Admission is $4.00, $3.50 for members; or get a book of ten for $25.00.

Goethe Institut — 170 Beacon St., Boston; 262-6050. German cinema, naturally. See classics from the silent Expressionists of the 1920s to recent stuff by Percy Adlon, one of the only German directors to make a name in a comedy (*Baghdad Cafe*). Films are free, usually shown on Friday and Saturday evenings.

Institute Of Contemporary Art — 955 Boylston St., Boston; 266-5152. Catch the latest in avant-garde and art films by national, international, and Boston filmmakers, in the intimate confines of the ICA Theatre. Sometimes these are introduced by the *auteurs* themselves. Admission is $5.00; $4.00 for students, seniors and ICA members.

Museum Of Fine Arts — 465 Huntington Ave., Boston; 267-9300, ext. 305. Another large, comfortable auditorium, the Remis, has an ambitious schedule of everything from unusual foreign films to rediscovered silent classics to festivals of animation and award-winning TV commercials. Admission is $5.00, and $4.50 for students, senior citizens, and MFA members. Entrance is from the new West Wing, by the parking lot; you don't have to buy admission to the museum to see the movies. No popcorn, of course, but the atmosphere is more casual than you may expect.

BROOKLINE

Brookline Public Library Programs — 361 Washington St., Brookline; 730-2368. Every Wednesday at 2:00 and 7:30 p.m., film buff Ted Kingsbury shows classic films upstairs in the main branch of the library in Brookline Village. He's been doing it for years, putting together a different theme each month and introducing the films himself. It's clearly a labor of love, and the choices are terrific—from the well-known to obscure gems. The themes may be tributes to stars or directors, or simply "Romantic Comedies." He runs a similar program on Thursdays at the Wellesley Free Library, 530 Washington St., Wellesley; 235-1610.

Films for senior citizens (but hey, anyone can go) are shown every Thursday at the Coolidge Corner Branch Library, 31 Pleasant St., Brookline; 730-2380. These can include anything from *An Evening with the Royal Ballet* to *The Way We Were*. Refreshments are at 1:00 p.m.; movies at 1:30.

CAMBRIDGE

Harvard-Epworth Film Series — 1555 Massachusetts Ave., Cambridge; 354-0837. Catch anything from silent-era comedies to the latest in Japanese cinema in this ongoing series at the Harvard-Epworth Methodist Church. Films are shown on Sunday nights at 8; tickets are $3.00.

Harvard Film Archive — Carpenter Center of Harvard University, 24 Quincy St., Cambridge; 495-4700. This most ambitious, long-running series embraces just about every kind of film imaginable: pop features, old-time classics, brand-new documentaries and world cinema. Most films are $5.00 for general admission and $4.00 for children, students and seniors. You can also purchase a book of fifteen admissions for $35.00.

NEWTON

Newton Free Library — 330 Homer St., Newton; 552-7145. This gorgeous, brand-new library shows movies on Wednesday evenings at 7:00. You never know what they'll show (well, you do if you pick up a schedule), from the Marx Brothers to a documentary on Spike Lee to Zeffirelli's *Romeo and Juliet*. They also run a family matinee on the first Saturday of each month. All free.

Other town libraries run free film programs, and many colleges show pop movies in their campus centers, often open to the public for a small fee. Check the ones in your area.

MUSEUMS

There are dozens and dozens of museums in the Boston area. The biggest of them are charging up to $6.00 or $7.00 admission these days, which can add up for a family or group; still, considering how much there is to see, you really get a good value for your money in most of these institutions.

Without the room to detail all of them, Mr. C wants to bring several to your attention which are free, very inexpensive, or have special free programs once you've paid your regular admission. Remember, to receive student or senior citizen discounts, you must show a valid ID!

BOSTON

The Computer Museum — 300 Congress St., Boston; 426-2800. Among its many exhibits, the Computer Museum—next to the Children's Museum on the wharf—features a giant personal computer big enough to walk through. Overcome your fear of these machines, or just find out what goes on in there! Lots of buttons to push, activities to do, and a theater showing computer animation videos. Regular admission is $6.00 for adults, $5.00 for students and seniors, and free for kids under five. Also, admission is cut in half for all ages on Saturdays from 10 a.m. to noon.

Institute Of Contemporary Art — 955 Boylston St., Boston; 266-5151. Several galleries and a video theater devoted to the very latest in cutting-edge art. Regular admission is $4.00; students $3.00, children and senior citizens $1.50. UMass and MIT students, $1.00. Also, the museum is free to the public on Thursday evenings from 5 to 8 p.m.

Isabella Stewart Gardner Museum — 280 The Fenway, Boston; 566-1401. Step inside the Gardner and you've left the city for another world. The rooms are filled with one of the greatest private col-

lections of art, and the central courtyard is a dazzling Mediterranean feast of trees and flowers. Regular admission is $6.00; students and seniors $3.00, children under twelve free. Also, the museum is free to all students on Wednesdays.

Museum Of Afro-American History — 46 Joy St., Boston; 742-1854. The historic African Meeting House on Beacon Hill, just below the State House, is the oldest black church still existing in the country. It offers a black version of the Freedom Trail, highlighting significant spots in the neighborhood. Admission is free to all, daily from 10 a.m. to 4 p.m.

Museum Of Fine Arts — 465 Huntington Ave., Boston; 267-9300. The MFA is one of the country's major collections of European, American, and Asian art. It's too much to see in one visit, but there are a few ways to keep the cost of return visits down. Regular admission is $6.00; students and seniors, $5.00; children ages six to seventeen, $3.00. Further discounts include $1.00 off all admissions on Thursday and Friday evenings from 5 to 10 p.m.; only the West Wing, with its cinema and special exhibits, is open. However, the entire museum is open, free to all, from 4 to 10

Mr. Cheap's Pick

✓ ***Museum Freebies!*** — Many museums in the Boston area offer free admission at certain times of the week. These are subject to change, so call first. **The Museum of Fine Arts** opens all but its West Wing to the public for free on Wednesday from 4 to 10 p.m.; **The Institute of Contemporary Art** is free on Thursday from 5 to 8 p.m.; **The Isabella Stewart Gardner Museum** is free to students all day on Wednesday; and **The Computer Museum** offers half-price admission before noon on Saturday.

---

p.m. on Wednesdays.

Free programs with general admission include gallery talks on particular changing topics, such as Orientalism or the pictorial history of flowers. These take place on various days and times; call extension 300 for details. Also, free introductory walks through the museum on Tuesdays through Fridays at 10:30 a.m. and 2:00 p.m., Wednesdays at 6:15 p.m., and Saturdays at 11:00 a.m. and 1:30 p.m., with a walk in Spanish on the first Saturday morning of each month at 11:30.

Old South Meeting House — 310 Washington St., Boston; 482-6439. Built in the early 1700s, this building has led a varied life as a church, meeting house, and even a horse stable. It's also the place where those uppity colonists first decided to throw a little tea party. Admission is $2.00, $1.50 for students and seniors, 75¢ for children under sixteen. Also the site for many lectures and concerts (see listings in those sections).

Paul Revere House — 19 North Square, Boston; 523-2338. You know, the place where the guy slept when he wasn't out riding. It's also the oldest building in the city of Boston, right in the lively North End. Admission is $2.00, students and seniors $1.50, children age five to seventeen, 75¢.

BROOKLINE

John F. Kennedy Birthplace — 83 Beals St. Brookline; 566-7937. See the place where our thirty-fifth president was born and spent his early years. This house near Coolidge Corner has just been renovated by the National Park Service. They also offer walking tours of the neighborhood, pointing out the sights Kennedy knew as a youth. Admission and programs are free.

Frederick Law Olmsted National Historic Site — 99 Warren St., Brookline; 566-1689. Visit the home of the architect who designed the Emerald Necklace and New York City's Central Park. Located south of Route 9, and west of Brookline Village. Admission is free.

Museum Of Transportation — Larz Anderson Park, 15 Newton St., Brookline; 522-6140. A fascinating collection of antique and classic cars of all kinds, with special exhibits on such topics as automotive inventions in New England. They also sponsor assemblages of vintage car clubs, weekend afternoons on the lawn during the warm months. General admission is $4.00, and $2.00 for students, seniors and kids over age three.

CHARLESTOWN

U.S.S. *Constitution* Museum— Charlestown Navy Yard, Charlestown; 426-1812. "Old Ironsides"

---

is the nation's oldest warship still commissioned—though it's hard to imagine her seeing battle at this point. Inside the adjacent museum are exhibits detailing maritime life in the early nineteenth century. Admission $2.00; $1.00 for kids age six to sixteen.

DORCHESTER

Commonwealth Museum — 220 Morrissey Blvd., Dorchester; 727-9268. The exhibits here focus on various themes related to life and culture in our fair state (er, commonwealth). Admission is free at all times; closed on Sundays.

ROXBURY

Museum Of The National Center Of Afro-American Artists — 300 Walnut Ave., Roxbury; 442-8614. Paintings, photography and sculpture by black artists from many different countries and cultures. Admission is $1.25, 50¢ for students and seniors. Open only from 1 to 5 p.m., Tuesdays through Sundays.

WALTHAM

Gore Place — 52 Gore St., Waltham; 894-2798. This restored Federalist-era mansion shows you what home furnishings were like during the period of 1780 to 1830. Admission is $4.00, students and seniors $3.00, kids five to twelve, $2.00. Closed Mondays and holidays. There are also forty acres of pasture grounds, open free to all.

And, of course, don't forget all of the exhibitions at our area's colleges. Perhaps the largest of these are the **Harvard University Art Museums** and **Harvard University Museums of Natural History**. There are actually three separate art museums. **The Busch-Reisinger Museum** (32 Quincy St.) concentrates on German and northern European works; the **Fogg Art Museum** (also 32 Quincy St.) has other European art as well as American; and the **Sackler Art Museum** (485 Broadway) features classical and Asian collections. Call 495-9400 for information. Admission to each museum is $4.00; $2.50 for students and seniors.

Harvard's natural history museum is also divided into four departments, but all in one building at 11 Divinity Avenue. **The Peabody Museum** displays different cultures of the world; **The Museum of Comparitive Zoology** studies modern animals and great fossils; **The Mineralogical Museum** has room upon room filled with the most amazing colors of rocks and minerals; and **The Botanical Museum** features the famous "Glass Flowers" display, absolutely lifelike plants and flowers of handblown glass. Admission to the building includes all four of these for $3.00; students and seniors, $2.00; children ages five to fifteen, $1.00. On Saturday mornings from 9:00 to 11:00, admission is free to all. Regular hours are 9:00 a.m. to 4:30 p.m. on weekdays, and Saturdays from 1:00 p.m. to 4:30 p.m.. For recorded information, call 495-1910.

Also of special note is the **MIT Museum**, 265 Massachusetts Ave., Cambridge. See demonstrations on holography, strobe light sculptures, and the remarkable photos of Doc Edgerton. A donation of $2.00 is suggested. Info: 253-4444.

Most other colleges have smaller galleries with changing exhibits that are free and open to the public.

MUSIC

CLASSICAL MUSIC

BOSTON

Boston Symphony Orchestra —
Symphony Hall, 301 Massachusetts Ave., Boston; 266-2378. Seiji Ozawa conducts the BSO in concerts from September through May. While these are not cheap—tix are $20.00 to $50.00—there are two alternatives. *Rush tickets*, $6.00 each, are set aside for concerts on Tuesday, Thursday, and Saturday evenings at 8, and Friday afternoons at 2. They are sold on the day of performance at the box office only, from 5 p.m. for evening concerts and 9 a.m. for Friday matinees. There is a limited supply, one to a customer, first-come first-served. *Open rehearsals* are another way to hear the BSO inexpensively. There is a separate series of these, usually on Wednesday evenings at 7:30 and Thursday mornings at 10:30. Each is preceded by a short discussion of the music to be heard, starting an hour before the rehearsal. Tickets are $10.00 and $9.50, respectively, with unreserved seating; these may be purchased in advance.

Also, The Boston Pops play a week of free concerts at the Hatch Shell on the Esplanade every summer. This kicks off, as everyone knows, with the Independence Day fireworks concert; they continue each night for the next week, with a rotating selection of show tunes and light classical favorites starting at 8 p.m.

Federal Reserve Bank Of Boston Concerts — 600 Atlantic Ave., Boston; 973-3453. That very modern building across the street from South Station hosts a regular series of free lunchtime concerts in its auditorium on the ground level. Ensembles from the area's music schools are most often featured; concerts begin at 12:30 on Thursdays.

Isabella Stewart Gardner Museum Concerts—280 The Fenway; 566-1401. Two sets of concerts take place in this lavish setting; The Chamber Music Series, Sundays at 1:30 p.m., and the Young Artist Showcase, Tuesdays at 6:30 p.m. Both feature soloists or small groups, including the Gardner's own chamber orchestra; both are free with museum admission.

King's Chapel Concerts—King's Chapel, corner of Tremont and School Streets, Boston; 227-2155. This stately edifice on the Freedom Trail between Park Street station and Government Center hosts several free concerts throughout the year, offering music by Mozart, Vivaldi, Bach, and others. Many works feature choral soloists. King's Chapel also has weekday lunch hour concerts on Tuesdays at 12:15 p.m., usually solo, duet, or small ensemble recitals. A freewill donation is requested.

Old South Meeting House — 310 Washington St., Boston; 482-6439. This historic building on the Freedom Trail has a regular series of lectures and concerts. Much of the music focuses on periods of American history; D.C. Hall's Concert and Quadrille Band, for example, recently presented a two-evening show on "Ireland and Irish America, 1820-1870." Concerts also make up part of the free "Middays at the Meeting House" lecture series, Thursdays at 12:15 p.m.

Old West Organ Society — Old West Church, 131 Cambridge St., Boston; 739-1340. This eminent Beacon Hill church houses one of the city's finest pipe organs, and there is a regular concert series featuring various musicians performing anything from baroque to twentieth-century organ music. Concerts are usually Tuesday evenings at 8 p.m., and admission is free.

Trinity Church Concerts—Copley Square, Boston; 536- 0944. One of Boston's largest and oldest churches, Trinity's huge pipe organ is usually the star of these free concerts; it's often accompanied by vocalists or brass ensembles. Most concerts take place on Sunday evenings at 8 p.m. A freewill donation is requested.

Trinity also has free lunchtime solo concerts on Fridays, beginning at 12:15 p.m. and lasting half an hour.

BROOKLINE
United Parish Church Concerts
— 210 Harvard St., Brookline; 277-6860. The United Parish Church in Coolidge Corner runs its ongoing "Music in the Parlor" series on selected Sunday afternoons at 4:00. Last year these featured the Zephyros Quintet, a local woodwind ensemble in residence. A suggested donation of $5.00 is requested at the door; $2.00 for children, students, and senior citizens.

CAMBRIDGE
Cambridge Center For Adult Education — 56 Brattle St., Cambridge; 547-6789. Among its many programs, CCAE's "Music for a Thursday Evening" series offers classical, folk, and jazz concerts each Thursday at 8 p.m. during the spring and fall. These feature local artists in ensembles and solo. Tickets are $3.50 at the door or in advance.

DORCHESTER
Ashmont Hill Chamber Music Series — All Saints Church, 209 Ashmont St., Dorchester; 495-1585. These Sunday afternoon concerts have been going on regularly for several seasons now. They feature small ensembles and choral music. Tickets are $8.00 at the door; $6.00 for students and senior citizens. Subscriptions are available too.

Mr. Cheap's Pick
✓ **Open Rehearsals at the BSO** — The Boston Symphony doesn't just have to be for the elite folks who can afford $50.00 tickets. Catch one of the regularly-scheduled "open rehearsals" for only $10.00, with a bit of behinds-the-scenes action into the bargain!

FOLK MUSIC

CAMBRIDGE

Christopher's — 1920 Massachusetts Ave., Cambridge; 876-5405. This popular Porter Square restaurant also features a separate room with folk music on Thursday through Sunday evenings. The cover price is usually around $5.00, and you can order anything from the restaurant while you listen.

The Middle East Restaurant — 472 Massachusetts Ave., Cambridge; 492-9181. Most evenings in the corner room (this restaurant has two separate storefronts; see listing in the Dining section), you can enjoy local folk bands while nibbling on kibby or kebabs. There is no cover charge, just the cost of the food, which is delicious and very reasonably priced. Check their window for the schedule.

The Nameless Coffeehouse—3 Church St., Cambridge; 864-1630. Right in Harvard Square, across from the movie theater, the Nameless has been a folkie institution for years. It's a showcase for rising singers, songwriters, and poets, held at 8 p.m. every Friday and Saturday night. Where else can you hear half a dozen different acts for a suggested donation of $2.00? The setting is lively and informal, with refreshments available at one end and the evening's performers hawking their tapes at the other. Cambridge at its most soulful.

Speaking of which, you can get all the free folk music you want almost any time the weather's nice in Harvard Square. The warmer months, of course, are particularly rich for these budding Bonnie Raitts and Tracy Chapmans. The best-known locations are in front of the Harvard Coop, Au Bon Pain, Grendel's Restaurant, and the corner of Brattle and Eliot Streets. You can while away a whole afternoon or evening by wandering from one to the next, for just a buck in each guitar case. Oh come on, they need it; it's still cheap.

Passim — 47 Palmer St., Cambridge; 492-7679. Once they've progressed from the streetcorners to the clubs, tomorrow's stars hope to make it to Passim. It's one of the best folk rooms in town, with music just about every night of the week. The cover varies from $6.00 to $10.00, depending on the artist; but, since they don't serve alcohol, you can enjoy an evening here very inexpensively. They do serve coffees, teas and desserts.

Mr. Cheap's Pick

✓ **Folk Stars of Tomorrow** — The **Nameless Coffeehouse** in Harvard Square offers a big lineup of folk performers every Friday and Saturday evening for just a $2.00 donation. It's considered an important stepping-stone to the professional circuit, and it's a fun, lively atmosphere.

JAZZ

BOSTON

Bay Tower Room — 60 State St., Boston; 723-1666. High atop Boston Harbor, the Bay Tower Room is known for rather pricy dining. However, you can sit at the bar to hear elegant piano jazz every night but Sunday, with no cover charge. Fridays and Saturdays after 9 p.m. the music shifts into swing. No extra charge for that great view, either. Do dress nicely.

CityPlace Atrium — Massachusetts Transportation Building, 8 Park Plaza, Boston. This spacious indoor atrium in the theater district offers free lunchtime concerts on weekdays at noon. The concerts feature local jazz artists and groups, and the performance area is lined with food establishments of all kinds.

Diamond Jim's Piano Bar — Lenox Hotel, 64 Exeter St., Boston; 536-5300. If cabaret's your thing and you feel inspired to sing it out, this is the place in Boston. Join right in as your host plays out Broadway hits and all-time standards. No cover charge.

Plaza Bar — Copley Plaza Hotel, Copley Square, Boston; 267-5300. Another swanky place where you can show good taste for the price of a nice jacket and a few drinks. Well, those may set you back some, but there is no cover charge to hear the great Dave McKenna tickle the ivories. He's been holding forth here for many years, much beloved by devout fans and players alike.

Wally's Cafe — 472 Massachusetts Ave., Boston; 424-1408. For jazz at its grittiest and most traditional, there is only one place—the smoke-filled room at Wally's. Just about every major combo in town has gotten started there. Sets begin around 9:00 each night and wail until 2:00 a.m., with no cover charge. The drinks won't run you out of dough, either. Monday night is an open blues jam, and there's another on Sunday afternoons.

CAMBRIDGE

Kendall Cafe—233 Cardinal Medeiros Way, Cambridge; 661-0993. More cabaret than jazz, this little club near Kendall Square has simple food and lively music most nights from 9 p.m. to 1 a.m., with no cover. Enjoy show tunes and pop songs with resident crooners, guest artists, and an open-mike night on Tuesdays. On Saturdays at 8 p.m., they offer a musical melodrama, "The Drunkard"; tickets for it are $10.00.

Regattabar Jazz — Charles Hotel, One Bennett St., Cambridge; 876-7777. The Regattabar? In the nouveau-ritz Charles Hotel? *That* can't be cheap! Well, no, but you can find a bargain here in Water Music's packed schedule of jazz greats from the national circuit. Players such as McCoy Tyner, Art Blakey, John Scofield, and Pat Metheny have all dazzled in this elegant room. Tickets are usually $10.00 to $14.00 per one-hour set; *but*, on Thursday nights you can usually hear two sets from the weekend's major artist for $10.00 total. Music starts around 9 p.m. Also, Tuesday and Wednesday evenings feature local artists at reasonable cover prices.

Mr. Cheap's Pick

✓ **Straight-Ahead Jazz** — For jazz at its rootsiest, **Wally's Cafe** is the place to be. Serious players, a smoke-filled room, and no cover charge.

NEWTON

Music At The Mall — Chestnut Hill Mall, Newton; 965-3037. Every Saturday and Sunday afternoon, the Chestnut Hill Mall offers free concerts from 2:00 to 3:30 in the large, airy central space on the main level. Local jazz groups and vocalists are the usual fare; sometimes you can hear a classical ensemble or the cast of one of Boston's musicals.

Not to be outdone, the newer, splashier Atrium Mall across the street (info: 527-1400) now offers a similar program on weekends; obviously they're both doing it to bring in shoppers, but hey—no one's going to twist your arm if you just want to listen.

SOMERVILLE

Willow Jazz Club — 699 Broadway, Somerville; 623-9874. The other cheap, cool jazz joint in town. The Willow is a must stop on the way up for local as well as national bands; it's tiny and often packed, but the music is worth it. Sets begin at 9:00 every night of the week, with cover charges from $4.00 to $12.00.

ROCK, POP, ETC.

There are so many bands in Boston and so many clubs in which to hear them. Here is a handpicked variety of venues that have live music for free or a low cover charge. Of course the club scene is ever-changing, so check the papers for current prices and policies.

ALLSTON

Kinvara Pub — 34 Harvard Ave., Allston; 783-9400. One of the many clubs lining the intersection of Harvard and Brighton Avenues in Allston, Kinvara serves Irish beers, cheap food (including a traditional Irish breakfast on Sundays) and live music on Thursday, Friday, and Saturday nights. Most bands play Irish traditional and rock, but straight-up rock is mixed in too. Cover is usually around $2.00.

In the neighborhood, check out other rock clubs such as **Allston Ale House, Bunrattys, Harper's Ferry** and **Molly's**.

BOSTON

Ed Burke's — 808 Huntington Ave., Boston; 232-2191. Famous for its gritty, no-fooling-around atmosphere, Ed Burke's is home to rock and blues bands on Thursday, Friday, and Saturday nights. Cover prices range from $2.00 to $7.00.

Limerick's — 33 Batterymarch St., Boston; 350-7975. In addition to buffalo wings, turkey melts, and shepherd's pie, Limerick's serves up Irish bands—sometimes rhythm and blues—on Thursday, Friday, and Saturday nights. There is no cover charge. They also have Guinness on tap. For the business suit crowd, mostly.

The Rathskeller — 528 Commonwealth Ave., Boston; 536-2750. It's probably safe to say that the Rat "is" Kenmore Square, as much as anything is. Two floors of live bands desperately seeking recording contracts. Downstairs has music every night, with a cover ranging from $4.00 to $10.00; on Friday and Saturday nights there are bands upstairs as well, with no cover charge. Good barbecue until 10 p.m., too.

Top Of The Hub — Prudential Tower, 52nd Floor, Boston; 536-1775. Open every night for dancing, with no cover charge—and that fabulous view from high atop Copley Square. Weeknights have a DJ spinning discs; Thursday, Friday, and Saturday nights offer live jazz.

Zanzibar — One Boylston Place, Boston; 451-1955. Had to throw in

---

Mr. Cheap's Pick

✓ **Hearing O' The Green** — Brighton's **Green Briar Pub** offers an Irish music jam session every Monday night. It's all acoustic and very casual. No cover.

---

a dance club. Zanzibar, in the alleyway behind Remington's in the theater district, is a lush tropical paradise here in the big city. It has gigantic pastel-colored palm trees reaching way up over your head, and cozy tables tucked into nooks along the walls; two floors offer you a choice of dancing on the spacious floor or watching the dancers from above. Admission is free on Wednesday and Thursday nights before 10:00, and $5.00 thereafter; Friday and Saturday, it's $4.00 before 10:00 and $8.00 after.

BRIGHTON

Green Briar Pub — 304 Washington St., Brighton; 789-4100. There is no shortage of Irish music pubs in Boston; Green Briar is one of the newer and nicer ones. Local Irish rock bands play every Friday and Saturday night, with cover charges of $2.00 to $5.00. Better yet is Monday night's traditional Irish jam session, with all acoustic instruments and no cover. Music starts after 9 p.m.; toward midnight the kitchen sends out free sandwiches for the players, and you can have one too.

CAMBRIDGE

Plough And Stars — 912 Massachusetts Ave., Cambridge; 492-9653. This sounds as though it should be another fine Irish music pub, after the famous O'Casey play; but in fact, it's good ol' American rock 'n roll spoken here. The owner, who is from Dublin, says flippantly, "There's no such thing as an American bar in Ireland; why

should there be an Irish bar in America?" Fortunately for the rest of us, other proprietors disagree. Meanwhile, this is a popular neighborhood hangout, boisterous and crowded at night. There is no cover charge for the live bands, which play every night and range from folk to reggae to blues. Great beers on tap.

JAMAICA PLAIN

Midway Cafe — 3496 Washington St., Jamaica Plain; 524-9038. This JP watering hole serves up blues, rock, and R & B every night, with a blues jam on Sundays. There is a $2.00 cover on Friday and Saturday nights; other shows are free, and the beer is plain and cheap.

SOMERVILLE

11th Chapter Saloon — 366A Somerville Ave., Somerville; 628-4300. A narrow bar in Union Square that happens to have great food (see listing in the Dining section). And somehow, they fit rock, folk, and blues bands in on Thursdays through Saturdays, with no cover charge. The atmosphere is dark and funky, with lots of good beers on tap and more in bottles.

Johnny D's — 17 Holland St., Somerville; 776-9667. This Davis Square joint has become legendary for great blues bands, good beer, and a packed dance floor. They have a blues jam on Sunday afternoons. Also, inexpensive dining through the day and evening. Cover is as low as $2.00, but can go up to about $8.00.

SUMMER SERIES

Summer is a great time to hear all kinds of music for free in special outdoor series. These can vary from year to year, so check the papers for advertisements. Here are some of the better-established programs.

Brookline Recreation Department Concerts take place each Wednesday in July at 7 p.m. in Amory Park, behind the 1100 block of Beacon Street in Brookline. Hear local bands play jazz, country, and pop oldies. Info: 730-2070.

Charles Square Summer Music Series, held in the courtyard outside the Charles Hotel, One Bennett Street, Cambridge (just outside of Harvard Square). These free concerts include jazz, folk, and rock bands from the New England area on Wednesday evenings at 6 p.m. Info: 491-5282.

Cambridgeside Galleria River Music Fest takes place outside of this sparkling new mall across from the Museum of Science. Concerts by major local jazz, blues, and pop bands are held on Thursday evenings at 6:30 on a barge in front of the lagoon fountain. Info: 621-8666.

Hatch Memorial Shell Concerts take place all summer on the Esplanade. Different music is heard on each night of the week; swing, folk, jazz, country, etc., starting at 7:30. You can also see dance and even films. Parking is permitted along Storrow Drive near the shell, during concerts only. Info: 727-5215.

Concerts at Jamaica Pond take place several nights a week in the gazebo beside the boathouse along the Riverway. Music can range from classical to jazz to march bands. Info: 725-4505, or the Jamaica Pond Ranger Station at 522-7159.

Jazz at Christopher Columbus Park, Atlantic Ave., Boston. Free Friday-evening concerts by groups like the White Heat Swing Orchestra, Didi Stewart and Friends, and other major local acts. Showtime is 6 p.m. Info: 725-3911.

Newton Arts in the Parks summer concerts present major folk and jazz performers in two locations. Tuesday night programs start at 7:15 at the Jackson Homestead, 527 Washington St., Newton. Admission is $4.00; seniors $2.00, kids $1.00. There are also free Sunday concerts starting at 6:15 p.m. on the green at Newton Centre. Info: 552-7130.

Oldies Concert Series, sponsored by Oldies 103 FM radio, have taken place for several summers now at City Hall Plaza. Concerts take place on Saturdays at 7 p.m. from mid-July through August. They bring back such groups as the Turtles, Jan and Dean, Herman's Hermits, and many others.

Summer Stage, a platform set up on Summer Street between Filene's and Jordan Marsh in Downtown Crossing, offers free concerts every Wednesday from mid-June to mid-August. The noontime shows include jazz vocalists, children's theater, tap dance groups, and more. Info: 482-2139.

OUTDOORS

GENERAL

BOSTON

Boston Common/Public Garden
— Boston; Info, Boston Park Rangers, 522-2639. During good weather, take a stroll through the Common during lunch hour and you'll see it teeming with people eating, talking, and watching street performers. Explore it on a weekend and find folks playing on its softball diamond and tennis courts, free to the public. Check out the Civil War Memorial.

Charles River Boat Company — Science Park, Boston; 742-4282. There are lots of harbor cruise boats in Boston, some of which can be pretty expensive. Steaming up the Charles, however, is a shorter, hence cheaper, outing. You still have the fun of being on the water, passing all the sailboats, and perhaps laughing at the cars crawling along Storrow Drive at rush hour. Forty-minute rides cost $6.00 for adults, $5.00 for senior citizens, and $4.00 for children. The season runs from May to October, with rides on the hour from noon to 4 p.m.

Community Boating — Charles River Esplanade, Boston; 523-1038. You've seen all those sailboats dotting the river on a sunny summer's day. Ever thought about trying it yourself? Located behind the Hatch Shell, Community Boating has for many years made the joys of sailing affordable to all. You can join for a month, two months, or the full spring-to-fall season. Membership includes everything

you need: Instruction, boats and equipment, and use of the boathouse, with a snack bar and showers. A thirty-day membership is just $80.00—not bad at all, if you go fairly often. A seventy-five-day membership is $175.00, and the full season costs $215.00. You can always bring guests along, too. Community Boating now offers windsurfing as well.

New England Aquarium Sea Lions — Central Wharf, Boston; 973-5200. Admission to the Aquarium is a bit pricy, though worth it; one thing you can see here for free, however, is the outdoor sea lion pool, during regular Aquarium hours. Watch half a dozen of these shiny, graceful mammals frolic and cavort in the water; if you're lucky, you may catch them at feeding time. It's endlessly fascinating, as the constant crowds prove.

The Swan Boats — Public Garden Lagoon, Boston; 522-1966. For a maritime activity of another sort, there are always those famous Swan Boats. Have you ridden one since your childhood? Y'know, we've had them since 1877; that's a lot of pedaling. Yes, it's one of the only human-powered forms of public transportation, even if you do end up where you started. Rides last about fifteen to twenty minutes, a little haven of quiet and charm in the middle of the city. And such a bargain! Only $1.75 for adults and 50¢ for the kids (hey, this boat

---

Mr. Cheap's Pick

✓ **Talk to The Animals** — **The Franklin Park Zoo** is having a resurgence lately, thanks to increased funding and the new African Tropical Forest habitat. Admission is free to all ages on Tuesdays.

✓ **Row Your Boat** — Need a country getaway without leaving the city? **The Charles River Canoe and Kayak Center** in Newton gives you a chance to while away an hour or two paddling along a quiet stretch of the Charles River. Rentals are inexpensive and easy.

---

makes kids of everyone). The boats run seven days a week, 10 a.m. to 4 p.m., from April to November. Don't forget to bring some bread to feed the ducks.

CAMBRIDGE

Mt. Auburn Cemetery — 580 Mt. Auburn St., Cambridge; 547-7105. If you're not uneasy about walking among tombstones, Mt. Auburn Cemetery also happens to be an idyllic place to stroll on a sunny day. Fully landscaped with lakes, hills, and huge old trees, there are so many pathways that they actually have street signs. Being a private cemetery, of course, not a public park, they do request "dignified behavior" from visitors; no lying on the grass, picnics, or ball playing. Instead, sign up for a walking tour of famous monuments, or an early morning bird-watching walk; the main house has brochures about Mt. Auburn's programs, which cost $5.00 each. The grounds are open every day of the year, free of charge, from 8 a.m. until 5 p.m., and until 7 p.m. in summer.

DORCHESTER

Franklin Park Zoo — Blue Hill Ave. & Columbia Rd., Dorchester; 442-2002. For many years a poor man's zoo fallen into neglect, the Franklin Park Zoo has had a ton of money poured into it recently, making it well worth a visit. In addition to its renowned aviary, where hundreds of rare birds flit all around you, the zoo has a brand-new walk-through habitat, the African Tropical Forest. It looks like a spaceship from the outside, but once you go in you'll see all kinds of gorillas, hippos, monkeys and snakes all living in full-size replicas of their natural habitats. Further down is that old favorite, the petting zoo, where kids can feed large animals. All of these are included with admission, which is $5.00 for adults and children over twelve; $2.50 for kids four to eleven; and free under age four. Admission is free to all on Tuesdays, from noon until closing. Open daily from 9 a.m. to 4 p.m., weekends and holidays 10 a.m. to 5 p.m.

JAMAICA PLAIN

Arnold Arboretum — 251 The Arborway, Jamaica Plain; 524-1717. One of the area's truly great places to get away to during spring, summer, and, of course, fall. In fact, the Arboretum is open every day of the year, from sunrise to sunset, free of charge. Designed by Frederick Law Olmsted, this is more than just a park; it's a living laboratory run by the botanical department of Harvard University. It has over 14,000 trees and shrubs from around the world, all grouped by family and labeled. The fields in between are perfect for picnicking or playing frisbee, and there are long, winding paths for strolling and even careful bicycling. The visitor center includes a gift shop and a video show about the place. To get there without a car, take the Orange Line to Forest Hills, or the "Arborway" bus.

NEWTON

Charles River Canoe and Kayak Center — 2401 Commonwealth Ave., Newton; 965-5110. Out by the unlikely junction of Commonwealth Avenue and Route 128,

you can actually find yourself a bit of natural bliss by renting a canoe and paddling for miles along the Charles. At $7.00 an hour, with room for up to three people per boat, it's a great cheap getaway from the city. Pass by lily pad bogs, tiny islands in the stream, or—if you must—glide right under the highway. They'll provide everything you need, including paddles and life jackets. Parking is across the river from the boathouse; walk back over the bridge to the docks.

SPORTS

BOSTON

Boston Red Sox Bleachers — Fenway Park, Brookline Ave. and Yawkey Way, Boston; 267-8661. No matter how the Sox are doing in the annual pennant race, tickets for their games are always at a premium. Fenway Park, one of the few "original" baseball parks left, is on the small side—and so most games sell out. Ticket prices nudge themselves up a few dollars every season. But you can always save a few bucks by sitting in the outfield bleachers, which cost about half of the box seat prices; this past year,

that meant $7.00, as opposed to $14.00. Buy them in advance at the box office or right before the game from windows along the back of the stadium, on Landsdowne Street.

When games are sold out, a limited number of standing room tickets are made available at the same price; since there are often no-shows, you can sometimes get in cheaply this way and then try to find an empty seat. Be nice about it, though, if the real ticket-holder comes along late!

Other Sports — If you find tickets for the **Celtics** and **Bruins** too expensive, and the Patriots too far away (with too little result), consider games at our area's many colleges. College sports can be just as exciting, easier to get into, and far less expensive. A **Boston University** football game, at the very modern Nickerson Field, costs only $10.00 for adults, and $5.00 for children. For you sports trivia fans: In another lifetime, this stadium was home to baseball's Boston Braves. Info: 353-3838. **Boston College** football has gotten more expensive, thanks to The House that Doug Built, with a top price of $19.00; but **BC Hockey** is still only $10.00 for seats and $8.00 for benches. Info: 552-3000. **Harvard University** football gives you a choice of $10.00 seats along the sidelines; $5.00 if you don't mind the end zone. Get your orders in early for the annual Yale game, though, for which all tix are $25.00. Info: 495-2211. And try a **UMass/Boston** basketball game in the Clark Athletic Center on the Columbia Point campus. Tickets are a mere $2.00 for some serious hoops.

WALKING TOURS

BOSTON

Boston Park Ranger Tours —
Info: 522-2639. During the warmer
months, the Boston Parks Department offers several free walking
tours every week in many areas of
the city. From the Public Garden to
Jamaica Pond, from bird watching
to architecture, these jaunts may
show you a side of Boston that
you've never seen before. All
events are free; call for schedules.

The Freedom Trail — Info: 242-
5642. Everybody knows the Freedom Trail—that red line painted
down the middle of the sidewalk
downtown. But have you ever actually *walked* it? Well, it's probably the
fastest history lesson you've ever
seen, and you'll get exercise too.
Nearly three miles of walking brings
you to a dozen colonial landmarks—some you'll know, some
you may not. And, unless you go
into some of them, like the Paul Revere House and the Constitution
Museum (which charge very small
fees), it won't cost you a cent. Pick
up a map at the beginning of the
trail, the Boston Common Visitor
Center on Tremont Street, and off
you go. From May through October
the National Park Service will take
you on a free ninety-minute guided
tour, starting from the Visitor Center
at the intersection of Devonshire
and State Streets, near City Hall.
Ask about maps for the Black
Heritage Trail, the Women's Heritage Trail, and the Harborwalk, too.

Historic Boston Tours — 2 Boylston St., Boston; 426-1885. A non-
profit organization dedicated to
researching and preserving knowl-
edge about our city's history, Historic Boston offers many walking
tours of areas like Beacon Hill,
which can tell you lots of things you
didn't know about places you see
all the time. Most tours cost about
$5.00; call for a schedule.

The State House — Beacon Hill,
Boston; 727-3676. Ever been inside

the state house? Designed by the
famous architect Charles Bulfinch,
it's a building as full of history as of
modern-day importance. They offer
tours every weekday from 10 a.m.
to 4 p.m., free of charge. See the
governor's "corner office," the Sen-
ate and House of Representatives
chambers, and perhaps a glimpse
of your senator or rep. It's a great
opportunity to observe the wacky
game of politics up close.

Victorian Society In America —
Info: 267-6338. The New England
Chapter of this nationwide organization offers inexpensive walking
tours of all parts of the city, from
Beacon Hill to the lower falls of Dorchester and Milton. Led by expert
historians, these tours focus on the
social and industrial aspects of a
city in development. (Did you know
that the above-mentioned lower
falls area was once known as
"Chocolate Village," because of the
candy factories there?) Tours are
usually on Sunday afternoons and
cost $5.00; $3.00 for VSA members.

CAMBRIDGE

Cambridge Historical Society —
Info: 547-4252. CHS offers ninety-
minute walking tours through many
different neighborhoods of this
large city, including the working-
class streets of East Cambridge,
the snooty estates of Brattle Street,
and the patrician homes of North
Cambridge. Most tours are $3.00,
and they go on rain or shine.

**Harvard University Walking
Tours** — Info: 495-1585. You can't
really pahk ya cah in Hahvahd
Yahd, but you can walk through this
oasis tucked away beside the bustling square. Find out what all the
buildings are and what their historical significance is. Free and open
to all.

CHARLESTOWN

Charlestown Navy Yard Tours —
Visitor Center, Charlestown Navy
Yard; 242-5601. Take a free ninety-
minute tour of the docks, the rope
walk, and the historic ships
moored here, sponsored by the
National Park Service. The visitor
center is located next to the
U.S.S. *Constitution.*

READINGS AND POETRY

BOSTON

Harvard Book Store Cafe Series
— At Boston Public Library, Copley Square, Boston; 536-0095. There are two Harvard Book Stores, and each runs its own authors' series. With a larger venue, this series gets the bigger names, like C. Everett Koop and Garrison Keillor. The readings take place on Tuesdays at 6 p.m. in the Rabb Lecture Hall of the BPL; they are followed by a chance to meet the authors and get them to sign copies of their books around the corner at the Harvard Book Store Cafe (190 Newbury St.). HBS runs two series, one in spring and one in the fall.

King's English Series — King's Chapel, corner of School and Tremont Sts., Boston; 227-2155. Every Thursday at 12:15 p.m., the stately King's Chapel presents free lunchtime poetry readings. These may be local poets reading from their works, or readings by famous poets.

New Writers' Collective — Community Church of Boston, 565 Boylston St., Boston; 267-8624. The New Writers' Collective is a group of poetry and prose authors who gather on Tuesday evenings to read their latest efforts. These are followed by an "open read" for anyone else who wishes to try something of their own in front of a constructive audience. Scheduled readings are at 8:30 p.m., with open reads at 9 p.m.

Trident Booksellers And Cafe — 338 Newbury St., Boston; 267-8688. Hear new pieces by local poets and prose writers on Sunday afternoons at 4 p.m. in this cozy bookstore. Seating is at tables, so you can sip a capuccino as you listen. A $2.00 donation is requested. The tables fill up, so get there early and browse.

CAMBRIDGE

Cambridge Center For Adult Education — 56 Brattle St., Cambridge; 547-6789. Poetry and prose readings by local writers take place on Monday evenings at 8:15 p.m.; admission is $2.00.

Harvard Book Store Series — Old Cambridge Baptist Church, 1151 Massachusetts Ave., Cambridge; 661-1515. The more intimate of the two HBS series (see Boston listing above). These readings present authors on Wednesday evenings at 6 p.m. in the church, then move across the street to the book store (1256 Massachusetts Ave.) for signings.

Longfellow National Historic Site — 105 Brattle St., Cambridge; 876-4491. This large, airy hall is the setting for readings of anything from poetry to storytelling. These usually take place on Sunday afternoons or evenings. Readings are free and open to the public; call for the current schedule.

Stone Soup Poetry — 227-0845. Stone Soup Poets gather every Monday evening from 8:00 to 10:30 at TT the Bear's Place, 10 Brookline Street in Central Square, Cambridge. TT's is a raucous rock n' roll bar most other nights, so the atmosphere is more funky than the bookstore cafe settings. Have a beer with your poetry instead of espresso. Admission is $3.00.

Mr. Cheap's Pick

✓ *Liven-up Your Lunch* — The city abounds with free entertainment every weekday at noon. Jazz at the **CityPlace Atrium**, poetry at **King's Chapel**, classical music and dance at the **Federal Reserve Building** are among the many hour-long entertainment options which make brown-bagging more fun.

Wordsworth Reading Series —
At the Brattle Theater, 40 Brattle St., Cambridge; 354-5201. This extremely popular series presents major writers reading selections from their latest releases; most take place on Tuesdays at 5:30 p.m. in the Brattle Theater. Among the authors heard this year: Helen Caldicott, Calvin Trillin, Sen. Albert Gore, and Gloria Steinem. Both novels and non-fiction are represented. The authors have a signing session afterwards, right in the theater.

These readings are free and open to the public, but WordsWorth requests that you bring a donation of canned food to the door. It'll be donated to the Cambridge Food Pantry Network. Even though the events are free, tickets are required; they "sell out" quickly, so call to get yours in advance.

JAMAICA PLAIN

Cornwall Gallery — 57 Cornwall St., Jamaica Plain; 524-8156. This gallery hosts a "Sunday Afternoon Poetry Series," weekly at 2 p.m. Admission is free, and you can buy homemade pastries and such.

NEWTON

Newton Arts Center — 61 Washington Park, Newton; 964-3424. NAC has poetry readings once a month, on Friday evenings at 8:00. Three local writers are presented at each event, making more of a full evening out. Admission is $2.00.

THEATER

Yes, shows downtown can be expensive. But Boston abounds with local professional troupes doing everything from Shakespeare to experimental work. Their ticket prices, usually from $8.00 and up, won't force you to refinance your car just for a simple evening of drama or a lighthearted musical. Let's start off with two major players for discounted cultural events:

BOSTON

Arts Mail — 100 Boylston St., Boston; 423-0372. Become a member of this mail-order organization and you'll receive their monthly newsletter filled with dozens of opportunities to see plays, dance, music, and more, usually at half-price or thereabouts. If you can schedule your culture in advance (there is generally a choice of dates for each show), you can save money big-time. Call for information.

Bostix — Faneuil Hall Marketplace, Boston; 723-5181. This booth beside Faneuil Hall sells half-price tickets to shows all over the Boston area, including the big shows downtown, when a batch of empty seats are made available by the individual box offices. Half-price tickets are sold for that day's performances only; Bostix also sells advance tickets at full price, as well as tickets for concerts, museums, and other events. Open Tuesdays-Saturdays from 11-6, Sundays 11-4, closed Mondays. Cash only.

Now here is a list of theater companies performing in the Boston area at affordable prices:

BOSTON

Mobius — 354 Congress St., Boston; 542-7416. Boston's longtime, dedicated avant-garde troupe. Run by its artist members, Mobius presents experimental works in theater as well as dance, music, and art installations. They offer a continuous schedule of performance art pieces, usually on weekends. Tickets $4.00 to $8.00.

New Theatre — 755 Boylston St., Boston; 247-7388. A local company dedicated to new and recent plays by Boston-based and nationally known writers. New Theatre presents an annual "NEWorks" festival of scripts in development, as well as performances by its own conservatory students. Tickets for these shows are around $6.00 to $8.00.

Wheelock Family Theatre — 180 The Riverway, Boston; 734-4760. Family theater here doesn't necessarily mean children's theater; WFT is dedicated to affordable plays that are appropriate for all ages. This can include classic musicals and even dramas, presented by a professional troupe in a large, comfortable auditorium on the Wheelock College campus. Tickets are around $8.00.

CAMBRIDGE

American Repertory Theatre — 64 Brattle St., Cambridge; 547-8300. With its Yale-Harvard pedigree and million-dollar-plus budget, the A.R.T. steals much of the theatrical thunder in town with its strong regular ensemble and lavish sets. Name players such as Christopher Lloyd and F. Murray Abraham occasionally strut and fret their hour upon this stage too, along with international directors and major contemporary playwrights. Ticket prices get steep, naturally, but here's a bit of a secret: The A.R.T.'s "Pay What You Can" program.

Each week, fifty tickets are set aside for the upcoming Saturday matinee. They go on sale Monday at 10 a.m. until they are gone; you must buy them in person, two tickets to a customer. And yes, you may literally pay whatever you can afford.

Back Alley Theater — 1253 Cambridge St., Cambridge; 576-1253. This small converted storefront in Inman Square has for several years been a showcase for local actors and local playwrights. See anything from Oscar Wilde to original scripts. Tickets are $10.00 to $15.00.

Nora Theatre Company — Harvard Union, Quincy St., Cambridge; 495-4530. Another professional company in residence on the Harvard campus, Nora presents an ambitious season of contemporary plays. Tickets are from $10.00 to $15.00.

Playwrights' Platform — At Agassiz Community School, 20 Sacramento St., Cambridge; 254-4482. This is a workshop group of local playwrights who develop new pieces through simple readings. Every Sunday night a new play is read out by local actors, so that the author can "hear" what's working and what isn't. You take your chances, of course, but hey—it's free. Be adventurous! Call ahead to confirm the program.

BROOKLINE

Puppet Showplace Theatre — 32 Station St., Brookline; 731-6400. Since 1974, Puppet Showplace in Brookline Village has been offering acclaimed performances using all kinds of puppetry to tell well-known and original children's tales. All tickets are $5.00. For adults, they also frequently present humorous shows by professional storytellers—usually on Friday or Saturday evenings. Tickets are about $8.00.

JAMAICA PLAIN

Jamaica Plain Multicultural Arts Center — 659 Centre St., Jamaica Plain; 524-3816. "The Firehouse"—which is what this building used to be—has local productions of new scripts, classics by college groups, and a variety of other music, dance and poetry performances. Tickets are usually under $10.00; sometimes, a donation is all that's asked.

Open Door Theatre — Jamaica Pond Park, Jamaica Plain; 524-4007. Each summer in the "Kettlebowl," a natural amphitheatre right there in the ground, the Open Door company offers outdoor theatre under the stars. Run with assistance from the Boston Parks Department, ODT offers Shakespeare, Tennes-

---

Mr. Cheap's Pick

✓ **Artsmail** — ArtsBoston makes two options available for those who want theater, music, and dance on a budget. Buy day-of-performance tickets at half-price, when available, at the Bostix booth at Faneuil Hall; or get the same deal in advance by ArtsMail, which costs nothing to join.

---

see Williams, and sometimes new works. Tickets are $10.00, and there is always a free night for Jamaica Plain residents.

NEWTON

Turtle Lane Playhouse — 283 Melrose St., Newton; 244-0169. Each summer for over a decade, Turtle Lane has presented high-quality local productions of popular musicals like *Fiddler on the Roof* and *Little Shop of Horrors*. Tickets are $14.00 to $16.00, with subscriptions available for greater savings.

NEWTON HIGHLANDS

New Repertory Theatre — 54 Lincoln St., Newton Highlands; 332-1646. A highly respected local professional ensemble presenting a variety of British and American plays from Noel Coward to Sam Shepard. Tickets start around $12.00, with subscriptions available for even lower prices. New Rep also has a "Platform Series," staged readings of new plays, with free admission. Discover a future masterpiece!

SOMERVILLE

The Performance Place — 277 Broadway, Somerville; 931-2000. A home for a wide range of Boston's experimental theater and dance companies that do not have theaters of their own. You can see anything here from modernized Greek drama to political theater to chamber opera. Tickets are usually $12.00.

Super-Cheap Tip: Many theaters, even some of the bigger ones, frequently seek volunteer ushers. All you have to do is dress nicely, show up a little early to learn the seating layout, and in return for half an hour's easy work, you can watch the show for free. Depending on how many people they need, you can even usher with a friend for a fun cheap date. Ushers are scheduled in advance; call theaters to inquire.

ET CETERA

BOSTON

Boston University Observatory
— 705 Commonwealth Ave., Boston; 353-2360. Wanna see stars? Go up on the roof to BU's tiny but workable observatory. On Wednesday nights at 8:30, in good weather, the telescope is open free to the public, and of course someone from the astronomy department is there to point you in the right direction. Call around 6 p.m. that evening to make sure they'll be open.

Christian Science Center "Mapparium"
— Massachusetts and Huntington Aves., Boston; 450-3790. Don't worry, Mr. C isn't getting religious on you! The publication building of the Christian Science Monitor happens to house one of Boston's unique treasures, something they call the "Mapparium." It's a giant-sized globe of the Earth—which you see from the inside. Walking along a bridgeway through this huge glass bubble, you can look above and below at the nations of the world, rendered in bright handpainted colors. Of course, it's impossible to change something like this, so you'll see the world as it was in the 1930s, when this was built. The way borders are changing these days, though, it'll probably be correct again in another year or so.

The Mapparium is also known for the wild acoustics of its round glass walls. Stand at one end and whisper to someone at the other; they'll hear you perfectly. Admission is free; hours are from 9:30 to 4:00 p.m. Mondays through Saturdays.

Commonwealth Brewery Tours
— 138 Portland St., Boston; 523-8383. If you've ever wondered how beer is made, you can see for yourself in the basement vats of the Commonwealth Brewing Company. Free tours are given every Saturday at 3:30 and Sunday at noon. Of course, this is a restaurant, so it's not *entirely* free; how can you pass up trying this fine home brew, once you've learned so much about it?

Mr. Cheap's Pick

✓ **See the World** — One of the best hidden gems in Boston is the **Mapparium** at the Christian Science Center on Massachusetts Avenue. Walk through the center of a giant glass globe with the nations of the world painted in bright colors. Also popular for its bizarre acoustics. Admission is free.

✓ **See Other Worlds** — Both **Boston University** and **Harvard University** offer free weekly Observatory Nights for stargazers. Look through powerful telescopes at the moon and the stars—weather permitting, of course. Call for hours.

John Hancock Observatory —
200 Clarendon St., Boston; 247-
1977. A different kind of observatory; this one is for looking down.
New England's tallest building af-
fords a spectacular view of our fair
city and the many hills and dales
beyond. Admission is $2.75 for
adults, $2.00 for senior citizens and
children; and you can stay up there
as long as you want. Hours: Mondays through Saturday from 9 a.m.
to 10 p.m., and Sundays from noon
to 10 p.m.

Prudential Center Skywalk —
800 Boylston St., Boston; 236-3318.
Okay, so it's not as tall as the Hancock. When you're this far up,
what's ten more floors? And besides, this one has a view on all
four sides, while the Hancock only
has three. It's all small potatoes,
though—again, the view will knock
your socks off. Admission here is
$2.75 for adults; $1.75 for children
ages five through fifteen and seniors; kids under five, free. Hours are
from 10 a.m. to 10 p.m. on Monday
through Saturday, and Sundays
from noon to 10 p.m.

CAMBRIDGE

Harvard University Observatory
— 60 Garden St., Cambridge; 495-
7461. Another place where you can
ascend to the heavens and leave
earthly bounds behind. The Har-
vard-Smithsonian Center for Astro-
physics presents a formal
forty-five-minute program on the
third Thursday of each month.
Again, be sure to call ahead if the
day's weather is in doubt (in Boston, when isn't it?).

JAMAICA PLAIN

Samuel Adams Brewery — 30
Germania St., Jamaica Plain; 522-
9080. Another place to see how
one of America's best beers is
made. Unlike the Commonwealth
Brewery (above), this is an actual
factory; but yes, they do give free
samples. Tours are given every
Thursday at 2 p.m. and on Saturdays at noon and 2 p.m. A donation of $1.00 is requested to defray
costs.

RESTAURANTS

Mr. Cheap's Picks
Tip-free Restaurants

The following fine establishments won't give you a dirty look if you head out the door without leaving a gratuity, God bless them.

ALLSTON
- ☐ Ali Baba Restaurant, 170
- ☐ Number 1 Kitchen, 175
- ☐ Riley's Roast Beef (and East Boston), 177

BOSTON
- ☐ Angora Coffee Shop, 179
- ☐ Blazing Salads, 180
- ☐ Buzzy's Roast Beef, 182
- ☐ Ej's Natural Foods, 185
- ☐ Kenmore Cafe, 188
- ☐ Kingston Deli & Grill, 188
- ☐ Mal's New York Style Delicatessen, 189
- ☐ Metro Deli, 190
- ☐ Paramount Restaurant & Deli, 191
- ☐ Province Place, 192
- ☐ Sami's, 193
- ☐ Sultan's Kitchen, 195
- ☐ Trattoria Il Panino (and Cambridge), 196

BRIGHTON
- ☐ BIll & Don's Cafe, 198
- ☐ Blake's Restaurant, 198
- ☐ Brighton Seafood, 199
- ☐ Jim's Deli And Restaurant, 200
- ☐ Peking Gardens, 201
- ☐ Wing It, 203

BROOKLINE
- ☐ Alicia's Chic-and-Pasta Restaurant, 204
- ☐ El Bandido Mexican Cafe, 205
- ☐ Imperial Restaurant, 206
- ☐ Jaffe's Pick-A-Chick, 206
- ☐ King Tut Coffee Shop, 206
- ☐ Pugsley's, 208
- ☐ Rami's (and Boston), 208
- ☐ Rose's Cafe and Deli, 209
- ☐ TJ's Taqueria, 209
- ☐ Yu's Take Out, 210

CAMBRIDGE
- ☐ Al's Lunch, 212
- ☐ Boca Grande, 213
- ☐ Cafe Mami, 214
- ☐ Cambridge Deli And Grill, 216
- ☐ Fresco's Cafe And Grille, 219
- ☐ Izzy's Restaurant, 222
- ☐ Jake And Earl's Dixie Barbecue, 223
- ☐ Moody's Falaffel Palace, 225
- ☐ The Skewers, 227
- ☐ Tommy's Lunch, 228

NEWTON
- ☐ Concept Cafe, 232
- ☐ La Rotisserie, 235
- ☐ Oh La La, 235
- ☐ Sandwich Works, 237

SOMERVILLE
- ☐ Mike's Restaurant, 239
- ☐ Picante Mexican Grill, 242
- ☐ Street Cafe, 243
- ☐ Worldly Wings, 244

WATERTOWN
- ☐ Demo's Restaurant, 249

ALLSTON

Ali Baba Restaurant — 514 Cambridge St., Allston; 254-4540. Middle Eastern food in Union Square is ably represented by Ali Baba, a recent addition offering cheap and healthy meals. The food is touted as all-natural, and it's good. The atmosphere is fast-food but clean; you eat from styrofoam plates, but each table has a couple of fresh roses for decor.

The selections are the traditional Mediterranean dishes—and the prices are great. The chicken and beef, in kebabs or shawarma style, are $3.50 for sandwiches (with lettuce, tomato and tahini sauce) or $4.95 for platters (with rice or fries, hummus, salad and pita bread). Either way, you shouldn't go hungry.

Falaffel, hummus and baba ganoush sandwiches are $2.95 each, as is the Greek salad. From 6 p.m. to 10 p.m. daily, there is an all-you-can-eat buffet of falaffel, salad, and tahini sauce for $4.95. For anyone not acquainted with Middle Eastern cuisine, Ali Baba offers free tastes of selected items.

Perhaps the best bargains are the rotisseried chicken dinners; the chicken plate ($4.75) consists of tender, fresh pieces of chicken pulled off the bones and placed on a bed of rice pilaf. It comes with salad, hummus, garlic sauce, and pita bread.

You can also get a whole rotisseried chicken, with garlic sauce and bread, for $6.50, or a half-chicken for $3.75. That's one cheap dinner. Ali Baba offers catering, take-out, or free delivery and is open daily until midnight.

Arbuckle's — 1249 Commonwealth Ave., Allston; 782-9508. Burgers, burgers, burgers—that's pretty much the story at Arbuckle's, a college hangout near that bustling intersection of Harvard and Commonwealth Avenues in Allston. Oh, but what burgers—twenty-one different kinds! Yes, there are other things to order here, but their burgers are a hard story to top.

Speaking of toppings, these go well beyond cheese. The basic model, served with lettuce, tomato, a pickle wedge and crisp, curly French fries, is $4.95. At the top of the line, just a dollar more, the choices are Mexican, with jalapeno peppers, salsa and a spicy cheese; or the Boston College, with turkey, lettuce, tomato, bacon and cheese.

In between are such options as teriyaki, guacamole, Cajun, reuben, and the "Brunch Burger"—topped with bacon and a fried egg. All of these cost between $5.25 and $5.75. And it should be pointed out that these are ten-ounce patties of fresh meat; even bigger than the half-pounders at most other reputable establishments. You'll really have to wrap your paws around one of these.

Another good bet at Arbuckle's is the chicken sandwich, made with an eight-ounce breast in barbecue, Cajun and teriyaki styles for $5.50 each. Again, you get fries, cole slaw, and a pickle. These are designated on the menu as "low cholesterol" items. Several salads are also in that category.

Arbuckle's has a long, dark wood bar, and a sports decor (which means plenty of TVs). The list of beers includes Bass Ale on tap, bottles of Corona and Dos Equis, and those big cans of Foster's Lager. House wines, coffee drinks, and creative cocktails with cutesy names complete the experience—a lively joint with a casual atmosphere. Oh yes, and huge hamburgers.

Arthur's Seafood And Deli — 204 Harvard Ave., Allston; 734-8343. Good seafood cheap—that's Arthur's, a small restaurant in the bustling intersection of Harvard and Commonwealth Avenues in Allston. The menu slants toward the Greek isles, and also features meat dishes and sandwiches. The place may be lean on atmosphere—your basic coffee shop look—but the fish is fresh, you get a lot, and the choices are extensive.

Lunch is the best deal here. Arthur's offers a full slate of daily specials, giving you an entree with one side dish for as little as $2.95 to $4.95.

The regular menu has a lot more choices, like the fried seafood platter ($5.90), a full plate of scallops, shrimp, clams and schrod. Each of these is available as an entree of its own for $5.95 ($5.50 for the haddock, or sole). These all come with French fries and cole slaw. So do the fish roll ($2.95), and the clam, shrimp or scallop rolls ($4.95 each). Fish and chips are just $3.95.

On the broiled side, starting at $4.50, you can get mackerel, bluefish, trout or smelts—along with two side dishes. Choose from fries, baked potato, salad, rice pilaf, or the day's cooked vegetable. Quite a deal. Haddock and sole plates are $5.50; swordfish, salmon and halibut are $7.95. The broiled combination plate ($6.95) consists of swordfish, halibut, scallops, shrimp and schrod, plus the sides.

Dinner versions get a bit fancier, with titles like "Haddock a la Grec" ($7.50), baked in a tomato sauce. Chicken seafood saute ($9.95) pushes the tab up, but it's a lovely mix of chicken, swordfish,

shrimp, and scallops in a mushroom and white wine sauce. There is a Cajun swordfish ($8.95), and baked stuffed crab is just $7.95, with a lobster/bread stuffing. Again, you get two side dishes.

Meat entrees at lunch and dinner include various shishkebabs, souvlaki, gyros, and loukaniko (Greek sausage), as well as pork chops, chicken, and hamburgers. These are all fine; but, when in Rome, as the saying goes . . . .

Barbeques International — 129 Brighton Ave., Allston; 782-6669. This is one restaurant that lives up to its name. BI serves up a varied menu of foods prepared in styles from around the world; from Mediterranean to Indian to good ol' Texas-style. It's like several restaurants all rolled up into one.

Most dinner entrees are under $10.00; many are in the $6.00 to $8.00 range. Want some chicken? You can have it barbecued, teriyaki, Cajun, or tandoori, each accompanied by the appropriate sides—be it French fries, rice pilaf, or warm Indian naan bread. The kitchen is outfitted with all the necessary tools and a clay oven to give each dish the proper taste.

The same approach is taken to beef and a couple of seafood dishes. Not all corners of the world are always available; the choices are rotated daily. The best deals, though, are the combination plates, like the "Beef 'n Bird" ($7.95). It's a packed plate of tender sirloin tips, a boneless chicken breast, fries, and cole slaw. You may wind up taking some home. The tandoori mix ($10.95) offers chicken, lamb, and shrimp in a yogurt sauce, served with naan bread.

Several beers are available to go along with the hot stuff. The restaurant has recently been renovated, looking very handsome with natural wood tables and glassbrick walls.

Bus Stop Pub — 252 Western Ave., Allston; 254-4086. The Bus Stop is a relaxed, neighborhood hangout where you can watch sports on the big screen TV, shoot a round of pool, and have good food cheap. All this was happening here well before the term "sports bar" became a buzzword. Located across from a park of baseball diamonds, it's a popular watering hole for local softball teams after games on summer nights.

The list of beers available is extensive, including Guinness Stout on tap. Appetizers are strictly the basics, with buffalo wings, potato skins, nachos, and a few others. These are a bit high-priced, from $2.25 to $4.95; the best bargain is the "Grande Nachos" ($4.95), topped with cheddar cheese, tomatoes, peppers, onions, chopped sirloin, and salsa. Or try a crock of chili with cheese on top for $3.00.

The dinner entrees and sandwiches are the real stars of the menu. Marinated steak tips ($5.95) are a hefty plate served with salad or crispy French fries. The tips are big and juicy. A boneless breast of barbecued chicken is the same price, with fries and cole slaw. The "Mixed Grille Medley" is a combination plate of grilled steak tips, lamb tips and sausage, with fries or salad for $6.95. They're all delicious. Daily specials are noted on the blackboard, but beware—they can run out quickly.

Just as filling, and cheaper, are the sandwiches. The steak sandwich ($3.95) is basically the steak tips on a sub roll, served with fries; add melted cheese for a quarter. It's yummy. Or try "Boardwalk Billy" for $3.75—sausage, onion, and cheese on a roll. There are also jumbo hot dogs, topped with chili and/or cheese ($2.50 to $3.25) and burgers ($2.95 to $3.75), all with fries.

Cafe Brazil — 421 Cambridge St., Allston; 789-5980. Cafe Brazil is a fun, funky, and friendly little place that has been serving up great South American food for several years now. The prices have gone up a bit over the years, with some dinners over Mr. C's limit of $10.00; but the portions are so generous that you'll probably take some home for leftovers anyway.

Brazilian cuisine is well seasoned, but is not generally spicy. The dishes of chicken, beef, and fish are flavored with things like cassava root, okra, onions, and garlic. Almost everything is served with rice and black beans. The menu is kind enough to explain many of the preparations, which are, after all, in Portuguese.

For a good introduction, Mr. C recommends the "Brazil 2001" platter ($9.95)—grilled pieces of chicken, beef, and linguica (nonspicy pork sausage) served over a bed of rice and sauteed cabbage. It also includes slices of fried banana and feijao tropeiro (a kind of stuffing made from black beans, cassava meal, bacon, sausage, eggs, garlic and onion).

Among the many fish dishes, moqueca a Mineira ($9.95) was a huge piece of steamed white fish with vegetables and herbs. Along with it you get a separate bowl of something called pirao: it is made from the cooking liquid used on the fish, which is mixed with cassava meal to make a thick sauce. Again, rice, beans, and enough fish to take home.

There are several beef and chicken dishes, with many of the same preparations, all from $8.95 to $12.95. Also, there is a vegetarian plate ($8.95) with fresh sauteed veggies, mandioca (cassava fried up like potatoes), fried banana, rice, and beans.

A cheaper way to try these out is to go at lunchtime (11:30 to 4:00), when exactly the same menu is offered. The portions are still generous, and the prices are about $3.00 lower per dish.

At night, however, you get the very romantic addition of live music, except on Mondays. The lights are low as a guitarist strums and sings the relaxing sound of bossa nova. Makes for a nice date.

Cao Palace — 137 Brighton Ave., Allston; 783-2340 or 254-9812. Cao Palace is a Vietnamese restaurant

Mr. Cheap's Picks
Allston

✓ **Arbuckle's** — Go for the burgers; some of the biggest you'll ever wrap your hands around.

✓ **Henry's Diner** — A classic, railroad car-shaped diner with a bit of funk and a huge, cheap menu.

✓ **Rama Thai** — Yes, it's in a shopping center; but think of the free parking! Pretty inside, and prices about a dollar less than most other Thai places in town.

✓ *Vietnamese Restaurants* — Several within a few blocks. Along Brighton Avenue, on either side of Harvard Avenue, check out **Cao Palace**, **Pho Pascal** and **V. Majestic**. Further up Harvard, toward the Pike, bank a left onto Cambridge street and you'll see the generically-named **Express Cuisine**, one of the few such restaurants with some hip style. Viet is *the* way to go for super-cheap, hearty meals these days.

and fish market. It holds down one end of the Brighton Avenue/Harvard Avenue intersection in Allston, while V. Majestic (below) reigns a block away at the opposite end. Together they make the neighborhood rich with inexpensive Vietnamese seafood.

At Cao Palace, the special style of cooking is "caramel," in which the food is sauteed in a way that brings its natural sugars to the outside for a slightly sweet taste. Caramel shrimp ($8.00) gives you a good portion served over steamed rice. There are also caramel fish, a whitefish ($8.00) and caramel pork ($7.00).

Those with more traditional tastes may have their seafood broiled or fried. Fried filet of sole is $6.50, with potato salad or French fries and salad or cole slaw. Other fried fish include cod ($5.50), catfish ($6.00), flounder ($6.50) and scallops ($7.00). The same fish are on the broiler menu, along with swordfish, tuna ($8.00 each) and shark ($7.25).

But for a treat, stick with the Vietnamese special dinners. For non-fish eaters, there is chicken lemon grass ($7.00), roasted in

honey and marinated in this tasty spice. Rolling beef ($7.00) is thinly-sliced beef marinated in a rich and slightly spicy sauce and wrapped in grape leaves. Or try an assortment of Vietnamese vegetables sauteed over rice ($5.50). Roast duck, sauteed lobster meat, and crab meat are among the other interesting items.

For appetizers, try the spring rolls (two for $2.00), which include turkey and crabmeat wrapped in rice paper; or one of the many unusual soups. Saigon soup ($3.50) contains fish, shrimp, and pineapple. Seaweed soup ($2.00) is better than it may sound, with your choice of shrimp, scallops, fish, pork, beef, or chicken.

Cao Palace offers several special luncheon deals, smaller portions of their main dishes at lower prices. Chicken lemon grass is just $4.00, or try the pan-fried whole fish of the day ($5.00). Fish and chips is just $1.75 for a small order, $3.50 for the large. And since this is a fish market, most dishes can be ordered to take out, or you can buy fresh fish to cook up yourself.

Express Cuisine — 431 Cambridge St., Allston; 254-3373. A nondescript name for one of the more interesting of Allston's many Vietnamese restaurants. Clean and spare but decorated with a touch of neon, it's a funkier look than the usual kitchen-style Viet place—kind of a Soho feel.

The appetizers are fine, and inexpensive; two spring rolls, filled with turkey, mushrooms, carrots, onion, and rice vermicelli, are $1.95. There are a half-dozen soups, most around $2.50—hearty, warming bowls based on chicken or seafood broths.

As with most such restaurants, caramel dishes are a house specialty. Try this sweet sauce on chicken ($5.55), salmon, or shrimp ($6.25 each). At these prices it's easy to try something new. Sauteed vegetable dishes are even cheaper; have them with rice sticks or noodles or in a special tomato sauce for just $4.55.

Vietnamese beef kebabs ($5.25 for four skewers) are marinated in soy sauce, lemon grass, sesame seeds, and other spices. Chicken lemon grass ($5.95) is another mildly spicy specialty.

Express Cuisine also offers daily lunch and dinner specials, most in the $3.00 to $5.00 range. The place is small and fills up easily, by the way; you may want to call ahead to see if they're busy.

Gerlando's Restaurant — 133 Brighton Ave., Allston; 782-3252. Mr. C has often found that bars and pubs offer some of the best food deals in town; these places make their money on liquor, so the dining values can be tremendous. The trade-off is ambience; many of these places look, well, a bit rough around the edges, though they often turn out to be just fine. Such a place is Gerlando's.

This is a neighborhood bar, with its regulars and maybe a motorcycle or two parked out front—but the folks who take your order are friendly and casual and happy to make a recommendation about the food. Italian dinners are the specialty here, like boneless chicken parmigiana for $5.25. Two large pieces came with a side of ziti or spaghetti, plus a roll and butter. A baked cheese lasagna dinner is just $3.95.

Burgers start at $2.50; hefty, fresh-ground-beef burgers, with fries for another dollar. Steak tips, $5.25, are another good bet for quantity and quality. You won't eat at Gerlando's and leave hungry, that's for sure. Pitchers of beer are just as cheap; plenty of sports games, too, to help you work up an appetite.

Henry's Diner — 270 Western Ave., Allston; 783-5844. People who are serious about diners hold one rule uppermost: A true diner must be in the shape of a railroad car, preferably in shining silver metal. Mr. C is such a person, and Henry's Diner is such a place. The joint has been operating, under a succession of names, for over seventy years on the same spot. Its newest owners have jazzed it up with some kitschy neon, hip music, and a "universal symbol" sign out front—a huge railroad crossing marker with a chef's hat on it. No words necessary; diner below.

The added funkiness doesn't come with higher prices, as with some more recent diners. Nothing on this menu tops $6.95, and that gets you the "Oceanside Platter"— clams, scallops, schrod, corn chowder, fries, corn bread, and cole slaw. Nothing fishy about these prices!

In fact, almost *every* item on the extensive menu seems to cost $3.95. All the beef dishes, from marinated sirloin tips with rice and vegetables to veal parmesan. All the chicken dishes—grilled, barbecued, or Southern fried. Plus the real diner fare: homemade meatloaf and lasagna, stuffed turkey breast, knockwurst and beans (with potato salad and corn bread) . . . you get the idea. Seafood dishes reel in just a bit more. Try the fried or broiled scallops for $5.95.

Then there's a heaping plate of linguini for $2.95, with meat sauce and a salad, perhaps the lowest-priced pasta in town. Get a bacon and cheddar burger with lettuce, tomato, onion, fries, and slaw for just $3.35.

Henry's is also a fun spot for weekend brunch, with big, thick slabs of French toast and eggs any way you like 'em. Even a request for eggs done without the yolks—no cholesterol—failed to raise an eyebrow!

Being a true diner, of course, seating is limited. They've packed a good number of counter stools and booths in, but at peak times you may have to wait. It's worth it.

Number 1 Kitchen — 5 North Beacon St., Allston; 782-7833. This small but cozy eatery is one of the cluster of ethnic restaurants that line Allston's Union Square. The staff is friendly, the service is quick, the place is clean; the food is average, but you do get large portions at very cheap prices.

Foremost among the bargains is the $2.00 luncheon—no, that's not a typo. For $2.00, you may choose two items from the several offerings at a special hot table. The choices include meatless fried rice, pork or chicken chow mein, roast pork lo mein, bean curd with vegetables, shrimp and pork with rice noodles, and more. They'll top it off with a chicken wing; you can also add other items inexpensively if you wish. It's available on weekdays from 11:30 to 2:30. Hard to beat.

Elsewhere on the clock there are lunch and dinner special combinations that are similarly cheap, ranging from $3.25 to $5.50. Pork with mixed vegetables, kung pao chicken, shrimp with lobster sauce, and beef with broccoli are among these plates, which come with white or pork-fried rice. For another $1.50 you can add an appetizer such as boneless spareribs, chicken fingers, or beef teriyaki. Appetizer combination plates are also available as specials. Regular

dishes are offered in small and large sizes, allowing you to spend only as much as you want to.

There are just a half-dozen tables or so in a clean, skylit setting. They do deliver in the evenings until 11:00, and the restaurant is open daily until midnight; that's good to remember when you have those late-night cravings.

Our House — 1277 Commonwealth Ave., Allston; 782-3228. Students in the Allston area have known about Our House for years—a truly casual place to party or relax. It's made to look like Mom 'n Dad's basement rec room, with a bar, big plush couches in front of TVs, and a pool table in the back.

More recently, it's been spruced up a bit; the "rec" area is rimmed by tables with white linen tablecloths, there is a separate "cafe" room, and the menu—still packed with burgers and sandwiches—now includes specials like the one Mr. C's friend ordered. On this plate, seven shrimp were lined up on seven wedges of pear, each wrapped in a basil leaf. These were served over rice pilaf, all topped by a caramel glaze sauce. It was a beauty to behold, as well as to eat. The dinner included a salad with fresh vegetables, and a basket of garlic bread (with real minced garlic), all for $8.95.

Yes, Our House has gone inexpensively yuppie, with pasta primavera ($6.25), beef brochette ($5.75) and chicken a la Suisse ($5.75)—chicken breast stuffed with ham, cheese, and a garlic herb sauce. Yet it's still a place where a hand-lettered sign tells you the "Shot of the Week" (Woo Woos for $3.00!) and the beers, mostly Buds and Millers, are in bottles only.

There are still a dozen different burgers, large and juicy, ranging from $4.25 to $5.50; Canadian, Texas, Italian, Teriyaki, and, of course, Yuppie. Best of all, the big appetizer menu is available until 1:30 a.m.—Buffalo wings for $4.25, five varieties of skins from $3.50 to $4.75, and "loaded fries" ($3.75)—

a big basket of spuds with melted cheddar and bacon bits. Friendly service, too.

Pho Pascal — 182 Brighton Ave., Allston; 254-3600. Pascal is part of the Brighton Ave. lineup of Vietnamese restaurants, probably the biggest cluster outside of Chinatown. Like the rest, the food here is incredibly cheap, and quite healthy too.

Just about anything you order comes in a very large soup bowl, even the entrees. Soup, though, is the main line of business; there are no fewer than twenty-one varieties on the menu. The biggest of the lot costs just $4.50 and could keep you going for a week. This "Special Combo X Large" consists of slices of steak, brisket, flanken, tendon, and tripe, along with a ton of vermicelli noodles, in a tasty scallion and onion broth.

Most of the soups are variations of this big daddy and are all priced from $3.00 to $4.00. Even the "smaller" versions are meals in themselves, again with lots of noodles—and the waitress will also bring you a plate of fresh bean sprouts on the side. Throw 'em in and let them cook in the broth. The meat in these soups is tender and delicious. There are a couple of seafood soups as well.

Other main dishes are served with rice or vermicelli too, hefty bowls or plates priced from $3.00 to $6.00. Many feature barbecued beef, which is delicious. Some come with spring rolls—small, crispy, and fun to munch on.

Pho Pascal also serves Chinese dishes, which are probably good too—but why bother with them in a Viet restaurant? They're also a bit higher-priced, most from $6.00 to $9.00.

Atmosphere at Pascal is the weakest of the Brighton Ave. bunch—Mr. C had very slow, unattentive service, and that was on a weeknight. Nevertheless, the food makes it worthwhile. A full, tummy-warming meal under $10.00—even around $5.00—is no problem.

Rama Thai — 181 Brighton Ave., Allston; 783-2434. Rama Thai is a lovely find amidst the rock-and-roll clubs and funky junk shops of Allston. Even more unlikely, it resides in a shopping center next to Dunkin Donuts, Domino's Pizza, and Osco Drug. But once you step inside the decor is light and clean and the atmosphere is peaceful. The menu is extensive, and cheaper than many comparable Thai restaurants in the area.

Start with appetizers like Thai rolls ($3.30), a plateful of tiny fried rolls with ground chicken, carrots, and bean thread, served with a sweet dipping sauce. A good order for the table. Chicken or beef satay ($3.80) is a traditional Thai nibble, chunks of meat grilled on skewers and served with a slightly spicy peanut sauce. There are also interesting soups, such as the Tom Yum Goong ($1.80), shrimp in a sweet-and-sour broth with mushrooms, scallions, and the popular Thai spices coriander and lemon grass.

The house specialties and seafood dishes are the pricier items on the menu, though you'll get plenty to eat with such dishes as Thai Ocean ($9.35), a mixture of shrimp, scallops, squid, fish filet, broccoli, carrots, onions, and baby corn. Duck Choo Chee ($8.30) is boneless roasted duck sauteed with vegetables in a curry sauce, and you can also order the "Garlic Sauce" plate with any main item from tofu to beef to shrimp ($6.25 to $7.85).

The "Chef's Specialties" offer the same treatment for a bit less: choose from tofu ($5.40), pork ($5.65), chicken or beef ($5.95), or shrimp ($6.65), and choose preparations such as basil leaf, ginger, sweet and sour, spicy bamboo shoot, or one of four different curry sauces.

For the true bargains, however, Mr. C recommends the many rice and noodle dishes. There is Pad Thai, of course ($4.85); it's a full plate of pan-fried rice noodles and bean sprouts with ground shrimp, chicken, eggs, tofu, and peanuts. There is also a vegetarian version for the same price. Rad Nah ($4.70) consists of heavier pan-fried egg noodles with broccoli and your choice of meat (or tofu) in a black bean sauce.

Green curry with thin rice noodles ($4.75) again gives you a choice of meat, in a green chili and coconut milk sauce with eggplant, green peppers, mushroom, and basil leaves. There is also a red curry version with a different taste. Spicy fried rice ($4.60) is chicken, beef, pork, or tofu in rice with chili, basil leaves, onions, and baby corn, served with tomato and cucumber. Or have it with shrimp for $4.95. You can also order a mixed vegetable plate ($4.95), either steamed with peanut sauce or stir-fried with oyster sauce.

Rama Thai offers a luncheon menu from 11:30 a.m. to 2:30 p.m., with many of these dishes at even lower prices. Most items are around $4.00, and may be ordered to take out. You'll get plenty, and it's well worth repeat visits to try the many unusual tastes.

Riley's Roast Beef — 140 Brighton Ave., Allston; 254-9592. Also, 259 Bennington St., East Boston; 567-9282. Anyone who's lived around the Boston area probably knows the Riley's sign—"Roast Beef 'Til 3 A.M."—as a local landmark. Mr. C. has always wanted to go in at 2:59 and order a peanut butter and jelly sandwich, just to see if a burly night cook would shout, "Roast beef! Ya gotta order roast beef! Can't ya read the sign??" Well, the good news is that you can in fact go to Riley's at just about any time of day, and choose from several different kinds of food.

Recently renovated, the Allston location is cleaner than it once was, well-lit, and decorated with plants for a cozier feel. It's really a fast-food joint, not what this book is meant to cover; but the food is pretty good, and there is more variety here than you'll find in any McChain.

Roast beef, of course, is the specialty of the house. It comes thin-sliced and hot on an onion roll in four sizes: junior ($1.75), regular ($2.89), the "Big 1" ($3.93) and deluxe ($5.19). All include cheese and barbecue sauce. It makes for a yummy, if messy, handful. You can add a medium order of fries and a soda for about a dollar more.

You can substitute pastrami, by the way, for the above sandwiches, at the same prices. There are burgers too, your average flat patty type, but they are char-broiled and the "Ranch burger" ($2.09) gives you two patties with lettuce and tomato.

Riley's also offers an assortment of fried munchies good for snacking, from egg rolls or broccoli and cheese rolls ($1.49 each) to chicken fingers ($2.59) to a scallop or clam plate ($3.99), which includes fries, onion rings, and cole slaw. There are soups too: clam chowder, minestrone, and chicken noodle ($1.69 each).

But it doesn't end there. Riley's has daily dinner specials, such as chicken pot pie ($3.99), which comes with corn bread and your choice of two side dishes. You can choose from baked beans, carrots, squash, zucchini, mashed potatoes, and rice pilaf. And there is rotisserie-marinated chicken, of which you can get a half bird for $3.99 with two of the above vegetables. That's quite a bargain.

Riley's even cooks breakfast, from 7 a.m. to 11 a.m., with omelettes from $2.29 or three eggs and bacon for $2.89 with toast, home fries, and coffee. And they have home-baked muffins for 69¢—blueberry, corn and bran.

Riley's East Boston location, in Day Square, is a bit more of a take-out stand than a sit-down eatery but offers most of the same foods.

The Sports Depot — 353 Cambridge St., Allston; 783-2300. What gives this place its character—is it the authentic brownstone train station of its origin? The autographed murals of Boston sports heroes? Or the nearly fifty TV sets scattered around the place, even in the bathrooms, so you never miss a second of the half-dozen games being shown at any one time?

Surely, it's all of these—not to mention the food, which could fill a stadium itself. Giant burgers and sandwiches, all around $5.00 to $6.00, complete chicken and steak dinners, with vegetables and fresh salads, about $10.00, individual pizzas for $3.25 and full-size for $6.99, fajita dinners for $8.95 . . . all with the basic intention of stuffing you silly. Big desserts, too.

Sunday through Thursday, the Depot offers two dinners for $12.95; choose from a BBQ half-chicken, lemon pepper schrod, shrimp alfredo, teriyaki steak tips, and several others. Salad and coffee are included. Great deal.

There are, of course, several bars of varying sizes around the cavernous room; but for an extra thrill, sit out in the enclosed patio that faces the train tracks. When ol' Casey Jones thunders by, you can practically reach out and touch the cars. Oh, and don't worry—there are TVs here as well.

V. Majestic Restaurant — 164 Brighton Ave., Allston; 782-6088. Part of the cluster of very good and cheap Vietnamese restaurants in Allston, V. Majestic offers excellent food at low prices. The surroundings are humble, but you won't mind once the food comes out.

Like most Viet kitchens, the emphasis here is on seafood. Most fish dishes come sauteed in ginger or "caramelized," the preparation that brings out the natural sugars of the food. Mr. C loved the caramel fish ($6.25), delicate pieces of salmon in this slightly sweet sauce, garnished with chunks of cooked pineapple. It comes with a heap of steamed rice and a simple salad.

For a variety of seafood, try the "Sea of Vietnam," a combo platter of scallops, shrimp, squid, and vegetables sauteed with rice. The small portion is $5.15, but large is a real bargain at $6.25.

Other great deals are the soups, many of which again feature fish. Crabmeat soup is just $3.00 for a large bowl of crab, shrimp, tomato, onion, and vermicelli noodles. Among appetizers, be sure to try the Vietnamese rolls ($2.40), a pair of large, uncooked rolls filled with lettuce, rice vermicelli, shrimp, and chicken and served with a not-too-spicy peanut dipping sauce.

Of course, there are also meat dishes. Glowing beef ($4.55) is thinly-sliced meat baked in special spices, served with vermicelli. Chicken lemon grass (small $4.15, large $6.95) is a tasty, mildly spiced dish flavored with a touch of honey. It comes with rice and salad.

Most entrees here range from $5.00 to $7.00, with good portions. The service is quick and attentive. V. Majestic is authentic Vietnamese food in a friendly, home-kitchen atmosphere.

BOSTON

Angora Coffee Shop — 1020A Commonwealth Ave., Boston; 232-1757. This BU favorite mixes Middle Eastern food with a variety of salads, sandwiches, soups, and individual pizzas for an eclectic and inexpensive menu. Much of the food is homemade, with ample portions.

Soups change daily, with such choices as clam chowder and cream curried chicken. Get soup and a half-sandwich for $3.95; these include brie, corned beef, and smoked turkey. Same deal for soup and quiche.

Salads start at $2.45; rotelli pasta ($3.85) is a winner, with baby corn, onions, carrots, and parmesan cheese tossed in. There are artichoke, avocado, and taco salads too.

A real treat are the Boboli pizzas—eight-inch pies covered with chunks of chicken and broccoli, beef and mushroom, or many other combinations, all around $4.50. They are filling and delicious.

The Mediterranean portion of the menu offers hummus, baba ganoush, tabouli and more, each served on pita bread for $3.45; for hearty appetites, you won't go wrong with the combination platter, which adds a Greek salad to the above, all for just $5.75.

Not to mention bagels from Kupel's, desserts from Rosie's Bakery, and Mrs. Miller's Muffins. Or follow a Greek specialty with a piece of homemade baklava. Lots of gourmet coffees, teas, juices, cappucino, and espresso to go along with these, too.

Ann's Restaurant — 2440 Cambridge St., Boston; 523-4606. Ann's, on the back of Beacon Hill, serves delicious Middle Eastern food in a pleasant cafe atmosphere. The wooden walls are a fresh white, with dark brown furni-

---

Mr. Cheap's Picks
Back Bay

✓ **Hsin Hsin Noodle Restaurant** — Simple, no frills noodle house. One of the better Chinese places outside of Chinatown.

✓ **Kenmore Cafe** — Flash! Fast-food chain replaced by honest cooking, cafeteria-style; emphasis on Middle Eastern.

✓ *Lively Student Hangouts* — A couple: **Dixie Kitchen** near Berklee offers great Cajun food in big portions; while **The Pour House** across from the Hynes is big, boisterous, and cheap.

✓ **Steve's Greek Cuisine** — One of the few hearty *and* affordable spots on Newbury Street.

---

ture and green linen—in short, nicer surroundings than you usually get with this kind of food.

Be sure to start off with the fattoush salad ($3.50/$4.25); even the small size is enormous. Greens and vegetables are mixed with mint, parsley, garlic and bits of toasted pita bread for a refreshing appetizer. Of course, all the other apps are there too: falaffel, baba ganoush, grape leaves, etc. Ann's falaffel is unusual, though—flatter and fried up crispier than most, while the inside remains moist. Just right.

Entrees give you more of the familiar choices, generally ranging from $6.00 to $9.00. Among the more interesting are the broccolinoodle casserole ($6.00), baked with mushrooms and Swiss and Parmesan cheeses. Kibby ($6.50), layers of ground beef and cracked wheat, is another house winner.

For a real bargain, order one of the ten combination plates ($6.00 to $8.25), with various trios of grilled chicken, spinach pie, falaffel, kafta, lamb kebabs and more, all served over rice pilaf. You get a basket of pita bread with your meal, too. Have a cup of Turkish coffee (95¢) and baklava ($1.25) for dessert.

Blazing Salads — 330 Washington St., Boston; 426-0864. In addition to being one of the better puns in the restaurant biz, Blazing Salads is an extremely popular lunchtime spot for office workers in the Downtown Crossing area. The food is cheap indeed, and very healthy.

Yes, there are lots of salads and vegetarian delights on the menu, but don't shy away, carnivores! There are also plenty of good ol' meat items as well. Common ground for those culinary mixed marriages. You're just as likely to find a "Blazing" hot dog with bacon and cheese ($2.63) as a broccoli and veggie pocket ($3.53). Don't ask about the odd prices . . . as long as they're this low, who cares?

The general flavor is Middle

Eastern; even burgers are served in pita bread. A quarter-pound of chopped sirloin, with various toppings, they go for $2.39 or $4.39. So do chicken sandwiches, such as the Calypso ($4.63), a sauteed boneless breast with rice pilaf, cauliflower, broccoli, and cheese packed in. Most entrees come with salad and tabouli. There are steak tip dishes ($4.67), falaffel, hoummos and other Mediterranean items, and rolled-up gyro sandwiches ($3-$5).

The atmosphere is bustling. Place your order, wait in line to pick it up, and then find a seat on one of three levels. At the front of the second floor, looking out over the street, a white upright piano tinkles out popular songs. There are al fresco tables on this balcony, fun if you can get one during good weather.

Bob The Chef's — 604 Columbus Ave., Boston; 536-6204. "Soul Cuisine at It's Finest," boasts the menu, and Mr. C. finds it hard to disagree. Bob the Chef's is located deep in the heart of the south— South End, that is. But not in the yuppified, trendy part of the South End; this is the older, grittier part of the neighborhood, and the joint has the authentic feel of a soul kitchen. You can sit on a stool at the long counter, or walk past the grill— where someone may be carving meat off of a leg bone—and settle into a booth.

This is heavy, down-home food done up properly, according to a friend of Mr. C's. "You have to have the ribs," he advised; and, being originally from Baton Rouge, he clearly knew what he was talking about. Bar-B-Qued Spareribs were a half-dozen or so meaty pork ribs in a sweet sauce, cooked so tender that the meat practically fell off. The dinner costs $9.50, but that includes two side dishes plus a plate of warm, fresh corn bread.

Each of the dinners, ranging from $7.00 to $9.50, offers the same deal. The side dishes include collard greens, (very) sweet pota-

---

Mr. Cheap's Pick
Beacon Hill

✔ **Metro Deli** — On the "back of the hill," a cafeteria that finds more ways to serve fresh turkey than you can shake a drumstick at. While you're eating, folks come around and offer you fresh fruit—no charge.

---

toes, black-eye peas, fresh-cut corn, rice and gravy, mashed turnips, and other southern delicacies. All told, you get a very big meal.

Other house specialties are chicken and dumplings ($8.00)—a large breast or leg quarter swimming in thick brown gravy over egg dumplings. These will stay with you for a long, long time. You can also have your chicken "Glorifried" in a crispy, golden crust. For the truly adventurous, try the "Soul Chitterlings" ($9.50). Our Louisiana expert describes these as "all the parts of a pig that you wouldn't want to eat," somehow cooked into a popular, traditional specialty.

Pan-fried porgy, "The Soul Fish," sells at market prices; but you can also have it in a sandwich version for $4.00. In fact, most of the dinner items can be had as sandwiches; from smothered steak and onions ($6.00) to fried chicken ($3.50). Add a side dish for $1.75 and you have a very cheap meal indeed.

Desserts are homemade and they all look great, if you can fit one in after this kind of meal. Still, try to aim for the pecan pie, $2.00 for a good-sized slice; sweet potato pie is $1.75. Service is nice and fast, by the way.

Boston Sail Loft — 80 Atlantic Ave., Boston; 227-7280. Also, 1 Memorial Drive, Cambridge; 225-2222. For an inexpensive meal that will seem like a big night out on the town, catch some fish at the Sail Loft. Located right on the waterfront, it offers a view of the harbor (very romantic at night). In warm weather you may be able to get a

table out on the deck and pretend you own one of the yachts moored below.

Meanwhile, the food is terrific and moderately priced. For fresh fish, such as bluefish, mako shark, and more, check the blackboard specials. Regular dinners include a huge platter of fish and chips ($7.95), fried shrimp, or scallops ($10.95), and fried boneless breast of chicken in a honey-mustard sauce ($6.95). These come with French fries and French bread, tartar sauce, and cole slaw.

Burgers are big and juicy, starting at $5.25. For a dollar more, though, try a havarti cheese burger or the Sail Loft burger, topped with Genoa salami, mozzarella, peppers, and mushrooms. A bowl of fresh clam chowder is $3.75; or have a cup with half a sandwich for $6.95.

Compared with most of the other joints in this classy neighborhood, the Sail Loft lets you dine like a captain—and may even give you a headstart on saving up for a boat.

Recently, Sail Loft opened a second branch near Kendall Square. Same great food, but alas, no view!

Buddha's Delight — 5 Beach St., Boston; 451-2395. One of the real finds in Chinatown, Buddha's Delight features "Vegetarian Specialties from the Orient." Here that seems to translate into "Vietnamese tofu," but read on: this is in no way a limited dining experience. In fact, it's a wonderful place that just about anyone will enjoy—and Mr. C has never been fond of tofu. But he certainly loved the food, and the prices.

The big secret of Buddha's Delight is the fact that someone has found a way to give tofu some taste; and, more importantly, texture. Try the barbecued tofu and vermicelli ($4.25), and you will think you're eating—yes, chewing on—sliced meat from a pork chop. It comes atop a huge bed of white vermicelli noodles, with a crunchy and delicious spring roll (also vegetarian).

The other substance found throughout the menu is gluten, a wheat product that is used to simulate seafood and chicken. Not all the substitutions are perfect imposters; "roast pork" comes close, and "chicken" slices are a bit less successful. But the point is that they *are* tasty, and you'll never complain that you feel as if you're munching on some sponge from the kitchen. The "gluten fried chicken," for example, comes in a few different preparations (each $6.75)—flavored with ginger, curry, or lemon grass. These give it a lightly spicy taste that isn't too hot to the tongue.

Among appetizers, there are the terrific spring rolls (two for $2.50) mentioned above; Vietnamese gluten and bean cakes ($3.25), which look a bit like deep-fried muffins, with cooked peanuts on top; and the unusual Vietnamese pizza ($3.75), which has nothing to do with dough, cheese, or tomato sauce. It actually looks more like a crispy omelette filled with "pork" tofu and vegetables. Noodle soups, most about $3.75, come in huge, deep bowls—try the steamed noodle with fried tofu and coconut milk.

The list goes on, with moo shi dishes, stir-fried noodles, and "seafood" dishes—all truly vegetarian, of course. For dessert, try one of the two-dozen or so blended fruit milk shakes, each about $2.00. "Pineapple milk with condensed milk shake" and "Pickled lemon with soda" are just a couple of the many exotic choices. Another after-dinner treat is the "Special Phin coffee with sweetened condensed milk" ($1.50)—very sweet, very

strong, and almost syrupy-thick.

A note about the service, which Mr. C rarely criticizes, having spent some time in kitchens himself. Though courteous, the waiter often seemed unattentive and confused; dishes arrived slowly, in random order. One appetizer did not show up until the end of the meal. An acquaintance of Mr. C's noted that this has happened to her a few times, so it is worth mentioning.

Nevertheless, she continues to eat at Buddha's Delight regularly. The restaurant itself is clean and comfortable, and the atmosphere was festive, with a packed house early on a Saturday evening. This is, after all, a place in which two people can eat like kings for a bill that may still come in under $20.00.

Buzzy's Fabulous Roast Beef — 327 Cambridge St., Boston; 523-4896. When Mr. C was first asked to report on the . . . "low-end" dining options around town, he decided to sample one of the area's best-known—and most-knocked—landmarks. Buzzy's has a prime (excuse the pun) location, tucked in between the Charles Street Jail and the Longfellow Bridge/Storrow Drive on-ramps. It offers, at practically any time of day or night, a thousand and one sandwiches and snacks. Can it be any good?

Well, Mr. C has lived to tell the tale. Actually, the food is not too bad, and it certainly is cheap. A double hamburger is $3.75, heavy on the grease. The trademark beef sandwiches start at $2.40, but you'll probably want the super size ($3.55), which is merely respectable. It comes with barbecue sauce and melted cheese.

These ingredients are only average. The meat can be gristly, but it's not grizzly. French fries are $1.75 for the small size, but wow—each fry is a half-potato.

Surprisingly, Buzzy's also has a number of homemade items, like chicken soup packed with meat and vegetables—$2.25 for a large container. There are also chili and beef knishes, and these are hearty.

If you're in the area and in a hurry, Buzzy's is quick and easy.

Crossroads Ale House — 495 Beacon St., Boston; 262-7371. Crossroads, near Kenmore Square, is a local watering hole that also serves up a varied menu of sandwiches and dinners. There are several good beers on tap, including Bass, Guinness, New Castle Brown Ale and Boston Ale, as well as Woodpecker Cider. The clientele is a mix of students and professionals, and the atmosphere is divey but comfortable.

For starters, a bowl of clam chowder (one of the changing soups du jour) is just $1.95. The tossed salad, at $1.95, is nondescript; but for an additional $1.95, you can have it topped with grilled, marinated chicken tenderloins. This is also available with the chef's and Greek salads.

Create your own pizzas, starting from $3.75 for one person and $5.95 for two. Toppings, about 75¢ each, include bacon, pepperoni, meatballs, sausage, and more. An order of buffalo wings is $3.95 for the small and $5.95 large; an unusual variation is the buffalo chicken fingers ($4.95), served with the traditional celery and bleu cheese dressing.

The appetizer combination platter gives you buffalo wings, potato skins, chicken or buffalo fingers, and mozzarella sticks for $5.95.

The chalkboard always lists a half-dozen daily specials, such as fish and chips ($4.95) or grilled shrimp ($6.95), which comes with cooked vegetables. There are various hot sandwiches, such as chicken parmagiana ($4.95) and barbecued beef ($5.25), all of which include your choice of soup, onion rings or hand-cut French fries. The menu also has lots of cold sandwiches, from turkey club ($5.95) to steak and cheese pocket ($3.95), with the same choice of sides.

Burgers, $4.95, are nice and big, made from fresh beef; for an extra 50¢ each you can top them with bacon, cheese, chili, or other items.

The decor is a "crossroads" of Irish pub and college frat house; the crowd can get a bit rowdy at times. Still, the joint is a neighborhood institution, and the food is pretty good.

Deli Haus — 476 Commonwealth Ave., Boston; 247-9712. Deli Haus has been a longtime hangout for the student and artist crowd who "live" in Kenmore Square. It boasts a large and varied menu and is one of the few restaurants in Boston that stay open until 2:00 in the morning—a good place for a bite after leaving one of the nearby clubs.

The atmosphere is mellow and funky. There is low lighting, a small counter, and high-backed wooden booths with individual jukeboxes. The prices are not rock bottom, but you won't leave hungry.

Appetizers include ethnic specialties like meat or potato knishes

---

Mr. Cheap's Picks
Chinatown

✔ **Buddha's Delight** — More than just a veggie heaven; one of the few to make tofu a treat. Delicious food and lively atmosphere.

✔ **Eldo Tea House** — At the other end of Beach Street, near the archway, a simple kitchen-with-tables setup. Their vast menu boasts tons of entrees around $4.00 to $5.00.

(three for $4.25) and homemade soups. Breakfast is not such a bargain, unless you can handle the "Beat the Haus" special: three eggs, five strips of bacon, German fries and three slices of toast for $5.75. Your arteries will love you for it.

There is a tremendous selection of sandwiches, both hot and cold: basic varieties range from egg salad ($2.95) to hot corned beef or roast brisket ($4.95). Or try Romanian pastrami, or imported sardines (a full tin!). Moving right along, "3-D's" are huge triple-deckers with combinations such as chopped liver with salami, lettuce, tomato, and Russian dressing; all are made on your choice of bread and come with potato chips for about $6.50.

Sloppy joes add another layer, for about another buck. Number 3, for example, packs turkey breast, corned beef, roast beef, and baked ham with lettuce, cole slaw and dressing for $7.85. Not cheap, but you could easily take half of it home for another chowdown.

In the hot category, the barbecued beef sandwich ($5.25) is thinly sliced beef dripping with a tangy sauce on a bulkie roll, served with plenty of French fries. German franks ("Two really big ones," as the menu says) can be boiled or broiled and come with baked beans and potato salad for $5.95. Big, charbroiled burgers are $4.65, with fries.

The dinners have similar prices, making better deals. The charbroiled "Chuckwagon" steak, at $7.25, comes in a sizzling sauce with salad, potato, and a vegetable. Or try a char-broiled half-chicken, with cranberry sauce, salad, and fries, for $6.25. You can also mix the two for $7.25. Baked eggplant parmagiana serves up a big helping with a salad for just $4.95.

The fill-you-up approach extends to the desserts, offering an array of giant ice cream sundaes such as the "Thursdae"— scoops of Dutch chocolate and Turkish coffee ice cream topped with coffee syrup, sliced bananas, toasted nuts, whipped cream and a cherry for $4.25. There are New York-style egg creams, too.

In fact, this place reminds Mr. C. very much of New York— the kind of joint you can wander into somewhere in the Village or on the upper West Side. Of course, these are not New York prices. Try it as a cheap getaway!

Deli Haus has beer and wine: there is also a take-out counter.

Dixie Kitchen — 182 Massachusetts Ave., Boston; 536-3068. Located along that international stretch of Mass. Ave. between the Berklee College of Music and Symphony Hall, the Dixie Kitchen serves up the cuisine that's music too: Cajun. Neon instruments beckon from the front windows, and zydeco music whoops it up on the speakers. The food will make you as happy as the music.

The menu and portions are large and the prices are small— Mr. C's kind of place. Start off with a huge bowl of gumbo; at $3.75, it's big enough for two to share. It's a thick, spicy stock filled with crab and shrimp, or chicken and sausage, and served with a plate of white rice to mix in.

Other appetizers include homemade Texas chili, baked oysters in a shrimp and garlic sauce, extra-spicy zydeco wings, and deep-fried alligator tail (yes, really!).

You may then want to move on to the hearty 'Po' Boy' sandwiches—fried catfish, shrimp, oysters or chicken on a French bread roll with a sharp remoulade sauce. Half-pound burgers come topped with your choice of jalapenos, chili, creole sauce or barbecue sauce, plus fries. These are all $5.00 to $6.00.

But then you'd miss out on the *real* Cajun delicacies. Jambalaya is a heaping plate of fried rice with smoked sausage, shrimp, and chicken mixed in, served with a dense, warm hunk of jalapeno corn bread—all for $6.95. Catfish Marguery ($7.95) is pan-cooked in a sauce of shrimp, mushrooms, parmesan cheese, and garlic. "Dixie Ribs" arrived hanging out over the edge of the plate—half a dozen meaty slabs in a tangy, not-hot barbecue sauce, sitting on a bed of rice, with cooked corn and beans on the side—all for $7.25. Plenty to share or take home.

Being much too full at the time to test them, Mr. C will have to return soon to try the pecan-breaded chicken or catfish, which sound wonderful too. Speaking of pecans, the desserts are homemade—pecan, apple and sweet potato pies, and a zippy bread pudding served with either whiskey or lemon sauce. Be sure to have a cup of "Cafe du Monde" with it; that's the name of the French Quarter spot famous for its strong coffee and "beignets," hot fried doughnuts. You can even pick up a box of beignet mix on your way out, in case y'all want to bring a bit of Dixie into your own kitchen.

EJ's Restaurant — 840 Commonwealth Ave., Boston; 731-6174. This spot on the Boston University campus has changed hands several times over the years, and changed cuisines along with the names. But whether Mexican, Italian, or Middle Eastern, it remains an inexpensive local fixture.

Currently known as EJ's, the menu mixes your basic pizza and calzones with more substantial Mediterranean fare. The falaffel, hummus, baba ganoush, and tabouli sandwiches are just $2.00, rolled in pita bread with lettuce, tomato, and tahini sauce. Meat kebab sandwiches, whether beef, chicken, kafta, or kibby, are $2.99, while lamb is $3.50. Perhaps the lowest prices around.

Also cheap are the combination platters, offering various groupings of three items. Vegetarian plates, offering combos such as falaffel, grape leaves, and baba ganoush, are $3.99. Meat versions, like the chicken, hummus, and

tabouli plate, are $4.99.

There are also daily specials: Eggplant with ground lamb and tomato, served over rice, was $3.95. All of the dinner platters are good-sized portions. Some items can be less than terrific in quality: the grilled chicken was tasty, but Mr. C found the falaffel overcooked and dry. You can check the food out behind the glass at the ordering counter; this may help in making your choices.

The atmosphere is cavernous, with all tables in high-backed booths clustered in one part of the otherwise empty space. The ceilings are very high, and the building has an industrial feel to it. Still, the clientele is lively, and being located across from BU's School for the Arts, it can be fun listening to conversations or just watching the folks go by.

Eldo Tea House — 57 Beach St., Boston; 338-2128. The Eldo Tea House is a tiny, simple room in Chinatown with a huge and varied menu that crosses the borders of several continents. After all, in what other Chinese restaurant can you order "Spam Ham and Egg Macaroni in Soup"? Many of the more interesting dishes here are combinations of Chinese and American items, as well as cooking styles from elsewhere in the Orient.

Almost everything is very inexpensive, and you can have a great meal—probably a healthy one, too—even for around $5.00. Lots of the bargain dishes are the unusual soups in big, deep bowls, like watercress and pork for two ($3.75) or sliced beef with noodles ($3.25). The house special soup is stocked with shrimp, squid, broccoli, noodles, and a piece of fried pork in the center. At $3.75, it's a meal all by itself.

Rice plates offer many inexpensive options and, again, strange combinations—such as rice with baby shrimps and scrambled eggs ($4.25). Veal chops with rice in a pepper-black bean sauce are just $4.50. And the more daring may want to try baked ox tongue with rice ($4.25).

Chinese spaghetti is another example of the cross-breeding here: try it topped with sliced beef in tomato sauce ($3.95); or with baked seafood ($4.95), which includes scallops, squid and shrimp.

There is, of course, plenty of more traditional Cantonese cooking. Most seafood dishes are priced between $6.00 to $9.00; beef and chicken dishes are all around $6.00. Preparations range from sweet and sour to satay to curry, which brings us back to the offbeat nature of the menu. There is a whole slew of entrees from Hong Kong and Singapore, which tend toward the spicy—like laksa, served in a large soup bowl with noodles and chicken, pork, beef, or shrimp ($3.95 each). The spices are tangy but not the kind that will set your mouth on fire.

By the way, you get your choice of noodle in many of these soups: pick from egg noodles, fat rice noodles, or rice vermicelli. This is definitely the kind of place where you will want to experiment with repeat visits—and at these prices, you can afford to do so.

Fajitas & 'Ritas — 25 West St., Boston; 426-1222. A novel approach to Mexican food: Mix and match your ingredients by circling exactly what you want—and how much of each item—on an order form. For example, a single chicken fajita plate is $8.10; additional orders will be $7.38 if you're going to share. There are also beef, shrimp, and vegetable fajitas. They all come to your table in a piping hot skillet, with guacamole, pico de gallo sauce, and tortillas.

Nachos are the other staple here, and they offer even more choices, allowing you to "build" your own nacho plate with such toppings as beans, chili, chicken, extra cheese, etc. The concept extends to the "'Ritas" as well—circle on the rocks or frozen, twelve-ounce or liter, regular or strawberry. Plenty of good beers on the list, too, including Pacifico, Tecate, Sierra Nevada and Lone Star; also, sangria and Sutter Home wines.

The atmosphere is part of the show at F & R; it's rollicking during the evenings, with the added fun of crayons and white paper table coverings so you can doodle while you eat. Past masterpieces are usually on display.

Hsin Hsin Chinese Noodle Restaurant — 25 Massachusetts Ave., Boston; 536-9852. Near Mass. Ave. and Beacon Street is a new restaurant that seems to belong in the heart of Chinatown. Hsin Hsin is a small, simple noodle house where you can get a lot of basic dishes for very reasonable prices.

The place has only about ten tables, and so is geared to take-out. The atmosphere is attractive, clean and casual, and so is the menu; noodles and soups, that's about it. Simple and good. The

---

Mr. Cheap's Picks
Downtown Boston

✓ **Sami's** — In the Longwood Medical Area, this convoy of food wagons has grown into take-out heaven. Each stand offers different cuisines, from Middle Eastern to Mexican to deli.

✓ **Sultan's Kitchen** — In the financial district, this place is packed every lunch hour. Great Mediterranean fare from a quick counter; find a table upstairs or take it back to the office.

soups include egg drop, wonton, or hot and sour, each about $1.75. Among appetizers, just the basics: Peking ravioli ($3.75), spring rolls ($2.50), scallion pancakes ($2.75), all yummy.

The main dishes divide into about five offerings each of soup noodles (all $4.75), fried noodles ($5.25 each), chow foon ($5.50), lo mein (around $5.50) and fried rice ($4.50). The portions are very generous, so you'll have plenty of leftovers.

Mr. C loved the egg drop soup, which was delicious and a bit salty, with mushrooms and scallions floating in it. Beef chow foon with pepper and onions consisted mostly of the wide rice noodles; not enough beef mixed in. Try the house special fried noodles ($6.50), crispy noodles with chicken, shrimp, beef, and vegetables. Cold sesame noodles are also tasty, with that slightly spicy, nutty sauce.

The service is friendly and attentive; Hsin Hsin is a great place for a quick, simple Chinese meal.

Kangaroo Restaurant — 738 Commonwealth Ave., Boston; 566-9288. This is one of Boston's many family-run Greek coffee shops; a place where you can always get a nice, big plate of food that will fill you up without emptying your wallet.

Much of the food is homemade, such as the soups, chili, and chowder (95¢ to $2.85). Spinach pies are $1.50. Pita sandwiches, appropriately called Kangaroo Pouches, can be filled with Greek salad ($2.89), thin-sliced steak ($3.69), or hummus, tabouli, and falaffel ($3.99). There are also regular deli-style sandwiches and quarter-pound burgers.

Apart from the two-skewer beef shish kebab dinner at $9.95, all of the hot dinners are in the $4.00-to-$7.00 range. These include Greek specialties like beef or chicken souvlaki, lokaniko sausage with rice and salad, and American food—fried chicken, fish and chips, or an open steak sandwich plate.

The Kangaroo is mostly a breakfast and lunch place, closing up by early evening and all day Sunday.

Kenmore Cafe — 539 Commonwealth Ave., Boston; 536-4444. A welcome addition to Kenmore Square—replacing a fast-food chicken place—is Kenmore Cafe. Its menu is infinitely more varied, interesting, and best of all, homemade.

Starting with breakfast at 6:00 every morning, the cafe offers three "Kenmore on the Run" quick specials for $2.75, such as scrambled eggs with bacon and cheese rolled up in pita bread. Steak and eggs are just $4.95, with home fries and toast.

Elsewhere the menu favors Middle Eastern fare, with falaffel sandwiches for $3.50, or "The Nile" ($5.50)—a plate of char-broiled spicy lamb and beef, served with rice, hummus, fatoosh, and a house sauce.

But there are plenty of American items too; Mr. C enjoyed the daily special, marinated grilled chicken ($4.95) with salad and a heap of very tasty rice pilaf. Fried chicken is also on the bill, and a grilled swordfish steak with fries is $5.95.

Then there are deli sandwiches, burgers (from $1.95), and sixteen-inch pizzas with your choice of up to five toppings, for $8.50. The food is delicious; and good news for the Square—it's served until 1 a.m. every night.

Kingston Deli And Grill — 83 Summer St., Boston; 338-8572. This large, clean cafeteria is a great place to escape the hustle and bustle of shoppers and business people racing around Downtown Crossing. It has two dining rooms and a large menu of breakfasts, sandwiches, and hot meals. Nothing is over $5.00.

For breakfast, two eggs and bacon with home fries and toast are $2.45. Omelettes are mostly $2.85. Sandwiches may be pouches, clubs and combos (all

$3.00 to $5.00), like the Black Russian— turkey, ham, salami, Swiss, lettuce, tomato, onion, cole slaw, and Russian dressing, all for $4.25.

Hot platters include chicken kebabs or steak tips over rice, with salad, each $4.95. Also in the same price range are roast beef, chicken, or turkey, with mashed potatoes and a vegetable. Check the billboard for daily soups and specials, too.

La Famiglia — 112 Salem St., Boston; 367-6711. Also, 19 Bennington St., East Boston; 567-1060. La Famiglia is a wonderful home-style kitchen featuring "Roman cooking at its best." The best thing about it is the value, because the portions here are enormous. Chances are you'll have leftovers to take with you.

The food is delicious. Pasta dishes, cooked to order in the open kitchen, range from the basic garlic and oil ziti ($4.95) to fettucine alfredo ($6.95), spinach lasagna ($7.95), mussels marinara with linguine ($6.95), tortellini with pesto ($8.95), and many more.

Chicken entrees range from $6.95 to $8.95, including piccata, parmigiana, or a version made with a ham, pea, and mushroom cream sauce. Veal dishes offer similar choices—the prices go over ten dollars, but again, you get a *lot*. Same goes for the house specials, easily big enough for two people to share. Try the La Famiglia Special ($13.95)—veal and chicken pieces with mushrooms and onions in a creamy pesto sauce, served over tri-color cheese tortellini. Mmmmmm.

There are also things like subs and steak tips, but you'll miss out on the true experience. Friendly wait staff, too. Gorge yourself.

La Piccola Venezia — 63 Salem St., Boston; 523-9802. Piccola Venezia is another of the great family-style pasta houses in the North End. This is the kind of place for basic, hearty home cooking, from a large plate of spaghetti and meat sauce ($3.95) to a tender, huge veal parmigiana ($9.95, with pasta).

The pasta dishes mostly range from $6.95 to $8.95, and again, they're big. There's baked ziti, spaghetti carbonara, manicotti, and many others to choose from. There are also veal, chicken, or sausage cacciatore ($8.50 each), with your choice of pasta, as well as tripe and polenta dishes.

There are salads and antipasto, soups like pasta with lentils or escarola with meatballs ($2.95 each), and several lunch specials, all around $4.00. Beer and wine are served.

The tables are crammed in and the atmosphere is always bustling around the dinner hour; there is often a line out the door. If you have a big appetite, the wait will be worth it.

Mal's New York Style Delicatessen — 708 Commonwealth Ave., Boston; 536-8676. Mal's is a longtime fixture on the Boston University campus, a place where both students and professionals are lunchtime regulars. It's a bustling little place packed with tables (there are a couple just outside the door, if the weather is nice); you call your order out at the counter, find a table if you can, and pick up the food.

Mal himself is usually cranking the orders out, a model of efficiency after all these years who still manages a smile amidst the din. He also makes a lot of the food himself. "I got chicken soup today," he answers a patron. "I got corn chowder, I got beef barley, I got . . ."

The soups are scrumptious, a good-sized bowl costing just $1.15, with a slice of fresh rye bread and butter. Chicken and rice had plenty of both; large pieces of white meat with rice, carrots and spices. Mal also makes homemade potato knishes, big and flaky, for $1.65; chopped liver (sandwich, $3.75); and broccoli and cheese calzones ($3.10) with huge stalks of broccoli sticking out at both ends.

Burgers are a big deal here, with several different varieties starting at $2.35 for a plain quarter pounder. For $3.60 there are six-ounce salsa and teriyaki burgers, and the half-pound "Jughead" tops the list at $3.95. All are made with fresh meat and come on an onion roll with lettuce, tomato, and a pickle. They're drippy, messy, and wonderful.

Sandwiches include hot roast beef, turkey, or reubens for $4.10; and several variations of chicken breast sandwiches, such as the cordon bleu or honey dijon, also $4.10 each. There are no French fries at Mal's (!); go for the homemade potato salad instead.

Mal's opens up early for breakfast, and you can really stuff yourself with the Country Breakfast ($3.75)—two eggs, pancakes, bacon, ham or sausage, toast, home fries and coffee. This is just a breakfast and lunch place, though, closed by late afternoon.

Massimino's Cucina Italiana —
207 Endicott St., Boston; 523-5959. Around the corner from North Station, Massimino's is an elegant, intimate little Italian bistro where the food is good and plentiful. Just about all the entrees are under $10.00.

Start off with a cup of escarole fagioli for $1.25. A shrimp cocktail or clams casino appetizer is $4.95. Most pasta dinners are priced at $5.95, including fettucine alfredo, spaghetti carbonara, and baked tortellini.

Among the other terrific entrees are veal Francaise ($6.95), steak pizzaiola ($8.95), and chicken saltinbocca ($7.95). Seafood dinners are a bit higher, such as shrimp scampi for $9.95; but they're still a good deal, with large portions.

There are several house specialties, too: Massimino's Special consists of shrimp, pasta, and broccoli in cheese sauce ($8.95, or $12.95 for two people). Or, try the sausage, chicken, potato, and peppers plate ($10.95).

All dinners come with pasta on the side. It's pretty hard to go away from here hungry, and this is

a pleasant alternative to the livelier restaurants of the North End.

Metro Deli — 160 Cambridge St.,
Boston; 720-4742. "We cook more turkey every day than any other Massachusetts restaurant," claims the Metro Deli. It's a bold claim, but hey, they could be right—this cafeteria on the back of Beacon Hill does serve up a lot of bird, and it is definitely the real, fresh stuff. Of course, that's not all you can have there.

The complete turkey dinner, at $5.30, consists of several slabs of white meat with stuffing, mashed potato, gravy, and a vegetable of the day. It's a full plate. There are many variations, mostly in sandwich form, such as the "Big Bird Syrian" ($3.95) which nestles stuffing and cranberry sauce in with the meat. A basic turkey sandwich is $2.95 and big. Oh, and don't forget "All-Natural Turkey Soup"—they've got plenty of bones to use, after all—for $1.90, a hearty stock in a bowl brimming with vegetables.

But there is more to life, and the Metro, than ol' Tom. The dinner plates all give you lots of food for around $5.00, like steak tips ($5.75) served oriental-style with peppers and onions over yellow rice. Baked lamb and baked stuffed chicken breast ($5.50 each) and a varying selection of fresh fish dinners such as baked haddock or swordfish ($5.75 each) are always on the menu. Check the chalkboard for other daily specials. Or, if you work by visual suggestion, you can look at all the selections behind the glass counter and just point.

The Metro has all the usual deli stuff, too; burgers (from $2.20), hot and cold sandwiches (open-faced corned beef, $3.75) and salads, including a salad bar.

Breakfast is good here too, with two eggs, home fries, and coffee at $2.10. They also have their own version of Egg McMuffins, with ham, bacon or sausage, for $1.85. And try the banana or blueberry pancakes ($2.75).

A delightful feature at the

Mr. Cheap's Pick
North End

✓ **La Famiglia** — Lines out the door tell the story. Gigantic portions at easy prices, with leftovers guaranteed. Mangia!

Metro is the person who shows up at your table carrying a tray filled with oranges, bananas and apples. Everybody at the table may choose one at no charge. In the evenings, as the day draws to a close, this person may show up more than once. Go ahead, take a couple. How often do you see a gesture like this anywhere?

Mike's Greasy Spoon — 1742 Washington St. (at Mass. Ave.), Boston; 536-1234. Mike's Greasy Spoon is one of those "retro" coffee shops that doesn't feel like a nostalgia show; it's just good, honest home cooking, with a little kitsch but not too much. You can sit at the counter on stools (you know, the kind that spin), or in the soda shop chairs at the tables. The long, narrow restaurant has plenty of each, all in a color scheme of black and white, including the tile floors and walls.

It's located in the up-and-coming part of Boston's South End that hasn't quite come up yet but probably will before too long. For now it's kind of an oasis, but the neighborhood—with its busy hospitals and renovated brownstones—isn't

too bad. And the folks at Mike's are relaxed and friendly.

Mike's serves breakfast and lunch, with plate specials and sandwiches. The morning bargain, weekdays until 10:30, is three eggs with bacon or sausage, served with home fries, toast, and coffee, all for $2.99. An eight-ounce steak and eggs, with fries and toast, is $5.95.

Sandwiches range from grilled cheese ($2.25) to roast beef ($3.75) and Mike's Homecooked Turkey ($4.45). Half-pound sirloin burgers ($2.95 to $3.70) can come with cheese, mushrooms or bacon. And you can always throw in a side of Mike's corned beef hash—a lunch counter fave—for $2.00.

Soups are delicious. Try the chili or the beef stew (each $2.50 per cup, $3.75 per bowl), made with a few zippy spices that Mom never added in. This is the South End, after all.

The platters are also great traditional diner fare. The hot turkey plate ($5.50, or $6.50 for all white meat) includes a nice, thick gravy, vegetables, and corn bread. Meatloaf ($4.95) and fried boneless chicken breast ($5.50) both include

---

Mr. Cheap's Picks
South End

✓ **Bob the Chef's** — Authentic soul food; huge meals under $10.00 that stick to your own ribs for a long time.

✓ **Mike's Greasy Spoon** — Fun and funky diner serving old-fashioned Americana, cheap.

✓ **Tim's Tavern** — The locals don't want you to know about this one. If you brave your way through the bar to the tables at the back, you'll find huge burgers for $2.00. Ribs, extra-large steaks, and seafood too.

---

mashed potatoes with gravy and the vegetable of the day.

Desserts ($2.50 to $2.95) are your basic—chocolate cake, carrot cake, cheese cake, and Boston cream pie. This may put your tab above $10.00, but you sure won't go away hungry.

Our House East — 52 Gainsborough St., Boston; 236-1890. Our House East is more like a sports bar than the cozy Allston original. Located near the New England Conservatory, the Huntington Theater, and Symphony Hall, it attracts a mixture of students and professionals. They all know it as one of the few restaurants in the area that is both affordable *and* attractive. The dining tables are natural blond wood, in a carpeted room adorned with polished brass.

The large menu seems at first glance to consist almost entirely of appetizers. From French onion soup ($2.50) and chili ($3.50) to more unusual items such as buffalo shrimp ($5.95) and boneless buffalo wings ($4.25), the apps alone offer quite a range. There are six different kinds of potato skins, each around $5.00 a plate, filled with cheese, chili, tomato sauce, sirloin tips, and more.

But don't worry, there are plenty of sandwiches and dinners. Nine different burgers are all $4.00 to $5.00; these are charbroiled half-pounders and come with chips, cole slaw, and pickles. Bigger still is the "Our House Burger" ($6.95), which packs— ready for this?— twelve ounces. Good luck.

On the dinner side, choose from a rotisseried half-chicken ($5.95), barbecued ribs ($8.95), chicken marsala ($7.25) and several others. The portions are substantial and nicely prepared.

Speaking of portions, the chef salad ($4.95) is gigantic. It's a brimming bowl of lettuce and spinach with heaps of thinly-sliced turkey, ham, and Swiss cheese. This is not a little nibble—it's a meal in itself.

Our House East also serves a big Sunday brunch from 12 p.m. to 3 p.m., where $4.25 gets you one of several cooked egg dishes along with a bagel and pastry buffet.

A separate bar area features wide-screen TV for sports events, with plenty of beers on tap in large mugs. A snack menu is available. A word to the health-conscious, though: The restaurant does not have a smoke-free area. Must be one of the last such places in Boston.

Paramount Restaurant & Deli — 44 Charles St., Boston; 523-8832. How these guys got into the chic world of Charles Street— with its pricy antique shops and trendy boutiques—is a mystery, but a happy one. Maybe you've blown a bit too much on a silver-plated chafing dish for your cat, and you're feeling a bit hungry yourself; but you'd never spend that much on your own meal. Step into the Paramount and have a roast chicken dinner for $4.95, or a cheeseburger from the grill for $1.95.

Yes, it's your basic cafeteria, somehow mixed in with the nobs. Grab a tray and tell the man what you want. Maybe baked macaroni and cheese ($3.25) or a huge bowl of beef stew ($3.55). Mr. C tried the chicken soup ($1.85), a large bowl of thick stock with bits of chicken, carrots, and rice.

Beef over rice or noodles ($4.75) is a hearty meal, as are the souvlaki or turkey dinners ($5.95 each). Or you can have a veal cutlet sandwich ($2.75); or breakfast all day, like two eggs and bacon for $3.25 or an omelette for $2.35.

The Paramount serves beer and wine and, unlike many such places, stays open in the evenings. Filling, heartwarming and cheap.

Pour House Restaurant — 907 Boylston St., Boston; 236-1767. People have found the Pour House out—it used to be a divey, unassuming sort of place to get a big meal cheap. More recently, it's been discovered by more and more students, yuppies and regular folks. So now, despite its two levels, you can have a tough time finding a booth, even on a weeknight.

Nevertheless, the joint remains a rowdy, funky place with good, cheap food. Diner food is big here, like the grilled meatloaf sandwich on white bread, served with mashed potatoes, gravy and vegetables for $4.25. Or, try one of the daily specials, such as spaghetti and meatballs with garlic bread for $3.95.

Burgers are also popular, starting at just $2.25 for the basic fresh quarter pounder. Best deal is the "Pour Boy," with two patties, bacon, cheese, and sauteed onions for $3.25. All come with fries and, for some reason, potato chips.

Mexican food makes up the flip side of the menu. As an appetizer, the Mexican pizza ($3.95) is a *huge* flour tortilla with enchilada sauce, cheddar cheese, onions, black olives, and jalapenos. Seven-pepper chili ($1.95 a cup) heats your mouth up slowly. And among the main dishes, the giant burrito ($5.25) is another big flour tortilla, filled with cheese and your choice of beef, chicken, or veggies and covered with enchilada sauce.

There are plenty of good beers to wash all this down, of course. In addition to all the booths, there are long, long bars both upstairs and down. Oh, and if you can make it to dessert, how about New York cheesecake with strawberries for just $2.25? Won't find it too often at that price. The Pour House is still a bargain after all these years.

Province Place — 44 Province St., Boston; 357-6861. Located on a side street around the corner from Filene's, Province Place is one of those breakfast and lunch places that mainly serve the business-suit crowd. It's popular and busy at lunch hour, a good sign from those finicky folks who, after all, eat lunch out every day. The prices here are not rock-bottom, but you do get a hefty sandwich for your money.

Breakfast, served from 7 a.m. to 11 a.m., ranges from two eggs (any style) with toast and home fries ($1.75) to mushroom omelottes, same fixings ($3.25) to sirloin steak and eggs ($6.25). For something cheap and quick, try a "Breakfast Sandwich"—a sunnyside egg and cheese on an English muffin—for just $1.40.

Most sandwiches are in the $6.00 range, but as noted above, you'll be stuffed. Check the board for daily specials such as the chicken cutlet sandwich: a whole breast of chicken, fried and topped with tomato sauce, served on a thick sesame bun.

Other sandwiches include barbecued beef, sirloin tips, veal parmagiana, and more. Tuna fish and chicken salads check in under $5.00. You can add a side of steamed vegetables for $1.25, but hey— heavy food calls for a plate of big, thick French fries ($1.50). All of the sandwiches can be ordered in platter form with vegetables, making a dinner-sized meal, for about $7.25.

Service is cafeteria-style; it's also a good place for take- out. Remember, as a business-world deli, they close around 3:00, and all day Sunday.

Remington's — 124 Boylston St., Boston; 574-9676. This venerable theater district restaurant is one of the few places in the area where you can have a full dinner or late night snack that isn't overpriced or over-trendy. It's a casual, comfortable place with dining rooms on two levels, and since they serve food until midnight, it's good for before or after the show.

Start off with appetizers, like several varieties of potato skins, deep-fried and filled with cheese, bacon, chili and the like. It's $3.50 for a plain plate and up to $4.75 for the "Chef's Assortment," which changes daily. Nachos with cheese and chili ($4.50), marinated chicken wings ($4.95) and a platter of cheese, fresh fruit, and French bread ($4.50) are also good choices.

There are lots of soups and salads to choose from, such as a crock of French onion bubbling with cheese ($2.95) or homemade beef stew with French bread ($4.50). Antipasto, Greek, and chef's salads are each $4.95; a garden salad is $2.95.

Burgers and sandwiches are terrific and cheap. "The Basic Burger" is $4.25, but for just 50¢ more you can add cheddar, American, or Swiss cheese and hot sauteed mushrooms or bacon. The Philly cheese steak sandwich ($4.95) includes onions, mushrooms, and melted cheese. A hefty corned beef on dark rye ($4.50) and crabmeat and seafood salad in a pita pocket ($4.95) are among the other highlights. All of the above come with fries, potato salad, or macaroni salad.

There are varying daily choices of a half-sandwich and soup or a half-sandwich and salad, each $4.50. And for $4.95 you can get a monster sandwich called Remy's Rathskellar—a "mile high" pile of corned beef, Swiss cheese, lettuce, tomato, potato salad, and Russian dressing on dark rye bread.

Moving up the scale to entrees, there are many inexpensive choices. Several dinners go for $6.95 to $7.95, including steak tips, broiled schrod, fish and chips, and Hawaiian chicken. Each comes with salad and fries or rice and makes for a fine meal.

The building that houses Remington's was originally a bank. Downstairs you can still see the giant vault and some of the stone foundation walls. It's nice to know, however, that even amidst the chic nightclubs and touristy restaurants, this is one place where you won't have to break the bank for dinner.

Sami's Outdoor Eatery — 299 Longwood Ave., Boston; 327-SAMI. The Longwood Medical Area may not sound like a place to dine, but anyone who works in the many hospitals or office buildings nearby knows that this place is always hopping at the lunch hour. The established king of the hill is Sami's, a booming enterprise that has grown from a falafel wagon to an en-

closed stand that operates (ooh, Mr. C apologizes for that pun) twenty-four hours a day, seven days a week.

What's more, Sami's has sprouted several sister wagons, making a sort of culinary convoy—each offering a different menu, from pizza to deli to Mexican. It all makes for a vast selection of good food at very cheap prices. There are over fifty choices on the Middle Eastern menu alone.

Falaffel and hummus, Sami's original bread and butter, come rolled up together in a foot-long pita for the picayune price of $3.48 (most of their prices are funny that way). The falafel is fresh and moist, and it's a meal in itself. All the usual choices are here: tabouli, baba ganoush, stuffed grape leaves, beef and chicken kebabs. The combinations are endless.

Shawarma, marinated meat that is slowly roasted and thinly sliced, also comes in a pita with lettuce, tomato, and dressing. The chicken or beef and lamb versions are each $3.95. You can have dinners too, such as chicken shish kebab over rice; or kafta, ground lamb and beef mixed with onions and spices, also over rice ($5.66 each).

There are also special daily items, such as a lentil soup ($1.50) that had a lemony tang to it. And do try the baklava for dessert (only 95¢), which is very light and very sweet.

On the Mexican side, a popular item is the nacho salad ($2.75), which consists of lettuce, tomatoes, sour cream, salsa, and olives, served on tortilla chips with melted cheese on top. It's pretty big, too. Add beans (25¢ extra), ground beef (50¢), guacamole (75¢), or have them all for $3.95.

Sami's also serves fajitas ($3.50), tacos ($1.60 to $2.50), chili ($1.50 a cup), and burrito salads, similar to the nacho salads, served in a crunchy tortilla bowl ($3.00 to $4.25).

Deli sandwiches offer such

choices as homemade roast pork ($3.25 in a pocket, or $3.85 on a large sub roll), or smoked turkey breast ($3.50 to $4.10). Cooked sandwiches include Polish kielbasa ($2.25); there are also charbroiled chicken dinners, from $2.00 for a leg and thigh served with garlic spread, to $4.95 for a half-chicken platter with salad and fries or rice pilaf.

You get the idea. You can have something different every day at Sami's, without repeating anything for quite a while. When the weather is nice, the tables outside the stand are packed; otherwise, you'll have to eat indoors somewhere.

Answering this need is the new Longwood Galleria mall, located across the street. It has an upstairs food court and atrium of the type found in most new malls, and nestled in among the fast-food chains is another Sami's outlet. The prices are slightly higher here, but just a bit. And the surroundings are much more pleasant than the busy street below.

Sorrento's Italian Gourmet — 86 Peterborough St., Boston; 424-7070. Part of the urban hip renaissance in the Fenway, Sorrento's is a warm, cozy upscale pasta and pizza spot. Its prices nudge up against Mr. C's limits, but you get good, hearty portions of delicious food.

Baked in a brick oven, the pizzas and calzones smell fabulous the minute you walk in. Pizzas start at $7.30 for a basic cheese; the large size is $9.40. Toppings are 85¢ each, with all the yuppie faves. Special pies include melanzana, with fried eggplant, tomato sauce, and romano and mozzarella cheeses. Napoli, their version of the works, has mushrooms, roasted pepper, prosciutto, and chicken pesto.

Fifteen different pasta dishes all range from $7.00 to $10.00. The most basic is rigatoni; have it with broccoli and chicken, or try linguine carbonara, pasta primavera, or Chicken a l'Abruzzi— chicken breast pate sauteed in olive oil with spinach. It's served with a basil cream sauce, over a bed of capellini, all for $8.80.

The atmosphere is casual and pleasant, with a black-and-white tile floor, natural wood chairs, and an open kitchen. Could just as easily be Soho.

Stars Ocean Chinese Seafood— 70-72 Kilmarnock St., Boston; 236-0384. Stars Ocean is a simple, unpretentious Chinese food restaurant in an out-of-the-way location: The Fenway. While it might have been lost in the sauce in China-town, here it stands out for good food, a large menu, and low prices.

For starters, Mr. C (guided by a newspaper clipping in the window) tried the Shanghai spring rolls (two for $2.75). Indeed, these were freshly made, served up hot and crisp, with a filling of cabbage and shrimp that was slightly tangy to the tongue. The menu specializes in Cantonese and Mandarin. Peking sesame chicken ($7.95), West

---

Mr. Cheap's Picks
Theater District

✔ **Remington's** — Comfortable (nearly fancy) surroundings and a varied menu that's actually affordable; good for after the show, too.

✔ **Sweetwater Cafe** — Around the corner in the Boylston Place alley, amidst yuppie discos, this place serves up Tex-Mex food at surprisingly good prices.

Lake beef ($8.95)—beef and scallops with vegetables in sauce—and pork fried with lemon grass ($6.95) are all interesting dishes. The portions are quite large and the sauces are tasty.

As the restaurant's name suggests, seafood is the specialty. There are over a dozen different choices for shrimp alone, such as Lake Tung Ting ($8.45), marinated shrimp and vegetables sauteed in a white wine sauce. Elsewhere, "Dragon and Phoenix" ($9.95) combines chicken and lobster meat with vegetables and scallions in a spicy tomato sauce.

Stars Ocean serves generous lunch specials, most for $4.95, with such choices as fried shrimp and chicken teriyaki, roast pork egg foo yong, or spring roll and boneless garlic chicken. Each plate comes with soup, chicken wings, a fried wonton and pork fried rice. Try to finish all that in one sitting. Stars Ocean is the kind of place every neighborhood should have—a basic, good-quality local Chinese restaurant.

Steve's Authentic Greek Cuisine — 316 Newbury St., Boston; 267-1817. Dining cheap on Newbury Street? It's true. If you don't need all those pretentious cafes with prices to match, Steve's is the place in this neighborhood. Most dinner platters are in the $6.00-to-$8.00 range, including gyros, souvlaki, moussaka, falaffel, and various shish kebabs. Each comes as a packed plate with plenty of meat, plus a Greek salad, rice, and pita bread.

Sandwich versions of the same go from $3.50 to $5.00 and still give you a lot to work on. There are also many appetizers, both hot and cold; the spanakopita ($2.65) is a big wedge of spinach and feta cheese inside layers of flaky filo dough, warmed up and served with homemade potato chips. Taramosalata ($3.35) is a caviar salad with potato and spices blended in; for $5.50 you can get a sampler plate combining this with stuffed grape leaves, hummus, eggplant, vegetables, spinach pie, and pita bread.

Desserts include the obligatory baklava, as well as galactobouriko (each around $1.50)—filo dough filled with a sweet custard. Mmmm.

Great for the budget Newbury Street shopper—stop in to refuel after cruising the secondhand clothing stores mentioned elsewhere in this book!

Sultan's Kitchen — 72 Broad St., Boston; 338-8509. Founded by a chef from Turkey, Sultan's Kitchen claims to be the only Turkish restaurant in Boston; it's probably true. It's also one of the great spots in the office building section of downtown—and it's jam-packed at lunchtime.

Fight your way in if you can. The food here is fresh, made with all-natural ingredients, and it's delicious. The setup consists of a counter where you order and pay for your food; then you look for a table nearby, or in the upstairs room, which is pleasantly decorated—though more like a country home than Constantinople.

Anyway, the food is yummy. Soups, at $2.85 for a large twelve-ounce bowl with pita bread, include egg lemon with chicken, a hearty stew; curried lentil; and, on the cold side, cacik (yogurt, cucumber, mint and garlic) and gazpacho.

There are all kinds of salads, from taramosalata, fish roe with olive oil and lemon juice, to well-known Middle Eastern fare such as falaffel, tabouli, and grape leaves. All cost around $5.00 a plate. The meze plate ($6.25) is a great combination of all these vegetarian dishes, with bread. There are soup/salad combinations available for $5.75.

Shish kebabs come in sandwich or dinner form, charcoal-grilled and tasty. Choose from lamb, chicken, kafta (ground lamb mixed with spices), beef or swordfish. The sandwiches, about $5, come with salad; dinners (around $7.00) include salad, rice pilaf, and feta cheese. Charbroiled burgers start at just $2.75, tucked into pita bread with lettuce and tomato.

Baklava, rice pudding, and other desserts are all under $2.00. In addition to coffees, teas, and fruit juices, beer and wines are available. Sultan's Kitchen is only open Monday to Friday, from 11 a.m. to 5 p.m.

Sweetwater Cafe — 3 Boylston Place, Boston; 357-7027. The alleyway between Boylston Street and the CityPlace Atrium, in Boston's theater district, is lined with bars and discos. Sweetwater Cafe, next to Zanzibar, is a rambunctious bar with great Tex-Mex food at very reasonable prices, considering the area.

A huge appetizer of chicken wings is $4.95; a pair of crunchy tacos, filled with beef or chicken ($3.95), comes on a bed of lettuce and olives. The sampler plate ($6.95) gets you a hefty batch of wings, nachos, and potato skins.

Burgers are half-pounders of fresh meat in various styles— Buffalo, barbecue, jalapeno—all in the $5.00-to-$6.00 range. A dinner of chicken fajitas is just $6.95, lower than many other places; and burritos are large at $4.95. Don't miss the chili either, just $1.75 for a cup.

The atmosphere is loud and funky, all in natural Western wood, like a Texas roadside grill. Elvis looks out over the proceedings, as do a shark and some gators. The jukebox bounces from Aretha to the B-52's to Sinatra. Pints of Bass, Sam Adams, and more are on tap.

Tim's Tavern — 329 Columbus Ave., Boston; 247-7894. This tiny nook in the South End has been known to locals for years as a funky neighborhood bar that serves up great, cheap food. Once renowned for Cajun dishes, the menu now mainly sticks to barbecue, with a bit of seafood thrown in.

The front of the joint is a divey bar with plenty of smoke, chatter, and good tunes. Walk through to the back and you'll find a cluster of formica tables, a waitress or two,

and the kitchen. The day's menu is posted on the wall; pick out what you want, tell the waitress, and watch the man at the back cook it for you.

The food, meanwhile, is incredible—and among the cheapest in town. Starting with the burgers, which are billed as "eight ounces or better," you will indeed have fun wrapping your hands around one. Order it loaded—with lettuce, tomato, onions, and mayonnaise. Even with all that the regular burger is $1.75; a cheeseburger is $2.25. Believe it! Crispy French fries or onion rings are a dollar extra.

For dinners there is a good selection, also cheap. How about a good-sized rack of barbecued baby back ribs for $5.50, with rice, rings, or fries—and *that's* the halfrack! A whole rack, at $9.95, will feed an army. Marinated steak tips or lamb skewers (each $4.95) come with the same choice of side dish.

In fact, one of the priciest items on the menu is the "X-Large Sirloin Steak, cut to order," at a whopping $7.50—and that's with a salad and rice or fries. And $7.95 will get you seafood specials like boiled lobster or baked stuffed shrimp.

Beers at the Tavern are strictly basic, like the food. There are no taps, and probably the fanciest bottle is Heineken. But hey, this is cheap, unpretentious dining—at its best.

Trattoria Il Panino — 11 Parmenter St., Boston; 720-1336. Also, 1001 Massachusetts Ave., Cambridge; 547-5818. Tucked into one of the side streets of the North End, Il Panino serves up great fresh pasta dishes quickly and inexpensively.

During the day they have lunch specials for $4.95 in the street-level room, which doubles as a sub shop. Don't be fooled. Each weekday there are two specials to choose from, such as tortellini Alfredo, a hefty slice of lasagna, or penne with mushrooms and broccoli in cream sauce. Every Friday it's lobster. Fresh bread comes with these.

After 3 p.m. the menu expands to over two dozen pasta dishes, all ranging from $6.95 to $9.95. Linguine with clams, ziti with three cheeses, tortellini with pesto, and more. There are also fra diavolo dishes—lobster, clams, calamari, or mussels—as well as chicken, gnocchi, eggplant parmigiana, and more.

For dinner, the trattoria downstairs is a warmer, cozy setting that feels like old Italy—wooden tables nestled against white stucco walls. Il Panino serves beer and wine, and much of its food is made fresh daily on the premises.

BRIGHTON

Bill & Don's Cafe — 386 Western Ave., Brighton; 254-9752. Located in a shopping center between Bed & Bath and Caldor, Bill & Don's Cafe is a great place for a quick meal during errands—your basic cafeteria, but with home cooking and cheap meals.

Breakfast, first of all, is served all day. But if you get there from 6:00 to 10:00 in the morning, you can snag one of the specials—like two eggs, bacon or sausage, home fries, toast, and coffee for $2.59. Daily newspapers are on sale by the register, too.

Later on the guys offer sandwiches, salads, and pizza. But dinners (well, they're only open until 4:00) are the real deals. How about sirloin tips or stir-fry chicken, each with rice or French fries, for just $3.99? Or spaghetti and meatballs for $3.50, chicken parmigiana with spaghetti for $4.50, and fish and chips for $4.75 . . . ?

There are also daily dinner specials five days a week. These offer the likes of salisbury steak, baked meatloaf, or baked breast of chicken dinners for $3.99, lasagna for $3.75, and a fried clam plate for $4.75.

Ambience is minimal at Bill & Don's—formica tables with the seats attached. But the service is friendly, and the regulars who keep stopping in attest to the quality of the food.

Blake's Restaurant — 1096 Commonwealth Ave., Brighton; 566-4144. Perhaps the best part about this luncheonette is not the cheap meals but the matron behind the counter who calls your order out to the cooks in an operatic, heavily-accented voice: "Haaaaammmmburger! Friiiies! One Co-oke!"

For many years this has been a popular spot with BU students and the working crowd. Different daily specials, along with your basic diner standbys ($1.85 for that burger), will stick with you for quite a while. Spaghetti ($3.35), franks and beans ($3.75), veal cutlet plate ($4.75), and chicken croquettes (same) are among the offerings. Most come with potato and vegetable.

Recently, Blake's remodeled with an attractive red and black tile look, individual tables, and ice-cream parlor chairs. They also extended their day to include dinner, serving until 8 p.m.

Bluestone Bistro — 1799 Commonwealth Ave., Brighton; 254-8309. Everyone said these folks were daft to put a funky bistro in the dead stretch of Comm. Ave. between BU and BC. Who would come to such a place? Answer: Everybody. There is an easygoing class about the Bluestone, which manages to be chic without trying too hard. The look of the place, dark marble walls and tables, is actually just painted on. Rhythm and blues give a little beat to the casual atmosphere.

And the food is first-rate, a triumph of cuisine over cash. Pizzas, pastas, and calzones comprise the menu—but these are the kind you'd expect to find on Beacon Hill, not in Brighton. For $6.95, two people can split a pizza with a thick, hot, chewy crust and Bluestone's own sauce. Then, for 75¢ each, add on a variety of toppings, from andouille sausage or artichoke hearts to bay shrimp, blackened chicken, pine nuts, smoked turkey, sun-dried tomatoes, and many more.

Such a pizza may look smallish on the tray, but it comes dense with stuff on top and is very filling and tasty. There are also pizzas for two to four people ($10.95) and just one ($3.95, toppings 50¢ each). Calzones, $5.95, contain five cheeses and your choice of fillings, like chicken with pesto.

The pastas are wonderful too, served with sourdough bread. Try the smoked chicken and herb cheese ravioli ($9.50) in a parsley and spinach sauce; or two-sausage pasta ($7.95) with andouille and chorizo sausages served over rosemary fettucine. There are several others to choose from; they are delicious and the portions are large.

Appetizers are good too, from fresh, thick minestrone ($1.95) or maple-glazed scallops wrapped in bacon ($3.95) to "Prairie Fire" ($4.75), spicy, warm beans with blue corn chips for dipping. It's all good, and popular; on weekends especially, get there early before tables—and many of the pasta dishes—run out. Makes a cool date without breaking the bank.

Brighton Seafood — 60 Washington St., Brighton; 734-0920. Here's a little hole-in-the-wall just below the intersection of Washington Street and Commonwealth Avenue. It's nothing fancy, but has good, basic fish—along with some meat dinners, sandwiches, and salads. The place is geared for take-out but has a half-dozen tables for eating on the premises.

Fish and chips are the store's main calling card. The small, thick chunks of fish are lightly breaded and fried, not greasy at all, though the fries are. A basic box, with three pieces of fish plus fries or Spanish rice, is $3.75; the dinner version, with twice as much fish, is $6.95 and comes with two side orders. The choices include fries, baked potato, salad, cole slaw, onion rings, or rice.

Other fish available, whether fried or broiled, are schrod (lunch $4.75, dinner $6.95); haddock ($5.50/$7.50); bluefish in season, broiled only ($5.50/$7.50); scallops ($6.50/$7.95); and also clams, calamari, shrimp, and sometimes swordfish.

After that, the menu takes a sharp turn: BBQ ribs and half-chicken for $5.95, with two sides; spicy chicken curry, also $5.95; cold tuna or seafood pasta salad, $3.95; stuffed shells, $4.95.

Brighton Seafood gets fresh fish daily and uses cholesterol-free, salt-free vegetable oil. The place is clean and the service is friendly.

Corrib Pub — 396 Market St., Brighton; 254-2880. Also, 201 Harvard St., Brookline; 232-8787, and 2030 Centre St., West Roxbury; 469-4177. The Corrib has been a landmark in Brighton Center for many years, and it is easy to see why. The atmosphere is relaxed, with a mix of locals and younger folks; the dark wood surroundings are pleasant; and the food is great and plentiful.

Both lunch and dinner are served, and in either case you'll get a lot. At dinner, Mr. C ordered grilled swordfish steak ($7.95), expecting perhaps a small center cut. What he netted instead was a huge, thick hunk of fish with a fine grilled taste. But that's not all. Each dinner entree comes with a good, fresh salad (or soup), potato or rice, and a side vegetable.

It's a sizeable platter indeed, costing as little as $5.95 (for the chicken marsala). Other dinners include chicken Maryland ($6.95) sauteed in orange juice, pineapple, and banana; steak tips ($7.50) marinated in a house sauce; and toppers on the menu (at $7.95) were broiled scallops or New York sirloin—a twelve-ounce center cut. There are also daily specials.

Homemade beef stew ($1.95 for a cup, $3.25 for a bowl) is a hearty one indeed. Burgers are large and fresh, starting at $3.60; they come with great, crisp French fries, as well as lettuce, tomato, and pickles. Sandwiches ($3.25 to $4.25) include hot pastrami, sliced chicken, and grilled barbecued roast beef. Again, these come with fries, lettuce, tomato, and pickles.

There are lots of great Irish and local beers on tap, friendly service and generously-portioned food. Corrib is a great place to stop in for a pint or a hearty, inexpensive meal. Recently, another Corrib opened in Coolidge Corner; they also have a location in West Roxbury.

Green Briar Restaurant And Pub

— 304-306 Washington St., Brighton; 789-4100. The Green Briar is a handsome recent addition to Brighton Center's strong Irish community. The food here, like so many pubs, is terrific; the bar, with its wide selection of Irish beers (including Murphy's Stout and Woodpecker Cider), is neatly partitioned from the restaurant area.

Lunch is quite reasonably priced, and though many dinner entrees go well above ten dollars, there are still plenty of cheaper options. The best bargains of all are found on Monday through Wednesday evenings, when a two-for-one special is offered at just $10.95. Patrons have a choice of four or five dishes, such as barbecued baby back ribs, teriyaki beef, or broiled schrod.

There are lots of appetizers, from buffalo chicken wings ($3.95) to fried zucchini and mushrooms ($3.95) and individual pizzas ($4.95) with your choice of toppings. Burgers start at just $3.95 for a thick half-pounder on a bulkie roll with lettuce, tomato, pickle, and steak fries. Additional toppings are 45¢ each, including various cheeses, bacon, mushrooms, and sauteed peppers and onions.

Among the dinner plates there is chicken teriyaki ($6.95) served over rice pilaf; fish and chips ($6.95)—large, plump haddock fillets, not greasy—and pork chops ($8.95)—two chops served with salad and vegetable. There are daily luncheon and dinner specials every weekday, and an all-you-can-eat Sunday brunch from 10:30 to 2:30 for a reasonable $6.95.

This is a good time to mention that the Green Briar is home to a regular "sesiun" on Monday nights: that's an open jam session on traditional Irish instruments. A good crowd gathers each Monday to bow the fiddle, or just listen in, from about 9 p.m. on. Unlike many Irish bands, this music is not amplified, which is the way it should be. Late in the evening, the pub even brings out complimentary sandwiches for all. It makes for one of Mr. C's favorite entertainment options.

Live music can also be heard at the Green Briar on Thursday, Friday, and Saturday nights from 9 p.m. to 1 a.m., featuring many of Boston's best Irish bands. The cover charge is only $2.00. Be sure to pick up a copy of "The Local" here, a free monthly magazine devoted to Irish music and the Boston pub scene.

Jim's Deli And Restaurant

— 371 Washington St., Brighton; 787-2626. Jim's is an interesting combination—a Greek-style cafeteria in an Irish neighborhood. It works. The place is simple, cheap and friendly. Nothing fancy here, just your basic deli and grill; grab a tray, tell the man what you want (you can look at most of the choices and point yours out) and pay for it at the end. There are plenty of tables, and the restaurant is pleasant and clean.

What's good here? The dinner plates will give you a lot for your money. There are always blackboard specials, like baked haddock ($5.25), chicken parmagiana ($4.25) or an open-face roast beef dinner ($4.95). These come with your choice of mashed or baked potato and rice or cooked vegetables. Whatever you choose, your plate will be heaped with food.

Regular dinners include spaghetti piled high with two huge meatballs ($3.85), fish and chips ($4.30), chicken kabobs ($4.60), sirloin tips ($4.90) and the slightly spicy Greek sausage, loukaniko

($4.90). There are many others, and most come with the above choice of side dishes.

Jim's has several seafood dinners, and the fish is quite good: the baked haddock, for example, was plump and moist, a good-sized serving. You can also try the clam plate ($6.60), though the scallop and shrimp plates verge on the expensive side. Stick with the salmon croquettes ($4.55), a true diner food if ever there was one.

Of course, it wouldn't be a deli without burgers and subs—just your basic—and reasonably priced; it wouldn't be a Greek deli without gyros. The sandwich, on pita bread, is $3.60 with French fries. Desserts include homemade bread pudding and baklava.

Jim's is also a nice breakfast spot. The $1.99 special offers two eggs any style, with home fries, toast, and coffee—with free refills. A cheese omelette is $2.95 with fries and toast, and two eggs with loukaniko are $3.95. Or go for the blueberry pancakes, $3.25 for a stack.

The quality of the food is fine, and the portions are large. The folks behind the counter are friendly and pressure-free. If the place isn't busy, they may even bring your food out to your table. What more could anyone ask of a cafeteria?

Mandy & Joe's Deli And Restaurant — 328 Washington St., Brighton; 254-9843. In spite of the name, Mandy & Joe's is really a coffee shop, just the kind you'd expect to find in the old-world heart of Brighton Center. It has a long, winding lunch counter and tables, a grill, and regular American diner food.

The meals include two or three daily specials, such as boneless chicken breast ($3.95); it comes with cooked vegetables, mashed potatoes, and cranberry sauce, all covered in gravy. While the breaded cutlet is the frozen kind, and the peas came out of a can, the potatoes were definitely homemade, as was the thick gravy. A decent, cheap meal.

Other good items were the sausage dinner ($3.25), with the same sides; fish cakes and beans ($2.75); and chicken pot pie or chicken croquettes (each $4.25). Better yet is the hot roast beef sandwich ($3.45), cooked with sliced onions and served on a roll with melted cheese over the top.

Mandy & Joe's also serves breakfast all day. Two eggs and bacon or sausage, with toast, costs $2.95; corned beef and hash with eggs is $3.95. Being that this is a breakfast and lunch place, though, it closes around 4 p.m.

Peking Gardens — 377 Washington St., Brighton; 787-0293. One of the many Chinese eat-in or take-out joints in the Brighton Center/Oak Square area. The food here is better than many other such places,

---

Mr. Cheap's Picks
Brighton

✓ **Bluestone Bistro** — Posh pizza for the well-heeled student crowd. Not that expensive, since you split it. Great pastas, too.

✓ **Corrib Pub** — Typical Irish pub, nothing fancy, but a ton of food for under $10.00.

✓ **Venice Ristorante** — Choose from over a dozen different gourmet pasta dishes, each $7.95, and see it being prepared. Large portions.

and the service is quick.

The menu, featuring Mandarin, Polynesian, and other specialties, offers no less than sixty combination specials, ranging in price from $4.50 to $8.00, available all day. There are another twenty served as luncheon specials (11:30 to 3:00 p.m.), priced from $3.50 to $6.00.

Mr. C sampled chicken wings, beef with broccoli, and pork fried rice ($6.75), and found the food tasty and fresh, with good portions. These are billed as dinners for one, and for one it's a good-sized meal.

Peking Gardens is happy to cook for special needs, using unsaturated vegetable oil or no MSG at your request. For vegetarians, there is the house special mixed vegetables dish ($5.25). They also deliver (not free) to Brighton, Allston, and Brookline from 5 p.m. to 10 p.m. and to 1 a.m. on weekends.

Pig 'n Whistle Diner — 226 North Beacon St., Brighton; 254-8058. Yet another true diner shines in Allston-Brighton. The Pig 'n Whistle is a cozy little place in the classic diner-car shape, paneled in aluminum and looking like it's been around forever. Inside, the folks are friendly, the lighting is warm, and the food is terrific diner fare.

Daily specials are the best bargains. For $4.50, how about a plate of sliced roast lamb in brown gravy, along with real mashed potatoes and a cooked vegetable . . . or, for $5.50, baked stuffed schrod with the trimmings. A huge bowl of homemade beef stew is $3.90, and a hot turkey sandwich—packed with slabs of dark and white meat— is $4.50, with potato and vegetable.

Lunch specials include such choices as a grilled ham steak sandwich ($4.95), which comes with a small drink, soup or potatoes, and a vegetable. Or try fried scallops ($6.95) with French fries, cole slaw, a roll and butter, and a small drink.

You can, of course, get sandwiches and burgers, omelettes,

and other breakfast specials, salads, and desserts. Oh, and the coffee is great.

Venice Ristorante — 957 Commonwealth Ave., Brighton; 787-7750. Also, 204 Cambridge St., Boston; 227-2094. There are two branches of this fine little eatery: the original is located on the back of Beacon Hill, and the larger, more recent outpost is on the west campus of Boston University. Both specialize in take-out and delivered food, but the BU spot is larger and more fancy, a nice place to sit amidst Venetian decor.

Black-and-white tile dominates the room, matched also by the canvas awning over the bar, which gives the feeling of being at an outdoor cafe indoors. The Venice recently acquired a liquor license and now serves house wines and a number of good local and international beers.

Pastas and pizzas are the specialty here, but not your average kinds. These folks have gotten creative. How about Hawaiian pizza, with ham, prosciutto and pineapple? Or pesto pizza, self-explanatory; and the ultimate in nouveau pizza, the "Yuppie." This comes with spinach, broccoli, and artichoke. There are eight choices in all, and each is $9.50 for the small (feeds two) and $13.95 for the large. You can also get an individual (seven-inch wide) pie for $2.75, with additional toppings 50¢ each. This is a great bargain.

On the pasta side, all dishes are $7.50. While this may not sound super cheap, you get a lot of pasta for your dough, along with hot garlic bread. The dishes are all cooked to order, and you can watch the chef working in the large, open kitchen. Choose from chicken agostino, which features a lemony cream sauce and broccoli; beef and pasta, sauteed ground beef with garlic, red wine, eggplant and tomatoes served over linguine; and fifteen other varieties. They are dee-lish.

Venice also serves calzone ($5.25 to $5.95), served with homemade tomato basil sauce on the side; deli-style sandwiches, burgers, soups and salads. There are daily specials on a blackboard outside. They also offer free delivery. Students are a large part of the business, but the clean and spiffy atmosphere put Venice Ristorante above the level of student hangout.

Wing It — 1153 Commonwealth Ave., Brighton; 783-BIRD (2473). The name says it all. Chicken wings have risen to a new height (sorry!) in this tiny barbecue palace. The emphasis here is on takeout, although there are a few tables and stools. Since they look wellworn by the student crowd that frequents the place, you may prefer to eat at home. Wing It offers free delivery in the BU/BC area, or you can call your order in and pick it up.

The food, meanwhile, is good stuff. The wings can be cooked six different ways. Buffalo and barbecue come in several grades of spiciness, from mild on up to "suicide." Honey hot and teriyaki explain themselves; then you have "teridactil," a unique blend of soy sauce and barbecue, and finally the most unusual of all—garlic and Parmesan. These last two are both interesting and worth a try.

A small order, for one person, is $3.95; for two, $7.10; for three, $10.50. Extra large, for up to six nib-

blers, is $15.20, and you can also order party platters of tremendous sizes.

But man does not live by wings alone, and neither does this establishment: the flip side here is baby back spare ribs. Again, they come in various sauces and spiciness. A half rack is $7.95, and the full is $12.95; for an extra $2.00, you can make a full dinner out of each by adding fries or onion rings and potato salad, cole slaw, or a side salad.

Both the ribs and the wings have plenty of meat on them, and the sauces are tasty indeed. A good and fun sampler here is the "Real Meal Deal," which gives you a half rack of ribs and five wings; you can mix and match the styles for each. It includes one side dish, all for $10.95. The "mega" size doubles the whole deal for $16.95. For one person, a small order of wings and a side dish is $5.55.

Probably the best bargain around, though, takes place every Wednesday night from 6 p.m. to 9 p.m. Yes folks, it's the all-you-can-eat hot buffalo wing buffet. For $4.95 you can chow down as much as your tongue can take. (This event must be the reason for the large sink in the middle of the room.) Try it if you dare!

BROOKLINE

Alicia's Chic-A-Pasta
Restaurant — 236 Washington St., Brookline; 734-4673. As the name implies, this small storefront restaurant has a large variety of foods on the menu. There are chicken dishes, pasta dishes, and of course, chicken and pasta dishes. Not to mention burgers, sandwiches, seafood, salads, soups, vegetables . . .

The food is homemade and the quantities are tremendous. Mr. C ordered the "half-portion" of chicken with broccoli and mushrooms over pasta shells in a cream sauce ($3.95) and just barely finished it. The full portion, only a dollar more, must be outrageous.

You have several choices to make in ordering such a dish, by the way. Choose your chicken: cacciatore, marsala, parmigiana. Then your pasta: linguine, fettucine, shells. Finally, sauce: alfredo, tomato, butter and garlic . . . .and then, there are the *seafood* and pasta plates!

Alicia's also serves something they call "Tenderwiches"—hot sandwiches like pork tenderloin or marinated chicken kebabs (each $3.85), on a baguette or in a pocket, with lettuce, tomato, and honey mustard dressing. The "Gourmet burgers" consist of six-ounce patties of fresh beef, starting at $2.50 for the basic. Half a dozen varieties range up to $4.35 for the deluxe. And there are several hot subs, pita sandwiches, and salads.

You can also get a whole or half rotisseried chicken; the half-chicken plate ($4.95) includes two side dishes from the list of hot vegetables—butternut squash, sauteed carrots, herbed corn, rice pilaf, and more. There are daily soups, such as spinach-mushroom, at $1.45 per cup or $2.55 per bowl. And top it off with homemade grapenut custard ($1.65) for dessert.

Alicia's has one row of tables and also does a lot of take- out business. In either case you place your order at the counter and have a seat. The place is clean and the folks behind the counter are very pleasant. It's a nice new addition to Brookline Village.

Captain's Wharf Seafood
Restaurant — 356 Harvard St., Brookline; 566-5590. A Coolidge Corner favorite, Captain's Wharf serves up a big catch of fresh seafood every day, and you won't have to put much bait on your hook.

The setting is simple—booths and formica tables—but there the comparisons to HoJo's end. Choose your fish steamed, broiled, or fried; there are a couple dozen options, most between $6.00 to $9.00. The steamed mussels dinner is $5.15; broiled sole, $7.95; fried clams, $8.25. All dinners include two sides—fries, baked potato, cole slaw, salad, and vegetable of the day.

Lunch versions are all one or two dollars less; there are also several daily "mini-lunch" specials, all $4.25, and you get plenty to eat. Be sure to start with a cup of homemade seafood chowder or clam chowder.

Lobster dinners start at $9.95 for a one-pounder; for two dollars more you can add steamed clams and mussels. When in season, the menu may also include bluefish, halibut and swordfish.

Captain's Wharf serves beer and wine. They close up early, around 10 p.m., and also fill up during lunch and dinner, so try to get there ahead of the rush.

"Dinner At The Mitton House" — Newbury College, 129 Fisher Ave., Brookline; 730-7037. Here's an unusual opportunity for a truly special meal. At Newbury College's culinary arts school, tucked way up in the fancy hills of Brookline near Chestnut Hill, students learn gourmet cooking techniques which will land them in many of the area's finer restaurants. For a fraction of that cost, you can dine here—in a mansion, no less.

The setting is the George Mitton House, the nineteenth century home of the founder of Jordan Marsh. Lunches and dinners are served on weekdays through the school year, with entrees such as lobster thermidor, medallions of veal "princess", and cuisines from around the world. Meals are complete, from appetizer through desserts, for one price; and everything is superbly made to order in their kitchens, including the delicate *garde manger* sculptures carved from fruits and vegetables.

Reservations must be made and paid for in advance; dinners cost $18.00 complete, lunches $8.00, and you can charge over the phone. With a capacity of only thirty-five to forty people, the tables get booked up well in advance. No alcohol is served, but you may bring your own wine. The service is excellent. You can really dine in high style, without going broke!

El Bandido Mexican Cafe — 1412 Beacon St., Brookline; 730-5663. Another of the recent arrivals of great, cheap Mexican food to Boston, El Bandido serves up quick, home-cooked food using all fresh ingredients. They are geared to take-out and delivery, or you can eat in the small, brightly painted shop.

Start with an order of nachos and cheese for $3.25, or a cheese quesadilla for $2.25. A taco salad is $4.75.

Solo plates range in price from about $4.00 to $6.00; these offer a pair of tamales, chimichangas, tostadas, etc., with sour cream and guacamole. The "veggie burrito," filled with beans, rice, cheese, lettuce, tomatoes, and salsa, is just $3.75. A combination plate, with your choice of two different items—tacos, enchiladas, flautas or burritos—plus rice and beans, is $6.45.

Specialties of the house include chile con carne or chile rellenos, each $6.50; and chicken mole, a traditional dish served with rice and tortilla, for $6.75.

El Bandido currently offers lunch specials from noon to 4 p.m. on weekdays: any one item with rice and beans for $3.75. Good deal. There is no liquor license, but plenty of juices, such as mango and papaya.

Family Restaurant — 1634 Beacon St., Brookline; 277-4466. True to its name, the Family Restaurant is a friendly mom 'n pop Greek diner, with tons of great food. The atmosphere is cozy, with plants in the windows; there are plenty of tables; or you can sit at the counter.

Greek specialties, of course, are the thing to have here. Mr. C ordered the moussaka dinner and was treated to a mountainous slab of ground beef, eggplant, cheese, and tomato sauce, with rice on the side, all for $6.25. It was too much to finish. Beef or chicken shish kebabs are each $7.95 for a full dinner which includes rice, cooked vegetables, a salad, and rice pudding for dessert.

There are sandwiches too; the souvlaki dinner is $5.75, but for $3.75 you can get a hefty sandwich in pita bread. Same prices for the gyros.

Seafood is nice and cheap, with a broiled swordfish dinner among the daily specials for $6.95. Fried haddock is $5.45, with French fries and cole slaw. Portions are good.

What would a diner be without burgers, starting at $2.00 for the basic up to $3.95 for the deluxe

model, with lettuce, tomato, bacon
and fries. And the Family is a popular spot for breakfast, with two eggs
and bacon or sausage for a mere
$2.85. Omelettes range from $2.75
for plain to $4.95 for the works.

The folks at the Family Restaurant use cholesterol-free oils and
maintain a committment to healthy
cooking. 'Course, this ain't exactly
health food to begin with—it's a
home-style filler-up!

Imperial Restaurant — 238 Harvard St., Brookline; 731-3322. Just
below Coolidge Corner, the Imperial looks like just another pizza and
sub shop. However, in addition to
great Italian pizza (crispy thin-crust
and Sicilian), calzone and sandwiches, they serve up hot plates of
wonderful, fresh pasta for only a
few bucks.

It's simply the basics here:
spaghetti, ziti, ravioli, and manicotti,
smothered in marinara sauce, and
also lasagna. You get a huge, filling
plate along with great-smelling,
warm Italian bread.

The pasta dishes all start at
$3.25, whether you order spaghetti,
ziti, or cheese-filled ravioli. Add sausage for 50¢ more; or a pair of
meatballs the size of tennis balls for
a dollar. The manicotti plate is
$4.00, and lasagna tops the menu
at $4.50 for a heaping slab.

The garden salad ($2.75)
comes on a plate the same size as
the dinner plates and, again, is
your basic lettuce, tomato, cucumber, onions, and black olives—but
everything is big and crisp. There
are also Greek ($3.75) and chef's
($4.00) salads.

The dinners are great bargains; but better yet are the daily
specials, when the price comes
down a bit more and—after 5
p.m.—you can add the garden
salad for only 99¢. One or two different menu items are offered each
day. So, for example, you can have
ziti and meatballs with salad and
bread for under $5.00. And it's all
fresh and delicious.

The Imperial also delivers from
5 p.m. until midnight, seven days a
week, for a $1.00 fee. It's really a bit
of the North End in Brookline.

Jaffe's Pick-A-Chick — 9 Babcock
St., Brookline; 738-3354. Ken Jaffe
has been making chicken for
years. He is part of a longtime food
tradition in Coolidge Corner; he
grew up working in his family's
shop on Harvard Street. The original Pick-a-Chick eventually closed
after many years as the premier
delicatessen in the area. Recently
Jaffe opened his own shop just
around the corner, giving it the
same name.

At Jaffe's, rotisserie chicken is
still the house specialty. For $4.95,
the basic plate gets you a half-
chicken covered in barbecue
sauce with two side orders—
mashed potatoes, stuffing, rice,
squash or several others. Or have
your chicken in sandwich form.

But there are plenty of other delicious foods, like barbecued ribs
($5.95 a half rack, $10.95 a full) and
sweet and sour meatballs ($4.95).
There are several deli combo sandwiches, hot reubens and the like, all
around $5.00 to $6.00.

Jaffe's also offers a different
lunch special for $4.95 every day;
you may see the barbecued beef
sandwich or the chili sloppy joe.
And on Saturdays the special is teriyaki chicken wings—all you can eat.

All the other usual Jewish delicacies are here, knishes and noodle pudding and, of course,
chicken soup and chopped liver.
The portions are big and the food
is wonderful.

King Tut Coffee Shop — 7 Station
St., Brookline; 277-0066. King Tut is
part of the influx of Middle Eastern
shops around Boston, and a very
good one indeed. This place takes
a great deal of care with the quality
of the food and the service. It's
strictly a take-out shop, located
across the street from the Brookline
Village T station, and so there is
also a selection of hot drinks and
pastries, both American and Mediterranean.

But the specialties are things
like falaffel or hummus and tabouli

Mr. Cheap's Picks
Brookline

✓ **Alicia's Chic-A-Pasta** — Crazy name, yet it's accurate. Pick from several different pasta and chicken dishes, or mix and match. Eat in or take out.

✓ **Jaffe's Pick-A-Chick** — Sounds the same, but the Jaffe family has been broiling birds in Brookline for generations. This is what Boston Chicken strives for.

✓ ***Mexican Double Bill*** — Two terrific, small Mexican food places on or near Beacon Street. **El Bandido** in Coolidge Corner offers good lunch specials cheap; **TJ's Taqueria** in Washington Square is perhaps the better of the two, but has almost no seating.

---

sandwiches (each $2.99), big and delicious; finger-sized stuffed grape leaves (35¢ each); warm, thick spinach pies ($1.50); and couscous salad ($4.25 a lb), crammed with diced peppers, scallions, carrots, and raisins for a taste that starts out slightly sweet, then kicks in with a bit of spice.

Various combinations are available as complete lunches, such as a tabouli, hummus, and couscous platter for $3.80. Larger, party-sized platters are available too.

This tiny storefront is only open Monday through Friday and usually closes around 6 p.m., though you may find the door still open even later. "If the lights are on, come on in," said the friendly man behind the counter.

Matt Garrett's — 299 Harvard St., Brookline; 738-5635. The venerable Matt Garrett's is a popular lunch, dinner, and late-evening meeting place. Its menu is one of those "everything under the sun" types— burgers, salads, seafood, pasta, Mexican, Italian, Jewish, Chinese . . . you name it.

The vast list of appetizers includes heaping helpings of chicken fingers ($4.95), buffalo wings ($3.95/$5.95) and a vegetarian platter of fresh-cut veggies, pita bread, hummus, and herbed cheese ($6.95). "Fingers and Rings for Two," at $7.95, is a huge order

served in an edible tortilla bowl. Again, these are not the cheapest prices, but you get a lot!

A sampling of the culinary choices at Matt Garrett's: a seafood salad platter ($7.95) with lots of shrimp and scallops; Mexican pizza ($3.95/$5.95) with spicy beef, olives, Monterey jack, and more on top; stir-fry chicken Oriental ($8.95); BBQ chicken breast ($7.95) grilled over real charcoal; fried scallops, clams or oysters (each $7.95); teriyaki steak tips ($9.95); pasta primavera ($7.95); also, half-pound burgers with fries, from $4.95; huge, deli-style sandwiches from $3.95; and even five kinds of yuppie-topped pizzas ($7-$8).

Portions are large, and most entrees come with sides of rice or potato (the fries are excellent), some with salads.

Garrett's also has weekday luncheon specials for $5.25, with choices like schrod, stir-fry, or pasta. And best of all are the early-bird dinner specials, when full meals are just $6.95. Grab them Mondays-Fridays from 3:30 to 5:30. Sunday brunch is a big deal here, too.

Matt Garrett's also has big desserts and sweet specialty drinks from the bar. The atmosphere is lively, and this is one of the few places that serves food until 1 a.m. on weekends. It's pretty much *the* late-night place in Brookline.

Niko's Restaurant — 187A Harvard St., Brookline; 277-2999. Tucked cozily into a row of stores a couple of blocks below Coolidge Corner, Niko's Restaurant is a terrific new arrival in Brookline. As you may guess by the name, Greek cuisine is spoken here; but Niko's is not like so many of the bustling coffee shops you see around town.

White linen cloths adorn the neat rows of tables, with a vase of fresh daisies on each one. Lively music of the Greek Isles plays in the background. A stately column rises up each wall—not real, of course, but not tacky either. The place has a light and pleasing look to it.

Here you don't have to be a king to eat like one. The Mediterranean specialties are delicious, full dinners with prices mostly in the $5.00-to-$7.50 range. Appetizers, at an all-around $2.50, include such exotic-sounding items as taramosalata, a dish made from roe, and tza tziki, a cucumber dip with yogurt and garlic.

A basket of warm pita bread arrives first, crisp and tasty. Then try the avgolemono ($2.65), egg lemon soup. Dinners come with a nice-sized garden salad made with fresh vegetables and feta cheese. Mr. C ordered the moussaka ($5.50), a hearty square of ground beef on layers of cooked eggplant and potato, with a fluffy cheese custard baked on top. Along with the salad, the price includes rice pilaf, made with tomato sauce. You can also choose mashed potatoes or French fries.

Zouzoukakia (just fun to say, isn't it?) is a dish of homemade meatballs simmered in a tomato and wine sauce. They come with the same sides for just $4.95, making it a very inexpensive dinner indeed. Cheaper still is the fried chicken dinner ($4.25), three pieces of chicken with French fries and cole slaw.

Desserts, all $1.45, include baklava, rice pudding, and daily specials; but Mr. C didn't have enough room left to try them! Another time.

Niko's also serves breakfast until 11:30 seven days a week. Two eggs, any style, with three sausage links or bacon strips, are $2.75. Home fries and toast are included. Omelettes are made with three eggs and go all the way up to $5.55 for the house special—which contains Greek sausage, feta cheese, mushrooms, peppers, and onions, and comes with toast.

Go for those great dinners, though, in an attractive and relaxing atmosphere. Niko's is an inexpensive bit of casual elegance.

Pugsley's — 41 Harvard St., Brookline; 739-9845.

This tiny storefront doesn't look like it serves up freshly-prepared seafood, salads, and sandwiches, but it does. An order of fish and chips ($4.50) gives you two large, thick pieces of fish, handcut fries, and tasty cole slaw; there are also fried haddock, clams, and scallops.

Roast beef and roast turkey are cooked in the store and hand-carved for big sandwiches, each around $4.00. Fresh-ground burgers weigh in under a half-pound but are juicy and served on fresh rolls with lettuce and tomato. The basic is $2.25; a double bacon cheeseburger is just $3.95.

Homemade soups include turkey noodle and clam chowder, $1.50 for a cup, $2.50 for a bowl. Pasta salad ($3.25) is made with rigatoni, fresh tomatoes, and basil.

Breakfast is also popular here. Have two eggs, home fries, toast, and bacon, ham or sausage for $2.75; French toast or pancakes with bacon for $2.95. Pugsley's is an early place, only open Monday through Friday from 7 a.m. to 5 p.m. and Saturday from 9 a.m. to 3 p.m.

Rami's — 324 Harvard St., Brookline; 738-3577. Also, 50 Winter St., Boston; 426-9770. There is no shortage of falafel in Coolidge Corner. Rami's is the newer kid on the block, looking like a Middle Eastern fast-food shop. The basic falaffel sandwich ($3.95), gives you eight of these babies packed into a pita bread pocket with tahini sauce and your choice of vegetables (lettuce, purple cabbage, tomato, cucumber, pickles, etc.). For 50¢ more, you may add a dollop of hummus or baba ganoush. There is also a homemade "sizzling hot sauce" available, but be sure to ask for it.

Whatever the combination, this is a delicious, satisfying meal, and super-cheap. It's also a messy one—but then, that's part of the fun. Of course, you can order the same foods in platter form and use a knife and fork.

Other dinners include grilled chicken ($4.95), cooked in spices and topped with minced onions and tahini sauce, with salad. Shawarma, usually made with lamb, is here a turkey-based meat dish in which thin shavings are sliced from a rotating block of seasoned, slowly-cooked meat. A shawarma sandwich in pita bread is $5.45, and you can also order it in combination with hummus, salad or falafel.

If you really can't decide, or just want to try it all, go for Rami's Special—a sampler plate of the kebab, falaffel, chicken, hummus and salad, all for $7.95. The place also offers its foods in quantity, such as hummus by the half-pound.

Another specialty here is the boreka—a hand-sized puffed pastry pie filled with chopped meat, spinach, or potato. The dough is crisp and flaky, topped with sesame seeds, making for a light snack item (it takes a couple to fill you up). These are all about $2.00 each. There is even an apple boreka, topped with powdered sugar, which can be a dessert. Speaking of which, baklava is on the menu too.

And here's a special tip from Mr. C: This is also a kosher restaurant, which means they close around 2:00 on Friday afternoon and stay closed on Saturday. Sometimes this results in special deals

on fresh items they can't keep. It's worth checking out if you're in the area on a Friday afternoon.

Recently, a second Rami's opened at the top of Winter Street in Downtown Crossing.

Rose's Cafe And Deli — 1009A Beacon St., Brookline; 566-6155. Rose's Cafe is a cozy little mom 'n pop with an eclectic menu that looks ordinary at first glance but is filled with surprises. Yes, you can get flame-broiled burgers, subs, omelettes, and the usual deli fare. But what's this? French bread pizza, with toppings from bacon to veggie . . . nice, big slabs, too ($1.50 plain to $3.50 with the works). The hot subs are huge, with veal or eggplant parmagiana for just $3.75 and barbecued chicken for $4.25.

And the surprises don't end there. Rose's has a variety of belly-stuffing hot plates that start around $3.00, for pasta or manicotti with sauce. Add meatballs for a buck. There's meatloaf ($4.75), sliced fresh turkey ($5.50) and barbecued steak tips ($5.75). Each of these is a very substantial portion and is served on a huge bed of rice pilaf (or with a side of pasta, where appropriate). A full plate of green salad comes with the entrees too.

So, have you guessed that the true flavor of the place is *Russian*? Surprise! Very few restaurants in Boston, cheap or not, offer such old world specialties as borscht, blintzes, pirozhki, and more. The folks who run the place are very proud of them; but the offerings change daily and aren't always on the menu, so be sure to ask about the Russian specials.

Rose's is kind of a hole-in-the-wall cafe, where you order at the counter and then find a seat at one of the few tables. At lunch it can be hard to get one, so many of the regulars take food out. They serve dinner too, but only until about 7:30 or 8.

TJ's Taqueria — 690 Washington St., Brookline; 734-TACO (8226). TJ's is a little storefront take-out restaurant serving Mexican food in a colorful, funky setting. They offer all the standard items at very reasonable prices.

Mr. C sampled the chicken tostada ($3.50), a round corn tortilla topped with shredded chicken, black beans, lettuce, cheese, and pico sauce. It's enough for a small appetite, but for anyone hungrier it's best to get something else with it. Guacamole and chips, for instance—the guac is homemade, chunky, and well-seasoned. Or a cup of Mexican fish stew, if it's on the day's menu.

Burritos are the heartiest items here, large sandwiches made in rolled-up soft flour tortillas. Bean and cheese is the lowest priced, at $3.95; most are $5.95, with such fillings as marinated grilled beef or shredded pork. Both are further stuffed with beans and guacamole, along with cilantro and onion.

The tacos, tortas, and other preparations all have similar choices of fillings; along with beef, chicken and pork, there is even the option of fried fish fillets. You also have your choice of salsa, blended in with the food or on the side.

There are no beers available, but TJ's does carry IBC sodas, several brands of mineral water, and fruit juices. There is flan for dessert ($2.00), as well as Mexican candies made from squash, coconut, and marzipan. Try a chili cookie (75¢), made with sugar and a dash of chili powder on top. "It's just like cinnamon," the man behind the counter assured Mr. C.

TJ's offers a choice of nine lunch specials Mondays through Fridays from 11:30 to 3:00. All are priced at $4.95, with combinations such as a taco, rice, beans, and a beverage, or a quesadilla, a cup of soup, and a beverage.

There are no tables for eating on the premises, but one wall has a counter with about half a dozen stools. Best bet is to take it home.

Yu's Take Out — 1374 Beacon St., Brookline; 734-2929. Yu's is a fast-rising newcomer in Coolidge Cor-

ner; beginning as a take-out place with a couple of stools by the window, they recently expanded into the space next door and became a full-fledged restaurant. Actually, Yu's is sort of a cross between restaurant and cafeteria. You place your order at the counter by the door, then go in and find a table. The service staff, and a friendly bunch they are, will bring the food to you as soon as it's ready, which is usually very soon indeed.

The menu is huge, with low prices and good portions. For appetizers, try the scallion pancakes—a pair of fried cakes the size of 45 rpm records—for $2.75. Spring rolls, $2.65 for two, are delicious. And the Peking ravioli ($3.65 for a half-dozen) will stick to your ribs. Speaking of ribs, these are great too. Vegetables fried in light, crispy tempura batter are $3.50. Or make your own combination platter: three items for $7.95, four items for $9.95.

Soups are another good bet, with several varieties including "Delights of Three" (clear broth with shrimp, chicken and ham, $5.25), corn soup with crabmeat ($5.50) and the house special: scallops, shrimp, and vegetables in an egg broth ($5.50). These are all portions for two people.

Most of the regular dishes at Yu's can be ordered in "small" or "regular" portions, making it possible to spend less if you wish to avoid leftovers—or if you just want to try more items. Lemon chicken, for example, is $7.50; but, there is enough for one in the small size at $4.75. Kan shao shredded beef, in a hot sauce with celery and carrots, is another good example. The full size is $6.95, the smaller portion just $4.65.

Also good and cheap are fried rice dishes from $3.00, lo meins from $3.35, chow meins from $3.50, and chop sueys from $3.35.

The real bargains, however, come in the bewildering array of combination platters that are available. Luncheon specials, offered every day, range from just $3.95 to

$4.75 for Yu-hsiang broccoli with straw mushrooms, shrimp with lobster sauce, or other choices. All plates come with white or fried rice and your choice of hot and sour or egg drop soup.

Dinner combos give you more choices. For $5.85 you can have egg foo yong, pork fried rice, and boneless ribs. $6.65 will get you pepper steak, fried rice, and chicken wings or spare ribs. Get the idea? The list goes on and on, and these options won't leave you hungry.

For the health-conscious, Yu's offers special dishes made without salt, corn starch, soybean oil, or sugar. Sliced chicken ($6.95) or large shrimp ($8.75) with mixed vegetables are some of the choices. And no MSG is used in the restaurant.

There is also a board of special items of the day, worth checking out. And at the side of the large dining room, decorated with folding screens, there is a condiment tray—take your own sauces to your table, as much as you like. You can also refill your own glass of hot tea from a large urn.

The atmosphere is very casual, and the service is quick. It's a great place to stop in if you're in a hurry.

CAMBRIDGE

Al's Lunch — 901 Main St., Cambridge; 661-5810. The prices at Al's may not strike you as low at first—but wait until you see what you get. This popular spot has a funky menu that ranges from comfort food to yuppie heaven. Wander through all the blackboard menus, step up to the counter and order a "Big Ham"—smoked ham, Havarti cheese, lettuce, tomato, and herb mayonnaise. Choose from wheat bread, pumpernickel, sourdough, or baguette. Find a table; they'll call you when it's ready.

Like all the sandwiches, this one comes in a full size ($4.75) or half ($3.35). Their half-size is what any other place would call full; it's served between thick, hand-cut slices of bread almost the size of a football. The full size gives you enough to take home for tomorrow.

There are other combos, basic sandwiches, and even good ol' "P.B. & J." ($3.00/$1.75). Try a pesto, pasta, and turkey salad plate for $4.45; and there are homemade soups also. On a recent hot day, Mr. C sipped a cold strawberry and watermelon soup—a huge bowl for just $1.90—delicious.

Al's is a hot spot for breakfast too, with daily specials and home-baked pastries. Have a bagel, egg and sausage sandwich, much more substantial than the McChain variety, for $2.50; the orange and grapefruit juices ($1.30) are fresh-squeezed.

The quick service is good for take-out; they like you to call your order ahead if you can. Meanwhile, true to its name, Al's Lunch is closed by nightfall.

Asmara Ethiopian Restaurant — 714 Massachusetts Ave., Cambridge; 864-7447. Of Boston's several (!) Ethiopian restaurants, Asmara in Central Square seems to be the least expensive. The food is wholesome and hearty, with all dinner prices under $9.00.

You'll probably notice there is no silverware on the tables. Ethiopian food is meant to be eaten with your hands; but you can have utensils if you prefer. Most orders come with injera bread, which is more like an open crepe. The waiter doles your food out onto the pancake, and you dig in—tear a piece of bread and use it to scoop up the food.

Many of the dishes are like thick stews, in either mild or spicy sauces. Alicha fitfit, for example, is diced beef with bits of carrot, rice, and potato; Asmara tibbs has beef sauteed with onions, green chilies, and butter. In fact, herbed butter flavors a lot of these dishes.

There are also chicken, lamb, and vegetarian entrees, many with a Middle Eastern style to them. The food is delicious. Be sure to have a cup of Asmara tea with it.

Bartley's Burger Cottage—1246 Massachusetts Ave., Cambridge; 354-6559. Ma Bartley probably does more with a hamburger, and for less money, than anyone you've ever met. The menu shows no less than forty-nine different creations, all made from seven ounces of beef, ground fresh daily. Most are priced from $3.50 to $5.00, from the Bagel Burger to the Reuben Burger to the Texas Barbeque Burger. Then there is the gourmet listing ($5.99 for most), featuring the

"Joe Kennedy"—bleu cheese and Canadian bacon, served with potato skins—and the "Stroganoff"— with sauteed mushrooms, sour cream, and onion rings. These range up to the "Macho Burger" ($7.25), a fourteen-ounce monstrosity served with fries, rings, and cole slaw. You can even design your own monster, with ingredients like guacamole, sprouts, green chili, tabouli, and more. They're all great, by the way.

But this doesn't even scratch the surface (the take-out menu is six pages long!). The half-chicken dinner ($5.25) includes corn bread and two side dishes, with such choices as homemade mashed potatoes, butternut squash, and baked beans. There is a vegetarian platter ($3.95), which comes with corn bread and three sides, fish and chips ($5.95), grilled frankfurters with potato salad ($3.95), open-faced hot turkey or roast beef sandwiches ($5.25 each), and so much more.

Also, over a dozen salads: Cobb, Caesar, Greek, fruit, pasta, shrimp . . . plus gigantic sodas, and homemade desserts such as pumpkin tart, grapenut custard, and hot apple pie.

It's all cheap, delicious and lively at Bartley's. The surroundings are somewhat cramped, and you may be seated at the long, long central table with perfect strangers, but hey—Ma says they're okay.

Boca Grande — 1728 Massachusetts Ave., Cambridge; 354-7400. Also, 149 First St., Cambridge; 354-5550. Boca Grande is a Mex-food chain that doesn't feel like a chain; at least, it certainly puts Taco Bell to shame. This is great food, cheap and delicious.

The atmosphere is hip, with an open kitchen, lots of plants, and walls painted in bright southwestern colors of clay and turquoise. The food is made to your order, with all fresh ingredients. You can have a full meal, like the half-chicken with warm tortillas and salsa for $4.95, or the Mexican plate, with your choice of beef, chicken, or spicy pork ("carnitas") plus beans, rice, and salsa for $4.50.

Or put a meal together from tacos, burritos, guacamole, chips, quesadilla, and more. The burritos grandes, by the way, are gigantic for just $4.15. The Mass. Ave. spot has tables by the window; the branch near the Cambridgeside Galleria has a separate room upstairs, which is a quiet and cozy way to dine.

Border Cafe — 32 Church St., Cambridge; 864-6100. Also, Route 1, Saugus; 233-5308. The Border Cafe has been for several years one of the most popular dining spots in Harvard Square, and it's easy to see why from the moment you step inside. The atmosphere is lively and hip, like a party that's always in full swing. The bright decor features painted wall signs, mostly old beer advertisements, looking like all of Tijuana compressed into one room. Stepping up into the bar area, you pass an old-fashioned bathtub that may once have swilled gin. Waiters and waitresses, accustomed to the crowds, zip past you with trays held high over their heads.

Another good reason for its popularity is the food itself. The menu is large, specializing in Mexican, Southwestern, and Cajun cuisine; and there is a great variety of meat, fish, and vegetarian dishes to choose from, many of which are at very reasonable prices. So Mr. C can chow down here all the time, and not tire of the choices.

Before you even get to the menu, someone has come by and placed a basket of warm (ah!) tortilla chips and salsa on your table— a welcoming gesture indeed. You may want to start this course off with a margarita—they'll take you off your budget, but they are quite generous. Starting at $3.50 (more if you want a name-brand tequila), they come frozen or on the rocks in a hefty goblet.

On to the appetizers, most of

which are in the $5.00 range—no, not cheap, but in good-enough portions to share. Cajun popcorn (crawfish), fried shrimp, quesadillas with or without meat, spicy chili with cheese . . . Order enough of these for the table to share and you may not even need dinner.

Dinners, in fact, are the real bargain here. Most are well under Mr. C's $10.00 limit and are served with fixings on the side to make for a full meal. A platter of soft tacos is just $4.45; enchiladas con pollo (chicken) are $4.95. Many dinners come with yellow rice with bits of peppers in it, and black beans; you can also add a side of chunky guacamole for another 95¢.

Some items blend Tex-Mex with nouvelle. Chicken Laredo ($5.95) gives you a breast of mesquite-broiled chicken served on a bed of cooked spinach—in a sauce made from smoked chili peppers, butter, and spices, served with the rice and beans. Chicken Santa Fe is a similar dish served on spinach fettucine noodles. These may not be authentic to the region, but the point is, at these prices, how many places even attempt to put such combinations on your plate?

You can get a mesquite-grilled burger for a very decent $3.99; or chorizo quesadillas, which are flour tortillas filled with melted monterey jack cheese, spicy sausage, and salsa for $5.29. Then there is the Cajun side. Catfish Mardi Gras ($6.89) is a couple of deep-fried filets cooked in a tomatoey Creole sauce and topped with shaved pecans. Jambalaya rice comes with it. Or try the blackened chicken, just $5.99.

The combinations are nearly endless. If you don't mind the boisterous surroundings, and are prepared to wait for a table, this is as close to a fiesta as you'll find north of the border.

Brookline Lunch/Jimmaize Cafe — 9 Brookline St., Cambridge; 354-9473. Strangely enough, Brookline Lunch is located in Cambridge's Central Square, just off Mass. Ave. on Brookline Street. That explains the name. To explain the food takes a bit longer, for this is a funky little coffee shop with an identity crisis.

First off, it's a popular breakfast spot, with its short counter and booth tables. Eggs Benedict is just $3.95, with home fries; omelettes start at $2.95, and the house special offers three pancakes, one egg, and sausage or bacon for a paltry $3.00. The coffee's good, too.

For lunch there are sandwiches like grilled cheese and bacon ($2.95) and burgers ($1.95), all served with fries and soup or a small salad; regular salads include spinach, tomato and herb, and cashew chicken, each $4.25.

But then, the menu veers from Cambridge health food to Middle Eastern delicacies—falaffel and hummus ($3.75), chicken, lamb or beef kebabs ($4.95), goat curry ($5.95), and more. Another sharp turn takes us to Europe—with chicken provencal ($4.95), shrimp scampi ($5.95), fettucine verdi ($3.95), and even "Snails Gormande" ($4.95).

With all these choices Mr. C couldn't sample everything; but the items he tried were tasty, and others he saw going by looked good. Most dinners come with vegetables, rice, and bread. And at these prices you can afford to go back and try it all. By the way, another paradox about the name: Brookline Lunch is open until 10:00 most evenings.

Cafe Mami — Porter Exchange Mall, 1815 Massachusetts Ave., Cambridge; 547-9130. Inside this Porter Square shopping center, upstairs from the trendy and overpriced Cottonwood Cafe, is a cluster of Japanese cafes that look like fast-food joints. In fact, they each offer different homemade oriental cuisines, and they are all inexpensive and delicious.

Cafe Mami, at the head of the row, is perhaps the most unusual—an offbeat hodgepodge of western foods prepared in eastern styles.

They often have funny-sounding jumbled names, like "Sunny Side Egg Hamburg Steak" or "Spicy Squid Ginger Vegetable"; the staff will be happy to help you out.

Mr. C sampled the "Garlic Lemon Chicken" ($6.80), which turned out to be balls of sauteed chicken mixed with lemon wedges in a tasty sauce. It was served with a plate of sticky white rice, an American-style salad, sprigs of cooked broccoli, and carrots. Like most dinners, it also came with a bowl of miso soup, a clear broth with scallions and chunks of tofu.

Other good bargains include tofu pan-fried noodles ($5.50), combining tofu with cabbage, bean sprouts, peppers, and onions in a tonkatsu sauce; and seafood spaghetti ($6.80) with mussels, shrimp, and squid served over a bed of noodles in a white garlic sauce.

You can, of course, order smaller items a la carte, like the miso soup ($1.00) or ongiri ($3.90), soup with two rolled-up rice balls. While eating, you may want to amuse yourself with something from the bookshelf of Japanese paperback comic books, which are a serious habit among all ages over there. You will often find groups of Asians hanging out at this and the other cafes, which have become an unofficial mecca for the Asian community.

Among the other establishments are Kotobukiya (354-6914), a handsome sushi bar: Six pieces of salmon maki-sushi cost $2.50. A combination plate of futomaki and inari sushi is $6.50. Tampopo (868-5457) offers fried tempura dinners, such as a shrimp and vegetable roll with a bowl of miso soup for $5.95, or assorted fried vegetables with soup and rice for $4.95. Ittyo (354-5944) is a traditional Japanese noodle shop, where $6.50 gets you a bowl of broth and noodles with a topping of curried beef, tempura, chicken, or boiled vegetables. And Sapporo Ramen (876- 4805) has even better noodle deals, such as $5.00 for a bowl of soy sauce-flavored ramen noodles with bamboo shoots, roast pork, bean sprouts, seaweed, and fish cake all mixed in together. All of these places are fun to return to and explore, along with the fancy shops displaying Eastern arts and crafts (alas, not so cheap!).

Cafe Troyka — 1154 Massachusetts Ave., Cambridge; 864-7476. New York may have the Russian Tea Room, in all its splendor; but here in cosmopolitan Harvard Square, Cafe Troyka gives you all that old world charm in a subdued—and much more affordable— setting. The food is delicious and quite different from so many other restaurants.

In fact, the menu is fun to just pore over, filled with all kinds of items large and small. You can order a full-sized entree or put several smaller dishes together into a hearty meal—that's where the fun comes in. Either way you can stay under $10.00 per person (no wine or beer is served, but patrons are welcome to bring their own).

Among the appetizer-type dishes, Mr. C enjoyed mushroom-barley soup ($2.35), a large bowl with whole fresh mushrooms in a clear, tasty broth with a dollop of sour cream at the bottom. Piroshki ($2.15) are crisp, flaky individual pies filled with meat, potato, or eggs and scallions. And a potato salad plate was big enough for two people, with potato wedges and vegetables in a light cream on a bed of lettuce.

There are larger dishes, such as pelmeni, or Russian dumplings ($5.85). Filled with meat or potato, these are evidence that different cuisines the world over are really variations on many of the same ideas. They could just as easily be filled wontons in a Chinese restaurant, or ravioli, or . . . Anyway, its a full plate of small, light dumplings served with mushroom sauce (potato) or soy sauce (meat).

Bigger still is the meat potato pie ($8.95), which combines layers of all of these; and the stuffed pepper or stuffed cabbage dinners ($8.00 to $9.00), which include a vegetable-tomato sauce and a side of black beans. Guriev kasha ($3.45) is listed as "a traditional St. Petersburg dish of sweet rice and raisins."

There are also blinchiki, which are like filled crepes; blini, Russian pancakes, topped with jam, lox, or caviar; oh, and of course hot or cold borscht. Desserts looked great, such as chocolate waffle torte and margarita cake (no, not the drink— layers of meringue, custard, and nuts), but Mr. C and his guest had so much fun trying the various dinner items that they had no room left. Another visit.

The atmosphere is cozy and intimate; each table has its own Orient Express brass lamp ("Paris—Istanbul"), and the walls are covered with framed photographs of famous Russian figures from Dostoevsky to Nabokov to Diaghilev. Not that any of them have eaten at the Troyka, but they would certainly have enjoyed it.

Cambridge Deli And Grill — 90 River St., Cambridge; 868-6740. Here's a great little spot tucked away just outside of Central Square. Don't blink or you'll miss it; and you'll be sorry, if you like barbecue.

You can take out or eat at one of the half-dozen tables. Mr. C loved the Texas-style ribs ($6.95), six meaty bones with lots of tangy sauce sitting atop a plate of fresh salad, shoestring fries, a slab of garlic bread, and a couple of crispy onion rings for good measure. A big, fun meal, complete with moist towelettes.

Chicken plates are available fried, barbecued, or Cajun- style. You can have it boneless or in shish kebabs, each on a bed of rice with salad. All variations cost around $6.00. The steak tip dinner is $6.50; but, for a truly cheap pig-out, go for the "Special Combo"— chicken, ribs and tips, with rice or fries and a salad, for $8.50.

There are seafood dinners as well, like fish and chips for $4.99 and a shrimp plate with fries, cole slaw, and potato salad for $7.25. And they have fresh quarter-pound burgers ($2.25 to $3.95), barbecue sandwiches, subs, salads, even stir-fry pita sandwiches, fresh pasta dinners, and homemade soups.

It's a big menu for a small place. They also offer catering, party platters, and chicken or ribs by the bucket. The guys behind the counter are relaxed and friendly, too. One catch, though; they're only open on weekdays. Grab it.

Charlie's Kitchen — 10 Eliot St., Cambridge; 492-9646. Charlie's Kitchen is one of those places that seems completely wrong for its surroundings; it's the opposite of almost every other restaurant in Harvard Square. Nestled among chic boutiques, across from the Charles Hotel, Charlie's is strictly a townie joint, where the long bar— with sports blaring on the TV— takes at least equal prominence with the dining booths. But don't be put off by its appearance; the guys are friendly and the waitress will call you "hon."

The menu sticks to basics, with food that sticks to your ribs. A plate of marinated steak tips ($5.95) is sure to keep you going for some time. Barbecued chicken, same price, is a hefty half-bird charbroiled in a tasty mild sauce, served up with lettuce, tomato, and plenty of shoestring french fries. Just about everything on the menu, from chicken to beef to pork chops, is in the $4.00-to-$6.00 price range.

Burgers, of course, are a mainstay here. The double cheeseburger special ($4.50) consists of two patties, each with cheese, and lettuce, tomato, pickles and fries. The patties are the pre-formed kind, but they're real beef, cooked on a flame grill. Add a bottle of Sam Adams and you can't go wrong.

Another good thing to know is that you can eat here late. Well, late is a relative term; at Charlie's you can still order food until midnight.

The appetizer menu, again, is the heavy basics: chicken fingers and wings, mozzarella sticks, potato skins, all from $2.00 to $4.00.

The decor is basic, too, with red formica and mirrored walls as the dominant design motif. It's strictly greasy spoon, but clean; and sometimes, after pushing your way through the crowds that have inexplicably gathered around some streetcorner mime, a joint like Charlie's can be just the sort of antidote you need in Le Square.

Christopher's — 1920 Massachusetts Ave., Cambridge; 876-9180. Christopher's is a popular Porter Square hangout with a huge menu, lots of international beers, all-natural food (much of it homemade), and good atmosphere, including a large fireplace. In fact, the only drawback is parking, which can be impossible in this area. There is a huge shopping center parking lot right across the street, but—even though there's plenty of room and the shops are closed at night—you can get towed or ticketed. Mr. C has warned you. However, the Porter Square T station (Red Line) is across the street too.

If all that makes you want to head south of the border, Christopher's can help in a big way—with lots of appetizers like Yucatan chicken wings ($4.95, large $6.95) marinated in citrus juice and mildly spicy; quesadillas filled with chicken and cheese ($3.50); and several varieties of nachos in the sizes regular, large and "elephantine" ($3.50 to $8.95). Dinners include six kinds of fajitas ($6.95 to $9.95), including shrimp and blackened tuna; as well as big enchiladas and chimichangas. But there is more to life than Mexican.

Moving around the menu, there are pasta dinners like whole wheat linguine with broccoli and marinated tofu ($7.95), stir-fry dishes (vegetables in ginger and garlic, $5.95) and grilled entrees such as chicken breast cooked in ginger, topped with molasses butter. Yuppie, yes, but then this is, as

the menu calls it, "Soon To Be Picturesque Porter Square."

So let's get back to regular stuff. Burgers are great here. They are large, fresh patties of ground sirloin served on whole-wheat buns with French fries that are thin and crispy. The basic "burgah" is $3.50; but for $4.95, choose from Cajun, barbecue, "Surfer" (with sprouts and guacamole, dude), or even Boursin.

The beer list is extensive, with brands like Courage, Guinness, and Cambridge's own Tall Tale Pale Ale on draft. In bottles there are over forty different brews, from Aass (Norway) to Xingu Black (Brazil). They have Woodpecker Cider, non-alcoholic beers, several wines, and coffee liqueur drinks.

Sandwiches are big, too. The Club Christopher ($4.95) is a big triple-decker with real turkey breast, bacon, lettuce, tomato, and those great fries. And then there is "Chuck's Veggie Peace Burgah" ($4.95), a vegetarian patty of mushrooms, brown rice, oats, cheese, chilies, egg whites, and several other healthy ingredients on a French roll or whole wheat bun. Part of the price goes to the "1% for Peace" fund; a portion of Visa card sales is also donated to the Boston Food Bank and Oxfam America. Cambridge at its best.

Christopher's features live folk and blues music with no cover charge on Thursday, Friday, and Saturday nights. Food is served until midnight. There is also a Sunday jazz brunch from 10:30 to 3:00.

Crystal Restaurant — 460 Massachusetts Ave., Cambridge; 576-1550. Among the many ethnic restaurants in Central Square, Crystal stands out with its large Chinese menu, low prices, and speedy, attentive service. They specialize in Szechuan cooking, with three levels of spiciness for any taste; but they offer Mandarin and Cantonese dishes as well.

The regular menu alone has almost two hundred items, from homemade Peking ravioli for just

$3.50 to seafood, moo shi, yu hsiang, chop suey, chow mein, and other noodle dishes, almost all of which are in the $5.00-to-$7.00 price range.

Chef's specialties go a bit higher; spiced duck is $9.95, sesame beef with broccoli is $8.95, and "Seafood Delight" at $8.75 consists of shrimp, scallops, and fish fillets in lobster sauce.

But there are real bargains to be had among the many choices: Minced pork tenderloins in lobster sauce is just $4.50, all of the rice and noodle dishes are in the $4.00-to-$6.00 range, and good ol' sweet and sour chicken is $5.95.

Luncheon specials, which are available from 11:30 all the way to 4:30, offer another forty or more deals, most of which are priced at $4.25 and come with a delicious, not too spicy, hot and sour soup. Chicken wings, chicken chow mein, and pork fried rice is one such plate; also beef with vegetables on rice and the wonderful "Three Delight Noodles."

These same specials are repeated as "late-night snacks" from 9 p.m. until closing, except on weekends. Whichever you go for, the portions are huge and the food is delicious.

E.B., A Rendezvous — 152 Columbia St., Cambridge; 661-8858. E.B's is a Creole snack shop tucked away on the sidestreets between Central and Inman Squares. It's the kind of place in which you order at the counter and they bring the food to your table. The menu consists mainly of lunch-size and dinner-size platters, both available at any time of day. Lunches range from $5.00 to $6.00, and dinners from $7.00 to $10.00; the choices are the same, only the dinner portions are larger.

There's baked chicken, fried pork, beef vegetable (a mildly spiced stew), fish, goat, conch, and ragou. "That's cow's feet," the waitress pointed out. Mr. C left it on the hoof. The beef and chicken were very tasty, though; each meal comes with rice and beans, fried

plantain, a bit of salad, and a lemonade. Extra drink options are the various juices and sodas imported from the Caribbean. The lunches are just enough for an average appetite, but a hungry person will want to go for the dinner.

The neighborhood is a little on the tough side, but the folks who come in are friendly—and the food is real home-style.

El Greco — 251-255 Cambridge St., Cambridge; 492-7232. True to its name, El Greco is a Greek-American diner offering traditional Mediterranean food. The portions are hearty, and the prices are unbelievably cheap. It's located across from the courthouse in East Cambridge, and around the corner from the Cambridge Multicultural Arts Center.

El Greco is a family-run restaurant in a working-class neighborhood. It is busiest during the day, when local folks stop in for lunch; but the place is open for dinner as well, with beer and wine available. There are pizzas and sandwiches, burgers and salads; dinners, though, are best of all.

All dinner entrees are under $6.00, and most come with potato and vegetables. Many also come with pita bread, which requires a moment of attention: this is no ordinary pita out of some plastic bag. El Greco makes its own pita, homemade and hot from the oven. It's thick and chewy, and it tastes great all by itself. Sandwiches are served in it; souvlaki, for example ($4.75) is large chunks of beef in a creamy garlic sauce, rolled up in a pita and toasted. It's delightfully messy and big enough to take some home for later. Gyros are $3.75.

Homemade soups, in three varieties, come also with bread. Egg lemon chicken soup is an unusual and tasty concoction, and there is a more conventional turkey soup (both $2.50). Beef stew is $3.25 for a good-sized bowl.

Meanwhile, back to the dinners. A chalkboard over the counter will alert you to the daily specials, which can be wonderful.

"Greek-style fish" ($4.95) is a large plate covered with broken-up pieces of flaky white fish (look out for bones, though!). It is served over slices of cooked potato and baked in a tomato and herb sauce. It's light and delicious.

Homemade meatloaf ($5.25) is a thick slab swimming in gravy, served with mashed potato and vegetables. A customer was heard to tell the hostess it was the best meatloaf in town. You can also get roast beef, turkey, and shish kebab dinners ($5.75 each); veal cutlet with spaghetti ($5.25); or fish and chips ($4.00).

El Greco is also open for breakfast from 6:30 a.m., except on Sunday (11 a.m.), with some of the lowest prices around. Two eggs with home fries, toast, and bacon, ham, or sausage are just $1.75. The "Grec" special adds another egg, an extra slice of meat, and coffee to the above—all for $3.50. Pancakes or French toast are $1.30, or $1.75 with bacon or sausage. Three-egg omelettes are $3.50 to $3.75 with toast and home fries.

Of course, you can just get a side order of pita bread for 75¢. Mmmmm.

El Rancho — 1126 Cambridge St., Cambridge; 868-2309. Located just outside of Inman Square, El Rancho is one of the few places in Boston where you can get "comidas tipicas" of El Salvador. This tiny storefront kitchen offers Mexican food as well, and it's all carefully prepared and flavorful, with sizeable portions.

The Mexican side of the menu offers the standard burritos, tostadas, etc. with prices in the $5.00-to-$6.00 range. Among the more interesting specialties was "Chicken el Sol" ($6.50), in which corn tortilla chips were neatly arranged around the rim of the plate, like a Mayan painting of the sun. A generous portion of rice was laid over this, topped by another layer of chips, and finally a layer of diced chicken in a tangy tomato sauce. It was absolutely delicious.

A special of the day was a vegetable chimichanga plate with rice, salad and frijole beans for just $5.35. Appetizers include nachos or guacamole and chips, each $4.99.

Mr. C also tried some of the Salvadoran cuisine; the most unusual of these were pupusas, soft corn tortillas filled with pork or cheese, with vegetables, and fried up brown and moist. A platter of three came with beans and a spicy cole slaw for a mere $4.50; again, a filling and yummy meal.

Among the other Salvadoran dishes are carne asada, a large, sizzling steak, for $8.25; and several egg dishes such as "Huevos Estrelladas" ($4.95), a fried egg plate. Sopa Mondongo, a tripe soup, comes in a hearty bowl for $2.75, with a tortilla.

With many of the meals you can add a side order of guacamole for 95¢. Also, there are bottles of hot sauce on the tables for those with spicier appetites. The service is friendly, if a bit slow, and the folks will be happy to explain the delicacies for you. Muy bueno.

Fresco's Cafe And Grille — 134 Massachusetts Ave., Cambridge; 491-8866. Along the M.I.T. stretch of Massachusetts Ave., Fresco's is a spiffy new cafe with a wide variety of food and great prices. From breakfast (the house special is two eggs, home fries, and toast for $1.49) through lunch and dinner (the place closes at 9 p.m.), there are all kinds of meals to choose from.

Gyros on pita bread ($2.99) is a good helping of delicious slices of meat with a cucumber-yogurt sauce for dipping. Make a dinner of it with fries or salad for $4.95. Also for $2.99 there is a chicken kebab or filet sandwich (dinner, $4.95). Fish and chips are only $3.95; and for $4.95, the swordfish kebab dinner is a steal. Plenty of charcoal-grilled chunks of fish over rice with a tomato sauce, and salad. Terrific.

Moving (not far) up the scale,

you can even get a barbecued half-chicken dinner for $5.25—with salad and rice or crispy French fries. Elsewhere on the menu, fried scallops, clams, or shrimp dinners are $6.95; fried haddock is $5.95. Veal or chicken cutlet with spaghetti is just $4.75.

For nibblers, the chef's salad is only $3.85, Greek salad is $3.75, and seafood salad is $4.15.

Fresco's also makes pizzas ($3.75 to $8.75) with all kinds of meat and vegetarian toppings, in large and small sizes. Hot and cold subs, including grilled steak subs, go from $2.45 to $4.45. Quarter-pound burgers and hot dogs are also available.

In short, this is the kind of place Mr. C loves. The prices are great and the place is clean and bright, with lots of tables and quick service. And you can keep going back all the time without having the same kind of food from day to day.

Goemon — One Kendall Square, Cambridge; 577-9595. Also, 267 Huntington Ave., Boston; 859-8669. Goemon is that rarest of rare birds; a restaurant that is trendy, healthy, and, of course, cheap. This recent addition to Boston's dining scene is a Japanese-style "noodle house" that is handsome to look at and fun to eat in. From the hostess who greets you in a traditional Japanese robe to the rice-paper screens and sparely-decorated tables, the atmosphere at Goemon is definitely different.

The main dining room features an open kitchen, where you can watch the chefs preparing huge vats of noodles, chopping vegetables, and so on. Off to one side there is a separate bar with the same look of elegance for a quiet drink.

As anyone who has seen the movie "Tampopo" knows, bowls of noodle soup are much more of a Japanese staple than sushi. At Goemon that's practically all there is—but it's by no means a limited selection. First you have to pick your noodle: soba, a thin buck-wheat noodle in a fish and sea vegetable broth; udon, a thicker, chewy version of the same; or ramen, a thin curly whole-wheat noodle in a pork and beef-based broth.

Now, what else will go into your soup? There is a variety of choices. Chashu ramen comes topped with roasted pork, bamboo shoots, spinach, and scallions. Kitsune features soba or udon noodles with sweet-fried tofu squares, fish cake, snowpeas, and scallions. Tempura substitutes large, crispy, battered shrimp for the tofu. Each of these dishes ranges in price from just $4.25 to $5.95 and is filling enough to be a meal in itself.

You may also "create your own" entree with anything from crispy, unflavored tempura to bean-sprouts, raw egg, toasted sea vegetables, and even smoked eel. It doesn't take much to produce a packed bowl that will fill you up for around $6.00 to $8.00.

For the heartier appetite, complete dinners are available, a noodle soup accompanied by one of Goemon's appetizers, such as shu-mai—shrimp and vegetable dumplings served with a dipping sauce. Other appetizers include yakitori, grilled skewers of chicken with scallions in a teriyaki sauce, and ika tempura, which is batter-fried squid.

Try a traditional Japanese drink with your meal, like a cup of green tea or an individual carafe of sake—the sweet plum wine that is served warm. Desserts consist of fresh fruit or ice cream with flavors like ginger or red bean.

Already a fixture in the music schools area, Goemon's second location is in the One Kendall Square complex, a handsome red-brick plaza that includes the Cambridge Brewing Company and is one of greater Boston's newest "happening" locales.

Good Stuff Cafe — 1908 Massachusetts Ave., Cambridge; 876-6645. Good Stuff is a pleasant little Porter Square eatery with a Mediterranean menu. The interior is warm and cozy, with booths and greenery. It's a nice place to hang out and chat.

And, of course, eat. All the Middle Eastern foods are here, with falaffel, baba ganoush, kebabs, and more. Most are available as entrees or sandwiches. Among the more interesting entrees are mujeddara, a plate of spiced lentil beans mixed with rice and onions. It's served with a side salad for $5.95. Msa'ah, an eggplant casserole, comes at the same price, as does the special of the day. On Mr. C's visit this was fasolia, chunks of lamb with lima beans and rice.

Kebab dinners are a bit higher, from $6.95 to $7.50, but you do get a good portion, served over rice pilaf. There are also delicious soups ($2.00); the lentil was thick with beans, celery, potato, and spinach.

Sandwiches, however, are the real bargains here. At $2.50, the falaffel pita comes rolled up with pieces of good falaffel, along with lettuce, tomato, and tahini sauce. It'll fill you up. Add hummus for $3.25. The kafta sandwich ($3.50) is yummy, a grilled mixture of beef, onion, and spices. Lamb, beef, and chicken kebab sandwiches are $3.80. There are also burgers ($4.80), in beef and tofu varieties.

For dessert, have a piece of baklava ($1.25). It's small but wonderfully sweet. Good Stuff is also a popular breakfast spot, with omelettes from $2.75; the house spe-

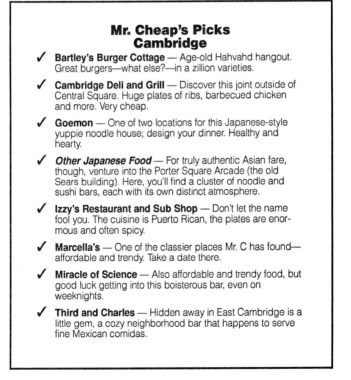

Mr. Cheap's Picks
Cambridge

✓ **Bartley's Burger Cottage** — Age-old Hahvahd hangout. Great burgers—what else?—in a zillion varieties.

✓ **Cambridge Deli and Grill** — Discover this joint outside of Central Square. Huge plates of ribs, barbecued chicken and more. Very cheap.

✓ **Goemon** — One of two locations for this Japanese-style yuppie noodle house; design your dinner. Healthy and hearty.

✓ *Other Japanese Food* — For truly authentic Asian fare, though, venture into the Porter Square Arcade (the old Sears building). Here, you'll find a cluster of noodle and sushi bars, each with its own distinct atmosphere.

✓ **Izzy's Restaurant and Sub Shop** — Don't let the name fool you. The cuisine is Puerto Rican, the plates are enormous and often spicy.

✓ **Marcella's** — One of the classier places Mr. C has found— affordable and trendy. Take a date there.

✓ **Miracle of Science** — Also affordable and trendy food, but good luck getting into this boisterous bar, even on weeknights.

✓ **Third and Charles** — Hidden away in East Cambridge is a little gem, a cozy neighborhood bar that happens to serve fine Mexican comidas.

cial, a dollar more, is filled with ground beef, onions, peppers, tomatoes, and olives. By the way, the place is great for take-out.

Indian Globe — 474 Massachusetts Ave., Cambridge; 868-1866. Located in the heart of Central Square, Indian Globe is one of the best Indian restaurants around. The atmosphere is casual, with music of India piped into a room of subdued lighting and authentic decor. Yet the service is very quick and attentive. The prices are about a dollar less per entree than many other Indian restaurants in the area (and there are many).

The meal begins as soon as you sit down, and a basket of pappad—sort of like curry-flavored lentil chips—is placed on the table. Mr. C also enjoyed a cup of tea that had a cinnamon flavor to it.

You will, of course, want to order one of the many warm breads with your meal. Paratha ($1.75) is a flaky, flat, whole-wheat bread about the size of a dinner plate. It's cooked in butter—soft and chewy, and piping hot. Onion kulcha ($2.25) is also good, made with a thin filling of onion and spices.

For appetizers, Mr. C recommends chicken pakora ($3.25): four large balls of rolled chicken, coated in a spicy batter, come with two different sauces for dipping. There is also a vegetable version for $2.25.

Chicken entrees dominate the menu, in fact, from the basic tandoori style ($7.50) to chicken tikka masala ($8.45), boneless pieces of white meat grilled in spices and served in a creamy tomato sauce. There are also plenty of lamb and seafood entrees, such as good ol' lamb curry ($7.65), made to your preference of spiciness. There are no beef items on the menu.

On the vegetarian side there are lots of choices too. Chana masala ($6.95) is a tasty preparation of chick peas in a tomato sauce with just a bit of zing to it, served with rice (as are all entrees). Or, try the mattar paneer ($6.95), homemade cottage cheese cooked

with peas and spices. For a real bargain you can order both as the Thai-E-House vegetarian special: the platter includes pappad, poori bread, raita (whipped yogurt with cucumber, potato, and tomato), rice, tea or coffee, and dessert, all for just $9.50. There is also a lamb and chicken version for $10.25.

Speaking of bargains, Indian Globe serves up daily luncheon plates from the main menu, most of which are $3.95—like keema mattar, ground lamb in a curry sauce with ginger and peas. And for the hefty appetite there is a buffet brunch offered every day from noon to 3 p.m., with all you can eat for $5.95. You can really put together quite a meal here, and it's all delicious.

Izzy's Restaurant And Sub Shop — 169 Harvard St., Cambridge; 661-3910. Izzy's is an out-of-the-way neighborhood kitchen serving up "Comidas Criollas"—native Puerto Rican food. It's a very homey establishment, as the many Latino faces at the tables prove. Despite the name, this is a great place to get hot meals.

When you walk in, the menu over the counter is bewildering. Each item is numbered, with items totaling well over a hundred. Yes, there are subs—even some unusual varieties, like fried pork or fajita subs—but more interesting here are the Spanish dishes. In many cases you can get a full meal for around five dollars.

You will also see menu items at Izzy's that aren't found at too many other places. Feel like some fried plantain ($1.50), a sweet, firm banana that is sliced and deep-fried? Have a taste for tripe soup ($2.50/$4.75), or a passion for pig feet stew ($4.65)? Here's where you'll find them, done to perfection. Even Mr. C, known to his friends as a devout banana-hater, loved the plantain.

Moving on to the dinners, there are endless combination plates. Many start off with black or red beans, rice, and salad (have this alone for just $3.25, to which you may add fried ribs ($4.65); a pair of pork chops or sirloin tips ($5.75 each); chorizo, a kind of sausage ($5.25); fajita ($5.75); and more. Or put it all together with the hearty montanero plate ($6.85): rice, beans, salad, steak, fried pork, fried egg, and plantain.

There is a set rotation of daily specials, which range from the exotic to the merely out-of-place. Tuesdays, for example, feature stewed goat, rice, and salad for $4.95. On Fridays, try the conch meat, rice, and plantain special for $5.75. Also on Fridays, though, you can get chicken cacciatore (!) with rice and salad for $5.35. Don't know how that got in there. Wash your meal down with one of the many interesting choices in the refrigerator case, like a non-alcoholic malt beverage or a bottle of pineapple soda.

There are ten tables or so, many decorated under their glass tops with postcards of Puerto Rico, for further atmosphere. The place fills up at the dinner hour, and so Izzy's also does a substantial take-out business. Either way, it's an experience.

Jake & Earl's Dixie B-B-Q —
1273 Cambridge St., Cambridge; 491-RIBS (7427). This Inman Square hole-in-the-wall is simply the other side of the kitchen—and a cheap alternative—to the pricey East Coast Grill next door. Both establishments have become popular spots for great southern-style food. They tout their 1989 mention in People magazine as one of the ten-best barbecue restaurants in the country.

Jake & Earl's creates a ton of atmosphere in a tiny space. The walls are lined with roadhouse decor: license plates, old-fashioned advertising signs, a bust of Elvis. As for dining amidst all this paraphernalia, well, there are about five stools along two walls, and that's it. The joint is really best suited for take-out.

What's good here? You guessed it: Ribs! The Memphis Dry

Rub Ribs plate ($7.50) is a house specialty—a half-dozen pork ribs rubbed in dry spices and slow-cooked to a smoky, not spicy, taste. They're served over—yes—a slice of white bread. *That's* down home. You also get cole slaw, some zingy pork and beans, and a hunk of watermelon. All plates come with these fixings.

Most other items on the limited menu are even cheaper. The pulled pork sandwich plate ($3.95) is marinated pork grilled to such tender juiciness that it's easily "pulled" off the bones and made into a nice, messy sandwich. Ditto for the brisket sandwich; there's even a "Burnt Ends" version ($4.25 either way) for those who like their meat *really* well done.

Poultry fans have two options: Jamaican "jerk" chicken ($7.00), with a smoky flavor—try it with banana guava ketchup—and barbecued chicken ($6.50). Both serve up half a bird with lots of flavor. And only the strong of heart (and tongue) may want to go for the "Hot, Hot West Indies Sausage" ($3.75).

Of course, there are all kinds of sauces to enhance your enjoyment: again, if you are brave, bottles of "Inner Beauty Real Hot Sauce" stand waiting. It must take a special kind of glass to contain this fiery condiment. Mercifully, there are milder sauces as well. Yow!

Jake & Earl's also offers daily items of unusual creativity from cuisines of the world: a recent special was Senegalese fish stew for $3.25, served with a side of corn bread. This actually consists of glorified leftovers from the restaurant side—but that can mean chunks of fresh tuna or marlin mixed with unusual vegetables. After all, the leftovers this place cooks with are bound to be pretty darned fancy.

Marcella's —
1808 Massachusetts Ave., Cambridge; 547-5000. Also, 1 Appleton St., Boston; 742-7382. If you're looking for a place that serves the carefully-prepared nouvelle cuisine of Boston's chic restaurants, without the trendy prices,

Marcella's is the answer. Or, to look at it another way, it's a *very* fancy take-out sandwich shop with a dozen white linen-topped tables at the back for dinner.

Either way, the food is great and affordable, if not exactly cheap. Mr. C still thinks it's a lovely place for a casual meal that seems elegant. Yes, the sandwiches are all priced from $6.00 to $8.00, but think of what you get: Roast beef with smoked mozzarella, sun-dried tomatoes, and Marcella's own house dressing. Or chicken salad made with apples and raisins, or Italian-style fresh tuna with imported sweet peppers, onions, lettuce, and dressing. The sandwiches are huge, served on fresh, crusty baguettes.

Dinners, in the same price range, may offer better values. Mr. C and his dining companion chose to share a few items, making a delicious, filling, and inexpensive meal. The specialty of the house is the "Pollo Platter" ($6.75), which puts a rotisseried, juicy half-chicken atop a garnish of tomatoes and cucumbers, with a side dish of oven-roasted potatoes. There's plenty of everything. Prosciutto and melon ($5.00) was the right combination of sweet and salty (eating here even makes you talk like a food critic), and again, there was enough to share. On the side was an order of Tuscan-style garlic bread ($2.00), several long crusts.

Marcella's also has salads, antipastos, pasta, and pizzas with such toppings as spinach, chicken pesto, fresh garlic, and ripe olives. The basic version is $6.75; the top of the line, for $12.75, features Scottish smoked salmon, capers, black pepper, and herb cheese. Split one and you'll eat fancy but still cheap!

With your meal there are several beers and house wines, by the bottle, half-carafe, or glass; and afterwards, splurge with an espresso, iced cappuccino, orzata (almond-flavored soda) and something from the bakery—cannoli, cakes, and pastries.

Recently, Marcella's opened a second, larger restaurant in the South End, at the corner of Tremont and Appleton Streets. The menu offers more in the way of full dinners, and is equally affordable: one special is a twenty-ounce steak, with oven-roasted potatoes and vegetable, for $7.95. Who needs Paris?

Middle East Restaurant And Cafe

— 472 Massachusetts Ave., Cambridge; 354-8238. How does one begin to describe the venerable Middle East? It's a bit of a Moroccan pleasure palace in the heart of Central Square, sprawling around a busy corner, offering in various chambers delicious food and adventurous music. It's big, yet each room is cozy, with a different atmosphere.

The main restaurant, three doors down from the corner of Brookline St., has the charm of Casablanca—with large, green plants everywhere, intimate booths and tables, and other Middle Eastern decor. Walk through to the back and you'll find the music room tucked away, like some kind of Persian speakeasy. There is a cover charge for the entertainment, which may be anything from cutting edge rock to progressive jazz; but you can stand in the breezeway for a moment and check out the act.

Connected (well, through the kitchen) is yet another dining room, which the staff refers to as the bakery. It's actually best entered from Mass. Ave. (the door at the corner), and is a smaller, less ornate space. You can indeed snack on a piece of homemade baklava and herbal tea; but in fact the same full menu is available here as in the other part of the restaurant. There is also a fairly extensive list of international beers, including Anchor Steam, Pilsner Urquell, Xingu, and New Castle Brown Ale.

The food itself is terrific, elaborate preparations of smooth stews, kebabs, and exotic bean dishes. Mr. C tasted the Mjudra ($6.50), a simple and tasty plate of lentils, rice, onions, and mild spices. The serving was big enough for leftovers. Among the other vegetarian dishes, Msa'ah ($7.25) was a delicious mixture of baked eggplant, sauteed onions, tomatoes, and chick peas, served over rice pilaf. Again, a hefty portion.

The kebab entrees, all priced from $7.50 to $8.95, include scallop, swordfish, and shrimp skewers along with the standard beef, lamb, and chicken. All are charcoal-grilled and come with rice pilaf. Also interesting is masbahet darwish ($8.50), a lamb stew made with zucchini, squash, eggplant, carrots, peppers, string beans, and chunks of lamb leg. It comes with salad and rice as one of the daily specials.

Lunch is an even better bargain at the Middle East, with all entrees ranging from $3.50 to $4.95, and generous portions. A falaffel sandwich at lunch is $2.85, and there are exotic salads and homemade soups as well.

Miracle Of Science — 321 Massachusetts Ave., Cambridge; 868-2866. Everyone assumes the theme of this bar has to do with its proximity to MIT, but there's no relation. The real miracle here is that this trendy place, with its hip futuristic design, serves such terrific food so cheaply.

Big half-pound burgers are $4.75, as is the grilled chicken sandwich; there are several Mexican appetizers as well. The true standouts, though, are the skewer plates—thick, juicy shish kebabs, creatively prepared. Try citrus thyme shrimp with chutney, or pomeroy beef and horseradish sauce. Each plate comes with tortillas, black beans, succotash, and mint cole slaw— nouvelle chic in a bar. One-skewer plates are just $3.75, and two skewers are $7.50. Big desserts, too.

Lots of great domestic and imported beers are available; what's not available most nights, unfortunately, is table space. The place is pretty small and extremely popular, so get there early if you plan to eat. Open for lunch and dinner.

Mom's Kitchen — 313 Massachusetts Ave., Cambridge; 492-9508. Yes, this dingy-looking storefront diner is really a great place for breakfast or lunch; and yes, there's really a "Mom" cooking up a storm behind the counter.

She opens up early for the working crowd, at 5:30 a.m.; grab two eggs, home fries, toast, and coffee for $1.75 until 9:00. Other morning fare, 'til about noon, includes blueberry pancakes ($3.25) and the "Flying Saucer" ($2.25)—a fried egg on a large, toasted sweet roll with three strips of bacon and melted cheese. Hey, who needs arteries, anyway?

Lunch offers the standards, like a hamburger and French fries for $2.50, and various sandwiches. But wait! Check out the specials menu, printed up daily. You may find a "Fisherman's Platter" of Maryland crab cakes, fried scallops, baked schrod, fried shrimp, French fries, cole slaw, and a roll—all for $6.95. Or two stuffed pork chops in gravy, with potatoes au gratin and cooked vegetables for $4.85. There are half-a-dozen specials like these each day. Wow!

Finish off with coffee and a slice of Mom's homemade apple pie ($1.60). Lunch ends the day, though—the joint locks up by 3:00. Closed Sundays, too.

Moody's Falaffel Palace — 25 Central Square, Cambridge; 864-0827. A relative newcomer, Moody's is perhaps one of the best of the area's many Middle Eastern eateries. Located just off of Mass. Ave., this tiny kitchen really puts out a ton of great, cheap food. The sandwiches—grape leaves, kebabs, and of course, falaffel—are giant, and all priced from $2.25 to $3.00. A cup of lentil soup, just 99¢, is light and tummy-warming, with bits of corn and peas mixed in.

The dinners are hearty too— the falaffel plate, with salad, is just $2.25. Chicken or beef kebabs, served over rice pilaf, are each $3.95, as is moussaka, kafta, kibby, or grape leaves, with rice or salad.

Nearing the top of the line are shawarma and rice ($5.00), grilled fish kebab with rice ($5.25), and the combination platter—chicken or beef kebabs, baba ganoush, hummus, and falafel, all for $5.75. There is also a vegetarian version for $4.25.

There are just a few stools by the window in this humble place, which is clean and bright. They are also open until midnight, seven days a week.

Peppercorn's Restaurant — 154 Prospect St., Cambridge; 661-2022. A cozy, casual, American-style restaurant just outside of Inman Square, good for sandwiches or dinner. The values here are incredible. The only item on the large menu that tops $10.00 (by a mere 49¢) is the prime rib, available only on weekend nights "while it lasts"—and you get fourteen ounces of meat, plus vegetable and salad.

Other entrees offer a bit of everything. A seafood casserole ($7.49) of baked scallops, shrimp, and cod with salad and potato; Cajun chicken breast with rice ($5.99); "A Pound" of pork chops ($7.89), either barbecued or Cajun; lamb shish kebab ($8.89) with rice or vegetables and salad.

Gourmet burgers have a half-pound of fresh beef on an onion roll with steak fries, tomato, and onion slices. There are eight varieties, most around $4.50. So are the deli sandwiches, like chicken parmesan, hot pastrami with cheese, "Texas Grande" (hot roast beef, cheddar, mushrooms), and "Mrs. Peppercorn's Spinach Pie," served with rice and salad.

Brunch is a big deal here. Saturdays and Sundays from 8 a.m. to 2:30 p.m. there is an all-you-can-eat buffet for $7.99 per person. The hot and cold buffet boasts forty-five items: quiche, muffins, seafood salad, fruit, veggies, and hot items from the kitchen. Order some Eggs Benedict, pancakes, or an omelette; it's all included. Come early, since there can be a wait for tables during the rush hour; and come hungry—you can really stuff yourself.

Pugliese's Bar And Restaurant — 635 Cambridge St., East Cambridge; 491-9616. "Pug's" is another divey bar that is a nice surprise if you don't mind downscale surroundings—such as folks at the bar smoking and chatting up a storm. There are plenty of tables, though they are packed in closely, and the crowd is mostly local regulars. But there's no need to feel unwelcome.

There's also no need to go hungry. What started out to look like a standard, cheap, pub meal on Mr. C's visit turned out to be a feast. Here's what happened. Mr. C's friend ordered steak tips ($4.95), which come, the menu said, with French fries or pasta. The friend requested the pasta. A few minutes later the waitress came out with a full-sized plate of linguini in tomato sauce, a meal by itself, along with grated cheese and a half-loaf of warm, crusty bread. This was followed by another plate with the steak, also a good-sized portion.

Needless to say, this was almost enough for two people—even though Mr. C had ordered a half-pound cheeseburger with lettuce, tomato, and fries. This came to a whopping $3.10. The burger was fresh, the fries were hand-cut, the pasta was nicely al dente. The tips were underdone, but the cook was happy to put them back on. Later he came out himself to ask if they were all right, which they were by then anyway.

As the bartender himself said, the place is a bit like your mom's kitchen—just go in and grab some food, lots of it. Other dinners include chicken parmigiana ($4.75), sirloin steak ($5.95), and a host of pasta dishes. Choose linguini ($3.75) or ravioli ($3.95), with meatballs, eggplant, or sausage, plus salad and bread.

There are also sandwiches, hot subs, calzones, and pizza. In fact, Wednesday is pizza night: all you can eat for just $2.00. Wash it down with Pug's own draft beer,

$1.00 for a twelve-ounce glass. Doesn't get much cheaper than this, folks.

The Skewers — 92 Mt. Auburn St., Cambridge; 491-3079. One flight below street level, across from the Garage Mall in Harvard Square, the Skewers is a Cambridge institution for great food cheap. It offers an eclectic mix of international cuisines, mostly Middle Eastern; this is odd, since the owners are from India, according to an article framed on the wall. No matter.

The falaffel is fresh and made with whole chick peas mixed into the filling, for a bit of crunch. You can get it in a pita sandwich for $2.95, including lettuce, tomato, cucumber, peppers, onions, and sauce. The dinner plate version is $4.95. Shish kebabs, in lamb, chicken, or beef, are $3.75 for sandwiches and $5.75 for dinners. Various combinations are available for $4.50 or $6.50.

The daddy of these combos is the maza plate for two ($13.00), with shawarma, beef kebabs, hummus, baba ganoush, falaffel, rice and salad. It's filling and healthy. The vegetarian version costs $5.95 ($10.95 for two). And another great dinner plate is the Middle East baked chicken: half a chicken marinated with raisins and mushrooms and cooked until the meat falls off the bones. It's served with rice pilaf, Greek salad, and bread, all for $6.25.

Then the menu turns strangely American, with burgers like the Southwestern, topped with avocado; and Eastern, with teriyaki beef or chicken. These are all $3.75 for sandwiches and $5.75 for dinners, with rice and salad.

For dessert, don't miss the baklava ($1.25). During Mr. C's visit, someone was heard to say it was the best baklava he had ever tasted.

The restaurant itself gives you a choice of table service or do-it-yourself counter service, allowing you to save an extra dollar or two. The table area at the back is nice and mellow, a rare commodity in the hubbub of Harvard Square.

Tasty Sandwich Shop — 2A J.F.K. St., Cambridge; 354-9016. "The Tasty," established in 1916 (it says so in the window), is indeed a long-time Harvard Square landmark—that tiny little lunch counter right on the corner facing Out Of Town News. Unlike so much of the chic Hah-vahd area, the Tasty ain't fancy and it ain't high-priced. There is only room for about a dozen people. It's a friendly place for a quick burger or sandwich, cup o' coffee, maybe a bowl of soup. And it's open all night.

It helps to love grease here. This is not a place for the healthiest of diets. Most food comes off the griddle, like the hamburger ($1.75) or cheeseburger ($2.00). These are thin patties, so Mr. C recommends the double versions of these ($2.75/$3.00). Grilled cheese sandwiches are $2.00; $3.00 with bacon and $3.75 with tuna. Grilled breast of chicken is a mere $2.50.

There are several deluxe sandwiches, all with appropriate local names like the Brattle Club—two burger patties, a fried egg, lettuce, and tomato on a bun, with French fries—all for $5.00. The Cape Cod Club is a fish fillet with lettuce, tomato, and fries for $4.50. And the Boston Plate consists of two frankfurters and beans, $5.00.

Egg dishes are also plentiful. A plain omelette is $2.50, and a western is $3.75; two eggs any style, with bacon or sausage, go for $3.75. French toast is $2.75, a dollar more for bacon.

And what better way to top off a heavy snack than with a good ol' Boston frappe? These are $2.75. Or try something from the inevitable pastry case (you know, the round kind with the glass top that sits on the counter. The Tasty is a truly great American hangout, a window on the world—the wacky world of Harvard Square, that is.

Third and Charles Bar and Grill — 202 East Third St., East Cambridge; 547-9310. This little hideaway is a little gem of a Mexican restaurant and bar. It's near, but not in the thick of, the chic area that has risen around the Cambridgeside Galleria mall; it's more in the older, residential part of east Cambridge, between Kendall Square and the big courthouse. So the atmosphere is a neighborhood bar all the way. Inside, the rooms are cozy, but with plenty of tables, and the service is friendly.

A basket of warm tortilla chips and salsa will be brought to you before you order, always a good sign. The well-stocked bar has plenty of Mexican beers and drinks on hand, including big frozen margaritas. For appetizers, along with the usual wings, fingers and nachos, you can get a generous quesadilla ($4.95) filled with your choice of chicken, steak and green chili, bacon and mushroom, or even spinach and broccoli (as you will see, this place does a couple of "Cambridge" turns on Mexican cuisine).

Mexican pizza for one ($2.95) can be ordered with a variety of meat or vegetable toppings, and you can have beef or chicken tacos, soft or hard shell, at $1.75 each (two for $3.00, three for $4.25). You can also have a taco platter, your choice of two tacos served with Mexican rice, for $4.50. With all appetizers, as well as entrees, the menu "dares" you to ask for your meal hot—or *very* hot.

The enchiladas are delicious—soft corn tortillas rolled with beef, chicken or "Florentine" (spinach and cheese) fillings, then topped with a zingy sauce and melted cheese. As with most items on the menu, you may order various combinations; the enchilada trio ($5.95) is a real bargain, with one of each type served over Mexican rice. They're soft, moist, and yummy.

Dinner entrees include fajitas ($5.50), slices of chicken or steak grilled with onions and peppers and served with rice and three warm tortillas so you can "roll your own." T & C Pollo ($5.75) is a boneless breast of chicken sauteed with mushrooms and bacon in a sour cream sauce, served on a bed of rice.

There are a few items from this side of the Tex-Mex border, such as a chicken and avocado salad and barbecued baby back ribs (each $5.95); but the real house specialties are clearly those south of the border. Mr. C suggests you get your posse on over there and rustle up some grub for yourself.

Tommy's Lunch — 49 Mt. Auburn St., Cambridge; 492-9540. Down a bit from Harvard Square, Tommy's Lunch is another of the area's many student hangouts—a good place for a quick plate of fries or a decent meal, cheap. Video games and discussions of global politics define the ambience of the place.

You can sit at the soda-fountain-style counter or take your tray to a table. There are four or five daily specials on the board in the window, like homemade lasagna served with a side salad and a roll for $4.85. Meatloaf ($4.75) comes with mashed potatoes, cooked vegetables, and a roll. Another dinner choice on a recent evening was a chicken cutlet, also $4.75, with lettuce, tomato, and French fries.

Soups are homemade too, and good. Chicken soup ($1.50 per cup, $2.25 for a bowl), contained noodles, vegetables, and a dash of spice. Lentil soup, beef stew, and chili were also on the menu. There is quite an array of sandwiches, from seafood salad in a pita pocket ($3.85) to a grilled chicken breast sandwich ($2.95) and all the usual deli choices.

Breakfast is super cheap, with three eggs, toast, and home fries for just $2.00. Add sausage for a total of $2.85. Tommy's also has baked pastries on display and is one of the few places in town to get a good lime rickey (90¢/$1.50). They also make floats, frappes, and egg creams.

Catering further to the college crowd, Tommy's stays open until 2:00 a.m.

JAMAICA PLAIN

Acapulco Restaurant — 464 Centre St., Jamaica Plain; 524-4328. Originally a local hole-in-the-wall, the Acapulco has grown into a successful Mexican eatery that will fill you up with fine home cooking for little dinero. The restaurant has recently expanded and renovated itself into a clean, cozy dining room.

The menu offers various combinations of the basics: tacos, burritos, enchiladas. Get any two on a plate with beans and rice for $5.35, or any three for $6.65. Be sure to try one of the platters featuring *mole* chocolate sauce, a traditional cooking sauce that is not sweet but very tasty.

There are many other plates to choose from, and just about all of them are priced around $5.00 to $8.00. A plate of nachos, to start, is $3.95. Wash it all down with a bottle of Tecate, or, for something a little different, a glass of mango juice.

Centre St. Cafe — 597 Centre St., Jamaica Plain; 524-9217. This is a place to discover, tucked into a little storefront near Pond Street. Taking Jamaica Plain's blend of cultures to heart with a nouvelle cuisine approach, Centre St. Cafe serves up huge, tasty platters from 5 p.m. to 10 p.m. each night.

Start off with a zippy, tomatoey gazpacho ($1.90 a cup), fresh guacamole and chips ($4.25) or a Caesar salad ($2.95). Drinks include a homemade cranberry cooler (non-alcoholic; there is no liquor served) and gingerade, made fresh and tangy with lemon juice.

The menu always includes a quesadilla of the day (*brie*?), as well as daily pasta and fish specials. The rest of the choices, all priced around $5.95 to $7.95, include a yummy Pad Thai and the "South American Stir Fry," rice cooked up spicy in chili butter with black beans, onions, broccoli, and carrots. With many of these dishes you may add your choice of tofu ($1.00 extra), chicken ($2.00), or shrimp ($4.00).

Take some of the meal home and save room for dessert, which includes such doozies as chocolate mousse brownie pie ($2.75) and key lime pie. Mr. C also advises you to arrive early, because after 7:30 or so it's hard to get one of the eight tables and you'll have to wait outside—or place an order to take out. Centre St. also serves up a big brunch from 9 a.m. to 3 p.m. on weekends.

Doyle's — 3484 Washington St., Jamaica Plain; 524-2345. "The Largest Selection of Draft Beers in New England," "Since 1882, Boston's Best Neighborhood Bar" . . . . You'll come across a lot of superlatives at F.J. Doyle & Co.—on the menu, in advertisements, and in conversation. Fact is, it's all true.

Doyle's is a legendary watering hole and eating spot; the only one, the story goes, to stay open throughout the Prohibition and survive to this day. Mayors, governors, and prominent city officials have been spotted there. It was James Michael Curley himself who, in 1933, declared the bar "officially" reopened. Ray Flynn holds court there to this day. "The Kennedys of Massachusetts" filmed scenes there. It's, y'know, historic.

It's also got great, cheap food. The burgers are immense half-pounders starting from $2.95;

the Pot Belly, a dollar more, adds cheese, bacon, mushrooms, and peppers. Further extras are 25¢ each, if you can manage to keep the thing together. A humongous side of fries or onion rings is $2.25.

Sandwiches range from $2.00 for grilled cheese to $3.95 for a reuben, and these are good-sized, too. Doyle's also serves its own pizzas (small $4.95, large $5.95), with a variety of toppings at 75¢ each. These are available until 11:30 every night.

Moving on to the full dinners, real bargains all: Barbecued steak tips are $5.95, as is veal parmigiana and spaghetti. You can get a knockwurst plate with sauerkraut and fries for just $2.95. And there are a dozen or so daily specials, such as broiled Cajun schrod ($7.95) or an eight-ounce sirloin steak ($5.95). Most dinners come with your choice of two sides: fries, rice, salad, or cooked vegetables.

But now to those beers. This must certainly be the largest collection around. On Mr. C's visit, he counted twenty-eight choices—and that's just on tap! Twenty-one more were available in bottles. The options range from plain old Schlitz ($1.50 a bottle) to something called Chimay Grand Reserve—a twenty-five-ounce bottle which goes for $8.95. Needless to say, Mr. C did not sample that one.

In between were all the varieties of J.P.'s own Sam Adams; all the Samuel Smiths; a tasty New England brew called Post Road Real Ale; Fuller's and Young's from Britain; and many more, including non-alcoholic beers. The list is updated from time to time.

So, have a seat next to Kevin White's signed photo, check out the huge old clocks and the wooden telephone booth, knock back a few, and have a great old time at Doyle's. What a way to get a history lesson.

Jean's Family Restaurant — 3383 Washington St., Jamaica Plain; 522-9680. As you should come to expect in the melting pot neighborhoods of JP, Jean's Family Restaurant is not your average sub shop. Oh sure, you can have a sub, but why would you, when you can have a pupusa instead? Along with El Rancho in Cambridge's Inman Square, this is one of the only places in town serving such Salvadoran delicacies.

Pupusas are flat, round pieces of bread fried up with fillings of cheese, pork, or beef. They only cost $1.00 to $1.50; have a few! They're hot and delicious and come with a spicy cole slaw.

Jean's also has Mexican foods, like fajitas ($7.00—lowest price around): Sizzling slices of beef cooked up with green peppers and onions. They're served with flour tortillas, a side of thick

---

Mr. Cheap's Picks
Jamaica Plain

✓ **Acapulco Restaurant** — Great Mexican food, one of many along Centre Street. Further up, try Tacos el Charro too.

✓ **Centre St. Cafe** — The other end of the JP spectrum—call it nouvelle world beat. A little Thai, a little South American, but all done up beautifully and inexpensively.

✓ **Doyle's** — What's left to be said about this Boston institution? Dozens of beers from around the world—drink with the pols. Great burgers and dinners, cheap.

guacamole, and rice with beans. Wash it all down with a beer—no fancy labels here, but then most restaurants of this ilk don't serve any.

Tacos El Charro — 349 Centre St., Jamaica Plain; 522-2578. Imagine a mom 'n pop, family-style Mexican restaurant—and you've got the idea of Tacos el Charro. It's the kind of place you'd find if you were actually *in* Mexico looking for an informal kitchen that just served up good home cooking. This makes eating at Tacos a very different experience from most of the other "Tex-Mex" restaurants in Boston.

It's bright inside, with a television playing Spanish programs in the corner. The walls are decorated with a few pieces of Mexican folk art. So this is not a place for atmosphere—just great food. It is clear immediately that each dish has been prepared to order—not stamped out on an assembly line. And the service is relaxed and friendly.

You can put together a fine meal from the appetizer menu alone. Mr. C particularly enjoyed the sopes ($3.95), fried dough shaped into a cup to hold a tasty mixture of beans and ground beef, with lettuce and cheese on top. Tacos ($1.60 each) come filled with beef, chicken, beef tongue, goat meat, or pork with pineapple (surprise—this is spicy!). Combine any two with rice, beans, and salad for $5.95. These are traditional soft tacos, but if you prefer "Tacos Dorados," the menu says, "we will gladly do those for you."

The fajitas are delicious. Chicken ($5.95) and beef ($7.95) are entrees in themselves, or great for splitting. The mixed fajitas ($8.95) include beef, chicken, and shrimp. There are also burritos, enchiladas, and tamales (two for $3.95), all prepared in a variety of styles. By the way, the salsa (mild or hot) and guacamole are homemade, chunky, and first-rate.

For something a little different, try the Plato Montanero (Colombian platter—$7.95), a stew of beans, pork, and beef served over rice. Avocado and plantain, a sweet kind of banana, are added on the side. There is also a goat stew plate ($7.95); sorry, Mr. C couldn't quite bring himself to try it. For dessert, vanilla flan ($2.50) is the obvious choice.

Tacos el Charro does not have a liquor license, so don't expect to wash this meal down with a margarita. Fortunately, there are several other delicious options, including a non-alcoholic sangria ($1.50). Best bet, though, is the virgin pina colada, made sweet with chunks of real pineapple. A tall glass is $2.00. They'll also whip up a fruit milkshake, also $2.00, that can go with the meal or be a dessert.

Even a soda here will make you think you're in a foreign country; when was the last time you drank Pepsi from a glass bottle? For something that really feels like a quick trip to Mexico, go to Tacos el Charro.

NEWTON

The Bagel — 1208 Boylston St. (Route 9), Chestnut Hill; 566-9404. No need to guess what kind of food is served at The Bagel. It's a nice, old-fashioned Jewish delicatessen and restaurant located across Route 9 from the Chestnut Hill Mall in Newton. The surroundings are basic and pleasant, with seating mostly in booths. The one next to you may be occupied by a yuppie couple going across the street to a movie, or by a white-haired lady taking her time over a glass of hot tea.

The food is quite good and very hearty. As with any deli, sandwiches are its bread and butter (sorry, Mr. C loves a bad pun). Anyway, these are enormous—corned beef, roast beef, turkey, and the rest are piled high on rye or pumpernickel bread and served with a pickle and cole slaw. Or try a nice hot reuben. They are all priced from $4.00 to $6.00, and unless you have a big appetite, you may want to take a half home.

Various hot and cold platters range from $4.95 to $7.95. Again, there are meats, like hot open-faced turkey ($6.95) served with gravy and potatoes; or fried chicken in a basket ($4.95) with French fries. A frequent special offers a barbecued half-chicken, with mashed potato and peas, for $4.95. There is also a sable platter (smoked whitefish), with lettuce, cold vegetables, and cole slaw ($6.95). Burgers are priced from $4.00 to $5.00.

Soups and salads are plentiful for those with lighter appetites; beef barley soup and clam chowder, for example, are just $1.10 for a cup and $1.65 for a bowl. A julienne salad ($5.95) is like a meal in itself. Or nosh on the traditional deli appetizers, such as kasha varnishkas (a mix of egg noodles and barley, with brown gravy), chopped liver, etc.

Of course, some mention must be made of the eponymous bagel. There are usually half-a-dozen varieties to choose from; they are fresh and big. Most dinners offer a bagel on the side, with butter or cream cheese. Breakfast, meanwhile, is available at any time of day: a bagel and cream cheese is $1.45, or $3.45 with lox spread. Egg platters start around $2.50. For a big Sunday kind of breakfast, try two eggs with bacon, sausage, or ham, served with home fries and, yes, a bagel with cream cheese, for $4.95.

The place fills up at weekend brunch times, and there may be a wait for tables. You can order just about any of the above at the take-out counter: sandwiches, chopped liver, knishes, herring, smoked fish, and all the rest.

Concept Cafe — 859 Washington St., Newtonville; 964-8322. Fabulous food at low prices—what a concept! This is a new storefront location for a company that has been in the catering business for over five years; they now have a huge kitchen that takes care of both the catering and the cafe, which means the public has access to Concept's creative, delicious cooking at low cost.

Beginning with breakfast (the cafe opens Monday through Friday at 6 a.m., Saturday at 7 a.m.), there are wonderful, fresh-baked muffins and pastries, like miniature strudels (85¢) and unusual varieties of scones (95¢)—be sure to try orange poppyseed or lemon ginger. There is also gourmet flavored coffee, a wide selection of herbal teas, and a non-caffeine alternative, hot vanilla ($1.00 a cup).

For lunch, the sandwiches are enormous. Chicken salad ($3.95) consists of huge chunks of chicken and celery in a light mayonnaise sauce. Virginia baked ham and cheese ($3.55) gives you a choice of American, Swiss, cheddar, provolone, or muenster; all sandwiches come on white, wheat, rye, pumpernickel, pita bread, French roll, or bagel, and all come with a pickle and your choice of potato salad, cole slaw, or chips.

There is a vegetarian sandwich of cucumber, sprouts, and herb cheese for $2.95; and salads include Caesar ($2.95), Greek ($3.25), antipasto ($4.25), and a chicken sesame salad plate ($4.25).

Dinners feature barbecued chicken by the piece, or as a half-chicken dinner ($5.50) with two side dishes (choose from baked beans, mashed potatoes, stuffing, cole slaw, vegetable of the day, or a garden salad). Extra sides are 75¢ each. Since they cook in quantity, Concept Cafe is also great for take-out; there are even pre-arranged chicken or lasagna dinners for two or four people that include salad, entree, side dishes, and dessert.

But we mustn't forget the daily specials. This is where the real fun comes in, where the chefs make things interesting. On a recent visit, Mr. C was delighted with a pot roast brisket in a honey sauce—out of this world. The generously sized platter consisted of cubes of brisket plus chunks of roasted potatoes, broccoli, zucchini, carrots, and summer squash. The gravy, as promised, was lightly sweetened with honey and brown sugar. Mother's was never like this—no offense, Mom. The meal came with bread and butter and a small garden salad, all for $4.50. What a bargain!

Don't leave out dessert—yummy homemade goodies like chocolate-peanut butter cookies, brownies, carrot cake, and cheesecake, with fruit topping. The latter is just $1.50 a slice, unheard-of these days.

The cafe itself is cozy and bright, small but not cramped. The folks behind the counter who put your order together may indeed be the ones who cooked it, and they're happy to chat about their recipes, too. There's a concept.

Dunn-Gaherin's Pub — 344 Eliot St., Newton; 527-6271. This is an out-of-the-way place that is worth finding— though you may as well forget it if you don't have a car. It's in Newton Upper Falls, south of Route 9, near some antique shops and one of the area's pricier dining rooms, the Mill Falls. Go to DG's; it's great food cheap, and much more fun.

Burgers are huge, starting at just $2.25. There are several varieties of toppings to choose from. A plate of onion rings goes for $3.25, but it's enormous; the fries here are great too. Sirloin steak tips ($4.95) are another good choice, and the chicken wings are speecy-spicy hot.

The menu goes beyond pub fare, though, and yet remains inexpensive. Mr. C's companion chose a daily special, the charbroiled swordfish tips, which were delicious—and there were plenty of them, served over a bed of rice pilaf. There are always several such specials to choose from, some of which are as far from pub food as can be—like the veggie melt sandwich in pita bread ($3.95).

The waitress, who had a lilting Irish accent, was friendly and fun. The atmosphere at Dunn-Gaherin's is similarly laid-back, with an odd mix of Americana decor amidst the Irish pub setting. The bar room, at the front of the restaurant, is nice and cozy; the perfect place to relax over a pint of Guinness or a black and tan.

George's On Washington Street

— 825 Washington St., Newtonville; 965-6628. George's is a warm and cozy neighborhood pub for the yuppie suburbs, a fine place to stop in for a full meal or just a drink and some munchies. It's also a popular spot for watching a football game on a Sunday afternoon with the guys. The mood inside is relaxed, with ceiling fans turning above polished hardwood tables and captain's chairs. Turn-of-the-century pictures of the area and antique posters adorn the walls, as do a pair of television sets over the bar.

But this is a full restaurant with a varied menu, where you can just as easily come in for breakfast (served all day) or lunch. For fun, try George's "Egg Skins" ($4.25)—four deep-fried potato skins filled with scrambled eggs, cheddar cheese, diced tomatoes, and scallions.

Salads are generous, ranging from $2.75 for a garden salad (greens, tomatoes, cucumbers, onions) to $4.95 for the chef, tuna, or fried chicken salad plates. The latter consists of warm chunks of chicken over greens and vegetables, served with a honey-mustard dressing. There are also soups: usually clam chowder and a daily special such as beef burgundy, for $2.25. You can order one with a salad for $4.50.

Sandwiches are big and tasty, from the deli varieties of turkey, corned beef etc., all around $4.00; build your own if you wish. Burgers are thick, handmade patties ranging from the basic ($4.25) to chili-topped ($5.25) or the Virginia, with ham and cheese ($5.50). You'll have to add fries, if you want them, for 95¢, but they're worth it—thick and crispy steak fries. Onion rings are good here too, with plenty of onion inside.

Speaking of appetizers, there is a full assortment, including the usual—spicy buffalo wings, potato skins, mozzarella sticks. But then there's fried ravioli—filled with ricotta cheese and deep-fried in bread crumbs, served with mari-

nara sauce for dipping ($3.95). Or homemade chili con carne ($3.95) with tortilla chips, also homemade.

Returning to sandwiches, the hot entrees are real bargains. Try the barbecued roast beef sandwich on a roll for just $4.75. The grilled reuben, as well as several variations of hot chicken breast sandwiches, are about $5.00. And for healthier diets, the "Californian" is a mix of fresh vegetables oven-baked with mozzarella cheese on top, served on whole-grain bread for $4.50.

The dinner menu has just enough variety in it. A half-pound steak is $8.95, served (as are all dinners) with the daily vegetable and potato or rice. There are meaty pork ribs in barbecue sauce ($7.25), barbecued chicken ($6.95), or a filling combination for $8.95.

There are a couple of pasta and seafood dishes, such as linguine in a homemade red sauce with salad and garlic bread for $5.25, or fettucine Alfredo for $5.95. Fresh, grilled rainbow trout in a lemon butter sauce is a very affordable $6.95.

George's has Bass Ale and other good beers on tap, along with house wines. Like everything else here, the range is limited to a worthwhile selection of choices. And it's just a nice place to hang out.

Golden Star — 817 Washington St., Newtonville; 244-0687. As suburban Chinese restaurants climb the upscale ladder, there are still some bargains to be found. At Golden Star, just across the Mass. Pike from the ritzy Weylu's (now departed) in Newtonville, the room is spacious, the atmosphere relaxed, and the service fast.

The vast Cantonese menu has lots of dishes in the $5.00-to-$6.00 range: a small order of pork chow mein, with crispy noodles, is just $3.00 (large, $4.80), or you can get beef chow mein ($3.35/$5.50) or one of fourteen other varieties. There are thirteen fried rice dishes, from chicken ($3.15/$5.05) to lobster (way up there at $5.05/$8.55) and seventeen kinds of chop suey. Golden Star also offers dinner combination plates, which are even better bargains. For $6.75 you can get an egg roll, pork strips, chicken chow mein, and a heap of pork fried rice—or, for $7.50, try beef teriyaki, chicken with broccoli, and the rice. There are a half-dozen such options, allowing you to eat hearty and still have leftovers for tomorrow's lunch.

Speaking of lunch, Golden Star offers about twenty different daily specials from 11:30 to 3:00 six days a week. Again, these are large combination platters, ranging from chicken wings, pork chow mein, and pork fried rice for just $3.75, to spareribs, chicken fingers, wings, and rice for $5.95.

Golden Star also has a full bar and is open until 1 a.m.— another rarity out in the 'burbs.

La Rotisserie — Chestnut Hill Shopping Center, Route 9, Chestnut Hill; 731-5335. Tucked in next to the Star Market, La Rotisserie is a long, narrow shop geared to take-out, though they do have several tables along one wall. You can get a whole barbecued chicken, rotisseried in their gingery sauce, for $6.95, or a lemon Cornish hen for $5.95. There is even crispy duck *a l'orange*, a bit pricier at $7.50 per pound.

Lunch and dinner plates come with two side orders; choose from real mashed potatoes, long-grain rice, squash, zucchini in tomato sauce, and others. The plates range from $4.00 to $5.50, including a half-chicken, barbecued ribs, a breast and rib combo, etc. Sandwich versions of these are all between $4.00 to $5.00. There are also homemade soups, salads, and pastas—not to mention their "famous" homemade gravy, available by the quart.

Mack's Restaurant and Pub — 761 Beacon St., Newton Centre; 244-9881. Mack's is a cozy, casual eatery with a bar on one side of the room and a restaurant on the other. The walls are done in handsome woods with brass rail features, and

the atmosphere is mellow. Yes, it's the suburbs again; but hey, for a relaxed meal, this is hard to beat.

Start with the extensive appetizer list, mostly $3.95 and under: shrimp cocktail, buffalo wings, mozzarella sticks, fried calamari, popcorn shrimp ($5.95), even a dish of linguine marinara. There are also individual pizzas, starting at $5.95, which you can customize with a variety of toppings.

Salads, all around $4.00, include grilled chicken and pasta, with strips of white meat over multicolored rotini pasta and garden vegetables. Among the sandwiches, mostly $4.00 to $5.00, are veal parmigiana on a roll and "Turkey in the Slaw"—a hot, open-faced sandwich with cole slaw and melted Swiss cheese on an English muffin. Fresh, juicy half-pound burgers start at $4.50, and you can add toppings for 50¢ each: Cajun spices, bleu cheese, chili, etc.

The dinners are reasonably priced and big. Each comes with rice, French fries, mashed potatoes (homemade and buttery!) or slaw, plus the vegetable of the day. There are three or four entrees each of steak, chicken, and pasta; lemon-pepper chicken ($7.95), eight-ounce sirloin steak ($8.95), and veal parmigiana with linguini and garlic bread ($9.95), to name a few.

There are even more options with fresh seafood, particularly on the specials blackboard. Fish and chips are $5.95, broiled schrod is $7.95, and so was a recent special of mussels marinara. Mack's has a children's menu too; and best of all, Mack's offers two dinners for $15.95 on Monday and Tuesday nights.

Oh La La French Cafe — 2-4 Hartford St., Newton Highlands; 332-6210. If you are reading this book, chances are you can't afford to pop over to Europe for a brioche and capuccino. No problem. Go instead to the Oh La La Cafe, just around the corner from the Green Line station at Newton Highlands. Here you'll find a quiet, relaxed atmosphere, lovely food, and a touch of Paris.

Oh La La serves everything from meals to snacks to sweets. Starting with breakfast: Have a vegetable or spinach and cheese omelette for $2.75, or eggs Benedict for $3.25. All egg dishes come with your choice of toast, croissant, bagel, or an English muffin. And be sure to have some of that great-smelling capuccino or espresso. For non-caffeine addicts, there is a variety of fruit juices and natural sodas. Sundays from 9 a.m. to noon, there is a buffet breakfast with eggs, quiches, croissants, muffins, and more for just $3.25 per person, $1.95 for children.

Sandwiches come on a good-sized baguette of French or whole-grain bread, or a croissant. Try the unusual combination of ham and brie ($3.95), or roast turkey and bacon ($4.20). These are not the most inexpensive sandwiches in town, but they are large enough, and you can also request Dijon mustard, horseradish, or garlic and herb cheese dressings. Check the board for daily specials.

The salad bar is small but stocked with lots of interesting items. In addition to greens and fresh veggies, you'll find hearts of palm and multicolored pasta in vinaigrette.

Dinners are again a limited but choice selection. Broiled scallops ($6.90), broiled stuffed shrimp

($7.50), beef stroganoff ($6.25), and chicken marsala ($6.50) are regulars on the menu, along with daily specials at similarly moderate prices.

For dessert, or just anytime you want to splurge, try a slice of peanut chocolate truffle cake ($2.75), a fruit tart ($2.10), or one of the various cookies, brownies, and other pastries. This is the kind of place where everything looks good!

The large dining room has lots of tables for two (or more), curtained windows, and a black-and-white tile floor. During the warm months you can also sit under the umbrellas outside. If you've stopped in by yourself, there are shelves with all kinds of books you can borrow. With a bestseller or a best friend, Oh La La is a great place to linger over an espresso—and to feel chic without a lot of cash.

Sabra — 45 Union St., Newton Centre; 527-5641. The spelling "Newton Centre" should tell you already that this is not the sort of neighborhood in which Mr. C often hangs out. Yet amidst the snooty boutiques of Picadilly Circle (puh- leese), across from the Green Line station, is the elegant Middle Eastern restaurant called Sabra. It combines inexpensive cuisine with refined surroundings.

The menu is a pedigree of Israeli, Lebanese, Greek and Armenian dishes; they all coexist quite

---

Mr. Cheap's Picks
Newton

✓ **The Bagel** — Across from the Chestnut Hill Cinema, a classic Jewish deli like from old neighborhood New York. Cheap daily specials.

✓ **Concept Cafe** — The concept: Successful catering company opens a storefront kitchen. Great lunch specials, different stuff all the time. They'll even share recipe tips.

✓ **Dunn-Gaherin's Pub** — Hard to pronounce and harder to find (it's in Newton Upper Falls, one of the forty-seven "Villages of Newton"), D-G is worth the drive. Cool, laid-back pub with wonderful food.

peacefully. Falaffel is the house specialty, served up as an appetizer ($3.95) that's great for sharing. It's fried golden brown, moist on the inside, and served on a bed of lettuce, with a sauce for dipping. Or try a bowl of lamb curry soup ($2.75) to lead off with a bit of spice.

The "Mazah Plate" ($13.95) is a sort of Mediterranean pu-pu platter for two, combining the appetizers: Armenian salad, baba ganoush, hummus, falaffel, spanakopita (spinach cheese pie) and meatless grape leaves. Great for vegetarians, by the way.

Sabra has many dinners priced under $10.00. Try the goulash ($8.95), chunks of beef cooked with carrots and string beans; or the shawarma plate ($9.50), ground beef and lamb mixed with spices. All dinner entrees include rice pilaf and a big salad.

Vegetarian dishes are priced lower. Dardara ($7.95) are lentil beans and rice sauteed with onions into a delicious and healthy blend. There are also more unusual specials, like "Pumpkin Kibbee," a mixture of bulgar (wheat), mashed pumpkin, onions, and herbs, fried into cakes and served over rice.

But the true bargains, Mr. C found, are the sandwiches. For just $4.95, the chicken kebab sandwich is a two-hands-on affair: tasty, hot chunks of chicken in tahini sauce, stuffed into pita bread with lots of lettuce and chopped vegetables. It'll keep you busy for quite a while. Or, for the same price, have beef, shawarma, or hummus and tabouli. Falaffel is just $3.95. Be warned, though, these are messy—and fun.

Finish your dinner with one of several liqueur coffees: Sabra (of course), Sambuca, Kahlua, and more. At $3.75, these are not cheap, but many bars charge more—and you'll have saved enough on dinner to splurge a bit!

The atmosphere is relaxed and inviting, with exposed brick walls and potted plants everywhere. There is also a cozy, separate bar area. The service is friendly and prompt. Sabra makes a nice place for an inexpensive date that definitely won't look cheap.

Sandwich Works — 827 Beacon St., Newton Centre; 332-6777. Also, 1284 Washington St., West Newton; 244-1211. Sandwich Works is a tasty little shop that's like a cross between a fast-food chain and a local deli. The service is over-the-counter and quick, with tables in a pleasant, if basic, eating area. Of course, it's also great for take-out. The food is good and cheap!

All your basic hot and cold sandwiches are here, from grilled cheese ($1.75) to BLT ($2.55) to roast beef ($3.75). You get your choice of breads and rolls, and side orders of cole slaw or "Red Bliss" potato salad are an extra 60¢ each.

What Mr. C really enjoys here are the special grilled sandwiches, like the "West Newton" ($3.65)—ham, turkey, Swiss cheese, and cream cheese on dark rye bread. It's grilled up hot and juicy, and there's plenty to wrap your hands around. Or try the chicken salad melt ($3.65), the chicken cutlet Parmesan ($3.55) or the garden pocket ($3.45)—broccoli, yellow squash, zucchini, peppers, and carrots marinated in a special dressing with cheese, served in a Syrian bread pocket.

There are also daily sandwich specials, along with changing varieties of soups and quiches. Broccoli and cheese quiche ($3.65) was a large and moist portion, served with lettuce and tomato on the side. New England clam chowder, beef stew, and chili (each $1.95 small, $2.65 large) round out the menu.

Sandwich Works has daily newspapers on sale inside, making this a nice place to relax over your lunch or dinner. (The Newton Centre branch is open to 8 p.m. every night but Sunday; West Newton is open until 7 p.m.) They also make note of their decision to use healthier, lighter cooking oils and recyclable materials. That's always to be applauded!

SOMERVILLE

Dolly's Late Night Restaurant —
382 Highland Ave., Somerville; 628-
0888. Attention night owls! Here is
a place you're going to love. Dolly's
Late Night truly lives up to its name,
by opening each night at 11:00; it
then serves food until 4:00 a.m. on
weekdays, 5 a.m. on weekends. It's
a plain old coffee shop, with a
counter and a handful of tables,
near Davis Square.

The menu couldn't be more
all-American. Have a grilled cheese
and tomato sandwich for $2.25, or
a hamburger with bacon, lettuce,
and tomato for $3.65. The chicken-
salad sandwich ($4.75), when it's
on the daily blackboard, is made
with giant hunks of chicken breast
piled high on a bed of lettuce in a
bulkie roll and served with fries.
Use both hands.

You can get a huge western
omelette ($5.25), an order of
chicken fingers ($3.95), French
toast ($2.55), or a tossed salad
($3.25). There is also a vast assort-
ment of combinations involving sirloin steak; a dinner of sirloin tips, for
example, is $5.99. Though even Mr.
C, a confirmed night person, finds
that a bit much for the hour.

Still, when you have that crav-
ing for a chocolate milkshake in the
middle of the night, Dolly's is the
place to go.

11th Chapter Saloon — 336A Union Square, Somerville; 628-4300.
In these troubled economic times,
most folks know what the term
"Chapter 11" means. Well, laying
low at the 11th Chapter Saloon is a
fine way to help anyone out of a fis-
cal crisis. This is a small but ele-
gant-looking bar with great
food—for very little cash-on-hand.

From the red brick walls to
the dark wooden bar, ceiling fans,
and green-shaded lamps, this
could be an insider's hangout on
Wall Street. Instead, it's a casual
spot to catch a Celtics game, or a
live band, over beers or dinner. The
menu is as small as the joint; but
both are high-quality.

Tight quarters put the kitchen
right behind the bar—a flame grill
that regularly flares up to add a little
drama, and great smells, to the atmosphere. Burgers are thick, round
half-pounders served on a big roll
with cheese, lettuce, tomato, and
French fries for $4.50. The grilled
steak ($4.50) or chicken breast
($4.25) sandwiches get similar treat-
ments.

The real bargains here,
though, are the entrees. Steak tips
($6.00) and pork chops ($6.25) are
thick and juicy cuts of meat, grilled
in a lip-smacking marinade. Mr. C
liked the chops particularly. Again,
these are served with fries, along
with a garnish of lettuce and carrot
sticks. There is a blackboard with
daily specials, such as grilled
striped marlin ($6.25).

For snacks, there are sandwiches ($3.75) and a chef's salad
($5.00) made with romaine lettuce
and fresh, crisp vegetables. On
the Tex-Mex side, there is chili
($2.50/$3.50) and nachos (veggie
$4.00, "super" $5.00). That's
about it.

For lunch you can get combination specials like a half-sandwich
and soup for $3.00 or a cup of chili
and a small salad for $3.25. And
full menu is available until 11 p.m.—
blue chip all the way.

There is a good selection of

beers, including Anchor Steam, Foster's Lager, and New Amsterdam. Thursdays through Saturdays, the 11th Chapter features entertainment with local bands. The bookings lean toward rhythm and blues. Space is tight, of course, but . . . hey, there's no cover charge. This is a good place to be bankrupt.

Jimy Mac's Southern Pit Bar-B-Q — 300 Beacon St., Somerville; 547-0000. Jimy Mac's has that authentic Southern feel to it—the sort of place that makes the food taste that much better. Not that it needs any help; it's delicious, finger-licking food that's fun to dive into. Jimy's is a small place with the kitchen at one end, tables for about two dozen at the other, and brightly colored signs advertising various specialties all around the room.

The menu is huge and seems to have just about every kind of down-home dish imaginable. The main features, of course, are chicken and ribs. Just about everything has a sharp, smoky flavor. The chicken comes barbecued or "Southern spicy fried"; there are back loin ribs, beef short ribs and "trash" ribs; in all cases you can order by the piece or by the plate. Two spare ribs alone cost $3.00; it's $6.00 for four, $8.00 for six, and so on. Similarly, you can order three mixed pieces of fried chicken for $3.75, four for $4.75, and up.

Chances are, though, that you will want one of the many combination plates, which add lots of yummy fixings on the side. The jumbo wing plate, for example, has seven wings plus cole slaw and rice or fries for $4.95 ("Jimy fries" are great—thin and curly). The smoked turkey plate ($5.95) comes with mashed potatoes, corn bread, and slaw.

All of the chicken, pork, and beef brisket is cooked so perfectly that it just falls off the bone. If you prefer, you can let Jimy's do that for you, with pulled pork, chicken, or brisket sandwiches. These come in various sizes, from $2.95 ("Just Enough") to $4.95 ("Giant"). Other sandwiches

available include Cajun meatloaf, crab cake, and fried catfish.

There are sausages of all kinds, like spicy beef "Hot Links" and smoked chicken. Texas chili with beans is served with corn bread. There's a barbecue house salad with pecan garlic dressing. And we haven't even gotten to the side order delicacies, like baked candied sweet potatoes and spiced "dirty" rice. And would you believe fried corn on the cob for a dollar? It's worth a try.

On Saturdays and Sundays from 11:30 a.m. to 2:30 p.m., there are "Country Weekend Breakfast" specials ($5.95) with main choices like dry cured bacon and smoked chicken hash, with sides like grits and cheese, fried green apples, and homemade muffins.

No liquor is served, but you can wash this great food down with IBC root beer or Sioux City birch beer. And for dessert, well, just try to choose from chocolate cookie pudding ($1.95), butterscotch pecan pie ($1.95), "Oh Yes! Sweet Potato Pie" ($2.95), lemon pecan pound cake ($1.50) and more. With fifteen possibilities on the menu (not all are available on a given day), there's something for every sweet tooth.

Jimy's sells its food in quantity, making great party food; they will also deliver or cater the whole thing for you.

Mike's Restaurant — 9 Davis Square, Somerville; 628-2379. From outside this prominent corner location in the heart of Davis Square, Mike's looks like your average pizza and sub shop— but when was the last time you saw a shrimp scampi pizza?

This place has a whole lot to offer beyond the basics, which are terrific to begin with. Along with round and Sicilian pizzas, hot subs, and calzone, Mike's offers pasta dishes, veal, chicken and seafood dinners, and more. The food is homemade, including fresh sauce and pizza dough made daily on the premises.

The prices make it easy to work your way through the vast menu. For just $3.75 you can get a hefty plate of ziti or spaghetti, with that fresh sauce and garlic bread. Or try the lobster ravioli or the homemade veggie lasagna. Fettucine Alfredo is $5.95, much lower than at other restaurants.

Veal and chicken dinners, around $9.00, come in all the traditional Italian styles—cacciatore, marsala, parmagiana, etc. Open some mussels marinara ($5.95) or scallops alfredo ($6.95). These dinners include pasta, salad, and garlic bread.

Speaking of seafood, there are those specialty pizzas. Try shrimp, calamari—or both for $12.99. Sounds like a lot to pay for a pizza, but since you'd certainly be sharing such a packed pie, the price works out to Mr. C's standards. Another unusual combination is the Hawaiian, topped with pineapple, ham, mozzarella, and sauce. There's even the George Bush favorite— broccoli and mozzarella. Both of these are $9.99.

Mike's also has an impressive selection of beverages to wash all this down: along with sodas and fruit juices, there are imported Italian drinks like Orzata, an almond-flavored soda commonly found in Europe. There is also a selection of red and white wines, as well as a beer list with over a hundred imported and American special brews.

With its bright orange formica tables, menu signs lining the walls, and hostesses calling your name over the microphone to pick up your order, Mike's is not big on "ambiance"; it's more of a family atmosphere. They also deliver in the Somerville area.

Mt. Vernon Restaurant — 14 Broadway, Somerville; 666-3830. On one side, Mt. Vernon is one of those venerable old family-style establishments where regular folks go for steaks and schrod or a "New England Boiled Dinner." Where people order baked padaydas with their meals. On the other side, it's a lively, casual pub with a separate menu and the Sox on the television.

The restaurant, of course, is pricier, but there are some bargains to be had. It's famous for its twin-serving dinner specials. Several nights a week you can actually get a pair of boiled lobster dinners, with

---

Mr. Cheap's Picks
Somerville

✓ **Dolly's Late Night Cafe** — Gotta love a place that *opens* at 11 p.m. Bizarre menu; plenty of good, heavy stuff you shouldn't eat at 3 a.m., like steak and eggs, grilled cheese sandwiches, and chocolate milk shakes.

✓ **11th Chapter Saloon** — Fabulous little watering hole, with a grill behind the bar. Good burgers, pork chops, and sandwiches.

✓ **Jimy Mac's Southern Bar-B-Q Pit** — As authentic and down home as Bob the Chef's; pulled pork, smoked chicken and chitterlings.

✓ **Neighborhood Restaurant** — A generic name for a cozy, bustling Portuguese kitchen in Union Square. Huge weekend brunch deals; they also bake their own bread, and you can buy a loaf for $1.00.

---

padaydas—er, potatoes—for $9.95. Baked stuffed lobsters go for $11.95. Wow. On other nights, there are similar deals, most for $11.95: Roast stuffed turkey one night, schrod the next, etc.

In the pub there is a larger menu of cheaper food, dinners and sandwiches. Here, you can have fish and chips for $5.95, macaroni and cheese for $2.95, or a broiled chicken dinner for $6.95. Dinners include salad, potato(!), vegetable, and bread. Burgers start at just $1.50. In some cases, both sides share the daily specials, such as chicken parmigiana and pasta for $5.95.

Whichever side you're on, you'll get plenty of food, with quick service. Mt. Vernon, by the way, is just over the Somerville line from Sullivan Square in Charlestown; getting there by car can be tricky, thanks to Route 93 and the bus station, but once you make it, they have plenty of parking in the back.

Neighborhood Restaurant and Bakery — 25 Bow St., Somerville; 628-9710. Somerville's Union Square has several Portuguese family- style restaurants, several of which are reasonably priced; any one of them is bound to be good, but Mr. C's favorite is the Neighborhood Restaurant. It's small and crowded, but the servings are huge and wonderful.

Let's start with breakfast. It's always good here, though it may not seem cheap; three eggs and toast are $4.39. But you get a large plate with fruit, home fries, coffee, and their fabulous homemade Portuguese sweet bread. The real deals are on the weekends, when you also have a choice of five brunch platters. For $5.95 you can get a Belgian waffle with homemade syrup, eggs, bacon, linguica sausage, corn bread, sweet bread, fruit, juice, and coffee.

Lunches and dinners, again, are big. Portuguese-style fish fillets ($8.95) is a plate of haddock, scallops, and shrimp; for even bigger appetites, go for the Mariscada a

Costa Brava ($13.95)—a large seafood platter in red sauce. Yes, it's over $10.00, but you'll have enough to take home. Same goes for the seafood paella, same price; chunks of fish, shrimp, sausage, and vegetables in a mountain of yellow rice. A friend of Mr. C's is such a regular, always ordering the paella, that the waiters have the take-out tray all ready to go. It really is two meals.

More moderately-priced choices on the large menu include Portuguese-style pork chops ($8.00), linguica sausage with fava beans ($6.95), mussels in tomato sauce ($7.00), fish and chips ($6.95), shrimp in garlic sauce ($9.95) and tortellini with sausage ($6.99). And don't miss the delicious homemade soup of the day ($1.75/$2.25), or flan for dessert ($1.25).

You can also buy loaves of that terrific sweet bread, just a dollar apiece; a day-old loaf, if available, is 75¢. Either one is a bargain.

O'Sullivan's Pub — 282 Beacon St., Somerville; 491-9638. If you look in the dictionary under "dive," you'll probably find a picture of O'Sullivan's Pub next to it. However, dives sometimes hide great food, and if you like burgers, check this place out.

The bar is a local hangout, a place to sit over a beer and watch the game. Still, it's not as dark and smoky as some bars, and the grill behind the bar yields one of the best burger deals in town.

Scanning the menu quickly— the entire list fits on one of those lighted mirror boards—Mr. C found four varieties of burgers, a couple of sandwiches, and hot dogs. So much for cuisine. Noting the prices, though, he decided to splurge for the deluxe burger. This consisted of a half-pound of fresh meat, nice and plump, on a big bulkie roll, with lettuce, tomato, mayonnaise, a slice of cheese, a strip of bacon, a slice of ham, plus a bag of potato chips. How much? Get ready—$3.00.

A pint of Bass Ale for $2.50 completed the picture beautifully. Guinness and other Irish brews are on tap, which fit in with the Ireland travel posters and the dart boards on the walls. The gentleman behind the bar was very friendly, and for that matter, the customers seemed accepting of outsiders too. If this is your kind of place, watch out—you could become a regular yourself.

Picante Mexican Grill — 217 Elm St., Somerville; 628-6394. Picante is good Mexican food for yuppies. The atmosphere is fun, but it's probably the only Mexican restaurant dominated by neon. It's located in a newly renovated building in Davis Square, right next to the latest mooring of the Daily Catch (not cheap, but also delicious and fun).

The menu at Picante is short and simple, with specials of the day and combination plates. A taco, cheese quesadilla, or flauta (soft corn tortilla filled with chicken and fried), served with rice, black beans, and salad, is $4.95; choose two items for $5.95.

An order of nachos is also $4.95, and with any order of chips you can avail yourself of the salsa bar, with lots of spicy sauces for dipping. Bring a cup back to your table.

Burritos are a good bet. A rolled-up tortilla is filled with cheese, rice, beans, a mild sauce, and your choice of such fillings as chicken, steak, or, for veggie fans, char-grilled squash and mushrooms. Each is $3.95; add a dollar for the deluxe, with sour cream and guacamole, or the ranchero, baked with sauce and cheese on top.

Taco salads ($4.95) are also huge, served in an edible crisp corn tortilla bowl. It's packed with lettuce, carrot sticks, and other vegetables, guacamole, sour cream, black beans, cheese, and sauteed chicken or steak.

There is no liquor license (and no smoking allowed anywhere), but the interesting drinks include a tasty non- alcoholic sangria ($2.00), various Latin sodas, and juices. Ask if they have agua de pina ($1.25), a tall, sweet cup of pineapple juice with chunks of fruit in it. It's

a refreshing way to wash things down. And if you have room for dessert, there's homemade flan for $3.00.

Rudy's Cafe — 248 Holland St., Somerville; 623-9201. Rudy's Cafe is a lot like the trendy Tex-Mex restaurants downtown, but in a neighborhood setting—and with neighborhood prices. The place seems to have a "mascot" of a big, colorful parrot, and you'll see stuffed, painted, and even neon varieties. They also have plenty of cactuses (cacti?) all around, and a full-sized motorcycle parked above the door. The atmosphere is bustling and fun.

The large menu has most entrees priced in the $5.00-to-$8.00 range. Appetizers include four different kinds of nachos ($3.25 to $5.50), topped with things like chili or guacamole. The guac is made fresh and is on the menu "when available." A meaty chili con carne is cheap at $1.50 per cup.

Tacos, burritos, and chimichangas are not exactly snack items here. They are big enough to be entrees in themselves. For $5.00 to $6.00, you can have three tacos, in your choice of crispy corn or soft flour tortillas, with beef, chicken or shrimp fillings. For the same prices, burros are single, large tortillas filled with beef, chicken, or beans and cheese, topped with enchilada sauce, melted cheeses, and sour cream. The chimichangas are the same as burros, but—in an unusual touch—deep-fried. Corn chips come on the side.

Some dishes get even bigger, but the prices don't. "El Grande" is the largest tortilla dish, filled with beef ($6.25) or chicken ($6.50) along with beans, cheeses, lettuce, and tomatoes. It's topped with sauce, cheese, sour cream, and guacamole. Should take care of most appetites. Rudy's even has lasagna ($5.75) and "Sky-High Eggplant Parmesan" ($5.75). Just the thing to take home if you've rented a spaghetti western.

The true bargains may be the half-dozen combination plates available, allowing you to sample many of the above treats. Combo #3, for example, consists of a guacamole taco, an enchilada verde (very spicy), and a small bean and cheese burro—with rice, sour cream, and guac on the side—for $6.50.

Dinner items include pollo al carbon ($7.75), a spicy grilled breast of marinated chicken; and pescado, a daily special of peppery grilled fish. There are a few things from the Tex side of the border, like baby back ribs ($8.75/$10.95) and the Santa Rosa chicken sandwich ($5.75), a chicken and avocado salad topped with bacon, tomato, and sprouts on whole-wheat bread. This takes you *far* north of the border. Other sandwiches and burgers start at $4.75.

The bar is stocked with a wide selection of American and international beers. Beyond the usual Mexican choices are such brands as Negra Medelo and Pacifico Clara; other nationalities represented include Foster's from Australia and Orval Trapiste Ale from Belgium. And there are several creative tequila drinks, from margaritas to the "Tijuana Taxi"—gold tequila, creme de cassis, and orange juice. There are even eight different kinds of tequila to choose from.

Meanwhile, if you still have room, desserts are hard to pass by. The brownie sundae ($2.75) starts with a large, thick chocolate brownie (nuts and chocolate chips inside), rising up to ice cream, chocolate sauce, and finally whipped cream on the top. The "Mud Ball" ($2.50) is coffee ice cream rolled in crushed Oreos and topped with sauce and whipped cream. There are also assorted coffee drinks and "Mocktails," non-alcoholic drinks like chocolate banana and raspberry lime fizz.

Street Cafe — 7 Holland St., Somerville; 625-6068. A recent addition to Davis Square, Street Cafe is located directly across from the Somerville Theater. It's a modest little Chinese restaurant where you place your order at the counter and the waitress brings your meal to you. The wide- ranging menu carries most favorites in various Chinese styles, and the food is freshly cooked to your order.

Soups are great here. Mr. C loved the chicken wonton soup ($2.50), which came in a plastic container (everything here comes in or on plastic—already geared to taking home your leftovers?). It was a big bowl, densely packed. Wontons with chicken filling, pea pods, water chestnuts, mushrooms, bok choy—there was barely any room for the broth.

Other appetizers come in small and large sizes, starting around $1.50 for an egg roll or spring roll with $2.50 for a small order of chicken wings (large, $4.75) and Peking ravioli for $2.00/$3.75. A pu-pu platter for one ($7.75) gives you a variety of these, including fried shrimp.

In addition to the usual sweet-and-sour offerings (such as chicken for $3.00/small, $6.00/large), Street Cafe also has sweet and sour shrimp or scallops ($3.50/$6.50 each) and wontons (super cheap at $2.00/$3.00). The small orders are plenty for one person. Lo mein and chow mein dishes are big and inexpensive: shrimp chow mein is $3.25/$5.50.

In fact, there are about 150 choices on this menu, with something for every Chinese food lover. For the real bargains, and to try several items, go for the luncheon specials (served from 11 a.m. to 3 p.m.) such as boneless spareribs, lobster sauce, and rice for $4.50.

There are also dinner combinations served all day, like beef and broccoli with spareribs and rice for just $6.25, and chicken teriyaki, egg roll and pork fried rice for $5.25. All of these platters come with good-sized portions of each item and make a full meal.

The service is very friendly. The restaurant itself is small; there are only about a half-dozen tables, so you may want to take your food out. Street Cafe also delivers in the Somerville area.

Tijuana — 290 Somerville Ave., Somerville; 628-7494. As the name implies, Tijuana takes us south of the border for what the menu tells us is authentic, carefully prepared Mexican food. This cuisine does not have to be heavy and greasy, the note mentions, and they're right. The food at Tijuana is light and yummy—and it doesn't even have to be spicy all the time, either.

Mr. C particularly enjoyed an entree simply called "Pollo a la Tijuana" ($8.95), which consisted of chicken marinated in an orange sauce, covered with crumbled corn flakes and baked up juicy. Whether or not this is authentic to Mexico, it's unusual and a nice change of pace for this kind of dining. Like most of the dishes, it's served with rice, refried beans, and a good, fresh salad.

Combination plates are a good bet for variety as well, each $8.95. Enchiladas (green or red) can be paired with a taco and your choice of burrito, tostada, or chimichanga. They're all tasty and filling.

Among the appetizers are napalitos ($3.75), for the more adventurous in taste—these are made with cactus meat. Mr. C somehow missed trying that one. Queso asado ($4.95) is a more standard choice to start—a tortilla baked with chicken and chorizo sausage. Or, try the tasty bean soup ($2.95) or fresh guacamole salad ($3.95). Tijuana does not have a liquor license.

Desserts, $2.00 to $3.00, include flan and elado frito—yes, that yummy fried ice cream.

Mexican wool tapestries form the brightly-colored decor here, and the Mexican music on the sound system keeps the atmosphere lively as well. Tijuana is one of the nicer such restaurants Mr. C has visited.

Worldly Wings — 711 Broadway, Somerville; 623-WING (9464). Here's a great new addition to the wing craze. Worldly Wings cooks up wings (natch), ribs, and sandwiches in your choice of fifteen different sauces. Four grades of Buffalo sauce, from mild to "Super-Wow," Cajun, teriyaki, garlic, Jamaican Jerk (ginger), honey mustard, even apricot chutney. If you're bewildered by this flotilla of flavors, they'll give you a taste of anything you'd like to try.

A seven-to-eight-piece order of wings is $3.95, and a double order is $6.95; the sizes go up to forty pieces and beyond, with party platters. Buffalo styles come with carrot and celery sticks, plus bleu cheese; other varieties come with cole slaw. Ribs are $7.25 for a good half-rack.

Another good deal is the chicken breast sandwich ($3.85), again, cooked in any of the sauces. Be sure to get an order of seasoned fries, done with a crunchy, flavorful coating. For dessert they have pints and bars of Ben and Jerry's ice cream.

Weekdays from 11 a.m. to 2 p.m., WW offers great lunch specials for just $2.85: an order of five wings, or a small chicken or roast beef sandwich, with fries and a soda. Tasty, and hard to beat.

ELSEWHERE AROUND TOWN

ARLINGTON

Arlington Restaurant And Diner
— 138 Massachusetts Ave., Arlington; 646-9266. Just over the border from Cambridge, the Arlington Diner is a bustling little place where the waitresses ask, "What would youse like?" Of course, they bring it out quickly—and it's all good stuff.

Everything looks good here. For breakfast, two eggs with bacon are $3.25; but for the hearty appetite, try one of the many interesting omelettes, like the Popeye, filled with spinach and mushrooms, or Eggs Muckonos, with feta cheese and tomatoes. These range from $2.95 to $4.50, and they are humongous. They come with home fries and toast, natch.

There are all kinds of sandwiches, such as a ham and swiss club with bacon, lettuce, tomato, pickles, cole slaw, and French fries, all for $4.30. The "Happy Waitress Special" ($3.95) is an open-face grilled cheese sandwich with bacon, tomato, and the fries, slaw, and pickles again.

On Fridays, try a cup of homemade clam chowder ($1.75). Otherwise, be sure to ask about the soup of the day. Greek salads are $3.95 and $4.95; five-ounce burgers start at $2.25.

Elsewhere on the large menu, the diner goes international. There's a section of Italian specialties (chicken parmigiana, $6.50 with salad and spaghetti), Greek specialties (lamb souvlaki, $7.95 with a Greek salad), and a whole separate list of "Saute Specialties" like shrimp scampi ($9.95) and even

"Chicken a la Arlington Diner" ($8.95). This consists of chicken breasts, broccoli, and ziti sauteed in white wine, garlic, and butter. Pretty fancy for a diner, but the cozy place pulls it off. Just enough Cambridge influence makes its way into this friendly, everyday establishment. Don't forget to check out the homemade baklava and other desserts, either.

Peter's Kitchen
— 166 Massachusetts Ave., Arlington; 648-9675. Peter's Kitchen is your basic Greek coffee shop; simple hot meals and sandwiches, quick and filling—and cheap. Dinners start at $3.95, with nothing higher than $7.95, and they all come with two side dishes: French fries or rice pilaf, and salad or cole slaw.

Greek dinners include shish kebabs (beef, $5.95; lamb, $6.50), souvlaki ($5.40/$5.75), mousaka ($4.95), stuffed grape leaves ($4.75), and several others. On the American side, sirloin tips are $5.85, pork chops are $5.95, and lamb chops are $7.95. Mr. C tried the broiled chicken ($5.25); it was so tender, the meat practically lifted itself off the bones.

There are also lots of seafood items, like broiled schrod ($6.25), fried clams ($7.45) and fish and chips ($5.85, sandwich $4.75). Check the blackboard for other daily specials.

Of course, there is plenty of diner fare: burgers and club sandwiches, omelettes, salads. Breakfast is served from 7 a.m., when you can have two eggs and bacon for $2.95 with home fries, toast, and coffee. Peter's is only open until 8 p.m., and closes at 1 p.m. on Sundays.

EAST BOSTON

Jeveli's Restaurant — 387 Chelsea St., East Boston; 567-9539. "Boston's Oldest Italian Restaurant," states the menu. Jeveli's is indeed a big old family-style dining room, very casual, with ample portions of Italian food. They give you quite a lot to choose from. While most of the dinner entrees are in the $7.00-to-$10.00 range, you'll come away stuffed.

Veal alone comes in seven different preparations, from cutlets to scallopini. Chicken marsala is a house specialty, served with a big, fresh salad and spaghetti for $8.25. Chicken and broccoli over linguine is $8.75, and eggplant parmigiana is $7.50. Again, you get a lot.

Seafood dishes are extensive. Starting with baked stuffed shrimp with salad and spaghetti (or potato and vegetable) for $9.50, the menu proceeds to mussels marinara with linguine ($7.25), broiled or baked haddock ($7.95), lobster pie ($9.95) and deep-fried squid ($7.75). The fish is fresh and light.

Pasta dishes are mostly in the $6.00-to-$8.00 range, with baked manicotti ($6.75), fettucine alfredo ($6.95), and even spaghetti with shrimp sauce ($8.75). There are, of course, daily specials along with everything else, and a children's menu section of dinners for just $2.99.

Jeveli's also has a pub side, with a "lighter fare" menu. It's a big, sprawling place with meals to match.

Mama Julia — 54 Bennington St., East Boston; 568-9020. East Boston may have the airport, but it also has a really cheap way to leave the country and head for South America. Visit Mama Julia's. This is a family-run Colombian kitchen, small but cozy. Food here is inexpensive and filling; the simple menu is printed in Spanish and English, and the friendly folks will help you out with any questions.

For starters, try the "morcilla" ($2.50)—Colombian black sausage, served with cornbread. "Bunuelos," cheese fritters, are $1.00. Different soups are served on particular days of the week: fish, chicken, tripe, or beef. They usually have a stock made with root vegetables like plantain, yucca, and potato.

You can also get a soup-of-the-day special meal for $8.50: soup with steak, rice, fried plaintains, and corn bread. The "bandeja tipica," or typical Colombian platter, is similar—steak and rice with salad, red beans, fried pork, yucca, potato, plaintain, and corn bread. A huge meal, all for $9.00.

Fried whole fish ($8.50) comes with fried green plaintains (isn't that a movie?), rice, salad, and corn bread; stewed chicken ($6.50) includes potatoes and the same sides. For the adventurous, try stewed beef tongue ($8.00).

Desserts include flan, of course, for $2.00, or rice pudding, and perhaps a special of the day. As at most Latin restaurants, there is no liquor license; you can have Colombian sodas with flavors like apple and cola champagne, or fruit juices mixed to order. "3 in 1" is

---

Mr. Cheap's Pick
East Boston

✓ **Mama Julia** — A Columbian kitchen with hearty, authentic food and a quiet, friendly atmosphere.

---

made with carrot, beet, and orange juices; you may prefer to try shakes made from passionfruit, blackberries, or pineapple. These are all $2.50.

Mama Julia's also serves

breakfast. You can go American, with scrambled eggs, corn bread, and cheese ($5.00), or Colombian, with "calentado" ($7.00)—spicy ground beef with rice and beans. Mama won't let you leave hungry.

ROSLINDALE

Pleasant Cafe & Restaurant — 4515 Washington St., Roslindale; 323-2111. Don't be fooled by the neon "pizza" sign and humble facade of the Pleasant Cafe, just outside of Forest Hills; this is no sub shop. Inside, it's a huge, folksy, family restaurant with a menu that's big on Italian food—and just plain big.

The dinners also include seafood, prime rib and other meats; all of these entrees range from $6.00 to $10.00, and most come with scali bread and pasta or vegetables. Chicken cacciatore ($6.95) is a vast plate with chunks of chicken breast, fresh half-mushrooms, peppers, and onions swimming in tomato sauce. It comes with spaghetti or ziti on the side, cooked just right.

Broiled swordfish is one of the half-dozen daily specials added in

on the blackboard—just $8.50. Or try lasagna and meatballs ($6.95), pork chops ($7.95) or veal marsala ($8.95)

They do, of course, have pizzas, made to your specifications on a nice, thin, crisp crust. These start at $6.75 and go up, depending on the toppings you choose. There are also sandwiches, like burgers for $3.25 or a veal cutlet sandwich for $5.50.

The portions are enormous. Even as they bring your dinner from the kitchen, the friendly waitresses tell you not to worry— the doggy bag is ready and waiting. The bar area is lively and boisterous, usually with a ball game on the tube; this room has lots of dining booths, but there are two other large rooms as well if you want (a bit) less noise.

Mr. Cheap's Pick
Roslindale

✓ **Pleasant Cafe** — Looks like a pizzeria, but it's so much more. A huge menu of Italian dinners, in a sprawling restaurant/bar where the old folks and young folks go for a casual, cheap big meal.

SOUTH BOSTON

Amrhein's Restaurant — 80 West Broadway, South Boston; 268-6189. This area of Southie isn't really that far from downtown, yet it often feels like another world—a simpler time and place. Amrhein's Restaurant is a big part of that. Operating since 1890, this Austrian pub in an Irish neighborhood has kept its old-world atmosphere. It's all dark

wood and brass with green trimmings and pressed tin ceilings; like Doyle's in Jamaica Plain, its heritage embraces famous and near-famous politicians. They also claim to have Boston's very first beer pump.

The food, meanwhile, will keep you full for another hundred years—especially if you go for the specials. Mr. C requested one,

---

Mr. Cheap's Pick
South Boston

✓ **Amrhein's** — Old world charm, and food to match, for the stout of heart (and stomach). Go for the weiner schnitzel and a nice brew. Handsome wood and brass bar.

---

roast pork tenderloin; it was a mound of slices in brown gravy, served with cooked vegetables and two warm rolls and butter, all for $5.45. There was enough for leftovers. Other early specials include chicken *and* veal parmigiana, with spaghetti, for $6.95; and a big chicken pot pie for $5.95.

Mondays through Wednesdays from 4 to 10 p.m., there are better bargains yet, with two-for-one specials such as chicken marsala and linguine, baked stuffed scallops with vegetables, and the house specialty, wiener schnitzel over noodles. Choose any two dinners for just $12.95!

Amrhein's is also the home of the twin roast-turkey dinner. From 11 a.m. to 3 p.m. on Saturdays, for $11.95, you get: turkey with stuffing, soup or salad, broccoli, squash, and mashed potatoes. Twice. Bring someone and stuff yourself.

Loaf & Ladle — 483 East Broadway, South Boston; 268-7006. Irish chic arrives in Southie! Loaf & Ladle is a bright, airy sandwich shop that would look just as fitting in Cambridge or Downtown Crossing. Plants hang in the windows. Sit at the counter, or at the natural wood tables, and have a traditional Irish breakfast of two eggs, Irish sausage, bacon, black and white pudding, home fries, and grilled tomato, along with Irish whole wheat bread and tea or coffee, all for $6.25.

If that's a bit much for your appetite, try three large pancakes ($2.75), or an egg and cheese sandwich with sausage or bacon ($1.25). Breakfast is served from 6 a.m. (except Sundays, from 9:30).

For lunch, a full selection of deli sandwiches ranges from $1.95 to $3.25, with corned beef, tuna melt, crabmeat salad, and more. Turkey, tuna, cheeseburger, or ham and cheese clubs are each $3.95, served with French fries. All soups and chowders are homemade, such as a brimming bowl of beef stew for $3.50.

There are always several daily lunch specials, though, such as barbequed steak tips for $5.95 or chicken curry, served over rice, for $4.95. They're hot and delicious. Any order can be made for takeout, too. Dinner is not served; they close at 4 p.m. every day. The Loaf & Ladle stands out in St. Patrick's Square; it's a modern, casual place.

WATERTOWN

Arsenal Diner — 356 Arsenal St., Watertown; 926-8371. This friendly little place has only been around for about a year. It's located on Arsenal Street, across and down a bit from the giant Arsenal Mall. Open from 6 a.m. to 3 p.m., it caters mostly to working folks—but, of course, anyone is welcome. Like so many good diners, the menu is Greek-American, the food is homemade, and the prices are great. The atmosphere is light and airy, with large windows and walls painted in a Mediterranean blue. The smoker's section is well separated from the non-smoker's (larger) area.

Mr. C started off with a cup of egg lemon soup ($1.50), which really turned out to be a chicken and rice soup with a tangy, creamy stock. Mmmm. He followed it with a plump half-chicken, rotisserie-barbecued, served with rice pilaf and cooked broccoli and carrots. Plenty of good eats for just $3.95.

Other such platters, all around $4.00, include hot openfaced turkey or roast beef, fish and chips, and spinach pie. A sirloin steak plate is priced at $5.95. There are also daily blackboard specials, such as meatloaf or chicken souvlaki.

The Arsenal offers hot and cold sandwiches at similarly good prices, like a hamburger club ($2.95), grilled breast of chicken ($2.50), or cold seafood salad ($2.65). Add fries to any of these for 75¢ more. A variety of salads include Greek salad for just $1.50/small or $2.25/large, or chef ($1.75/$2.75); and for $2.95 you can get tuna or chicken with cole slaw and potato salad on a bed of lettuce.

Breakfast at the Arsenal is really cheap. Three eggs and ham, bacon, or sausage costs $2.95; steak and eggs are just $5.45. Omelettes start at $1.65, going up to $3.75 for the works (ham, peppers, onions, cheese, mushrooms, linguica sausage, and tomato sauce). Of course, all of these include home fries, toast, and a bottomless cup of coffee.

They also make pancakes (plain, fruit, chocolate chip), waffles and French toast, all under $3.00. Also a treat is the assortment of homemade muffins, including corn, apple cinnamon, and bran; a recent special deal offered a muffin and coffee for just 95¢.

Demo's Restaurant — 64 Mt. Auburn St., Watertown; 924-9660. Demo's is a longtime local Greek favorite just outside of Watertown Square where a full meal comes in for well under $10.00. "Our Specialty, Shish Kebab," the menu says prominently; and for $7.30 you can get two gigantic skewers of beef, chicken, baked lamb, or a combination; they are barbecued, hot and

juicy, and served on a heaping bed of rice with tomato sauce. The price includes an equally large plate of Greek salad and a slice of pita bread.

Unless you have a voracious appetite, you may even end up with leftovers for lunch. If your stomach is smaller and you don't want a doggy bag, get the "open sandwich" version—one large kebab, salad, rice, and bread for just $3.80 (chicken $4.05). With those thick chunks of meat, it's still a filling meal. Amazingly cheap.

Another favorite of Mr. C is the beef stew. It's a tasty bowl with large, tender chunks of meat in a tomato stock, served with rice or French fries and a salad for $3.50. Or, as an appetizer, try a cup of chicken and rice or black bean soup (just 85¢ each!), and then move on to a Greek sausage plate ($4.50) or the veal cutlet ($3.80), both with rice or fries and a salad. Finish off with a piece of baklava for $1.15.

Demo's is a good deal, and it shows. The atmosphere is bustling and friendly, with lots of families. The system is a hybrid: Stand in line to place your order and pay, find a table, and the counter staff will miraculously find you and bring the food when it's ready. There is also a full bar with cocktails, beer (house drafts for $1.15), and domestic and Greek wines.

The place does a lot of business, and you may have to share part of a long table if you don't want to wait for an individual one. No frills here, but at these prices, who's complaining?

Kareem's Restaurant — 600 Mt. Auburn St., Watertown; 926-1867. Located in the heart of this Middle Eastern enclave of markets and restaurants, Kareem's is a delightfully cozy cafe all done up in natural blond woods—tables, ceiling fans, and walls, even in the open kitchen. It's also very popular with diners of all cultures. Mr. C was there on a Monday night, and the place was hopping.

This is probably because Kareem's serves up a menu of fifteen different Mediterranean entrees, all priced at $5.95 or $6.95. Each gives you a full plate, with toasted pita bread and a huge, fresh salad spiced with mint and garlic.

There are all the standard meat and vegetarian plates: Falafel, eggplant, kibby, shish kebabs, kafta, stuffed grape leaves. For something a little different, try the Yahkni al Sabanikh, spinach cooked in olive oil and topped with melted cheese. It's served with a side of moist, delicious, crackedwheat pilaf.

Meat dishes fall into two categories—chicken and lamb. The kebabs have huge-sized chunks. There are also sandwich versions of many entrees (at about $4.00 each), served in Syrian pockets. A word of warning, though: The appetizers tend to be rather small portions for the money. Strange, since everything else is so generous.

The specials board usually lists several fresh-squeezed fruit drinks, like apple, grapefruit, and carrot. Dessert includes several homemade pastries and sweets, from barazick to rice pudding. Lunch is served from noon until 2 p.m., and dinner from 5 p.m. to 8 p.m.; there is also brunch on Saturday and Sunday mornings, with specials such as waffles with fresh bananas.

New Yorker Diner — 39 Mt. Auburn St., Watertown; 924-9772. For some reason, Watertown is blessed with more good ol' friendly diners than any other part of Boston. The New Yorker is a longtime favorite. Nothing fancy, just the basics. An "early bird" breakfast special actually runs until 11 a.m., with two eggs, toast, home fries, and coffee, plus ham, bacon, sausage, or hash, for $2.99. Nice touch: scali bread for the toast.

You can also get scali French toast for $3.75, or $5.00 with bacon, hash, etc. Omelettes are a bit pricy, but large and cooked just right. They range from $4.50 to $5.75, packed with lots of broccoli, sausage, or whatever you choose.

Burgers and sandwiches are good-sized. A bacon cheeseburger is $3.80; a turkey club is $5.45. There are daily specials, too, like a ham plate for $4.95.

Breakfast, of course, is served all day; however, that's only until 2 p.m., seven days a week. In the spirit of the Big Apple, though, the diner reopens on Wednesday through Saturday nights from 11 p.m. to 4 a.m.

Around the corner from the New Yorker you'll find Pat's Diner at 11 North Beacon Street (924-9872); and further up Mt. Auburn, heading toward Cambridge, is the dining-

---

Mr. Cheap's Picks
Watertown

✓ **Demo's Kitchen** — In the square, a kebab house that packs 'em in and offers huge chunks of grilled meats on a huge bed of rice for about $5.00. Just *try* and finish the full dinner (two skewers, $8.00).

✓ **Diners, Diners, Diners** — For some reason, Watertown has got to be diner central. **Pat's Diner** is only open late at night; The **Arsenal Diner** only serves breakfast and lunch. The **New Yorker Diner** manages to burn the candle at both ends. And, further up Mt. Auburn St., don't forget the **Town Diner** as well. In various shapes and sizes, they're all casually old-fashioned.

car-shaped Town Diner, at 627 Mt. Auburn Street (924-9789). Both offer similar fare and similar old-time eating experiences. Fill up that coffee again, willya?

Verona Restaurant — 18 Mt. Auburn St., Watertown; 926-0010. Like many of its Watertown Square neighbors, the Verona is a humble local establishment with a loyal following and great value. Just because one cannot afford high prices, Mr. C says, one should not have to give up variety! So this is the kind of restaurant he loves— where one could dine every night for a month without having the same meal twice.

Starting with pasta, choices are already upon you. Pick spaghetti, shells, or ziti, and top it with homemade meat sauce and parmesan cheese for $6.95; with meat sauce and sausage or meatballs for $8.25; white clam sauce and cheese for $8.50; and more. Or have these with homemade fettucine for $1.00 extra.

Moving on to other dishes, baked lasagna ($7.95) is a mountainous slab with fresh sauce poured over the top. Eggplant parmigiana ($8.50) gets the same treatment. The Italian combo plate

($9.75) is also generous, with a veal cutlet, ravioli, meatballs, shells, and sausage. And there is a full page of daily specials.

With most of the entrees you get a side order of pasta, as well as a choice of cooked vegetables; but the dinners themselves go well beyond Italian fare. Try the homemade lobster cutlets, with a crabmeat sauce ($9.50), or good old Boston schrod ($8.50) cooked in lemon butter. All seafood is brought in fresh daily.

You can also opt for salads and sandwiches. A toasted crabmeat salad roll, with French fries, is $6.75; the veal parmigiana sandwich is $4.95.

The Verona offers several interesting desserts, including "Creme Brulee à la Ritz" ($2.50), a sweet custard topped with caramel sauce. There are tapiocas, grapenut custard, and bread pudding too.

The restaurant has a family atmosphere; the menu is printed on the placemats, and most of the tables are booths. But don't be fooled by the plain surroundings— at the Verona, you'll stuff yourself with large portions of great home cooking.

INDEX

C

D

E

F

G

H

T

U